DANCING

ON THE

EDGE

DANCING ON THE EDGE

A JOURNEY OF LIVING, LOVING, AND TUMBLING THROUGH HOLLYWOOD

RUSS TAMBLYN

WITH **SARAH TOMLINSON**

BLACK STONE
PUBLISHING

This book is a memoir. The events are portrayed to the best of
Russ Tamblyn's memory. It reflects the author's present recollections
of experiences over time.

Printed in the United States of America

First edition: 2024
ISBN 979-8-212-27331-2
Biography & Autobiography / Personal Memoirs

Version 1

Blackstone Publishing
31 Mistletoe Rd.
Ashland, OR 97520

www.BlackstonePublishing.com

For Bonnie, my forever love

CONTENTS

INTRODUCTION OF A STORYTELLER

Don't be too good at telling stories, or you could end up getting lost in them for decades—I learned that the hard way. It's not like I didn't know I'd had a special life with more than its fair share of unusual adventures. But I was always surprised when our neighbors at our little complex in Santa Monica, where my wife, Bonnie, and I have lived for forty years, would call out, "Tell us another story, Russ!" at our holiday gatherings in the courtyard. I was happy to oblige, especially with a bottle of quality tequila in hand.

There was the one about how, early on, I had a small part in the movie *As Young as You Feel,* and on set I encountered an unknown blond actress who would become the Hollywood legend Marilyn Monroe. Or there was the one about how I lent Howard Hughes ten dollars at a gas station. Or how Paul Newman ended up in the trunk of my Austin-Healey while I was driving off the MGM lot one day. Believe me, I could tell these kinds of tales all night, as the breadth of my career practically spans the history of cinema itself.

I finally decided to collect all these tales by writing a book, thanks to the suggestion of Dr. David Soren, a brilliant archaeologist and the Regents Professor of Classics and Anthropology at the University of Arizona in Tucson. He completed an expansive and well-researched biography about my life and was very gracious when I told him that I wanted to rewrite the manuscript in my own voice, using his excellent raw material as my foundation.

Neither I nor Bonnie had any idea what a big job it would be. We spent a year rummaging through dusty old boxes of my tattered memorabilia: clippings from my early days, when Lloyd Bridges gave me my start in a play at age thirteen and I had my first film role in *The Boy with Green Hair*, and records of my work for Cecil B. DeMille, my heyday as an MGM player, and my starring roles in such iconic pictures as *Seven Brides for Seven Brothers* and *West Side Story*. Then there were all the art and memories from my role in the sixties counterculture, following my radical decision to drop out of Hollywood and become a fine artist in Topanga Canyon as part of the West Coast Beat scene. In addition to this was memorabilia from my resurgence in the early nineties, when I was directed by David Lynch in *Twin Peaks*, and then my role as our daughter Amber's manager when she landed her first role on *General Hospital* at age eleven, launching her own distinguished career as an actress and soon-to-be writer, director, and political activist.

Organizing my early archives was a daunting task, and I would rather have been creating art, which inspired me in the present, than writing about another lifetime that was all in the past. But Bonnie kept me grounded and on task. She made an outline of my entire career, from my start in films in the late forties to what was then the eve of the twenty-first century. We included information about my dad and mom, Eddie and Sally Tamblyn, who had gotten their start in vaudeville on the Orpheum Circuit.

More than just offering readers a glittering mirage of Hollywood legends, I wanted to take them on a more intimate journey that recounts my personal awakening. How, at the height of my career, I turned my back on cinematic glamour and sought a deeper, more connected existence. In some ways, all my wonderful adventures as a child star and leading man, as well as the easy money and available women that fell in my path, perhaps kept me from maturing quite as quickly as others. After all, I was living in the fantasyland of the films in which I starred.

It wasn't until my consciousness was cracked open by the writing and artwork of some of the greatest, most iconoclastic artists of the twentieth-century counterculture, from Henry Miller to Wallace Berman, that my real growth began. When I sacrificed the only life I had ever known for a craggy perch on a mountaintop in Topanga Canyon, I began to come of age as an artist and a man. But nothing grew me up faster or better than becoming a dad in my early fifties— to two beautiful, talented daughters, who were both their own kinds of happy surprises, and one of whom was an actual secret from me for years, as will be revealed later. I had always been a free spirit, following my instincts into pleasure, film parts, and the visual arts, but now I wasn't so concerned with myself anymore. I had been an acrobat, an actor, a dancer, and a fine artist, and now I was a family guy—a father with a lineage and legacy I had never thought about before. My daughter Amber, who is an established author, would go on to give me helpful insights as I prepared this book, showing me that some of the stories from my days as a young Hollywood rascal, although titillating and innocent enough, weren't so appropriate. So they will remain my secrets! Don't worry, though—there are still plenty of juicy, behind-the-scenes back lot moments.

Sadly, my story must include the loss of many of the great artists who were also my dear friends and who passed during the two decades I was writing. My hope is that they will live again in the pages of this book, in the stories of the times we had together, making movies, making artwork, and—what we never would have believed back then—making cultural history.

As you open these pages, know that this is a story of more than eighty years of living. As an actor, dancer, choreographer, director, artist, and father, I have experienced fame, rejection, awakenings, loss, and love. Come with me on my journey, from the beginnings of my career as a young kid in show business, through the Hollywood heydays and my escape from the grind, to finally finding purpose, meaning, and true and lasting love.

Nomination
Assemblage by Russ Tamblyn

1957 Russ Tamblyn Academy Award nomination for *Peyton Place*,
recreated as a work of art in the seventies.

PART 1

HOLLYWOOD HEYDAYS

CHAPTER 1

Leaping into Life

It almost feels like I haven't chosen anything in my life. It's more like I fell into everything that happened to me. Or more accurately, I leaped and tumbled and climbed. From an early age, I found that I was nimbler than the other kids. I also possessed a total fearlessness about heights, imagining I was Tarzan and able to swing from tree branch to tree branch or climb anything like a monkey. When I was a young boy in Inglewood, California, I once shimmied to the top of a telephone pole in front of my house, as the neighborhood kids started betting against me. And then I did a handstand on top of it.

When my mother came out and looked up at what the kids were staring at, she became petrified. I had braced my arms between two sets of two-by-fours that were placed about four or five inches apart at the top of the pole. I remember it being much easier than it looked, but of course, my mother couldn't know that from far below. She later told me that she wanted to scream at me but was afraid I would get startled and fall or touch the high-voltage wires only a few feet away from me. After I came out of the handstand, she yelled at me to get down carefully, which I did. But before she could lecture me, I collected almost a dollar in change from the neighborhood kids who had bet I couldn't do it. I suppose, in a way, this was my first paid gig.

Whenever I've had the urge to do something, instead of worrying about what could go wrong or what people might think, I've just done it. And you know what? It's gotten me into a few scrapes, but most of the time, it's worked out pretty well for me.

In fact, you might say I owe my career in Hollywood to this way of thinking. One example is the time I put on an impromptu show at age ten at the Granada Theatre in Inglewood. In the early 1940s, Saturday morning was kids' time at the theater, with weekly showings of serials and cartoons, plus screenings of my favorite movies, like *The Cisco Kid*, *Superman*, and *Flash Gordon*. Performing was in my blood on both sides of my family. Both my parents, Eddie and Sally Tamblyn, had been on the Orpheum Circuit, a nationwide theater chain featuring vaudeville shows. My parents had recently taken me to see my father's performance in the 1933 movie *The Sweetheart of Sigma Chi*. I was amazed at how much larger than life he appeared up there on the screen. It had such an impact, and I wanted to be just like him. So I found a way to be.

A few kids used to rib me and call me a girl because I had curly hair. Looking to compensate for this somehow, I ran onto the stage and started hamming it up, doing cartwheels, falling down, and rolling backward up to a headstand. The audience of kids exploded with laughter, which further fueled my antics.

When the manager ran down the aisle to corral me, I flew off the stage and scooted under the seats like a garden snake. After a few weeks of doing these kinds of performances, I found the manager one Saturday waiting for me in the wings. He grabbed me by the shirt collar and marched me into his office. I was scared to death. When he asked me if I knew my phone number, like a fool I said yes. He called my mom and said I was making a pest of myself. When I got home, instead of punishing me, Mom asked if I would like dancing lessons.

That's how I first studied dance when I was eleven years old with a very short, portly, and enthusiastic teacher named Bob Cole, who looked a little like Bob Hope. Sweat just poured out of him onto the dance floor, to the point where I feared I would slip and fall when I was doing my number. I guess I was a pretty good hoofer in my first year, learning the waltz clog and then working my way up to more demanding moves. When Mom told Dad I was taking lessons, he wasn't too happy, perhaps fearing my interest in the performing arts would lead me to experience the same heartache he had, but eventually he capitulated. He reluctantly attended my first recital, and once he saw me perform, he beamed. Mom later told me that he said, "Well, it's no wonder. Dancing's in his blood." There wasn't much money in our family to promote my interest in dancing, so my mother played the piano for Cole to cover the lesson costs.

Cole saw such promise in me that he guided me to an acting coach, Grace Bowman, whose studio was in a big, old, wooden Craftsman home on a street north of Hollywood Boulevard. She had built a small stage in her front room, where I would give monologues. She had a great flair for acting, and she made it fun. A grand old Hollywood dame, she wore large floral muumuus and lots of gaudy costume jewelry, which clattered on her arms when she clapped for me. She would chain-smoke with a long cigarette holder and say, "Attaboy, Russell!" At the end of my lessons, I would walk down her wide cement steps on my hands.

Encouraging me to join the Screen Children's Guild so I could act and dance in union productions in the area, Cole helped me to gain my first onstage experience in USO shows during World War II. And then when he felt he had taught me everything he could, he recommended me as a student to famed Black tap dancer Willie Covan, whose dancing was so smooth it was described as "poetry in motion." He was the head dance instructor at MGM, having once worked with legendary tapper and stair dancer Bill "Bojangles" Robinson. Bojangles had taught Shirley Temple to tap, worked with Debbie Reynolds, and designed routines for Ann Miller, Mae West, and Mickey Rooney. When I started working with Covan, he had a little studio in downtown Los Angeles, and to cover the cost of my lessons, my mother would once again play piano for his classes. He was a high-spirited, upbeat soul who laughed a lot, but he was not a flashy dancer. Instead, his dancing was very subtle and low key, with lots of heel and toe action and extra taps done in an easy style. Even so, he also perspired a good bit when he danced, so he taught with a towel in one hand and a cane in the other, tapping out the rhythm he wanted his students to emulate. My dancing lessons were followed by acting lessons, and soon I was landing my first roles on stage and screen. And it was, perhaps, the most fateful instance of me leaping into life without thinking about it.

———

I was born into a show business family, and it was the only existence I knew. My father, Eddie, had seemed bound for stardom when he landed a spot on the Gus Edwards Revue at age fourteen. Edwards, the songwriter behind such classics as "By the Light of the Silvery Moon," was nicknamed the Star Maker for having discovered many luminaries of the day. Once Dad became too old for the Edwards Revue, he found work as an understudy, small-part player, and specialty dancer known for his fantastic Charleston ability.

Dad danced a lot like James Cagney. They were both little guys, and they loved to dance, straight backed and jaunty, without a lot of arm movements, in a style that came out of the Celtic tradition. Dad was very stylish and had a great grin and a wonderful sense of humor. He was always the center of attention. One of Dad's specialties was to appear to be drunk and dance himself into a precarious situation, as if he were about to fall into the orchestra pit. His moves definitely inspired my impromptu dance at the Granada, and he was the first Tamblyn to dance on the edge.

After five years on the vaudeville circuit, where his tours lasted as long as fifty-eight weeks, he broke into Broadway as a juvenile lead dancer, eventually being dubbed within the industry "Broadway's Juvenile." "Juveniles" were male teenage performers who shone during routines in shows and films that expressed the mood of the early 1920s. Dad took whatever small parts he could land and formed his own group of "exhibition and specialty dancers," called the Vernon Revue or the Vernon Four. On a road tour that included 4,026 performances, all of them featuring my dad, he met my mother, Sally, who was then a sixteen-year-old chorus girl. She had lied about her age to land the part. Although he was a decade older, they were both diminutive—Sally was five feet two to Eddie's five feet six. They fell madly in love and married as soon as she turned seventeen. They continued to tour together and performed as an act together, after hours in clubs, with Mom playing piano and Dad dancing and singing. And then, when Mom was eighteen, she became pregnant with my older brother, Warren.

Dad tried his hardest to earn a good living for his young family, but he had difficulty breaking out of juvenile roles, especially as cinema became the dominant form of entertainment. He had done well in vaudeville as an emcee and eccentric dancer, and he showed promise in a few small roles in early film shorts, but by the mid-1930s, the juvenile type was passé. Eddie wasn't quite a juvenile any longer, either, but he couldn't seem to transition to character roles. Dad made at least sixteen films between 1931 and 1937, including his small roles in Will Rogers's production of *A Connecticut Yankee* and *Two Seconds*, a star vehicle for Edward G. Robinson. But the parts got smaller and increasingly harder to land.

Perhaps Dad's biggest role was in the 1933 film *The Sweetheart of Sigma Chi*, which my parents had taken me to see. At the time it was released, the picture had garnered some fan attention, which was encouraging for my ever-hopeful father, but the momentum for his career began to slow down, and he lost his agent, Max Shagrin. Dad always hoped to someday revive his career in the entertainment industry, but he eventually had to admit that it wasn't going to happen for him. So whenever he couldn't find steady work, he would run a hot dog stand in our neighborhood. Sometimes, we joined him there for dinner, which my older brother and I loved.

Mom worked too. A good piano player, she sometimes performed in cocktail lounges and taught singing and played piano for a children's dance school. She suffered a great deal because of Dad's failing career, which led to his growing depression and bursts of rage. She tried to help out financially as much as she could, but somehow it was never enough.

Whenever I hear "Claire de lune," I think of my mother's wonderful piano rendition and how sweet and nurturing she was. She tried to shield Warren and me from Dad's temper, but he yelled at us for the smallest things. I remember how we would all brace ourselves for the storm, never knowing when he was going to blow. Occasionally, he would clip me from behind with a smack upside my head, and I never knew why.

Our family seemed to be falling apart. In fact, Dad's last film, *Mountain Music*, proved to be the last straw, not only for his failing career but also for his marriage. His personal scrapbook, so diligently kept by my mother, sadly ends at Christmas 1935. The subsequent years of his career's slow decline, amid the strain of the continuing Great Depression, were difficult indeed. My parents finally divorced in 1938, when I was just four years old.

It was incredibly difficult for a single woman with children to get by in the Depression. I was placed with a foster family named Peters while my mother worked to make ends meet. I was miserable and missed my father terribly. Although I was only about four years old, I can clearly recall, with dread, how I sat at the dinner table with half a dozen other kids, being forced to eat liver. I hated liver! I eventually developed the skill to palm it, stick it in my pocket, and later flush it down the toilet. Actually, that began a big interest in magic for me, especially sleight of hand. (Years later, I would use that skill while playing Dr. Jacoby in the television series *Twin Peaks*.)

I have shadowy memories of a sense of terrible loneliness, isolation, and abandonment. Somehow, I remembered Dad telling me he lived only a few blocks away, probably to reassure me. So one day during my naptime, I climbed out of my bed, went outside, and grabbed a wagon. I pulled it over to the gate, climbed up, and unlatched it. Off I went, in search of my daddy. I quickly got lost. A police car found me and took me to the station.

"Are you hungry?" an officer asked.

"Yes, but please don't give me any liver!"

They laughed and gave me ice cream instead. It was the best time I had ever had up until then, but the police officers brought me back to the Peters. Apparently, my escape act was very tough for my folks. I think it might have helped them to reconsider their divorce. Reluctantly, Mom began seeing Dad once again, hoping to bring our shattered family back together. By now, show business had left Dad completely behind, and parts didn't come his way anymore. He promised Mom he would not be so moody, distant, and explosive. Mom wasn't sure it was a good idea to take him back. But it was so hard to make a go of it on her own. After two years of separation, Sally and Eddie remarried in 1940. Gradually, we learned to stay out of range if Dad seemed likely to go ballistic.

During World War II, Mom became pregnant again, and on February 5, 1943, she gave birth to Lawrence Arnold Tamblyn (who would grow up to be part of rock 'n' roll history as the lead singer of the Standells). Ironically, the war finally provided us with stability. Dad went to school to upgrade his skills and worked in a defense plant, building airplanes. Our family was able to buy a small house at 517 Florence Avenue in Inglewood, California.

Eddie and Sally remained an act of sorts, but it was only at home now, entertaining family members and guests. Mom later told me that around friends, Dad would brag about his boys. That came as a big surprise to me. I remembered him yelling at my brothers and me, clipping the back of my head with his open palm. As a boy, I had cut my left knee when I fell on a bottle while playing in a vacant lot about a block from our house. We went to the doctor, who sewed me up with eighteen stitches. But as soon as I healed, I fell on glass again—this time on my right knee—and my father was so frustrated that he decided not to take me to the doctor because it cost too much money. Instead, he patched me up himself, which hurt like hell. I don't remember him ever showing me affection, and I never felt close to him. But looking back, I can see how much my father influenced my decision to go into show business and how, as fellow hoofers and actors, we had a great deal in common. For such a little guy, Dad was larger than life to me. I also owe a great debt to my mother, who was very talented, and whose musicality and gumption allowed her to trade her piano playing for my first dance lessons. As a young actor with a rising star, I wasn't so in tune with my family lineage, but I've become proud of having carried forward the Tamblyn talents and name in ways my parents could only dream.

—

My big break came at age thirteen. After several years of dancing, acting lessons, and local performances at places like the Sawtelle Veterans Home, I was discovered by Lloyd Bridges. I auditioned for his first play, *The Stone Jungle*, which he directed and starred in at the Coronet Theatre in Hollywood in April 1948. I was cast as Pie-Eye, for which I received a salary of thirty-five dollars a week—a lot of money at the time, at least for me. On opening night, I received a warm note from Lloyd that read, *You do some great acting in this show Rusty—really extraordinary talent! I know you'll keep building your ability and your career—always count on me to help in any way I can. Thanks for working so hard on this play with me.*

The next day, we were all excited because the reviews were so positive, including one from the *Los Angeles Daily News*, which said my performance was a "sensitive portrayal of the little boy." The production had a limited engagement, so we did not reach our goal of taking the show to Broadway, but it was a great experience for me. I learned how to be onstage for the first time and how to work with other actors, although I found both always came naturally to me. I also found that I loved acting and, of course, all the attention. Lloyd wrote to my mom and dad, telling them they were "parents to a genius child actor."

"Look at that, son!" Dad said to me with a smile. "That must make you feel good!" What really made me feel good was that, for once, Dad was proud of me and showed it.

From there, I signed with my first agent, Edith Jackson, who was friends with Lloyd. Director Joseph Losey, who had seen my performance at the Coronet, quickly cast me in a small role as a schoolkid in RKO's 1948 film *The Boy with Green Hair*. It starred my fellow child actor Dean Stockwell, who would become my longtime best friend. Because of his beautiful, angelic face, Dean always played the tormented child, who inevitably had a crying scene. However, in real life, he had a great sense of humor, couldn't stand people fawning over him, and was by then channeling his copious amounts of energy into mastering the drums.

In one of our scenes together, Dean had his green hair cut off, and after we were done filming, I had the urge to grab a handful of his shorn locks and stick them in my pocket as a souvenir. (Years later, I would incorporate items like these from my past into my art pieces.) After the movie wrapped, Dean and I palled around together, going to the cinema with his older brother, Guy. We sat up in the balcony, making obnoxious noises and talking back to the screen until the usher threw us out on at least one occasion.

By the time I attended North Hollywood Junior High, I had made a name for myself with my gymnastic prowess and drew attention from girls for my curly hair. But I was hooked on Hollywood and would begin spending less and less time at my regular school. In 1949, I landed parts in three films: *Samson and Delilah*; *Captain Carey, U.S.A.*; and *The Kid from Cleveland*, in which I played the title role. This was my first time filming on location and flying in an airplane. Back in 1949, planes were propeller driven and much slower, so the flight from LA to Cleveland took ten to twelve hours. I was glued to the window the whole time, enjoying every second of flying over the epic Rocky Mountains, the mind-blowing Grand Canyon, and the glistening glow of the sun reflecting off the many lakes and rivers. When we hit turbulence, I wasn't scared. It was all a grand adventure, and the bumpier the better, as far as I was concerned.

Once I arrived in Cleveland, the production office gave me a book of taxi coupons to travel to the neighborhoods where we filmed. Sometimes, my mom accompanied me on the set, but one day, she stayed at the hotel. When we finished shooting for the day, I invited a pretty sixteen-year-old who had been watching me film a scene to go for a ride in my taxi. We rode for miles along the Lake Erie coastline, and unfortunately, I used up nearly all my coupons. (I think I really impressed her!) My mother screamed at me for being so frivolous. For the next few weeks, I had to pay my own taxi fares, but it was worth it. I was a budding Romeo, and for many years, I would pursue even the most fleeting on-set romances.

Our director, Herbert Kline, was looking to cast a local as the villain, who, like Fagin, leads a gang of young delinquents, including myself. None of the area theater actors seemed right. However, one of the players from the baseball team then known as the Cleveland Indians, who were featured in the film, had clear potential. John Beradino was a tall, strong-featured Italian American who had the look of a stereotypical gangster. He and I read together for his audition, and Herbert asked me what I thought. When I got over my surprise that our director trusted the opinion of a fourteen-year-old novice actor, I told him, "I think his acting is pretty good, and he looks perfect for the role." Well, John got the part, and it launched his four-decade career, in which he made more than thirty movies and appeared in at least thirty-five television shows.

Acting was a great adventure that became even more adventurous when my agent sent me to Paramount to try out for a part in *Samson and Delilah*, which was being directed by the legendary (and terrifying) filmmaker Cecil B. DeMille. My audition was held in a room that was dominated by a huge one-way mirror. When my session was over, DeMille marched out from behind the secret room, followed by his entourage of secretaries and assistants. He was in full regalia, including knee-high leather boots and a riding crop.

"Excellent, young man, you've got the part of young King Saul," he boomed at me.

De Mille was known to be a fiery autocrat who moved actors about like cattle. A crew member constantly followed DeMille with a chair so that whenever he wanted it, his seat would be right behind him. Most of the time, he didn't even look before he sat down. The chair had better be where it was supposed to be (and it always was!). The film opened with a long voice-over from God. Guess whose voice DeMille used?

A stickler for perfection, DeMille was determined and ruthless to get what he wanted. During the filming of the coliseum scene, for instance, DeMille separated two out of hundreds of extras because the colors of their costumes clashed, and he thought it was an offense to the eye. My own costume had me draped in off-the-shoulder buckskin, with my trusty slingshot wrapped around my forehead like a headband.

In one of my scenes, I had to run up to Victor Mature in the temple and indicate my slingshot on my head while saying, "We can fight our way out of here."

After I went through the scene the first time, DeMille stalked up to me and commanded, "Rusty, when you point to the slingshot on your head, don't block your face with your hand." We did the scene again, and I screwed up again. DeMille was visibly pissed off at me. "No, Rusty!" he said, sternly. "Didn't you hear what I just said?" Angrily, he grabbed my hand. "I told you to put your hand here," he said, banging it against the side of my head. "Not here," he said, banging it against the front of my head.

As always, a crew member was holding a microphone in front of DeMille's mouth, so his words resonated all over the soundstage. The extras and everyone else on the set could hear everything he said. I was only fourteen years old and so humiliated that tears welled up in my eyes. As was the studio rule, my mother was on set to chaperone me, and I wondered why she didn't intervene. She must have been afraid of DeMille too. Back then, child actors were expected to perform like mini adults. Another child actor named Bobby Driscoll told me that one time, right before a sad scene, the director told him his dog had died. Bobby was devastated, especially after the scene, when the director admitted he lied to get Bobby to cry. DeMille didn't go quite that far, but he was stern.

Our film's star, Victor Mature, had the look of a Greek god, and he photographed superbly as Samson, but in fact, he was horribly unfit. At the beginning of the shoot, DeMille charged into the wardrobe department and gave him a harsh once-over. "Vic, you've got to get into shape!" he chided him. "Can you do push-ups like this?" DeMille got down on the carpet and did ten brisk push-ups. Vic tried, but he was struggling by the third one and collapsed onto the floor. Vic appeared to have a great build, but it was actually flab. In one scene, I had to grab his arm, and after a few takes, DeMille thundered, "Just pretend to grab him. You're making him wobble like jelly!"

Vic was attracted to his costar Hedy Lamarr, who played Delilah (and who wouldn't be?). I thought she was the most beautiful woman I had ever seen, and I used to fawn all over her. I was also impressed by her gentleness, kindness, and intelligence. She seemed shy and retiring and didn't talk much. Once, though, when we broke for lunch, she surprised and thrilled me by asking, "Would you like to go to the Paramount commissary and have lunch with me?"

"Yes, thank you," I replied. I tried to play it cool, but I was thrilled! On our way there, we popped into a neighboring soundstage to say hello to one of her friends. They were shooting *My Friend Irma*, which was the screen debut of two young comedians—Dean Martin and Jerry Lewis. The whole set was bubbling with laughter, and Hedy and I stopped and watched for a bit. Jerry was smoking and making lots of wisecracks. When he noticed the long ash on his cigarette, he unzipped Dean's fly and flicked the ash into his pants. Dean made a face of disgust that mimicked the famous TV comedian Jack Benny, and everyone on the set howled with laughter, especially me. Clearly, these guys were going to be huge stars.

The studios were their own small communities, and it was common for actors to pop onto other sets between takes. Just about everyone on the Paramount lot knew about the tremendous coliseum that had been built on our stage, and stars including Bob Hope, Paulette Goddard, and Gloria Swanson stopped by to check it out. For only my fourth film role, this was quite an experience. I think it's fair to say I was hooked on the magic of show business.

Paramount took up almost half a square mile, from Santa Monica Boulevard to Melrose. During the filming of *Samson*, there were long periods when I wasn't needed on set, but I still had to attend school on the lot. I took my usual bus and streetcar route from our home in North Hollywood to the stop that was closest to the studio.

Some of my fondest memories are of riding the Red Cars, the trolleys that were early public transportation in LA. The ride was a thrilling, rattling event. The Red Cars had large windows you could lean out of while you took in the view across the then-unpopulated San Fernando Valley. You could see a few ranches, cattle, and lots of dry, sandy riverbeds called washes that collected into rain rivers when winter came.

There were farms and orchard crops, and fields of orange and lemon trees that emitted a delicious scent that seemed to shoot right up my nose as I passed. Then suddenly, the clickity-clack of the Red Car tracks got louder as the train sped across the LA River bridge. At the right moment, I would stick my torso as far as I could out the window and drop a stone, hoping for a direct hit in the middle of the river.

I also loved the ride from the top of the Cahuenga Pass, which cuts through the Hollywood Hills, down into that most famous neighborhood of the city. It was the fastest part of the ride, as we sped by the sweet chaparral and oak trees. The wheels on the steel rails sounded like a machine gun out of a James Cagney movie, and the squeaking breaks signaled that we were getting close. We would pass the Hollywood Bowl and then slow down even more.

Back when I had regularly traveled into the city for my weekly acting and dance lessons, I would always hop off the streetcar in the heart of Hollywood, at Hollywood Boulevard and Highland Avenue. I would immediately head over to a nearby tall building and climb the stairs to the top floor. I knew where to find the door that led to the rooftop and my private path to Vine Street, where I leaped from building top to building top.

Now, I walked half a mile to the gates of Paramount, and then it was nearly the same distance across the studio lot to reach the schoolhouse. I thought there must be an easier way. One morning, when I got off the Red Car on Santa Monica Boulevard, I made a discovery. By climbing up a cemetery wall next to the studio, I could reach the wall circling Paramount and drop down at the back of the lot. Then it was only a short distance to school, which cut a full mile off my usual route.

When I reached the top of the wall, I noticed they were filming below, right on my favorite landing spot. I walked farther until I finally found a place where I could jump down. A guy was resting in a chair, getting some sun. I was light on my feet, but I landed on a piece of tin, which startled him, and he jumped up.

"Where the hell did you come from?" he asked in a remarkably deep voice.

I couldn't help staring at him, as it was dawning on me that this was Alan Ladd, the star of 1940s noir classics such as *This Gun for Hire* and *The Blue Dahlia*.

I quickly explained my schoolhouse dilemma, causing him to laugh.

"Next time, give me a little warning before you come in for a landing," he said. Although I never again almost clobbered him on the Paramount lot, he would be the star of my next film, *Captain Carey, U.S.A.*

Projects kept coming my way, and although my parts were often small, I always loved being on set. Working with talented actors and directors taught me a great deal about show business and my craft, as when I was cast as Bart Tare, a troubled youth obsessed with guns, in the cult classic 1950 film *Gun Crazy* (a.k.a. *Deadly is the Female*). It was directed by iconic noir director Joseph H. Lewis and written by Millard Kaufman, one of the pen names used by the brilliant writer Dalton Trumbo, who had been blacklisted by the House Un-American Activities Committee after he had refused to testify in 1947, during their witch hunt against communism in Hollywood. After breaking a window and stealing a pistol from a gun store, my character is caught and sent to prison. John Dall plays the role of the adult Bart Tare after he has been released.

Joe spent considerable time helping me develop my acting skills, and he was the first director who talked with me intimately about a character's motivations. He got me to dig deeply into myself so I could express how I would respond as this boy who was actually nonviolent but obsessed with guns. In the movie, there is a scene where I aim a gun at a mountain lion but can't bring myself to shoot him. Joe asked me if I had anything I could draw on for that scene. Well, just a couple of years earlier, I had been shooting at cans in the backyard of my house with a BB gun. A bird had landed in a tree, and I shot at it, just to see if I could hit it. Unfortunately, I did—and I killed it. I felt so horrible that I dropped the gun and cried. Then I put the bird in a box and buried it in the backyard. I was so upset I couldn't eat my dinner that night. So I learned how to bring that emotional experience into the scene. Now was my chance to *not* shoot the bird. That's what I was thinking when I aimed at the lion.

Just after my fifteenth birthday, in early 1950, I landed a nice little part as Spencer Tracy's son (and Elizabeth Taylor's brother) in MGM's *Father of the Bride*, directed by Vincente Minnelli. I wasn't given much to do in the movie, but I was awestruck by the chance to film a few scenes with a master actor like Spencer Tracy.

During my first day filming, Spencer strolled onto the set, scratching his head, glancing at his script, and seeming completely lost. This was not at all what I was expecting from such a pro. During our rehearsal of the first scene, he stuttered and stalled, mumbling and missing line after line. If another actor had bungled a scene like this, he probably would have been replaced immediately.

Oh my God, we're never going to get through this scene, I thought.

"Oh, what the hell," Spencer finally said. "Let's just try one."

So Vincente Minnelli shouted, "Roll 'em."

Suddenly, Spencer came to life, deftly executing the scene without missing a single line. He nailed it! I was flabbergasted. I wasn't sure if the bumbling was all a trick or just his method, but his acting looked so natural and spontaneous, it amazed me to no end. I wondered how he could deliver such a spot-on performance, which made me aspire to be as good.

My first agent, Edith Jackson, passed away in 1950, and I was now represented by Milton Garfield. My career showed no sign of slowing down, even if my next part was in the 1951 sequel *Father's Little Dividend*, which was somewhat less successful than its predecessor and found me with far less screen time. I was not yet under contract to MGM, but they still paid me during the weeks when I wasn't needed on set and had me attend their famous "Little Red Schoolhouse," which was frequently featured in movie magazines because among the child stars who had been taught there were Freddie Bartholomew, Judy Garland, Mickey Rooney, Margaret O'Brien, Ann Rutherford, Jackie Cooper, and my *Father of the Bride* costar Elizabeth Taylor, as well as my friend Dean Stockwell.

Our teacher, Miss McDonald, looked and acted like an old-time schoolmarm. Her hair was parted in the middle and pulled back in a bun. She wore little glasses and a black dress with a lace collar that seemed to choke her neck. One day, Elizabeth raised her hand to ask to go to the bathroom. Miss McDonald granted her permission to go, but when Liz didn't return for ten or fifteen minutes, Miss McDonald became visibly concerned. Finally, we heard the toilet flush. Dean and I gave each other a look that said, *Boy, she's in trouble!* Out came Liz, returning to her desk.

"Elizabeth, you couldn't possibly have been going to the bathroom all this time!" Miss McDonald said.

"I was too," replied Elizabeth. "Do you wanna go in there and smell?"

On the day of Elizabeth's graduation, the movie magazines were all there, covering the event. Miss McDonald kept a vigilant eye on everyone, making sure no one got out of line. One photographer had just put a fresh roll of film in his camera and wanted to shoot a few more pictures of Elizabeth outside on the school steps. He convinced her to throw her books up in the air to suggest she was now happily finished with school. Miss McDonald grabbed the photographer's camera and ripped the film out of it, shrieking, "Don't you *dare* take pictures of Elizabeth throwing schoolbooks up in the air! What kind of message do you think that sends to the children in this country?"

Dean and I couldn't stop laughing. Dean was already an MGM player and had a dressing room above the rehearsal hall near the schoolhouse. We would go up there during our lunch breaks and have ourselves little parties. One time after we smoked a cigarette, we started wrestling on his carpeted floor. We knocked over a table, and a heavy lamp fell with a loud crash. Suddenly, there was a knock at Dean's door. We opened it to find Gene Kelly standing there.

"Hey, guys!" he said. "I'm just underneath you, and I'm trying to take a little nap. Could you hold it down a bit?" Then he made a face as he smelled the cigarette smoke. Recognizing Dean, with whom he had costarred in *Anchors Aweigh*, his face grew stern. "Dean! You surprise me. Does your mom know you're smoking cigarettes?"

"No, sir," Dean replied.

Gene shook his head as if to say, *Shame on you*, but instead, he smiled and said, "Well—I won't tell."

Of course, Dean and I admired Gene greatly, and we were incredibly embarrassed. We gave up our wrestling matches and spent the rest of our lunch breaks in the school's recreation room, playing table tennis. Dean beat me in every game. Of course, he had already been at MGM for a few years, giving him ample time to practice, so he was a whiz.

In 1950, I had several small parts in films that have not withstood the test of time, but one of them, *As Young as You Feel*, was notable for my encounter with a blond, up-and-coming actress who had a small part as a secretary. She told me how much she loved my curly hair and asked if she could run her fingers through it. Normally, I would have protested, but she was so beautiful I couldn't resist. I bent over like a puppy starved for affection and let her stroke my curls, basking in the moment. That night in bed, I couldn't stop thinking about her. At the time, the actress was under contract to 20th Century Fox, just one of many pretty young starlets on the lot who filmed small parts in movies. Early nude photos of her appeared, which were quite scandalous for the times, and her popularity increased enormously. Of course, she would go on to become Hollywood legend Marilyn Monroe.

My *Gun Crazy* director, Joseph H. Lewis, came back into my life when he was casting a heavy drama about the retreat of American marines from the Changjin Reservoir in Korea (better known as the Battle of Chosin Reservoir) called *Retreat, Hell!* for Warner Brothers. He wanted me for the part of Jimmy W. McDermid, a strong role for me. Joe had me test for the movie, but Warner Brothers thought I looked too young and wanted to replace me with an older actor. However, Joe stood up for me, saying if they took me off the film, he would have to be replaced too. Joe won, and I ended up doing the part.

I was only sixteen but portrayed a seventeen-year-old forced to witness the horrors of war, including the death of my own brother. The movie was shot at Camp Pendleton in California, and we all stayed in a motel in Carlsbad, right by the sea. It was the first time in my young career that I was completely on my own, with only a schoolteacher, who didn't watch me very closely, as my chaperone. I loved that location. At night, I would leap over the motel wall and run down to the beach for a swim. I became obsessed with the Marine Corps and put its eagle, globe, and anchor emblem on the cover of my school notebook.

Most of filming was a lark, but there was one strange scene that would haunt me. In it, I rounded a corner, looking for my older brother, who was also a marine. I discovered about a dozen bodies under blankets—marines who were killed in battle. I had to check their dog tags to see which one was my brother. When I finally found him, I had to drop down on my knees and weep over his body. The deceased marines were actually played by real marines. The covered marine, who was supposed to be my brother, started to giggle when I held him.

"Cut!" Joe said.

He looked at the platoon's sergeant, who was on set to supervise his men, and nodded for him to say something. The sergeant reminded the soldiers that they were all going overseas the next week and would have to face real warfare. Suddenly, all of them were silent, and we quickly finished the scene. Tragically, I later got word that all of them were killed in Korea.

Just a teenager, I wasn't fully aware of the real cost of the war, and my life rolled on. I had graduated to North Hollywood High and would return there between film projects. It wasn't as exciting as a movie set, but I actually liked public school. I joined the gymnastics team and did very well, winning lots of medals in tumbling and free exercise. One of my high school buddies, Bob Six, was the son of Warner Brothers still photographer Bert Six, who shot what would become famous headshots of WB stars and then went to work for Howard Hughes at his film studio, RKO. One day, Bob and I pulled into a gas station in the San Fernando Valley.

"Do you see that big guy over there, the one getting out of the convertible?" Bob said as we filled up our car. "That's Howard Hughes. Come on. I'll introduce you to him."

Hughes was quite friendly. "I'm so glad I ran into you guys," he said. "I'm out of cash and forgot to bring my wallet. I need to pay for the gas I just bought. Do either of you guys have ten dollars you could loan me?"

Bob didn't have that much cash on him, so I ended up lending ten dollars to Howard Hughes. He said he would pay me back, but he never did.

Meanwhile, Joe Lewis, who had a reputation for recognizing talent and getting good performances from his actors, was touting me to MGM executives at every opportunity. Convinced after his two films with me that I had the makings of a future star, Joe screened *Retreat, Hell!* for MGM's studio chief, Dore Schary. MGM offered me a seven-year contract. And so by the time I was sixteen, I had already achieved more success and financial stability than my father.

Young Rusty, age eight, first professional shot.

Mother,
Sally Aileen Triplett,
chorus girl and dancer.

Father, Eddie Tamblyn,
with dance partner
Madeline Sheffield.

Dean Stockwell, Johnny Calkins, and Russ on the set for *The Boy with Green Hair* (1948).

Samson and Delilah (1949): Russ as young King Saul with Victor Mature.

The Kid from Cleveland (1949): first title role as Johnny Barrows.

Gun Crazy (1950):
Russ as young Bart Tare
seeing the gun in a store
window.

Gun Crazy: caught by the teacher.

Father of the Bride (1950): learning from Spencer Tracy, with Elizabeth Taylor, Don Taylor, and Joan Bennett.

Elizabeth Taylor's graduation with (left to right) Dean Stockwell, Mary Jane Smith, Elizabeth, Russ, and Tom Irish.

CHAPTER 2

RISING STARS AND DARKENING CLOUDS

By the time I was eighteen, my habit of leaping into life was working out pretty darn well. I was part of the last generation of actors who came up under the studio system. Much has been written about the downsides of this sometimes insular world, and I would eventually outgrow my role as an MGM player and bristle against its limitations. But for now, I was having the adventure of a lifetime. My personality, especially at this age, was particularly well suited to being a studio player. I didn't overthink my persona (or think about it at all, honestly) or worry about the gravitas of the roles I was offered. Maybe it was partly the lingering impact of having watched my dad struggle to support our family during the Great Depression while never quite letting go of his Hollywood dreams. But I was grateful to be earning very good money. This helped me to contribute to the family budget, even buying them a new car, while getting to act and have fun. Every day when I turned up on set, there was a new adventure to be had with my costars, during and in between takes, and I loved almost every minute of it.

I was soon being offered the kinds of parts that would help my star to rise even further and cement my reputation as a gymnastic dancer. The 1950s was the decade of the big studio musical, and I was lucky enough to appear in a few of the classics, including *Seven Brides for*

Seven Brothers, starring Jane Powell and Howard Keel, who had already starred in several hit MGM musicals such as *Annie Get Your Gun* and *Show Boat*. Ironically, *Seven Brides*, which would become quite iconic and boost my career to another level, almost didn't happen.

It was the pet project of Louis B. Mayer's nephew, Jack Cummings, who had worked his way up the MGM ladder over many years to become a producer. After Dore Schary replaced Mayer as the head of MGM, it seemed like the film might not get financed. However, Jack had already lined up director Stanley Donen, who codirected and choreographed *On the Town* and *Singin' in the Rain* alongside Gene Kelly, and an excellent hot young Broadway choreographer named Michael Kidd, who would go on to become the first choreographer to win five Tonys. The studio decided to make the film, but no one expected it to do much business because its budget was relatively small, especially after money was siphoned from it and given to the production of *Brigadoon*, starring Gene Kelly. On top of that, to shoot in CinemaScope, we had to film on the largest stage at MGM, and even that wasn't big enough, so they quickly built on an addition. The wardrobe and makeup people were relegated to tents outside the stage.

As for casting, Howard was brother number one. For his six siblings, Michael had wanted professional dancers, but MGM had a passel of male contract players and insisted Michael use some of them. A compromise was reached. Michael could cast four dancers: Marc Platt of the renowned Ballet Russe; Jacques d'Amboise, star of the New York City Ballet; Matt Mattox, great Broadway dancer and choreographer; and Tommy Rall, fabulous tap dancer and acrobat. But Michael had to use two contract players: me and an ex–baseball player turned actor, Jeff Richards, who danced like a broken windup toy. Going into filming, he made fun of male dancers, saying they were a bunch of sissies. Of course, once Jeff got to know his brothers and saw how talented and masculine they were, he liked them a great deal and changed his tune.

It wasn't just our steps that needed to be in sync, either. All of us Pontipee brothers had to be redheads. So I experienced my first dye job in order to become Gideon, the youngest brother. Once filming was underway, Howard would drive all seven of us wild-looking redheaded brothers to lunch in his big convertible Cadillac. He'd put his top down, and when we pulled up to a local drive-in, still in our makeup, we made quite an impression. Other diners openly stared at us, clearly wondering where the hell we came from and who we were.

As the title of the film suggested, all these brothers had to have brides. At the time, I never thought twice about the misogynistic way we essentially kidnapped our brides-to-be, but sensibilities were very different then. Among the actresses cast was the statuesque Julie Newmar in her first major role (she would later play Catwoman in the midsixties hit TV show *Batman*). She earned quite a reputation on set, for a most unusual reason. Every morning after rehearsing for a couple of hours, we would smell a horrific odor, and we couldn't figure out its source. One afternoon, when we broke for lunch, Jacques ran up to me and said excitedly, "I just discovered where that stinky smell is coming from. It's coming from Julie Newmar."

Every morning, she would put a piece of cheese between her breasts until lunchtime because she preferred her cheese warm and ripe. Finally, after being confronted, she changed her diet, or at least her habits. (You can't make this stuff up!)

Jeff and I were only supposed to act in the film—no dancing for us—but after a week, I got antsy and went to the hall where Michael was rehearsing his dancers. He approached me right away with a warm smile. "Hey, Rusty, I heard you're a tumbler," he said. "Is that true?"

I answered yes and immediately did a backflip.

"Great! Some tumbling will be perfect in the barn dance sequence."

"Wait a minute, Michael," I said. "I can't possibly dance alongside the likes of all these great dancers."

"Nonsense!" Michael said. "It's only square dancing."

My tumbling and stunts proved to be an invaluable skill in Hollywood. When making a comedy, I could easily take pratfalls. In westerns, I could leap onto horseback. In musicals, I could do inventive and daring acrobatic dancing. In fight scenes, I could fly through the air backward from a punch. In *Seven Brides*, I got to show off several of these techniques at once.

True to his word, Michael gave me a lot of great acrobatic stuff to do in the barn dance, and thanks to his eye for choreography, I felt comfortable and looked like an excellent dancer. During my tap days with Willie Covan, I used to perform a dance with a cane, even jumping over it. I showed Michael this move, and he suggested using an ax. Of course, the steel-edged head on the handle was changed to rubber, making it lighter and safer. The *real* challenge was performing this move by consecutively jumping back and forth over the ax four or five times on a narrow wooden plank that was elevated several feet off the ground. It took twenty-seven takes to get it right. That was a record for me!

During another sequence centered on the barn raising, various "accidents" occurred, as the young, rival townsmen surreptitiously attacked the brothers with planks and hammers. When my character got wise to what was happening, I initiated a brawl that raged up and down the multistory barn. About fourteen people were involved in the fight, and it was all intricately choreographed, like a dance number. I was in my element here, getting thrown out of windows, sliding down poles, and eventually climbing up a rope on the side of the barn to the roof, then jumping down onto the group below. The action was so calamitous we eventually knocked down the entire barn!

One day, Michael was a little late returning from lunch. When he finally appeared on set, he was with Gene Kelly, one of my dancing heroes. Gene stood and watched us run through the whole fight scene. Of course, knowing he was watching, we really exerted ourselves.

"Well, guys, there's nothing left for you to do except cut yourselves and bleed," he said when we finished.

That would have been enough to make the film a success for me. I had even more reason to be pleased when it was released in July 1954. Although no one had expected much from it, *Seven Brides* was a smash hit for MGM and earned five Oscar nominations. It also made me a household name and a celebrated dancer, with my picture in *Dance and Dancers* magazine.

Next, MGM assigned me to appear in *The Fastest Gun Alive*. They explained this was a serious western, starring Glenn Ford, that needed a light dance number to break up the weighty drama. When asked by the studio who I wanted to do my choreography, I had one answer: Alex Romero. We had gotten along well on *Seven Brides for Seven Brothers*, where he had been one of Michael's assistant choreographers. We had about a week to put together the routine, and I knew we could collaborate well and come up with a pretty good dance number. We did even better than that when we had the brainstorm that I should dance on two shovels as if they were stilts. No one had ever seen anything like that, and we knew it would be a sensation.

The only problem was how to keep the shovels against the bottoms of my boots. Walking was easy but dancing was very difficult. So we had the prop department build me a second pair of shovels, with a second pair of boots bolted to a piece of iron that was attached to the top of the blades. Now, every time I lifted my feet, the shovels automatically stuck to my boots. Thanks to a well-timed cutaway, I was able to slip into the special boots, and off I went. (This might have been the first important shovel moment in my career, but oddly enough, it would not be the last, although the other two incidents would happen decades apart.)

I also unleashed a number of acrobatic stunts, swinging from the rafters on a rope and leaping over five-foot horse stalls. The studio thought the dance number was amazing, but when Glenn Ford saw it, he was not amused. He went to the head of the studio and demanded the number be cut from the film's preview, where it would be screened for a test audience.

"This is a serious black-and-white western, and suddenly you've got a guy dancing all over the barn like in a big colorful MGM musical!" he said.

The studio complied. Lucky for me, however, they didn't cut the end credits of the film, which included one that read, "Russ Tamblyn's dance number choreographed by Alex Romero." When the test audience filled out their survey cards, 95 percent responded, "Where was Tamblyn's dance number?" So they put my dance back in the film! And it has actually had greater longevity than the movie itself. A clip of it has been posted on YouTube and viewed by hundreds of thousands of people over the years.

Shortly before Christmas 1954, I attended a party hosted by Christina Crawford, daughter of Joan Crawford and author of the infamous tell-all biography *Mommie Dearest*. Also in attendance was a beautiful young blond named Venetia Stevenson. The London-born daughter of British actress Anna Lee and British director Robert Stevenson (of *Mary Poppins* fame), she was a vision of youthful elegance and glamour.

I was instantly smitten, and we soon began dating. There was an effervescent excitement surrounding us, as both of our careers were exploding. After being discovered by famed pinup photographer Peter Gowland at age fourteen and having a brief but very successful stint as a model, Venetia would sign with RKO in 1956, just before the studio went out of business. That didn't slow her down, though; she signed with powerful agent Dick Clayton, who represented me at the time, and appeared on many magazine covers, eventually beating out four thousand contestants for the title of "the most photogenic girl in the world" from *Popular Photography*. She was also frequently featured in fan magazines, linked by the studios to gay actors Anthony Perkins and Tab Hunter, in an attempt to divert suspicion away from their true sexual orientation. She became close friends with both men.

In February 1955, *Hit the Deck*, the MGM musical I had starred in opposite Debbie Reynolds, opened at Radio City Music Hall to good reviews. I had adored being Debbie's romantic and dance partner in the film. I loved her so much as a friend that I kept a picture of us from the film in my wallet for years. When she married Eddie Fisher that September, she was hounded by paparazzi, who recognized her car. So I traded vehicles with her so they could sneak out to Palm Springs for their honeymoon without fanfare.

I was now seen as an MGM musical star after back-to-back hits in this genre. Even strangers on the MGM lot recognized me and said hello in passing, and my salary jumped to $550 a week. This was very good money, especially since I was only twenty years old.

By mid-1955, my romance with seventeen-year-old Venetia had become widely publicized, thanks to a spectacular picture that ran in *Life* magazine in June, becoming an instant classic. While walking down a street in Beverly Hills, I had an idea for the pic: I ran down the sidewalk and did a roundoff backflip next to Venetia. The photographer stood in front of us and snapped at exactly the right time. While I was upside down in the air, I put one foot slightly in front of the other, and it looked as if I were walking upside down next to her. Despite what this photo suggested, however, my relationship with Venetia wasn't always so buoyant; it was actually more up and down.

To me, Venetia was as beautiful as a Greek statue, and she had a quality about her like no other girl I had ever met. Of course, it's not like I knew much of the world, as I was only twenty years old myself. This point was made to me in a striking fashion when Venetia and I attended a star-studded party at the home of famed movie columnist Louella Parsons, where I overheard an actor with a distinctive voice. Instantly, I recognized it as belonging to Vincent Price, who had sized up me and Venetia and remarked to a friend, "He's too young to appreciate that beauty."

Venetia seemed worldly to me, maybe because her father was very British, and her mother, Anna Lee, was famous for her supporting role in John Ford's *How Green Was My Valley*. Venetia often played at being a dumb blond, but she was really smart and funny. I had never encountered anyone so fascinating and complex. Plus, she was the first girl I had ever met who didn't wear a bra. This was the 1950s, when there were strict conventions about how women should dress and behave. Yet she was very casual about being such a rebel, and I thought that was pretty bold. I was so struck by her.

But as I soon learned, Venetia could be moody, icy, and cool, even cold. And we were from opposite worlds—she had attended private schools and had a very different upbringing from mine. If I hadn't been so young and lacking in perspective, if not romantic experience, I probably would have seen that we were not a good match. Despite some fun times together, her moodiness used to drive me crazy. Still, I was so smitten that I rushed ahead and proposed to her.

Shortly before we married, Venetia visited her father, who was directing a film on location. While they were away, I accepted a dinner invitation from Venetia's new stepmother, Frances. After our meal, she mentioned trips she had taken to Europe and how free the culture was. When she got to how sexy the young men were, I began to find the conversation a little inappropriate and uncomfortable. Suddenly, she started coming on to me more directly, asking me to spend the night with her. I was shocked and embarrassed and quickly excused myself, saying I had somewhere else to be.

When Venetia returned from her trip, I got up the nerve to tell her what had happened. I thought she would be devastated, but all she did was laugh. That *really* shocked me. Maybe I wasn't worldly, but the thought of getting into bed with my future mother-in-law was too much for me! I never understood how Venetia could think an episode like that was so funny.

Venetia had experienced a profound personal trauma as a teenager, and left to process the difficult experience with no family support, she struggled with depression and was often mercurial. Sometimes she was joyous, and a moment later she would be distraught. And yet, I ignored all the warning signs, and we were married on Valentine's Day in 1956. The small wedding was held at the beautiful, all-glass Wayfarers Chapel, on a hill overlooking the ocean in Rancho Palos Verdes, California. As Venetia approached me waiting at the pulpit, the organ music stopped, and we turned to face the preacher. It had been a gray morning, but at that exact moment, the fog lifted, and the sun came out, magically illuminating the entire church. I thought this was a sign from God that our marriage was going to last forever. (Spoiler alert: a more accurate guess would have been eleven months.) In retrospect, perhaps God was really trying to tell us to "see the light" and part ways before it was too late. But it was already way too late.

I was thrilled about the marriage, and so was MGM. On our wedding night, they put us up in a beautiful suite at the luxurious Hotel Bel-Air. The next morning, we flew to the premiere of *The Last Hunt*, a film I had recently appeared in. It was about buffalo hunters, and so its debut was held in Rapid City, South Dakota. We traveled with its stars, Stewart Granger and Robert Taylor, in Robert's little Twin Beech airplane, called Missy, which he piloted.

During the flight, Stewart asked Robert what he had thought about working with Greta Garbo in *Camille*. "She was a very strange woman," he said. "I really respected her acting ability, but you never knew what mood she could drop into. One minute she was joking around, and suddenly she was so depressed she would just sit and sulk. You had to constantly be on your toes to follow her moods."

I looked at Venetia, seated next to me, wondering if she had heard. To me, it was as if he were talking about the time we had been preparing to celebrate her birthday. She was putting on makeup in our bathroom when suddenly I heard crying and rushed in.

"What's wrong?" I asked.

Venetia stood before the mirror looking like perfection itself, like a young goddess. "Look at me. I'm getting so old. My face will be getting wrinkles soon."

No matter how robustly I reassured her during these spells, she was not moved. Still, that was mostly a happy time. After Rapid City, Venetia and I went to New York for another *Last Hunt* premiere. While there, we got a call from Venetia's old friend Tab Hunter, who came up to our suite at the Park Plaza for Dom Pérignon champagne and Russian beluga caviar. When we opened the champagne, the cork hit the ceiling and landed in Venetia's vichyssoise. It splashed all over her, and we burst into laughter. Finally, Venetia and I went to Vermont for our honeymoon. We celebrated mightily, like a couple of spoiled rich kids. Unfortunately, in actuality, we were only a couple of lost kids, and we had no idea of the dark cloud that had yet to pass over us.

We were way too young to have gotten married, and she was a very troubled young lady who I was too immature to handle. Often, she was incapable of making eye contact, and when we went to a friend's house, she would retreat to a corner or even to another room.

This was a high time for me. I was a young celebrity with such a bright future to look forward to, and I was loving the perks of being an MGM player. Even when I wasn't filming, I often spent time at the studio and hung out with my fellow actors. Just visiting different soundstages could be an adventure, like the time in 1956 I found myself on the set of *Somebody Up There Likes Me*. I wanted to say hello to Pier Angeli, who was playing the wife of middleweight boxing legend Rocky Graziano, portrayed by Paul Newman. I'd gotten to know Pier through Vic Damone, who I had been friendly with since we had filmed *Hit the Deck* together. Pier and I were having a little chat in her dressing room when Paul showed up. Pier introduced us and then left for a dinner date with Vic. Paul and I hit it off and easily fell into a long, far-ranging conversation.

Finally, Paul told me that he was having his car washed at the corner gas station, which was just at the end of the block, outside the main studio gate. "Would you mind driving me to my car?" he asked.

"Sure, but I have a little two-seater Austin-Healey, and the front seat is filled with boxes," I said. "I'll just have to move it all into the trunk, which is empty."

"Oh, don't bother. I'll ride in the trunk. I'll hold it open a crack so I can breathe."

I laughed at this image, but sure, it sounded like a reasonable plan to me. We walked out to my car together, and Paul curled up in the trunk, grasping the door from the inside. That's how I found myself driving off the MGM lot with Paul Newman as a stowaway. As was often the case, about a dozen fans waited at the entrance gate. Seeing me, they swarmed my car to ask for an autograph. When I finished signing, they all backed away, but I called over to them, "Hey, don't you want Paul Newman's autograph? He's in my trunk."

They all laughed, thinking I was joking, and nobody took me up on my offer. With a big grin on my face, I drove to the gas station. When we arrived, Paul jumped out of the trunk, flashing that classic wry, tough-guy smile. "Thanks a lot, asshole," he said.

"No problem!" I quipped with a smile of my own.

I was in the orbit of other young Hollywood actors, and it was a relatively small and comradely world, at least in my experience. Later that year, in December, I made an appearance on *The Walter Winchell Show*, a half-hour live variety television program, hosted by the famous entertainment reporter. The night was memorable, that's for sure. I performed a dance with Filipino actress and dancer Neile Adams. The number had been choreographed to show off my acrobatic abilities. However, when I was lifting Neile down, as she jumped off the piano, her dress blew up over my head, and I was trapped beneath her flaring skirt. I extricated myself fairly quickly, but because we were filming live, the audience at home saw the whole bizarre sequence. In my experience, it was one of the wilder and funnier moments from the days of live television. Others must agree, as the clip survives on the internet.

That wasn't the only notable happening that week. In the days before we broadcast, Neile brought her boyfriend to a rehearsal. During our lunch break, I spent some time chatting with him. He told me he was an actor and had just done a part in his first movie, *Somebody Up There Likes Me* with Paul Newman.

"Great, I was just visiting that set myself!" I told him about driving off the lot with Paul in the trunk of my car, which made us both laugh. "Did you have a good part in the film?" I asked.

"No, not really," he said. "It was just a bit part. I didn't even get billing, but I'm hoping something better comes along soon!"

I had seen how long "something better" could take, so I gave him some advice. "You might be better off finding some other kind of job, because so many actors are out of work in Hollywood, and the chances of you getting anywhere are pretty slim."

He nodded thoughtfully, taking in my words. But thankfully, he decided not to listen to me and went on to pursue his acting dream. It wasn't long before I and everyone else around the world knew his name: Steve McQueen.

I was having fun, acting and kicking around Hollywood, but because of my marriage, this period in my life was often nothing short of miserable. Venetia couldn't overcome her painful past or her terrible depression, and I couldn't cope with the strain. And yet, I wasn't ready to separate. We kept up a good front for the press, but underneath it all, we were falling apart.

Finally, less than a year into our marriage, she broke the bad news to me: she was ending it. She wanted to concentrate more on her career and live alone while doing it. Rather than being relieved, I couldn't believe her.

"Why?" I asked.

"I'm not good for you. Look, Rusty, some day, when you grow up, you'll see I was right. You'll come back to me and say, 'Thank you.'"

Devastated, I left our apartment and careened down Sunset Boulevard, unsure where I was going. When the divorce papers were delivered to me a few days later, I just looked at them. I had no idea what to do. So I went to see the man I considered my mentor, Joseph H. Lewis, who had directed me so wisely in *Gun Crazy*. He comforted me and helped me to retain his brother, Ben, to be my lawyer. Although the divorce was initially painful for me, Venetia and I remained on speaking terms, and I always rooted for her in her career. She went on to land parts in films and shows like *Darby's Rangers* and *Cheyenne*. After a brief affair with Elvis and a long relationship with Ricky Nelson, she married Don Everly of the country-pop duo the Everly Brothers.

Moving out of the apartment Venetia and I had shared didn't feel like an auspicious start to 1957, even though I liked my new beach house in Malibu. January was not a happy month, but by February, I was starting to rebound. I still had my thriving career, and soon I had a brand-new film to absorb me. Based on a hit 1956 William Brinkley novel, *Don't Go Near the Water* was a comedy about navy public relations in the South Pacific, starring Glenn Ford and Gia Scala. It was to film in March on MGM's back lot, which they had made over to look like a tropical island.

I had a supporting role and wasn't always needed on set. So, being the young bachelor I was, I stayed up partying almost every night, especially when I didn't have a big scene the next day. By now, I was fairly comfortable with the moviemaking routine, including the long wait times between scene changes, as well as the set lighting that seemed to take forever. Luckily, the stand-ins were the ones who had to endure the heat of the arc lights for long periods while the cameramen made sure we actors would look good when we performed. Some people read books and others, like Fred Clark, who played the commanding officer, did crossword puzzles.

Since I was often hungover and sleep deprived, I usually managed to nap in my dressing room between takes. And by noon, I had gotten all the sleep I needed. But one night before a shoot when I knew I only had one scene with two short lines, I didn't go to bed at all. The next morning, we filmed the commander, played by Glenn, giving a long speech to a crowd. All I had to do was spit out my two lines. But I was seated next to Glenn, and the camera was on him—and therefore on me—when I fell asleep. Our director shook me awake and said, "Russ, do you realize that you just fell asleep in the middle of a scene?"

Groggily, I looked around. Everyone was staring at me. I was terribly embarrassed. Talk about an unprofessional moment. That was the last time I ever stayed up all night when I had to work the next morning.

Not only was I learning how to be a leading man, but I was feeling more at home in Hollywood, having met many lovers and compatriots on my films. During this shoot, Glenn and I got along well, and I soon confronted him about trying to cut my dance out of *The Fastest Gun Alive*. He sheepishly admitted to having taken this action but said it was nothing personal. "Look, Rusty, I'm married to a dancer," he said.

I nodded, knowing his wife was movie-musical star Eleanor Powell, one of the greats.

"I love dancers!" he continued. "I just didn't think it was appropriate for my little western."

We had a good laugh about that and became fast and lasting friends.

Seven Brides for Seven Brothers (1954): Russ as Gideon, the youngest brother, doing his famous axe jump.

Learning to dance during the number "Goin' Courtin'" with the Pontipee brothers. From left to right: Matt Mattox, Marc Platt, Jane Powell, Russ, Jacques d'Amboise, Jeff Richards, and Tommy Rall.

The Fastest Gun Alive (1956): Russ as Eric Doolittle doing his famous shovel dance.

The young Hollywood couple: Russ with first wife Venetia Stevenson.

Head over heels with Venetia in Beverly Hills (from the iconic 1955 *Life* magazine article).

Hit the Deck (1955):
with dance partner
Debbie Reynolds.

Debbie and Russ relaxing on
the set—
Russ kept this photo in his
wallet for years.

CHAPTER 3

MGM Days

By this point, I was becoming increasingly enmeshed in the MGM universe. With my multiyear contract and newfound fame from my recent hit films and high-profile marriage, I was an asset to the studio, and they took care of me. They provided me with the services of well-known MGM publicist Dore Freeman, who handled nearly all my publicity. Mostly, this meant photo spreads and movie premieres, which were easy and fun. However, one day, I received a call from Howard Strickling, the head of the publicity department. He wanted me to come see him regarding an important matter.

Oh my God, I've knocked up some girl and my career is over! I thought.

When I walked into Howard's office, he asked me to sit down across from him. "I have some very bad news for you, Russ, but MGM will do everything in its power to help you out of this mess," he said.

My heart sank, landing in my guts with a thud. I knew it had to be something serious for Howard to be handling the matter himself. He then showed me a torn-up marriage certificate with my signature on it, accompanied by a very long, nasty letter from a girl in El Paso, Texas. She wrote how much she hated me for taking her across the border to get married in Juárez and then disappearing the next morning. I was too confused to really panic, especially when I looked at the signature and could see it wasn't my handwriting. Also, the date on the marriage certificate proved I couldn't have been with her in Mexico, because I had been attending an MGM premiere. I outlined all of this for Howard.

"Don't worry about it," he said. "I'll write her a letter, explaining that it was obviously someone posing as you."

What a relief! Although it was a little unsettling that someone was going around using my name and my fame to marry unsuspecting girls, it seemed relatively harmless. I felt glad for the studio's support and to know the situation had been resolved. Well, at least for the moment.

As a studio player, I no longer had to audition for roles. Even better, after the popularity of *Seven Brides for Seven Brothers*, I was now getting my pick of parts—and not just in MGM pictures. I was approached by director Mark Robson about a film he was doing for 20th Century Fox. It was an adaptation of the novel *Peyton Place*, which had been a bestselling and scandalous literary sensation and was sure to pack movie theaters. Robson explained several roles in the project could be good for me, and it was my choice. After reading the script, I decided to tackle the character of Norman Page, a role that appealed to me because he was the least like me in many ways. To personify his quiet awkwardness, I drew myself inward, using physical details, like combing my hair forward and fidgeting, to help me feel closer to the character and bring him to life on screen.

I was the first to be cast in the film, and Mark asked me to read with several actresses who were auditioning for the young female lead, Allison. We had some big scenes together, so the chemistry between us had to be just right. Every actress came in with an impressive résumé and photo album, claiming she had read the book and really wanted the part. Finally, Diane Varsi stepped up to read. Unlike the others, she had no portfolio or publicity photos and said she had not read the book. When asked what she had acted in, she said her only experience was a drama class and one play. Also, she was candid that she wasn't even positive she wanted to do the film—she liked to write poetry and seemed unsure of everything else. But there was nothing uncertain about her performance. We read the scene, and both Mark and I knew we had found our Allison. We contained our enthusiasm until she left. Then we agreed it had been an odd audition, but she seemed perfect to play the shy and troubled writer, as that was who she was in real life.

Off I went to Rockland, Maine, to begin filming. I was playing an innocent, introverted young man who discovered first love with an equally uncertain young woman, played by Diane. Our characters' delicate friendship developed primarily because we both had troubled home lives, which were played out in dramatic scenes that gave us both an opportunity to flex our acting chops.

Working in Rockland was an amazing experience, and I enjoyed everything about my time there. Right after we arrived, a wealthy local man welcomed us with a lobster bake. For the festivities, we all boarded his large, beautiful schooner and sailed to a small island he owned. Someone had gone ahead and dug an impressive firepit in which to cook the many live lobsters we brought with us. The lobsters were delicious, and everyone had a fabulous time. On the way back to the mainland, our host pointed out a tiny isle that was for sale. It was less than an acre but very scenic, and the thought of owning an island excited me. I decided, right then and there, I would buy it! Unfortunately, when I went to make an offer, the land had just been sold.

Although he was two decades older than me and played the part of the film's villain, Arthur Kennedy impressed me with his acting talent. We bonded immediately, becoming great friends and hanging out together whenever we could. One afternoon, while on location, which was twenty or thirty miles from our hotel, we were told we wouldn't be needed for several hours. There was a shallow river gently flowing into the bay, so we borrowed a rowboat from a local. We were having a terrific time, singing, laughing, and yelling like pirates, when suddenly the rowboat ran aground. We hadn't noticed how shallow the water had become. We decided to leave the boat where it was and walk a little farther up the streambed, just to see what was ahead. When we returned, to our great surprise, we discovered that the boat was now resting on a completely dry riverbed. We realized the river was tidal, and as the tide went out, the water was rapidly disappearing. We had merrily rowed about half a mile upstream from where we had started, and we were about to be stranded. Panicking, we struggled to pick up the heavy boat and toiled our way down the creek bed with it, as fast as we could. Heavy as the boat was, it took us a full ten minutes to catch up with the receding water. Thankfully we did, because we never would have gotten the boat back on foot.

While we were on location, Diane and I both stayed at the Thorndike Hotel in Rockland, and her room was right down the hall from mine. In keeping with my penchant for dancing on the edge, I could be fairly lighthearted and impulsive, and I loved doing pratfalls and playing pranks on my costars. Diane did not have that type of sense of humor. In fact, she didn't seem to have any sense of humor at all. She had a sweet demeanor, but it was easy to see that beneath her quiet exterior, she was a deeply complicated person. Instead of hanging out with the rest of the cast and crew, she kept to herself and spent much of her time in her room, writing dark poetry. She reminded me of Venetia, from the fact that they were both Pisces to the deeper truth that they were both very troubled. Maybe it was because I was still pining for Venetia, or maybe I was developing a habit of rescuing tragic beauties, but I was fascinated by Diane.

The night before our first big scene together, I called Diane in her room. "Would you like to run through our scene tonight?" I asked.

"Yes, but not in the hotel," she said. "Maybe outside in the woods somewhere."

"Okay, but it will be dark in the woods."

"That's all right. I don't care."

I called our director, Mark, and told him about Diane's suggestion.

"Great," he said, "I'll bring a flashlight. Meet me downstairs in fifteen minutes."

I walked down with Diane, and there was Mark, waiting in the lobby. The three of us left the town behind, setting out into the shadowy woods. It was a strange, still, moonless night. When we found a clearing among dense trees, we paused and arranged ourselves for the scene. As Diane and I began to run our lines, Mark shone the flashlight in our faces so we could see each other's expressions and play off each other. Our rehearsal went well and was helpful, but undoubtedly, it was the most unconventional scene run-through I ever did.

As we had established, Diane and I had obvious chemistry, on screen and off. We became closer as filming progressed. Late one Saturday night, when I was returning to my hotel room from the bar, I noticed Diane down the hall, sitting in front of her door. I leaned down toward her. "Are you okay?" I asked.

"No, I'm depressed," she said.

When I expressed my sympathy, she invited me in and explained how unhappy she was in her marriage. I could tell she needed to vent, and I settled in for what seemed likely to be a lengthy conversation. Thankfully, it was Saturday night, and we didn't have to work the next day. After I had listened for a while, I smiled sympathetically and let her know I could relate. "I just went through a divorce myself, and it was really hard at first, but it's actually starting to feel good to be free," I said.

This seemed to cheer her up, or maybe it was just having a sympathetic ear to unburden herself to, after weeks of doing her best to be professional around the rest of the cast and crew. I was happy to be a friend to Diane, but at that time in my life, it was not in my nature to be very introspective. I had also just had a few beers and was feeling a little high, so I leaped up on her bed, my hands outstretched.

"I've got just the thing for you," I said. "It's called 'The Divorce Dance.'" I jumped up and down to demonstrate. "Come on, join me!"

Diane stood on the mattress with me, uncertainly at first, but she soon had a broad smile on her face. "This is crazy, but I like it. I'm starting to feel better!"

We jumped up and down, higher and higher, kicking our legs out in front of us and flailing our arms in the air. We began laughing so hard that we both lost our balance and fell onto the bed. Now that we were lying next to each other in a big heap of tangled limbs, the mood shifted again. We began kissing and soon made love. Over the next few weeks, our attraction developed into an on-set romance. After we had gotten to know each other, she was warm and easy to be with, and I felt a deep connection to her during our brief time together.

One Friday night, after the day's filming, I was sitting on my bed, writing a letter to my parents. My in-room phone rang. It was George Pal, who had produced such hits as *Destination Moon* and *The War of the Worlds*, telling me that he would be helming my next film assignment for MGM, a musical version of the Brothers Grimm fairy tale "Tom Thumb." He was bursting with enthusiasm, and it was catching. So the next morning I went to Rockland's public library and found the collected fairy tales. As I sat there poring over "Tom Thumb," I became more and more excited. *What a dynamic story!* It was very dark and full of poetry, and I loved the almost surreal image of a team of mice pulling Tom Thumb's tiny coffin after he had been killed by a poisonous spider. I could hardly wait to hear the music and read the script.

I was beginning to feel better than I had since the early days of my marriage. Being on location, working on a film that stretched me as an actor and allowed me to form deep and meaningful relationships, was a wonderful balm for my heartbreak, and being on set was a welcome distraction from my real-life pain. And my career was on an unstoppable upward trajectory. I couldn't wait for whatever adventure would come next. But then, as I was wrapping up my time in Rockland, I received some devastating news from home.

My mother called, telling me that Dad was on his deathbed. He had been diagnosed with brain cancer the previous year, and he had been hospitalized for treatment. The experience had been very emotional for me, especially as I was only twenty-two years old and still on the cusp of manhood myself. Even though my father and I weren't close, as he had never really been there for me, seeing him hospitalized at only age fifty was very hard for me. I still had very mixed emotions about him, and it seemed impossible to know where to put my anger now that he was dying. As I listened to my mother, I touched my right knee, which was still weak from his amateur repair job. This was now a professional liability, as I was known for my dancing and tumbling in the movies. But all my past anger and sadness seemed to fall away.

Although Dad never hugged me when I was a child, and we never sat and talked as adults, we had shared one surprising moment of tenderness—the best I ever had with him—after his brain operation. He had been lying on his hospital bed with his head all bandaged up, but his eyes were clear and bright. When he looked over at me, seated by his bedside, he smiled. Then he reached out and held my hand. He had never done that before. In fact, it was the first time I could remember him showing me any affection, and it was just as I was about to lose his presence in my life forever. As we sat and held hands, I wept. Remembering this made me feel tender toward Dad and eager to see him one last time.

The next morning, I filmed my final scene and left for the airport immediately, catching the earliest flight I could book. On the plane, an attractive flight attendant recognized me and said hello. We got along well enough that I invited her to come see me at my beach house in Malibu. When she turned up a few days later, she brought along some marijuana. It was my first experience smoking pot, but I immediately took to it. Although it hadn't become mainstream yet in the late fifties, it wasn't hard to find in LA, and I partook often in those days.

When I landed, I raced straight to my mother's house. I wanted to be there when my father passed, but I arrived a few hours too late. He died while I was in midair. After the adrenaline-filled day of filming and cross-country travel, I sank onto the couch beside my mother. I was awash in a swirl of emotions, and I found myself unsure what to do or say. I wasn't thinking about the loss of my father as much as I was worried about my mother and how I could support her in her grief. So I stayed close to her and let her express her emotions.

Mom and I hadn't seen each other since before I left for Rockland. She said that about a month earlier, Dad had awoken from a sound sleep and told her about a terrible nightmare. He had dreamed there was a violent thunderstorm, and he could feel himself being lifted into it.

"The strange thing," she said, "is that last night, there was a huge thunderstorm when he passed away. It was the worst summer storm we've had in years."

Mom and I sat on her couch in silence. I put my arm around her, attempting to console her. But no matter how much we had tried to prepare ourselves for Dad's passing, it remained incomprehensible, as it always is to lose a loved one. Suddenly, I had an idea. I knew Mom had never been to Europe, so I told her I would soon be going to London to film *tom thumb* (George Pal insisted the film title always be written in all lowercase letters, to play up the diminutive size of my character). "Would you like to go with me?" I asked.

"Yes," she said, smiling for the first time all day.

"Is there any particular place in Europe you've always wanted to visit?"

"The Isle of Capri," she said, without needing to consider.

"You got it!" I said. "We'll go over early, rent a car, and drive across the continent. MGM will take care of everything."

As I was beginning to learn, being a movie star came with all the perks I could have wanted and more. I knew our trip couldn't bring Dad back, but it could give Mom an exciting distraction and allow us to spend time together in a new way.

Still depressed about my personal life and experiencing culture shock after having been tucked away in a sleepy and picturesque Maine town, I headed home to Malibu. When I arrived at my rented beach house, which I hadn't seen in several months, I received another shock. There was an eviction notice on my front door. Apparently, while I was away, the neighbors had complained to the owner about all the partying on weekends. Checking on his property, he had been appalled by what he found. I soon realized he wasn't just being an old fuddy-duddy, either. When I walked in, I couldn't believe my eyes. It was a mess! In my absence, I had lent the house to my new friend Elvis Presley. I had met him as he was preparing to film *Jailhouse Rock*, which was an MGM picture. My friend Alex Romero was helping with the choreography and had me give Elvis some pointers for his dance moves in the film. One afternoon, Elvis and I were having lunch in his dressing room on the set. Afterward, we started fooling around with some dance steps. He liked the way I could quickly pop my knees in more dramatically than he could. "Can you teach me how you did that?" he asked.

"Sure," I said, showing him the move again. "Just exaggerate what you're already doing. You've got the right moves. You just need to give it a little more oomph."

He mimicked what I had done, and I worked with him for the rest of the lunch break. When we headed back to the set, he showed Alex what he'd learned. Alex was very impressed and gave me a thumbs-up. This would become one of his signature moves. Elvis was a hard worker, and it certainly paid off for him in that film. I thought it was one of his best.

Elvis and I got along well, so I had invited him to stop by for a visit in Malibu, an offer he accepted several days later.

The first time he walked into my house, I was playing a record on the turntable, and he stopped in his tracks, listening intently. "What's that? Who is that?" he asked, clearly smitten with the sound.

"It's 'Jelly, Jelly' by Josh White," I said.

"Can I borrow the record?" he asked.

Having just watched Elvis Presley fall in love with one of my favorite musicians, I happily obliged. Of course, I never got the record back. It was the same with all the girlfriends I had around that time—I introduced them to Elvis, and I never got them back. That's not a joke, either. Who could compete with him?

Even so, I liked Elvis, and again, he was Elvis Presley! Of course it was fun to hang around with him. So before I left for Rockland, I was only too happy to oblige when he made a small request of me: "Hey, Russ, while you're gone, can I use the house as a quiet getaway on weekends?"

Yes, I knew he traveled with a large entourage—his cousins, girlfriends, and bodyguards—and they liked to have a good time. But I definitely was not prepared for the chaos they unleashed. My house was a total shambles. Half-eaten peanut-butter-and-banana sandwiches had been left just about everywhere, even down inside the bedsheets and in the drawers of the bedside tables. Of the more than two dozen glasses I had owned, which had been stored in a kitchen cupboard, only two remained. Many of the broken shards were strewn all over the floor, along with piles of trash. It was such a mess I had to use a rake to clean up the big stuff before I could even bring in a broom. So much for what Elvis had originally asked of me (a quiet getaway, my ass!).

When I confronted Elvis about the utter destruction he had wrought, he apologized profusely and admitted things had gotten a little out of hand. He had his manager, Colonel Tom Parker, send me a check to cover the damages. Of course, most of the money went to the owner so I could avoid being evicted.

After I had finally cleaned up my place, I sat on the deck for several days, staring at the ocean and thinking about Dad. Although he had experienced disappointment and hardship in his life that had led him to be a distant and volatile man, it didn't take much digging to turn up good memories of times we had spent together: embarking on crazy fishing trips, scarfing down chili hot dogs at the Hugo's stand, playing games of croquet on our front lawn, camping under the epic trees in Sequoia, and singing and dancing for company with Mom at our house. Once he taught me his eccentric drunk dance for a performance during which I sang "Show Me the Way to Go Home" at the Seville Theatre in Inglewood. Yes, he had greatly influenced my career in such a powerful way.

A week later, we held Dad's funeral at Forest Lawn Memorial Park. It was a very sad day, and Mom's tears flowed throughout the ceremony. Their marriage had been far from perfect, but they had clearly patched things up, getting back together and having another son. I felt I had to be strong, to support my mother and younger brother, Larry. I knew there was nothing I could say to make them feel better, but I comforted Mom as much as I could, telling her to try to think about our upcoming trip to Europe. It was difficult, but we managed to get through it together.

Although we had finished our location shoot in Maine, I still had a few scenes to do for *Peyton Place*, which meant filming on the Fox lot in Los Angeles, where all of Lana Turner's scenes were shot. One morning, I arrived about an hour early and headed for my dressing room. While walking down the second-floor hallway, I recognized Robert Mitchum coming the other way with a big guy who resembled him. Mitchum's dressing room was right across the hall from mine, and we arrived in front of our doors at the same time.

"Good morning, Mr. Mitchum," I said, a little starstruck.

"Call me Mitch. You're Russ, right?" He invited me in and introduced me to his friend, who was his stand-in. The first thing he did was open his window, complaining about how he needed air. Then he abruptly lit a cigarette. Next, he went to the refrigerator and made himself and his friend double Bloody Marys.

"Want one?" he asked.

"No, thanks," I said. It was seven thirty in the morning.

Mitch started going on about how much he liked musicals, especially *Seven Brides*, because the male dancers in the film were masculine. While he was telling me about several songs he had written, the phone rang. His friend answered it and told Mitch the publicity department wanted him to do some sort of benefit for the film he was shooting. "Tell them, 'Thanks but no thanks!'" Mitch said.

A few minutes later, the phone rang again. It was the same publicity person, pursuing the same request. While still talking to me, Mitch grabbed the phone, ripped it out of the wall, walked over to the window, and threw it out. It was remarkable how he could be both so calm and ill tempered at the same time.

I couldn't help but smile—this was the same Mitch who was already a legend in my mind. I had always been a big fan, and not only of his acting. After his arrest in 1948 for possession of marijuana, the booking sergeant asked Mitch for his occupation. "Well, before this arrest, I used to be an actor," he replied.

But my favorite Mitchum line was delivered after he served his fifty-day jail sentence. A reporter asked him how he had liked the desert prison farm. "I thought it was just great," he said. "Kind of like Palm Springs without the riffraff."

I was just starting to smoke marijuana around the time that I met him. But I had always found it bizarre that people cared what Mitch or anyone else did, and that they only seemed satisfied when he quit marijuana, which was then illegal, and smoked cigarettes instead. Unfortunately, of course, it was the cigarettes that would kill him in the end—not the pot.

Before I went back to my own dressing room, Mitch invited me to visit him on the set of his current picture, *The Enemy Below*. A few days later, I had some free time, so I hung out for several hours in his trailer. At one point, Mitch and I started sharing stories about our various drug escapades, and I told him about the time I almost got swept up in a heroin bust while attending a party at Barbara Burns's house. Luckily, the cops who were hiding outside in the bushes had waited until I left to charge in, a story I only heard from an officer who served as a consultant when I filmed *High School Confidential*.

After we had been talking and laughing for a while, Mitch's costar Theodore Bikel came in with his guitar and played a few folk songs for us. They were amazing, and I was very impressed by his talent. I invited both Mitch and Theodore to an upcoming party I was having at my beach house. Mitch had something else going on that night, but Theo accepted. I asked him to bring his guitar if he felt like it, and surprisingly, he did. It was a great party! Among the guests were some of my friends from *Peyton Place*, including Diane Varsi, Terry Moore, David Nelson, and Arthur Kennedy, and my drinking pals Rod Taylor and Jeff Richards. Nick Adams brought Natalie Wood. Dennis Hopper came by himself. At some point, Theo began playing his guitar. Everyone sat around, amazed as this phenomenal talent vigorously slapped his guitar strings and passionately belted out folk songs in Russian, Yiddish, and English. Several weeks later, Theo recorded a wonderful album, *Songs of a Russian Gypsy*. Also, that year, he originated the role of Captain von Trapp in the Broadway production of *The Sound of Music* and starred as Tevye in a stage version of *Fiddler on the Roof*.

After the other guests left my party that night, Diane hung around, clearly needing a friend. Not long after that, she came to see me again, and I sensed something was really bothering her. We took a walk along the beach, and she opened up to me. "I hate the Hollywood life, and I'm thinking of moving back East," she said.

"You should try to stick it out a little longer, because you are really going to be in demand when *Peyton Place* is released."

She nodded her head absently, like she heard me but was past caring.

As it turned out, we were both nominated for Academy Awards in 1958, and the Academy Awards ceremony was the last time I ever saw her. Not long after that, she abruptly left Los Angeles and moved to Vermont. She just couldn't stand all the attention and hype that came with Hollywood and preferred a quieter life.

After Arthur Kennedy and I worked together, we remained good friends for several years. Everyone who knew him called him Johnny— his real name was John Kennedy, but when he started acting, people told him that an up-and-coming politician from Massachusetts had the same name, so Johnny decided to go by his middle name, Arthur. He was a great actor, and although he never won an Academy Award, he was nominated five times. He lived in New York, but during these years, whenever he came to California, he would call me. He was also close friends with Anthony Quinn, who had a house in Pacific Palisades. We had dinner there one night, and Tony showed us many Gothic, religious-looking paintings he had acquired. However, he had painted most of the paintings on his walls himself. He had a whole house full of interesting art, and I was very impressed. He was probably one of the first people I knew in Hollywood who showed me that it was possible to pursue other passions in addition to acting.

On another evening, Johnny brought Tony by my beach house. Three pretty girls were visiting me. Tony boldly hit on one of them right away and tried to get her into the top bunk, although the rest of us were in the room. It was awkward for the girl, and I grew embarrassed, rolling my eyes and giving Johnny a dirty look. He just shrugged his shoulders, smiled, and whispered in my ear, "That's Tony."

I didn't say anything to Johnny, but I was disappointed that an actor I admired as much as Anthony Quinn could be so tactless, and I never again invited him over. Of course, I would soon have several girls living with me in the same room, but the mood was different—very light—as they were all women who had chosen to enjoy free love and an unconventional lifestyle with me.

I couldn't have been more excited to work with George Pal, who had made a name for himself as a pioneer in the fields of special effects, science fiction, and fantasy filmmaking. He had begun his career with his Puppetoons, a unique new form of animation featuring three-dimensional objects that were carefully photographed, frame by frame, with slight changes of position each time, so they appeared like cartoons. For *tom thumb*, he planned to use Puppetoons and actors, an idea that excited me.

Unfortunately, after reading the Brothers Grimm fairy tale, I found George's script of *tom thumb* to be a big disappointment. The title was styled in lowercase, which was about all I liked about the adaptation. I thought his version was sweet but a silly, fluffy reupholstering of the original. For the first time since I'd broken out in Hollywood, I wasn't sure about the quality of the material or the use of my time. I drove to MGM and went straight in to see George. When I told him how upset I was, he explained there were many versions of the story, and I must have read one of the darker ones. Besides, he had just signed Peggy Lee to pen some of the music. Not only was she writing a special song for me, "Tom Thumb's Tune," but she also wanted to meet me.

That made me feel better about the whole endeavor. I admired Peggy Lee's sultry, jazz-tinged pop music; one of my favorite songs was "Fever." I had several of her albums at home, including one of her more obscure gems, *Sea Shells*, which I loved.

Sure enough, Peggy called me up that evening and invited me to a small party. She resided in a gorgeous mansion in Bel Air, with a swimming pool and an elegant, formal Japanese garden. I was particularly impressed by a magnificent chandelier she had purchased at a flea market in Paris. I was so excited to be there, in her presence, as I had always been such a fan. The whole time I was at her house, I noticed her observing me. At one point, she saw me looking at her and came over.

"Excuse me for staring at you, but I'm going to write a song about you for *tom thumb*, and I want it to be just right," she said.

"I'm honored," I said, beaming. "I have several of your albums and am a big fan of yours." *Oh my God, she's going to get into me and write something that really fits me!* I thought. When I got home, I called several friends and bragged about how Peggy Lee was penning an in-depth song about me.

A week or so later, George called and told me to come in and listen to "Tom Thumb's Tune." I raced to the studio, sat down in George's office, and heard:

Too-dee, do-dee, dum-dum-dum.

George loved it, but part of his charm was his childlike enthusiasm and the creative twinkle in his brain. All the way home, I kept thinking, *Too-dee, do-dee, dum, dum, DUMB!* After my initial disappointment, however, the song did grow on me, and I was excited to be working with Peggy.

Mom was so thrilled about our trip to Europe, she couldn't sleep for a week before we left. MGM booked us in a first-class, two-bedroom suite on the SS *Île de France*, sailing from New York to its home port in Le Havre, France. The ship was extraordinary, with a cutting-edge style; it was the first ocean liner with an art deco interior. The luxurious dining room rose three decks high, and in my tux, I walked Mom down the grand staircase to dinner every night.

We rented a car in Paris and drove south through the beautiful French countryside. While we were traversing the French Alps, a torrential downpour pummeled our car. I did my best to negotiate a sharp curve, but our car slid down an embankment and stopped just short of a little farmhouse. A woman ran out, screaming in French. She motioned for both of us to come inside, taking us down a flight of stairs to an adjacent wine cellar. She pointed up to the ceiling, and much to our amazement, we realized our car was resting on the roof. We were extremely lucky it hadn't come smashing through. The lady was nice enough to call us a tow truck and even offered us a glass of wine.

After arriving in Rome and visiting popular tourist sites, from the Colosseum to the Pantheon, I took Mom to dinner at Alfredo alla Scrofa, which everyone called Alfredo's. It was one of Italy's most famous restaurants, as it was where fettuccine Alfredo was invented. *Seven Brides* had been very popular in Italy, and I was immediately recognized and given the royal treatment. They put us at the best table. The owner himself, with his big thick mustache, served us the now-world-famous pasta dish. I was even allowed to use the golden fork and spoon that had been gifted to Alfredo by Mary Pickford and Douglas Fairbanks, two of Hollywood's Golden Age film stars, during frequent meals there on their honeymoon.

Mom couldn't stop smiling, especially when we took a ferry from Naples to Capri, where we visited the Blue Grotto and other attractions. I had told Mom that I would occasionally be going out by myself on this trip and didn't want any complaints if I returned late. One night, I went to a bar in Capri and met an English girl who was traveling around the continent. We had a great time talking, and I didn't go back until midnight. I knocked on Mom's bedroom door, but she wasn't there. I waited for two hours, growing more and more worried. Finally, she strolled in, and I told her how upset I was and scolded her for not calling me. Laughing, she reminded me of how many times I had come home late when *she* was scared half to death. Touché, Mom!

When we arrived in London, my mom was due to leave the next day. George Pal gave her a beautiful bouquet of flowers as a farewell gift, and I was very happy to have been able to fulfill her dreams. I would be working at the legendary Elstree Studios (which was later used to film *Star Wars* and *Superman*), and I was treated like a major star. MGM had rented me a luxurious flat with two spacious bedrooms; plus, I had a per diem that added up to a thousand dollars a week (in British pounds) and a chauffeured limousine at my disposal twenty-four hours a day.

Alex Romero and I had worked out some of the dance routines in the rehearsal hall back at MGM, but the majority of our choreography had to be created in conjunction with huge sets being built in London. One amazing production number, "Talented Shoes," had been inspired by one of Fred Astaire's dance numbers in *Royal Wedding*. In my version, I appeared to dance across a cobbler's bench, pulled by shoes given to me by the cobbler. To create the effect, a ninety-foot-long and thirty-five-foot-high bench was constructed, balancing like a seesaw, on a piece of steel. The bench cost $40,000 to build, and the scene took six days to film.

Another fabulous set built for me was a giant crib, on which I performed Peggy Lee's profound song, inspired by me—"Too-dee, do-dee-do." As my character was only meant to be five inches tall, the camera was usually shooting me from about one hundred feet away to create this illusion. So I had to respond to everything in as big a way as I could. For example, when the two crooks, Tony (played by Peter Sellers) and Ivan (played by Terry-Thomas), chased me, I couldn't just make a fearful face, as it would never register in the shot. So I jumped up in the air, throwing my arms out to the side, as if to say, *Oh my God, they're after me!* I soon realized this was probably going to be the broadest performance of my career. I couldn't talk in a normal voice; I had to yell almost all my lines. In addition to using a Tom Thumb doll, they filmed me against a blue screen and then added me into scenes. After many colors were tested, it was blue that worked the best. Since then, the blue (or green) screen technique has become industry standard.

It was during the auditions for interesting-looking background players and dancers that Alex Romero alerted me to a showgirl named Elizabeth Kempton auditioning for a small part. She was gorgeous. "Hire her!" I said, oblivious to the fact that I had just met my future second wife.

At Christmastime in London, Alex and I decided to do something for the children who lived in one of the city's poorest neighborhoods. I bought a bunch of toys that Alex and I gift wrapped and put in the back of our car from the studio. We drove to a run-down area and parked. Then we got out of the car with our bags of gifts, like a couple of Santa Clauses, and stood beneath a row of apartment flats.

"Merry Christmas to all of the children!" we hollered over and over.

It didn't take long for kids to start coming around to check us out, and we gave each of them a toy or a doll. I was a few days away from my twenty-third birthday and had found myself living an unbelievable life of joyous creativity and abundant wealth. It felt wonderful to be able to give back, and to see the smiling faces of these surprised children with their new gifts.

Peyton Place (1957): director Mark Robson and Russ discuss a scene.

Relaxing by the ocean at his Malibu beach house.

Russ and Diane Varsi on the set of *Peyton Place*.

With second wife, Elizabeth, who Russ met while shooting *tom thumb* (1958) in London.

Promo shot from *tom thumb*.

Working with
choreographer Alex
Romero, Russ tries on
the "talented shoes" in
tom thumb.

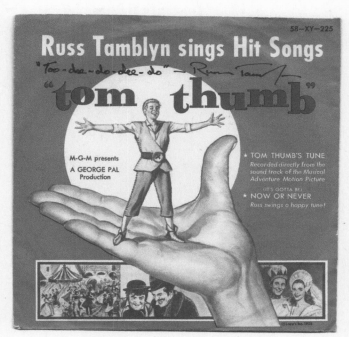

tom thumb:
45 rpm vinyl of
the theme song.

Little Tom Thumb balancing on a paintbrush in the dance with the toys.

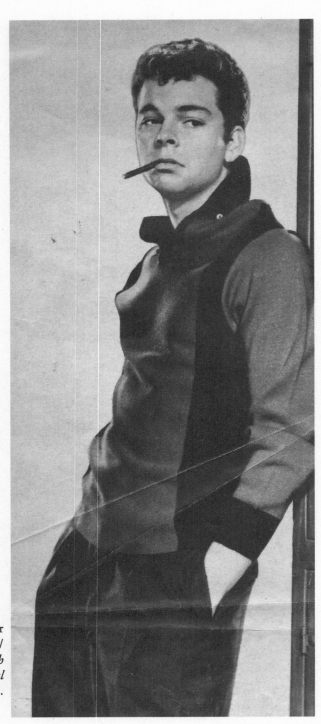

Russ as undercover agent (Tony Baker / Mike Wilson) in *High School Confidential* (1958).

Advertisement for "teensploitation" movie.

CHAPTER 4

A JET ALL THE WAY

At the height of my fame, I was drafted into the army. MGM had assigned me to make one last film before basic training. They flew me back from London, picked me up in a limo on the tarmac, and rushed me to the set of *High School Confidential*. It was an exploitation film masquerading as an exposé about teenage gangs, marijuana, and heroin trafficking. I was obliged to do this corny project because of my contract, but my first scene was with the femme fatale Mamie Van Doren, so things were looking up. The other sweetener was that I got to act with some heirs to Hollywood royalty, including a Barrymore (John Drew) and Charlie Chaplin Jr., as well as Jackie Coogan. The best was hanging out with Jerry Lee Lewis, who taught me some boogie-woogie licks on the piano. The film was good fun to make, and although I didn't realize it at the time, it would become a cult classic.

I then reported to the army at Fort Ord, where I began a two-year stint, during which time I excelled with my physical fitness but not much else. As I began my military career, I had quite the culture shock, finding myself scrambling up a hillside, firing blanks at signs that kept popping up with the message I AM THE ENEMY, while my drill sergeant yelled, "Aim! Aim!" Turning around, I could see Central California's historically rich Monterey Peninsula.

What a sight, I thought. *I can't believe I'm looking at this incredible view while my sergeant's yelling for me to aim blanks at signs.*

Suddenly, the sergeant grabbed me from behind and spun me around. "Get up that hill, Tamblyn, aim at those signs, and kill the enemy!" he yelled at me in a gruff voice.

The next morning, we were standing in formation when the sergeant stopped in front of me and barked, "Tamblyn! The trouble with you is ya been livin' in a make-believe world too long." Unable to adapt to my new celibate lifestyle, I first got in trouble for sneaking off base during basic training for a secret rendezvous with a young starlet, who leaked our meetup to the press. The army was definitely a culture shock, but I enjoyed perks my fellow soldiers did not. One day, a cake from a "Mr. A" arrived. I had no idea who that was, or who would even send me a cake, except maybe my mother? Suddenly, it dawned on me: "Mr. A" was Jackie Coogan's character in *High School Confidential*. Sure enough, my friend had seen fit to take care of me: there in the middle of the pastry was a Prince Albert can that was packed with pot. None of my superiors were any the wiser, and it made my days off far more fun, that's for sure.

After that, I was stationed at Fort Sill in Oklahoma and assigned to the entertainment section of Special Services, which found me organizing dances, talent contests, and fashion shows for the sergeants' wives. Not only was this a cushy military assignment, but I was allowed to live at a motel near the base and take a thirty-day leave to promote my film *tom thumb*. The press junket included riding on a float in the Macy's Thanksgiving Day Parade (which was when I first saw *West Side Story* on Broadway) and traveling to San Francisco, where I visited City Lights Bookstore and bought books by iconic poets who would later become friends, including Allen Ginsberg and Michael McClure.

Unfortunately, I made what I thought were some off-the-record comments about what a joke the army was to a reporter, who clearly knew this story would be big—and it was, when it got picked up by the Associated Press. I was briefly demoted to the much less fabulous tank company. Thankfully, I was soon able to talk my way back into Special Services, where my main duty was to teach a weekly trampoline class to officers' wives, and I got away with smoking contraband pot sent to me hidden in a cake by actor Jackie Coogan. I was even allowed to take long weekends in Dallas, as well as a break to film a remake of the classic 1931 western *Cimarron* with my old friend Glenn Ford. I finished my stint in the army as a corporal, the lowest rank of noncommissioned officers, but I was no longer the lowest of the low, and I felt like a general! I had gained a bit of discipline, an appreciation for the sacrifices of our enlisted men, and the companionship of a gorgeous waitress, who traveled back to California with me.

Once out of uniform, I dated around a bit and then decided what I needed to be happy was a lifestyle that would be called polyamorous today (at the time, I thought of it as my harem). I found the perfect bachelor pad, a house in Malibu with private beach access and a fireplace that filled the air with sweet pine smoke that drifted up to a bunk bed with an ocean view. I invited half a dozen women to move in, and we would lounge on the beach and deck all day and then party late, before I went to bed with one of the women each night. While it might have been an unconventional setup for many, we were all getting along and enjoying ourselves.

And then in May 1960, I received a call from my old friend Sammy Davis Jr. A beautiful Dunes showgirl named Elizabeth Kempton, who I had met in Europe in late 1957 while filming *tom thumb*, was looking to reconnect with me. Our love affair had been sweet but brief, and she had given me a sexy pinup photo, which I kept with me while in the army.

When Elizabeth and I reunited in Las Vegas, we impulsively married on our first day together. So maybe it wasn't a harem I wanted after all. I called home to let my girlfriends know they needed to leave, as I would be returning with my wife. Although the ladies had departed, they left chaos behind. One of the first things Elizabeth noticed was that my two cooking pots were all dented. She held one up with a perplexed expression on her face and asked, "What happened?"

"We've been using them for drums and cymbals," I said. My answer did not seem to clarify the matter for her. "I'll buy you all new ones!" I continued.

She nodded but was still looking at me like I was nuts as she began cleaning up the empty bottles, overflowing ashtrays, discarded women's underwear, and general dirtiness.

Unfortunately, Elizabeth wasn't the only one of us to wonder what we had gotten into with this hasty marriage. Right after our nuptials had been announced in the press, all my Hollywood friends began calling me with congratulations.

When Glenn Ford rang me up, he said, "Rusty, I read you got married. What did you do with all your girls?" Of course, that was what he was really interested in! Glenn told me that he wanted to throw Elizabeth and me a party to celebrate our union. I was utterly surprised because he was such a notorious cheapskate. Sure enough, when the soiree did happen, it was actually hosted by Van Johnson and his wife, Evie. Evie and actress Rosalind Russell hosted the event at the Johnsons' plush Beverly Hills mansion. Many celebrities attended, including Henry Fonda, Jack Lemmon, and of course Glenn Ford.

I was having a great time with my old friends, but this Hollywood crowd seemed to overwhelm Elizabeth. She got drunk on champagne and made a pass at Glenn, grabbing his crotch in a very forward way. As Elizabeth and I were leaving the party, Glenn pulled me aside to tell me what had happened and advised me to get rid of her and get an annulment.

My cheeks burned with shame and anger, although I also hadn't been entirely faithful since we had tied the knot, nor would I be for the nineteen years of our marriage. These were obviously bad omens, but something made me stay with her.

Later that night, Elizabeth and I fought about the incident with Glenn. She was still too drunk to explain her actions or remember them in detail, so she denied them at first. Then, when she finally realized what she had done, she threw her wedding ring on the floor and wept. Of course, the next morning she apologized, and I forgave her. Looking back, I can see that I was simply getting a taste of my own medicine, but I had internalized the double standards of the times. I didn't realize that if one partner has the right to fool around, the other one does too.

Unfortunately, infidelity would be just one of our issues over the years, but we both did our best to make a go of it, at least in the beginning.

Not long into our marriage, I embarked on what would be the most challenging movie I ever made and probably the best film of my career, *West Side Story*. It had been a smash hit on Broadway, which was where I had seen the show. I wanted the lead part of Tony, so much so that I had already memorized several songs. As soon as I'd heard about the film adaptation, I had been hoping to land the role. The only catch was it was a United Artists movie, and I was an MGM player—if I got the part, the studio would have to agree to loan me out.

It seemed like a good sign when the studio heads said I could test for Tony opposite several actresses who were trying out to play Maria. I put my heart and guts into my audition. Plus, I had an inside track to the film's producer and codirector, Robert Wise, as we had the same agent, Phil Gersh.

Almost every day, I called Phil and asked him what was going on with the part. "It's really narrowed down now," he kept saying. "It's between you and another actor."

Hearing this made me feel anxious and on edge, especially the second or third time around. It was beginning to seem like they would never decide.

Finally, one evening, Phil called me. I could tell from his voice he had bad news. "Russ, I'm so sorry, but the part of Tony went to Richard Beymer. But—the company offered you the role of Riff."

"What?!" I exclaimed. "Playing Riff never even occurred to me. I'm mainly an acrobat, and I'm not sure I could handle all the tough technical dancing Riff has to do in the 'Cool' number." Of course, after pausing a few seconds to think about the opportunity, I came to my senses. "Okay, I'll be Riff!"

"Not so fast," Phil said. "You're under contract to MGM, and they've turned it down."

I had known I would need MGM's permission to do the film, but that had seemed like a technicality. I couldn't believe I was so close to what I already sensed would be the role of a lifetime, and I might be forbidden from taking it.

The next morning, I called Benny Thau, head of MGM, and asked to see him. I was so determined to be in this film, I took his first available time slot and raced over to try to persuade him to reconsider. In his cavernous office, sitting at a huge desk once occupied by Louis B. Mayer, Benny argued that playing the gang leader Riff would go against my clean-cut image. "You have a good reputation here, Russ," he said. "And your career will be ruined if you do this part. You'll have to sing this song 'Gee, Officer Krupke,' which goes, 'My parents treat me rough. With all their marijuana, they won't give me a puff,' and 'My sister wears a mustache. My brother wears a dress'! This just does not fit your image here at MGM. Besides, Russ, we've already cast you in a movie that will be much better for you. It's called *Where the Boys Are* with Connie Francis."

I cringed. A teen musical with Connie Francis was the last thing I wanted to do (and if he knew how much marijuana I was smoking in my private life, he might not have thought of me as quite so clean cut, but I certainly wasn't going to tell him that). Now that I was getting more interested in art and culture, having had my mind expanded during my stint in the army, I was beginning to chafe at the inane subject matter of the average Hollywood studio fare, not to mention the rigidity of the Hollywood studio system, which made me feel like a teenager petitioning a strict parent for my freedom. But if anything was worth fighting for, it was this project. I knew from the outset that *WSS* was something special and would be a challenge worth attempting. I was all in—if I could only convince the studio.

I begged Benny to change his mind and let me do *WSS*. I told him that I had been wanting to do this musical ever since I saw it on Broadway, and I would be absolutely devastated if I couldn't be in it. Benny said he would think about it and get back to me in a couple of days. Of course, he ultimately did give his blessing for me to do the movie, although reluctantly. (Years later, I would find out that MGM's protestations hadn't really been about the film's edgy subject matter; they had been a savvy bargaining tactic to get United Artists to pay me $7,500 a week. Since my salary was only $2,000 a week, MGM pocketed the difference with me none the wiser. But I would get them back after *Where the Boys Are* was aired on television. Thousands of dollars in residuals started pouring in even though I was never in the movie.)

My first meeting at United Artists Studio, to discuss my role as Riff, was with Robert Wise and Jerome Robbins. I was already well known for my on-screen acrobatic dancing. So I had some dance chops. But dancing for the great Jerome Robbins, the visionary choreographer behind *WSS*, was an entirely different matter. Robbins had written, choreographed, and directed the theatrical version of *West Side Story*, which featured the extraordinary score by Leonard Bernstein and was the lyrical debut of iconic composer and lyricist Stephen Sondheim.

Bob was very quiet in the meeting, but Jerry had a lot to say. I was all ears, wanting to learn as much as I could from this artistic force who was a powerful figure in the dance world and an acknowledged genius. I was a little shocked, though, by his directness.

"Listen, Russ," Jerry said. "I know you've tumbled and done gymnastics in all the musicals you've made, but Riff is not an acrobat! You're going to have to do straight dancing in this."

We exchanged a long look, and I could see how much passion he brought to the project.

"I promise I will work hard," I replied. "I'll do the best I can, and I'll try to keep up with the rest of the dancers."

My declaration of intent seemed to placate Jerry—now I had to actually prove myself. We started out rehearsing in Hollywood on the United Artists Studio Lot, also known as Samuel Goldwyn Studio. First up were the wardrobe tests. I arrived early with one of my Jets, David Winters, and we found that we weren't needed for another hour.

"Hey, they're auditioning some dancers on one of the stages," David said. "Let's go check 'em out."

We stood at the back, watching Jerry's first assistant, Howard Jeffrey, audition about thirty dancers. Suddenly, Howard noticed us and became irate. "Russ Tamblyn, you and David get off the stage—I'm auditioning!" he yelled.

All the dancers turned and looked at us. We were embarrassed and quickly left. As we were walking back to our set, David turned to me. "Jesus, Russ, you're a star," he said. "He has no right to treat you that way. How come you let him get away with talking to you like that?"

The more I thought about it, the angrier I became. By the time we all gathered in front of the camera for the wardrobe tests—the Jets and Sharks, Bob Wise, Jerry Robbins, and Howard Jeffrey—I couldn't contain myself anymore. As everyone else watched, I grabbed Howard by the collar and pulled his face up close to mine. "If you ever speak to me like that again, I am going to knock you on your ass—do you hear me?" I asked.

"Yes, sir," he replied.

Maybe my reaction was a little strong, but it had two benefits. Howard never yelled at me again, and my gang of actors told me, "You are definitely the leader of the Jets."

Another positive resolution came regarding the costumes. The original concept featured colorful and corny uniform-like outfits. We looked like background dancers in a 1950s musical. Thankfully, Bob Wise rejected them, and we ended up wearing street clothes.

Soon, it was time to start rehearsing our dance numbers in downtown Los Angeles. All of us danced for block after block, practicing the opening prologue, up and down the streets. Accompanying us was Betty Walberg playing a piano perched on the back of a flatbed truck. From the start, there was a feeling of tension on the set. Jerry was a first-time film director, given the opportunity by Bob to be his codirector. More than that, he had a reputation for being emotionally abusive to his dancers, and he did correct us with a rigor I hadn't experienced before. He never yelled at me, but if one of the dancers missed a step three or four times when we were rehearsing, Jerry would make them go sit in the corner, like the dunce of dance.

After more than a year of preparation, on August 10, 1960, a typically muggy summer day in New York City, we finally started shooting the film's opening prologue. It was a sinuous sequence of intricately choreographed dancing. And it established the tribalism and simmering conflict of two street gangs, the Jets and the Sharks, based on the two warring families in William Shakespeare's *Romeo and Juliet*. The increasingly intense standoffs culminated with my iconic line "Beat it," spoken to the rival gang leader, Bernardo.

The temperature often rose above a hundred degrees during the filming of that scene, not to mention the dense humidity, which made it feel like we were dancing with wet bags of sand on our limbs. After jumping up and down all day on the steaming asphalt, I repeatedly went back to the Warwick Hotel with shin splints. This inflammation of the leg bone was caused by dancing for hours on the hot New York City concrete. There was nothing I could do to make the severe pain go away, either with ice or with massage. Finally, after days of dancing at our most energetic pace while being scalded by the relentless heat, we couldn't take it anymore. During a break, the actors playing the Jets were fooling around when someone started doing our version of a rain dance. Everyone joined in, and we were soon dancing around playfully, encouraging the rain to come. However, it wasn't so lighthearted when a sudden thunderstorm stopped us from shooting for the whole afternoon. The following morning, the day's call sheet included a memo: *No more rain dances!*

I had promised to do my best, and I really did give it my all. Jerry was known as a perfectionist with a unique vision about even the tiniest details. He never gave me a hard time and was always nice to me. In fact, he once privately told me that his idea to update *Romeo and Juliet*, his concept behind *WSS*, was not completely his own inspiration; it had sprung from an idea presented by his lover, Montgomery Clift, one night at a party on Fire Island. Jerry and I had a mostly warm relationship, but we sometimes had our creative differences. For instance, when Riff first confronts Bernardo, the line in the script read, *Huh!* Knowing how a camera magnifies an actor's every expression and sound, I read it as a subtle scoff.

"Cut!" Jerry yelled.

I stood on my mark, awaiting his instruction.

"Say it louder," Jerry said.

I looked into the lens, which was tight on my face. His direction didn't feel right. I knew it was bold of me to disagree with the great Jerome Robbins, but I thought it would come off as overacting.

"That's the way it was done onstage," he insisted.

But I wouldn't back down.

"Yes, Jerry, that's onstage, but movie close-ups are different."

We began arguing intently. Since shooting had already been disrupted, we took a walk down the block, trying to work out our differing opinions.

Finally, Bob approached us and said, "Listen, guys, why don't we shoot it both ways, and we'll use the best one?"

We agreed, and when I saw the finished film, I learned that they had ended up using my version. Jerry was a master of the stage and made substantial contributions to the movie's brilliance, but I was an experienced film actor, and I knew my medium well.

I witnessed many instances when Jerry was downright mean to some of the dancers. Bob seemed pleased with how the production was going, but Jerry always wanted more. As we shot one of the main dance sequences, he demanded that the routine be reshot with the dancers doing all the steps on the opposite foot, even though he liked the first take. This, of course, is a dancer's worst nightmare, as it requires a lot of time to relearn the steps. It's not so simple to switch a routine completely in one's brain and to suddenly dance it in reverse. Plus, what's the difference anyway?

Some of the dancers would argue that Jerry was such a genius choreographer that he had to have a good reason, but I couldn't buy into that explanation. He never seemed happy unless our feet were bleeding. Meanwhile, Bob kept looking at his watch. I felt this was just another example of Jerry's sometimes pointless perfectionism that caused the filming to go way over schedule. After forty-five days of shooting, we were twenty-four days behind. The Mirisch brothers, who were producing the film, grew increasingly concerned as the production threatened to go over budget. And the well-known consensus among Hollywood insiders was that the movie would never be finished with Jerry at the helm.

While the conditions surrounding the filming were stressful, I was very happy with my new bride, who stayed with me in New York City for the months we were on location. Elizabeth was supportive and always kind. As a result of her upbringing in England, she had wonderful manners in public and knew all the best champagnes and wines. She taught me table manners that I have used for the rest of my life. On more formal occasions she was unfailingly polite and quiet, but when alone with people we knew, she laughed easily and had a wonderful, cutting wit. Although she sometimes drank too much, it wasn't yet a regular occurrence, and I didn't think too much about it. We were young and newly married, and following our extremely short courtship, we were still getting to know each other and our life together.

We became friends with Chita Rivera, who had starred as Anita in the original Broadway cast of *WSS* and was married to Tony Mordente, who played Action, one of my Jets in the film. She was appearing on Broadway in *Bye Bye Birdie* with Dick Van Dyke, who had yet to become famous for his beloved TV show. Chita was great fun to spend time with, and the four of us often had dinner and even took a boat trip around Manhattan.

Having filmed the street scenes on location in the sweltering heat of New York City in late August, we were sent home before the production was due to pick up back in Los Angeles. Then, during the fall of 1960, we were told the film was going on hiatus. I was really blue after how hard I had fought to be in this epic project and how much I had committed myself to it. I called my agent, Phil, to find out what he knew. Apparently, the movie was way over budget, and the producers didn't know if we would be allowed to continue.

During this break, Elizabeth and I took a road trip, down California State Route 1, which hugs the coastline, offering vertigo-inducing views and a straight shot through Big Sur. This was sacred ground because I knew this small coastal town was home to the writer Henry Miller.

I had been a big fan of his semiautobiographical novels *Tropic of Cancer* and *Tropic of Capricorn* ever since I had been turned on to him by my friend Joe Gray, a well-read Hollywood extra and stuntman. We used to sit around and discuss Miller's wild bohemian lifestyle and controversial writing, which at that time was banned in America. I even bought an album on which radio and TV personality Ben Grauer interviewed Henry. I listened to it over and over until the vinyl got scratched to the point where it became unplayable. Henry stressed the difference between making entertainment, which meant working to please others, and making art, which often required walking away from the commercially viable. He was even willing to suffer to do what he wanted to please himself. As a Hollywood movie star, my mission was to entertain, and yet I felt an intense kinship with Henry. His courageous individuality stirred faint longings within me, which would grow stronger over the next few years.

I hadn't been planning to make a pilgrimage exactly, but I felt moved to connect with Henry in some way, so I decided to pull over to the side of the highway. In a grove of redwood trees, I found a low-slung, clapboard-covered bookstore that, after Henry's death, would become the Henry Miller Memorial Library. I went in and poked around and bought several books, feeling like I was at the source of so much that interested and excited me. As I paid for my purchases, I struck up a conversation with the man who was working there. "Does Henry Miller live around here?" I asked. "I would love to leave him a note or something."

"Yeah, he lives on the highway, down a ways," he said. "You could leave a note in his mailbox. It says *Miller* on it."

I thanked him for his help, and Elizabeth and I got back in the car and drove farther along the road to see what we could find. At the bottom of a steep hill, where a few houses were perched among windswept trees, there was a huddled group of weather-beaten mailboxes. On the metal door of one of them, painted in all caps, was the name MILLER. Just to be sure, I reached inside, where I found some letters that were addressed to Henry Miller. So I ran back to my car and jotted down a note that basically said, *I don't know if you know who I am. I'm an actor, Russ Tamblyn. I'm a big fan of yours and would love to meet you sometime.* I guess it was a little bit like tossing a message in a bottle into the vast ocean. But I admired his writing and everything he stood for so much, I figured, if nothing else, it would be nice to let him know.

Back in Los Angeles, Phil called me again with the good news that the production would resume after all, as well as some interesting news. "Guess what?" he said. "Jerry's been fired!"

I couldn't believe it. Even though I knew he could be difficult to work with, this was his project. Clearly, I wasn't the only one who felt this way, because when I told the dancers about Jerry's dismissal on our first day back, most of them were distraught. I have to admit, I was surprised at first. After all, I had heard them complain about how badly he had treated them. So I thought for sure they would be glad to see him go. I was wrong. Almost all of them were in a state of shock and couldn't believe the movie could continue without him. I considered it a great honor to have danced for him, in what has since been recognized as an iconic moment in cinema (and dance) history. But the fact of the matter is that *West Side Story* could never have been completed with Jerry at the helm! We would still be shooting it, to this day.

When we later picked up filming in Los Angeles, I was also reunited with my old friend Natalie Wood, who I had known for years as a fellow child actor. She was not well liked on set, in part because she had been fawned over by Jerry, who was known to adore his stars and be very tough on his dancers and the other actors. She was also very aloof, in part because she had not been on location with the rest of the actors and dancers in New York, so she had not bonded with the cast. Not only did she refuse to spend time with her castmates, but also, she found fault with any members of the cast or crew who she perceived to have crossed her, especially her romantic lead, Richard Beymer. Natalie had wanted Warren Beatty, her *Splendor in the Grass* costar, to play the part of Tony, and she let her displeasure be known. She infamously put up a "shit list" on the wall of her dressing room, on which Richard always seemed to find his name at the top.

Richard confided in me that he hated the experience of filming *WSS*. And I could understand why. He was a nice guy from Indiana who was being tasked with embodying the role of a tough, urban street punk. From what I could see, the direction he received from Jerry didn't do anything to help him. My feeling was that while Jerry lived openly as a gay man, he was conflicted about his sexuality, which was common at the time, as there was such a strong cultural stigma against homosexuality. I believe this caused Jerry to fetishize the love between Tony and Maria so much that he seemed to want Richard to worship Natalie like the Madonna. I watched Jerry drive Richard to play Tony with more idealism, more passion, more of everything, to the point where it made Richard insecure about his performance—and even his masculinity and his personal experience of how he would love and pursue a woman. It was very unnerving to witness them working together. For this reason and many others, the mood on the set could become so intense it was nearly toxic. It was crucial to know how to treat filming as a job and to leave tensions behind at the end of the day. On top of that, Natalie refused to talk to Richard, which added to the general unease and must have been uncomfortable and embarrassing for him. I also felt bad for Natalie, who seemed near the breaking point, as rumors were flying that things weren't going well in her marriage to Robert John Wagner, who we all called RJ.

Not long after filming was finally finished, Natalie asked to stop by my beach house with Marty Crowley. Not only was Mart Nat's longtime assistant, but he was also a very talented writer. He was penning what would become the iconic musical *The Boys in the Band*, which ran on Broadway in the late 1960s and became a film. Nat had just broken up with RJ and wanted to talk to me. I knew Nat needed a confidant, so I asked Elizabeth to stay with Mart in the house while Nat and I walked down the beach.

Natalie was quiet and visibly nervous. She kept throwing stones into the ocean. We didn't talk much, but when we did, it was small talk, which was fine with me. I decided to just listen and let her take her time in opening up. We stopped at a cool little spot that was at the bottom of Sunset Boulevard until it burned down in the midsixties and was replaced with a big commercial restaurant called Gladstones. Nat and I entered by climbing a little-known wooden ladder from the beach, which took us right up into the dining room. We headed straight for the bar. After ordering two Bloody Marys, we talked for about an hour. Nat was childlike, and when things didn't go her way, she took it very hard. I just wanted to comfort her and tried to be encouraging.

On the way back, we sat on the sand while she had a good cry. Her career was skyrocketing, but her private life was sinking into an abyss of confusion and sadness. I put my arm around her and tried to convince her that this would pass, but I'm not so sure I got through. She asked me not to tell anyone about our talk, and I'm only sharing it now to show how her aloofness was a form of self-protection. She was actually very sweet and earnest.

I was impressed that she managed to hold it together as well as she did, at least in front of the camera. She was under tremendous pressure in many areas of her life. I remembered the time I had invited RJ and Natalie over for dinner with Mart and Tony Mordente before we had left to film in New York. After dinner, I had suggested we play the game "Truth." The main rule was that you had to be on your honor to tell the truth, no matter the topic. Everyone loved the idea, and all was going well until I decided to spice it up a bit by turning to Nat and asking her, "If you had a choice of being guaranteed you'd receive the Best Actress Oscar for *WSS*, but as a stipulation, you would have to divorce RJ, what would you do?"

After a moment she said, "I'd take the Oscar."

RJ was visibly pissed. He pounded on the table, stood up, and stared daggers at Nat. Then he ran out of the house and down to the beach. Tony Mordente went after him to try to calm him down, but the party was clearly over.

Natalie turned to me and said, "I should have said that I could always marry RJ again, but I didn't know if I'd ever get the chance to win another Oscar."

I tried to reassure her that it would all blow over, but when RJ and Tony came back, RJ said to Nat, "I think we'd better leave."

That was the last time I ever played that game!

———

Looking back, I think there's a reason I gravitated toward many of the other child stars I met during my years in Hollywood. I've had deep friendships with other actors and artists throughout my life, but there was a bond I had with Natalie Wood, Bobby Driscoll, and especially Dean Stockwell. It was based on our innate understanding not just of what it was like to achieve success and fame so young but also of the pressures of remaining innocent and wholesome in a business that could be very cruel. We didn't often discuss these matters, especially in our younger days, but I think we felt safe with each other in a world that sometimes exploited us. That was an incredible gift, especially as we began to mature, and our lives grew so much more complicated—both on screen and off.

Russ as Riff in *West Side Story* (1961).

Russ with his Jets. Left to right: Tony Mordente, David Bean, David Winters, Harvey Evans, Tucker Smith, and Russ.

Russ and George Chakiris as rivals Riff and Bernardo face off on the set of *West Side Story*.

West Side Story set mischief: tearing down a Sharks banner.

Getting a better
view on the set of
West Side Story.

Russ with Jet Bobby Banas and choreographer Jerome Robbins.

Discussing a scene with director Robert Wise.

Blocking the dance on the streets of New York while the crowd looks on.

Directors and production team prep with the Jets.

Eliot Feld, Tucker Smith, David Winters, Tony Mordente, and David Bean, with Russ, getting notes from Jerome Robbins.

Taking flight on the streets of New York.

Indiscretions and Other Growing Pains

Elizabeth and I settled into beach life. I loved being out of the city, and it was the perfect setting for me to indulge in my artistic stirrings. I was inspired by the spark of nonconformity and freedom in the books I was reading by Henry Miller and the Beat writers, including poets Michael McClure and Allen Ginsberg. But that was just in my free time; when I was done filming *WSS*, I remained under contract to MGM, which generally kept me busy with two film projects a year. My life was still very much that of a Hollywood insider.

In early November 1960, I was surprised to receive a letter in the mail with a red printed return address that read: *Henry Miller, Big Sur, California*. On the back, there was a red artist's print almost the entire length of the envelope. I couldn't believe it—my message had reached its mark, and my literary hero had written me back! Inside, I actually found a wonderful, conversational letter from Henry's then wife, Eve Miller. She wrote, *Dear Russ Tamblyn, certainly we know of you. Possibly Henry wouldn't have, if his children weren't the ages they are. He wouldn't have seen the same movies without them. As it is, he is a first-rate champion of the worst westerns you can imagine.* (I had to laugh that my hero thought I had been in some of the worst westerns imaginable.) She continued: *He insists they are noble and inspiring, the romantic of the German in him no doubt. At the moment, and for several months to come, he's in Europe again. Only returned in July from the last trip. This occasion he'll settle a while in Málaga and get into the next volume of Nexus. I remain home happily with the office, good life, children, et cetera. Thank you very much for writing. Eve Miller.*

I was thrilled. I had made contact. But I didn't have any particular plan for following up or making our meeting come to pass someday.

———

Before the public release of *West Side Story* in the fall of 1961, we had an invitational premiere at the Carthay Circle Theatre in Beverly Hills. This was a fitting launch for a film that would go on to earn ten Academy Awards and become a celebrated classic. The theater had been one of the most famous movie palaces of Hollywood's Golden Age, with films such as *Snow White and the Seven Dwarfs*, *Gone with the Wind*, and, fittingly, *Romeo and Juliet* having premiered there. Built in 1926, the main auditorium was shaped in a perfect circle. The interior's walls were lined with forty-foot paintings of historic scenes, and the exterior's octagonal bell tower, topped with a neon light, could be seen from a distance of several miles.

The night they first screened *WSS*, by invitation only, just about everyone who was anyone attended. The theater's 1,500 seats were all occupied, and when the movie ended, everyone cheered and gave it a standing ovation. As I walked up the aisle from my seat, I was buzzing with the excitement of seeing myself in a film I was so proud of and the warm congratulations from my peers, including a who's who of Hollywood legends. About halfway up the theater's aisle, I felt a gentle tug on my shoulder. I turned and there was my dancing hero, Fred Astaire. I leaned in to hear him amid the din of conversation in the packed room. "What a great dancer you are. I'm such a big fan!" he said.

Needless to say, that was all I could think about for the rest of the evening, and all these years later, it's still one of the highlights of my dancing life. That night, however, is topped by the most memorable screening of the film I attended. When it was shown in London at a Royal Command Performance for Queen Elizabeth and her family, I was seated in the royal box behind Her Royal Highness and next to my onetime costar Peter Sellers. Although I knew him to be very shy and the first one to tell you how uncomfortable he was when he had to be himself, he certainly didn't show it on this night. As the lights dimmed when the overture was finished, Peter leaned forward and whispered in Queen Elizabeth's left ear, "Lady, would you mind taking your crown off?" Her Majesty didn't so much as blink, twitch, or even smile. However, as I was exiting the box after the screening, I did earn a raised eyebrow from Princess Margaret, who seemed to be making a pass at me. Her social secretary even asked me if I would care to join the princess's party that evening. I thanked her but let her know I was already booked for the rest of the night. Later, I asked Peter how he could possibly have spoken in this way to the queen of England. "We're all going to end up in the Tower of London!" I said.

"It's okay," he replied out of the side of his mouth, with a little mischievous grin. "I'll go to the palace for lunch, and she'll tell me how funny it was."

During this same period, I had a day off and was taking a dip in front of my beach house. I was bobbing in the ocean, about twenty-five yards from shore, when I heard a shout from land. I turned and recognized my friend Joe Gray on my deck. He waved to me, as did the man next to him, who I could recognize even from this distance with his long face and bald head. There he was, my hero, Henry Miller. What an incredible surprise!

I quickly swam to shore, dried off, and hurried to join them. Joe told me about how he had spotted Henry at a bookstore and introduced himself. Because of Joe's great knowledge of books, the two of them had fallen into a deep conversation and immediately become friends. Of course, I invited them inside. Elizabeth brought out some red wine and a cheese platter for everyone to enjoy in the living room. Henry was delighted.

The three of us sat together talking for several hours. We discussed art, moviemaking, and writing.

"Do you like the Beats?" I asked.

"I only like the work of Jack Kerouac, because of his unconventional writing style," Henry said.

This surprised me, but I certainly didn't push back on the wisdom of the great Henry Miller, especially about writing. If you're wondering if I was intimidated to be sitting there in conversation with the man I considered one of the greatest, freshest writers of our generation, the answer is yes! I mostly just listened a lot, which felt like a huge honor, in and of itself.

At the time, art was more of a hobby for me than anything else. I was always very passionate about it, but it was something I did on the side when I wasn't busy with my acting career. My work wasn't particularly cutting edge. It was mostly the kind of normal stuff art students might paint—still lifes and that sort of thing—and the canvases were scattered all over my house. The next thing I knew, Henry Miller was strolling around in his slow, thoughtful way, looking at everything. One by one, he walked up to each of my paintings, sized it up, and then said, "Hmm. Hmm." I eagerly waited to hear what he would say next, but that was it. *Hmm. Hmm. What does that mean?!*

Once he had examined my paintings, I did talk to him a bit about my own artistic process. "I'm having a little trouble painting faces perfectly," I said.

"Don't worry about it," he replied. "If you want a perfect face, don't paint it; just take a photo."

I couldn't argue with that, could I? As the sun set over the ocean, we wrapped up the afternoon with cheerful goodbyes. He gave me the phone number for the house where he was staying with a friend, a little farther down the beach. And so began our friendship. Just like that, my creative passions were being encouraged by one of my heroes in ways I had never expected. I was used to spending time with movie stars and even titans of the cinema, but to have the chance to sit in conversation with such a great thinker was truly remarkable. And still, I couldn't yet conceive of a life where I counted myself among fine artists.

For the next few years, the perks of being a movie star in the MGM stable outweighed the fact that I was not always thrilled by the material or the expectations that went along with being a contract player in a rigid system. Many of the films I starred in during this period were shot on location in Europe. I always jumped at the chance to go abroad, especially when the studio rented a house for Elizabeth and me, and we could travel before and after shooting.

In July 1961, I had mixed feelings when I learned MGM had assigned me to make another fairy-tale film, this time for the ultrawide screen format of Cinerama—a short-lived filming process whereby three cameras were attached together and aimed at slightly different angles in order to film both directions at the same time. The resulting films were meant to be more lifelike, requiring three projectors, running simultaneously, to be screened. But they were ridiculous for the actors, who were often placed in front of different cameras within a scene. The cameraman then gave us both a spot to gaze at to (hopefully) appear as though we were looking at each other. Even back then, when it took less technology to razzle-dazzle an audience, the results were often mixed.

But since I was to be featured in a fairy tale from *The Wonderful World of the Brothers Grimm*, the good news was that I would eventually be filming in Bavaria. I was to play the Woodsman, and my dance sequences were to be enacted with the Dancing Princess, played by Yvette Mimieux. The studio asked me who I wanted to do my choreography, and my first and only answer was Alex Romero, as we had worked so well together on *Seven Brides*, *Fastest Gun*, and *tom thumb*.

Alex and I rehearsed for a few days on the MGM lot. The next day, Yvette was scheduled to join us. Only she was two hours late. When she arrived, she explained that on the way to the studio, she had seen an open field of wildflowers. So she decided to stop, wander around, and gather up an armful, which she brought to the rehearsal hall to give to us. How can you be mad at someone who is such a free spirit and brings you beautiful flowers?

Yvette soon revealed that she was well versed in classical music and art, especially for a twenty-year-old actress. She happened to mention that Henry Miller was one of her favorite writers. Of course, I tried to impress her by dropping that I was friends with the great man himself. It worked. When I asked her if she would like to meet him, she jumped at the chance. I had been around Hollywood stars for so long by now that I didn't think twice about it—they were just my peers and pals. But to my new, more intellectual friends such as Henry Miller, I had access to a desirable and rarefied world. This was particularly true because it contained stunning young starlets, such as Yvette. As Henry was the first to acknowledge, he had a keen appreciation for attractive women.

I arranged all the details and then called Henry. I picked him up and drove him to Yvette's house, which was on a mountaintop off Mulholland Drive, high above Brentwood. She was clearly as excited to meet him and as fascinated by his conversation as I had been the first time I'd had the honor of talking with him. I was very surprised by how much she knew about Henry and his work and what intelligent questions she asked. She was a terrific hostess, and we had a truly delicious afternoon. Henry talked about her beauty all the way down the hill and back to the Palisades.

Every time I went to see Henry at his house or met him for lunch, I hung on his every word and came home feeling invigorated and inspired. I was especially grateful for our friendship because he was my only real opportunity to have the kind of thoughtful, cultural conversations I craved, as I was making my first tentative foray into the arts myself.

When it was time to film on location in Bavaria, Elizabeth and I decided to go to Europe a few weeks early and do some sightseeing. We took a train to New York, boarded the *Queen Mary*, and sailed for England. Every night, we dined with director Blake Edwards and his wife, Patricia. This was a few years before they divorced and he married Julie Andrews. Blake was on his way to London to direct the first *Pink Panther* film, which he had also written. The other couple at our table was Henry Mancini and his wife, Ginny. Hank and Blake were longtime collaborators, going back to when Hank had composed "Moon River" for Blake's *Breakfast at Tiffany's*. I felt honored to be spending such quality time with these two extremely talented, nice guys and their wives. Crossing the Atlantic became a major event in and of itself—the six of us ate, danced, and partied all the way to the British Isles. At the end of the night, when everyone else went back to their cabins, I developed a habit of going to the bow of the ship. I would climb over a small railing and sit on the very front of the boat (decades before Leo in *Titanic*, I might add). Rough seas arose on several occasions, and riding the gigantic waves with a powerful wind blowing in my face was one of the most exhilarating highs I've ever had.

Jane Scott, Elizabeth's sister, met us in Southampton, where we docked. I liked her right away. She was very British but very down to earth at the same time. She was also extremely wealthy and drove us in her big silver Bentley to her estate, Field Place in Surrey, where we were to stay for a few days.

The next morning, Jane had to pop into London. She asked Elizabeth and me to accompany her. She wanted to take us to the city's most famous tearoom. She warned me that it was the height of elegance, so I had to be on my absolute best behavior. *Oh, you don't say!* When we reached the top of the wide, thickly carpeted stairs that led into the hushed, fancy room, my mischievous nature simply could not be contained. I faked a trip and tumbled head over heels down the stairs, bouncing as I went. This is a pratfall I've performed in many of my films, and so I really made it look like a tremendous fall. I could hear teacups rattling and high-pitched shrieks of terror. I got up with a shrug, raised my eyebrows, and proceeded to our table as if nothing had happened. When Elizabeth and Jane sat down, I thought they were going to kill me. Later, of course, it became Jane's favorite funny story to tell. (And years later, Chevy Chase, the comedian known for falling down in the funniest of ways, told me, "You're where I got my pratfalls from.")

Elizabeth and I spent a few weeks touring around Ireland, with me checking in with MGM at every major city. We visited some of the Emerald Isle's most spectacularly scenic spots, from the Dingle Peninsula to Kilkenny. At Blarney Castle, I even kissed the famous Blarney Stone, which is known to give you the gift of gab. Finally, when we reached Galway Bay, I was told that our director, George Pal, needed me in Bavaria ASAP. We returned to London, where Elizabeth stayed behind because her father was ill. I wasn't surprised his health had taken a turn, as he was a severe alcoholic, but I knew it was upsetting for her.

I had been summoned because George wanted me to choreograph my stunts. It took me several days of rehearsal to figure out what I was capable of doing. It was a complicated scene with an element of danger, but I felt it was worth the risk, especially since the sequence was to be shot in Cinerama. After an intricate series of leaps and tumbles, on and off a speeding horse-drawn carriage, I had to cross a long treacherous bridge made of rope and wooden planks. George found a real bridge over a deep gorge for this scene. However, they did remove several planks and replace them with balsa wood. My challenge was to stagger across, step on the breakaway planks, and catch myself with my arms without falling through. George wanted to build a net underneath, but I talked him out of it. Even though a plunge into the gorge, several hundred feet below, would have proved fatal, I was confident I could do this stunt safely. The only way I would have fallen through was if I had held my arms tightly against my body, and there was no way I was going to do that.

The whole morning was spent prepping the bridge and securing the huge Cinerama camera to one side of the canyon walls. Extending another camera on a crane, way out over the gorge, made for a terrifically scary shot. Before filming began, we broke for lunch. George came over to me with his particularly puckish grin. I've always described George as "a man with a twinkle in his brain," and I immediately knew he was up to some mischief. His secretary, Gae Griffith, was coming to set, and he wanted to play a little joke on her.

Soon after Gae joined us for lunch, we were ready to go back to work. George had her sit in a chair with a clear view of the scene. The camera rolled, and I staggered across the bridge. I stepped on the fake planks, they broke, and as I started to drop, Gae jumped up and screamed in horror. Then, as I caught myself without falling through, she froze. Poor Gae actually thought I was plunging to my death and almost had a heart attack! But she soon forgave us when she could tell that George and I had gotten an exciting scene in the can.

My costar Yvette arrived, and we started shooting together. Sometimes we would take walks while running our lines, and the autumn weather was absolutely perfect. Bright yellow, pink, orange, and red autumnal leaves sparked the forests and meadows with their magic. We were both in our twenties and got along well, so we really enjoyed working together. Our relationship was close but not intimate. When we weren't on set, we played chess. But one night, toward the end of shooting, Yvette and I were in the dining room of the main lodge and decided to have a match. The chess set was in her room, so we went there. We laughed a lot and played through one game before suddenly Yvette perked up. "I've got an idea! Let's hike up to Swan Lake and jump in!"

How could I resist? It was late, and I had an early call in the morning, but it seemed more than worth it to at least visit the lake, known locally as Schwansee. The moon was full, and it was a beautiful night, albeit quite cold. We grabbed towels and took off. When we got there, the moon was shining on the lake, with swans in the near distance, and the reflection was like a Maxfield Parrish painting. I felt higher than a faraway star.

Yvette walked to the end of a small fishing pier. She dropped all her clothes in the silhouette of the full moon and stood there, a naked beauty on the dock. Then she jumped into the lake. "Come on in!" she yelled.

I tested the water, which felt like it was about ten degrees. I realized I needed to go in quickly, so I stripped and took the plunge. God, it was cold! It felt like submerging myself in one of those ice tubs used to chill beer and soda. Neither of us stayed in the lake very long, but when we got out, we both felt like we could run over the Bavarian Alps. We dried off, dressed, and trotted down the winding path like a couple of mountain goats.

Back in her room, we took a hot shower together that verged on a nirvanic experience. It was the best shower I've ever had. We made love, and I didn't leave Yvette's bed until two in the morning. Even though we were both married, the intoxication of being in this beautiful setting was too much to resist. She was mesmerizing. We had both been swept away.

When I got back to the main lodge, the front door was locked, and there was no doorbell. My room was on the second floor, but I did have a balcony. Somehow, I managed to scale the wall, like Gene Kelly in *The Three Musketeers*. Then I crept along a ledge, inconspicuously passing another guest's window. Finally, I reached my balcony. Thankfully, I had left the door unlocked. I set my clock for three hours later and passed out. When my alarm sounded, I could barely rouse myself. I was late getting to makeup and hadn't yet had a cup of coffee. The makeup lady made one for me and asked if I had stayed up late. Still under the spell of the previous evening, I told her about our adventure—except for the lovemaking—but it was enough for her to infer what else had happened.

Later in the day, Yvette confronted me. I confessed, while making it clear I hadn't told the makeup woman *everything*. Still, Yvette was very hurt, and rightfully so. "How could you?" she said. "That was personal and private." Then, before I could say anything else, she turned and walked away. Yvette barely spoke to me for the next two days. At least we were at the end of the shoot. But our friendship never recovered. Me and my big mouth. I knew I should never have kissed that Blarney Stone! Yvette was right, and I felt terrible.

I didn't want to hurt my wife—or the other women who would be my lovers during these years. But I was still very much under the sway of several powerful influences. My mother's skewed view of the world had left me with a lack of understanding about how love and sex went together. My parents had sometimes played raunchy songs like "Johnny's Little Yo-Yo" when company came over, and Mom would laugh uproariously. But then she told me I would go crazy if I touched myself when I was a boy. So "Johnny's little Yo-Yo" was funny, while mine was a no-no.

As a result, I thought love was one thing and sex was something else, something dirty and yet something I needed. So I required a relationship with a mate but also sex on the side. I just couldn't combine the two, even with Elizabeth. At first, we'd had such a great physical attraction and friendship, but it hadn't taken long for my eye to wander, and it wasn't until I was more mature that I could ever successfully make my wife my lover.

Also, as I've mentioned, I was deeply influenced by Henry Miller, not just by his writing but by the lifestyle he seemed to advocate. He had mentioned how in Europe it was much more common, and even accepted, for men to have mistresses. So to emulate him, I thought this was something I should do too. As I can see now, my womanizing only made my tenuous bond with Elizabeth more frayed, and yet, I didn't make this connection back then. Having other lovers seemed totally normal to me. I would like to be able to say I learned from my one-nighter with Yvette, but because the relationships formed on film sets were so fleeting, it was easy to put her anger out of my mind as soon as I got home. And it wasn't long before I would be swept away again—and again, and again.

HENRY MILLER
BIG SUR, CALIFORNIA

Mr. Russ Tamblyn
18242 West Pacific Coast-Highway
Malibu
California

Russ's letter to Henry Miller is
answered by Henry's wife, Eve.

Henry Miller taking in Russ's
artwork on his first visit.

Russ's pinup girl during the army years and his second wife, Elizabeth Kempton.

The Wonderful World of the Brothers Grimm (1962): Russ as the Woodsman with Yvette Mimieux, the Dancing Princess.

Russ checks out his next stunt on the bridge: it's a long way down.

Leaping onto the speeding coach: timing is everything.

CHAPTER 6

THE END OF AN ERA

For the first few years of our marriage, Elizabeth and I were on location more than we were in LA. Even when a script was lacking, I could always find something to enjoy about a production. Film sets had been my life for more than a decade, and I felt at home there. I always became captivated by some interesting aspect of my performance or the blocking and choreography. I was comfortable around other actors, and I enjoyed spending time with my costars in the beautiful locales where we filmed.

When I was sent the script for *Follow the Boys*, the sequel to *Where the Boys Are*, starring Connie Francis, there was no denying the material was pretty bad. But then I got the news it would be filmed in the South of France, and I was reminded I couldn't say no contractually. So Elizabeth and I made another trip to Europe and enjoyed ourselves immensely during the summer of 1962. (Coincidentally, my brother Larry Tamblyn and his successful 1960s garage band, the Standells, played the incidental music for this film, although they wouldn't achieve their real fame until 1966, when they had their big breakout hit, "Dirty Water.")

Next, MGM asked me to do a small part in a big movie. I was to play a Confederate deserter in *How the West Was Won*, which was one of those mega all-star epics from the Golden Age of Hollywood, with an incredible lineup that included John Wayne, James Stewart, and

Henry Fonda. After *The Wonderful World of the Brothers Grimm*, this was my second film in Cinerama, making me the only credited actor to ever appear in two Cinerama movies. The film featured five unique segments, each with its own cast and crew, and the legendary director John Ford helmed the segment in which I appeared.

In some ways, it was actually better to have a minor role in the film, because I had less responsibility. During the five days I was on set, I was able to relax and absorb the atmosphere while watching these greats at work. I had been friendly with Henry Fonda for several years, thanks to our mutual friend Glenn Ford. But John Wayne was the costar with whom I had actually had the most interesting experience. A few years earlier, when I was still married to my first wife, Venetia, we were invited down to Venezuela to get in on a land-development opportunity. Unfortunately, the deal ended up being a bust because of the country's unstable political climate. But it was almost worth the money I lost in the venture just for the experience I had on my return flight from Caracas to the States.

Venetia took a pill on the flight and fell into a deep sleep. Intensely bored, I headed to the rear of the cabin, where John Wayne and producer Tony Owen, who was married to Donna Reed and would become a friend of mine, were sitting in a comfortable conference section. The Duke had already belted down several Scotches and was feeling pretty loose. He was a big guy, about six feet four inches, and he had an imposing presence. He was down to earth but much more opinionated than I ever would have imagined. When he invited me to join them, he was in the middle of a passionate political discussion, which culminated in him saying, "Them goddamn commies, they oughta send 'em all to Siberia and let 'em freeze their asses off." Crushing out his cigarette and quickly lighting another, he said with his trademark twang, "That sure is a pretty lady you got there, Russ. She looks like she just slid off the cover of one of them fashion magazines."

"Thank you," I said. I couldn't help but be pleased, especially because this was as much as he had said to me on the whole trip besides "glad to meetcha."

Now that we were on the topic of women, the conversation segued into lovers. He launched into a story about Marlene Dietrich, with whom he had worked on the film *Seven Sinners* back in 1940. While he was just starting out, Marlene was six years older and already famous as a femme fatale.

Apparently, the Duke developed a huge crush on Marlene and kept asking her out, all through filming, but she always refused. Even though he constantly kidded her about all the reasons she should go out with him, she only wanted to focus on acting together. Then, the day the movie finished, her assistant knocked on his dressing room door and told him that Miss Dietrich would love for him to drive her home after work. Surprised and excited, he left his car at the studio because she insisted that he drive her car, saying she would get him back to the studio later.

"Okay, where are we goin'?" he asked once he was sitting behind the wheel.

"We go that way!" she answered in her thick Teutonic accent, pointing forward.

The Duke couldn't believe how far they drove. She took him to a cabin in Big Bear in the San Bernardino Mountains that she kept as a hideaway. For three days straight, she made love to him. She cooked for him, massaged him, read him poetry, and took him on long walks in the woods. After three days of this heavenly bliss, he was dumbfounded. When they left, he was practically paralyzed, unable to speak. After they parted, he couldn't do or think of anything else but her for several days. Finally, he called her up to keep the affair going, but she refused to answer the phone. When he did reach her, she told him it was time to move on.

As the Duke stared off into space, ruminating on what might have been, I didn't have the heart to tell him that I had actually been at a lunch with Marlene a few years earlier. During the meal, she dominated the conversation, mainly talking about men she had known all around the world. One of her guests, British actor Stewart Granger, asked her who made the best lovers. She thought for a moment. "English generals."

I could barely hold back from saying, *Too bad you weren't an English general, Duke!* But I could tell he wasn't up for such a joke in that moment, nor would he ever be.

———

I was only on set for *How the West Was Won* for five days, but I was thrilled to be directed by Ford. He had the reputation of being one of the greats of all time, right up there alongside Frank Capra, Alfred Hitchcock, William Wyler, Cecil B. DeMille, and Orson Welles. Working with him on set had a surreal quality. It was almost like he was playing the part of an eccentric director, except he really was one. When I first met him in his office, he did not at all disappoint. He sat in a big chair, puffing a pipe. He wore dark glasses due to his poor eyesight, with a patch under the lens that covered his left eye, which had been injured on a previous shoot.

Every day on set, he wore an old hat that was dirty and crumpled, and he kept chewing on his handkerchief. Suddenly, he would walk over to me and wipe my cheek with his hankie. Then he would go back to his chair. Before long he would be chewing on it again. I could never figure it out—I guess it was part of his process.

The set was big. There were extras everywhere, all of them dressed up in Civil War uniforms. My segment featured John Wayne, Andy Devine, George Peppard, and Harry Morgan. Between setups, a musician would play the concertina, and I really felt like I had traveled back in time and was on a Civil War battlefield.

But the real fighting happened between Ford and his star, John Wayne. Ford ragged on Wayne all morning. Although from what I could tell, it was done in a very calculated way.

"Jesus, Duke, when are you going to learn how to act?" Ford said.

These kinds of insults went on and on.

Peppard told me that nobody else could talk to the Duke in that manner. Ford seemed constantly annoyed and frustrated and kept berating John, but he never flinched; he just took it all in stride. "Yes, sir. Well, let's just try it again," John was always saying.

When Ford finally settled on a take, he wasn't exactly glowing in his praise. "I guess that's about as good as it's gonna get! All right, print it."

While it was amazing to have the opportunity to work with such film legends, I continued to feel less and less inspired by my life as a Hollywood actor. I had even tried to decline my role in *The Haunting* (which would end up being the final film I would do for MGM), but the studio told me that I couldn't pass. So, late in 1962, I traveled to the MGM-British Studios in London to begin work. Based on Shirley Jackson's novel *The Haunting of Hill House*, the film was mainly about the character named Eleanor, played by stage actress Julie Harris. Eleanor was a shy neurotic who, along with a few other guests, was invited to spend a night at a supposedly haunted mansion.

I portrayed Luke, a spoiled playboy and wise guy (typecasting, obviously) who was the nephew of the manor's owner and the one who stood to inherit the ninety-year-old house. I had tried to turn down the part because I really didn't want to play such a jerk in a serious film about a haunted house, even though it was being directed by Bob Wise, who I had worked with on *WSS*.

We had a strong cast, but the real star was the house. Bob and the film's writer, Nelson Gidding, had originally done location scouting in New England, where the story takes place. But none of the sites there seemed quite right. Bob was determined, though, to find a real haunted house for the exterior. Finally, he ended up in London at a society that kept track of British homes with paranormal activity. On their list, he found Ettington Park, a formidable manor that turned out to be the perfect locale. Located several miles outside Stratford-upon-Avon, it was being used as a pub and inn. The grounds in back of the hall had a little graveyard next to a small chapel. It purported to have several ghosts that had been seen numerous times for more than a hundred years, including one known as Lady Emma. She normally appeared inside the hotel, where she would glide along the corridors at night and then vanish into the wall.

I wasn't exactly a believer in ghosts, but I really wanted to see one during the single night we filmed at the hotel. So I guess that did make me kind of a believer. When the light and noise from our all-night shoot kept me awake, I headed to the back of the inn, where the chapel and graves were. It was very dark. I could hardly see anything in front of me but walked very slowly on the dimly lit path until I sensed I was fairly close to the chapel. I stopped and turned around to look back at the inn. Suddenly, I felt like someone had put a brick of ice on the back of my neck. The chill was so pronounced I stopped in my tracks and bent forward in a state of fear. It was more than just mental; it felt physical, like someone pushing down on my shoulders with frozen hands. Somehow, I knew if I did turn around, I would see the specter. I reasoned with myself: *That's why I came out here in the first place!* But now that I was faced with the prospect of an actual ghost, I was terrified and rushed back to the inn. Safe in my room, I felt a little embarrassed by how scared I had been, and I never told anyone about my weird experience that night. Ever since, I have wanted another chance to face a ghost, but it has never happened.

Thankfully, the rest of the shoot went smoothly, and I was pleasantly surprised by the quality of the production. Although I hadn't particularly liked my character when I read the script, the more involved I became, the more I connected with him, and the more I committed myself to the film. Sensing my enthusiasm, Bob let me expand the role, and *The Haunting* ended up being one of my favorite films in my career.

———

I was grateful to go out on a high note, but as my stint with MGM came to an end in 1963, to be honest, I was glad. I liked working, and I found it stressful to lose that reassurance of the next guaranteed project on the horizon, but I preferred my freedom over a regular paycheck.

I couldn't deny it any longer; acting was no longer inspiring me creatively. Even without a contract, I would keep busy with regular film and TV work, but I felt more alive on my days off, when I could lose myself in my new passion for my artwork, especially for painting with acrylics. But Elizabeth and I did have a great deal of overhead, especially after I bought us a five-bedroom, four-bathroom house on Goucher Street in Pacific Palisades.

When my agent, Phil Gersh, called while I was in London working on *The Haunting*, I had to at least entertain his offer. "Would you like to guest star on a television pilot about the circus?" he asked me. "It stars Jack Palance, and you'd play opposite Tuesday Weld. This would be your first project away from MGM, and you'd be paid seven thousand five hundred dollars. But you would have to do it immediately when you got back to the US."

That was a lot of money at the time for guest starring on a TV show, but it seemed a little too rushed for me. "Thanks, but I think I'll pass," I said.

The next day, the phone rang again, and it was Lucille Ball. She told me that she had a project called *The Greatest Show on Earth* and that she desperately wanted me to do it. Lucy had just bought out her ex-husband, Desi, in November of 1962, and this was one of her first ventures as a studio head. In fact, Lucy was the first woman to ever run a studio, making her the most powerful woman in Hollywood at the time. Of course, I couldn't turn her down, even though I had to fly directly from London to Sarasota, Florida, to shoot the pilot at the headquarters of the Ringling Bros. and Barnum & Bailey Circus. I admitted to her that I was a little anxious about diving into the new role so quickly.

"Don't worry about it, Russ. This part is perfect for you, and I really would love to have you do it," she said. "If you would, I'll pay you ten thousand dollars."

The more I thought about it, the more excited I became. My role in the episode "Silent Love, Secret Love" was as a clown, and during filming, I actually got to appear as a clown in one of the Ringling Brothers' circus performances. I walked around the ring, juggling, tumbling, and doing pratfalls. I was in makeup, so the audience didn't know who I was. The applause I received was as a circus performer, not a well-known actor. That was very exciting and something I had only dreamed about as a kid. It was also great seeing Tuesday Weld again and reminiscing about the wild and crazy times we had experienced together in the late 1950s, when we had dated casually and I would take her to the Peppermint Club to see my brother Larry Tamblyn in the band he was in before the Standells.

Money was becoming less and less of a draw for me, as were traditional Hollywood scripts, but I was always enticed by the possibility of international travel, as was Elizabeth. Although I was no longer under contract to MGM, the studio approached me in March 1963 with an offer for *The Long Ships*, to be filmed in Beograd (Belgrade), Yugoslavia. It was a Viking movie starring Richard Widmark, Sidney Poitier, and me in the role of Orm. Robert Wagner was originally scheduled to play the part, but he had backed out at the last minute. So when I got the offer, I had to agree immediately. I was indifferent to doing the film itself, as my on-screen roles had come to feel increasingly meaningless, but it did seem like an adventure.

Elizabeth and I once again packed up—she with her eighteen suitcases—and flew to New York to spend the night at the Plaza Hotel. Early the next morning, we boarded the *Queen Elizabeth* and set sail for England. Although I was still living the rarefied life of a movie star, it no longer made me happy. I wasn't excited by the prospect of the movie in which I would soon be acting. Elizabeth and I were already becoming quite disconnected in our daily life. We experienced a brief respite when we stayed at her sister Jane's beautiful three-story manor, Gilford. From the moment we arrived, driven through a big brick gate and down a long driveway, past barns and a lake, I felt inspired by the great beauty of the nature surrounding us. During our time there, I lost myself in painting while the two of them went shopping in London for a few days. Increasingly, this was my greatest pleasure, and I even managed to finish a small painting that I gave to Jane before we left England.

Then we flew to Paris, where we had to spend the night because our flight to Belgrade wasn't until the following afternoon. While looking in the entertainment section of the newspaper for something to do, I noticed an old acquaintance of mine—jazz legend Chet Baker—was performing at a local club. In the early 1950s, I had often gone to see him play with the Gerry Mulligan Quartet at the Haig in Hollywood. My friend Bobby Driscoll, another former child star, whose life had taken a darker turn when he'd become addicted to heroin, always seemed to be there. I would sit with him between sets until Chet came over to our table, and after a short visit, the two of them took off together. I surmised they were going somewhere to shoot up.

More recently, Bobby would come over to play pool with me at my house in Pacific Palisades. One day, we were driving to lunch when we started talking about experimenting with drugs. The subject of heroin came up.

"I wouldn't mind trying it sometime," I said.

"Why don't you pull over, and I'll turn you on to something cheaper than heroin that will give you the same effect," Bobby said.

Intrigued, I parked alongside the curb, not knowing what to expect.

"Now, just take one shoe and sock off, start eating your foot, and see how much of yourself you can eat."

I sat there for a second, chuckling quietly. But he was staring at me intently, and I realized he was serious. A little shaken, I eased into traffic and continued driving us to the café.

I had been successfully warned off heroin, but I was still a Chet Baker fan.

Elizabeth and I went to see Chet at this little smoky, dark hole-in-the-wall in Paris. When he took the stage, I hardly recognized him. His face was pockmarked, and his teeth looked like they were rotting out of his head. He didn't sing that night, but he sure played beautifully. One piece in particular was stunning. It was a long, slow, almost classical number he'd written during his stint in an Italian prison.

He sat with us following his performance, and after we'd caught up a bit, I asked him about prison, where he'd served several years for drug possession. He told me they had taken away his horn for a good portion of his sentence and that it was his most miserable period.

"What did you do without your trumpet?" I asked.

He thought for a moment. "I swatted flies," he finally answered. "When I got to five thousand, I quit counting."

We laughed at this, but it was clear the experience had marked him.

"I'm leaving for Yugoslavia tomorrow," I said. "Do you know where I could get some weed to take with me?"

"Sure, but you're better off taking hashish, because it's safer to travel to another country with," he said.

"Sounds good to me," I said, knowing he was the expert.

He explained that he would need to take me himself. The next morning, I took a taxi to his apartment, close to Montmartre. I climbed the stairs to his small flat and banged on the door, but no one answered. Finally, just as I was about to leave, he came to the door in his skivvies. "Just a minute, let me throw something on," he said.

"Yeah, you don't wanna go out in your skivvies!" I joked, while trying to hurry him up by letting him know I had to make my plane to Yugoslavia in two hours.

He took me to an Arab or Afghan section of Paris that could only be entered on foot. The narrow rues zigzagged like a snake, writhing through the close-knit clusters of broken-down shops and poverty-stricken housing. Without Chet, I never would have found my way in or out of the neighborhood. We stopped and entered a small corner café. I could tell Chet had made this trip many times before. The smoke was heavy with the odor of marijuana. We sat down and ordered a demitasse of the strongest black coffee I had ever tasted. Then the waiter brought a handwritten menu of different grades of pot and hashish to the table so we could place our order. I had bought pot plenty of times, but I was perplexed by the many options.

"You should buy the strongest hash because a little goes a long way," Chet said. "It'll be easier to hide in one of your pieces of luggage, and it has less of an aroma than pot."

I took his word for it—he obviously knew his stuff. When we completed our transaction, I hurried back to my hotel to get Elizabeth. Chet and I parted with a warm goodbye and a promise to see each other again in whatever city we both rolled into at the same time.

Yugoslav Airlines flew us to Belgrade, which was my first experience in a communist country. As we were driven into the city, a gigantic, five-story photograph of the country's first president, Marshal Tito, loomed over us. He was the head of the Socialist Federal Republic of Yugoslavia and the first socialist leader to defy Stalin.

Walking through Belgrade, soaking up the sights, I quickly noticed the lack of variety in its stores. Not only that, but when I went to an electronics shop to buy a portable radio, there were about fifty of them in the display window, but all of them were the same brand; being communist, the country only manufactured one brand of everything that was for sale.

The Long Ships was quite a big production. It took almost five months to complete—from April to August 1963—and we were in Yugoslavia for much of that time. The movie was in trouble from the very first day. Sidney Poitier arrived on the set at Avala Studios in Belgrade, where a Moorish city had been built for our first week of filming, only to find that all his Moorish men, who were supposed to be Black like him, were actually local Yugoslav extras with a lot of black makeup on their faces. So Sidney walked up to the producer, Irving Allen. "Where is my Black army?" Sidney asked in his commanding voice.

"We couldn't find any Black men in Yugoslavia," Irving said.

"Go to Africa," Sidney replied. "I think you might find some there. Meanwhile, I'll be waiting back in my hotel room until you do."

Finally, after two days, a group of about thirty Black extras was flown in from Africa, and we started to film. Sidney quickly became my hero. He somehow managed to be intense yet cool, and he was a very intelligent and elegant man. Plus, I admired how ready he was to stand up to the status quo. We had to duel each other in a sword fight and became pals for the rest of the shoot, spending a lot of time together. While we were still filming in Belgrade, his then girlfriend, actress Diahann Carroll, came to visit him. She played opposite him in the 1961 Paul Newman / Joanne Woodward movie *Paris Blues* and is probably best remembered for being the first Black actress to star in her own television show, *Julia*, winning a Golden Globe in 1968 for playing the title role.

When the weather grew sweltering, Sidney suggested we get cots from the studio and sleep under the stars outside one of our dressing room trailers. Elizabeth thought this sounded better than going back to our bland hotel. It turned out to be a sensational idea. The four of us climbed onto our cots and stared up at that magical region beyond the earth's atmosphere. It was a super clear night, and there was no city light pollution. Falling stars were abundant, and we could feel the earth moving beneath us. As Sidney pointed out the constellations and Diahann sighed every time a star fell, I felt like an astronomy student seeing space for the first time.

It was an intense shoot for a variety of reasons. We spent five days on an extremely difficult scene that involved all the Vikings being chained together and dragged through the city's dirt streets by the Moors, led by Moorish king Aly Mansuh (played by Sidney). Aly's men rode on horseback, whipping us along. We had lots of blood, sweat, and dirt makeup all over our bodies and couldn't wait to finish this exhausting sequence. When we finally did wrap, we were so relieved that we broke out into spontaneous applause.

Two days later, the first assistant director informed us that we were going to have to shoot the scenes over again. We all laughed, assuming he was pranking us. And then we got the bad news: When our production company had taken the undeveloped film to the new Belgrade airport to send off for development in London, Yugoslav customs officers opened the sealed cans in the sunlight to check what was in them. All the negative film was ruined! And yes, an unbelievable week of misery had to be repeated.

There was trouble behind the scenes as well. The director, Jack Cardiff, was a very sensitive, quiet man who was best known for his remarkable cinematography for such films as *The Red Shoes* and *The African Queen*. When he switched to directing, he was nominated for an Oscar for his adaptation of D. H. Lawrence's novel, *Sons and Lovers*. Unfortunately, *The Long Ships*, with its hundreds of extras, was not the kind of film Cardiff was best suited to direct, and everyone soon knew it. Actor Richard Widmark was constantly berating him for not being a more boisterous and exuberant director. Richard told me in no uncertain terms that our film needed a stronger and rowdier leader, such as Sam Fuller or John Ford. And Richard basically took over the directing at times. He would grab the bullhorn and scream at the Yugoslav extras.

When we left Belgrade, we touched down at several beautiful locations in rural Yugoslavia, including the Aman Sveti Stefan, which is a small, gorgeous resort on an islet connected to the mainland of Montenegro by a very narrow isthmus. Then we had some filming to do on a long stretch of beach, south of the most southern town in Yugoslavia. It was only about thirty-five miles from Sveti Stefan to Ulcinj, but our company told us that the drive there would take a horrific three to four hours because of bad roads. Richard had a better idea. He rented a big yacht and invited a few of us to go with him. Included were three stuntmen, Sidney, me, and two other actors he liked. We drank champagne, gazed at the amazing coastline, and laughed all the way to our destination. On that day, Richard was pleasant for a change. However, our relationship took a turn for the worse not long after this ocean adventure.

One night, Elizabeth and I were in our hotel room after dinner, and I had smoked some hashish. I sprawled on our bed and was drifting in and out on the undulating waves of my high until I finally fell asleep. I came to a little later, and Elizabeth was gone. For some reason, I knew exactly where she was. I went down the hall to Richard's room. His door was slightly ajar, so I pushed it open without knocking and strode into the room. Elizabeth was lying on the bed with him. They were dressed, but that was small comfort.

"Get out of here!" I yelled at Elizabeth.

She slunk back to our room, and I grabbed Richard by the collar. "That's my wife," I said.

We managed to avoid coming to blows, but I was really pissed off about the whole thing. After that, he and I just stuck to business and got through the rest of the shoot. I felt so betrayed by Elizabeth that I sent her to stay with her family in England for several weeks. She did finally rejoin me on location, but I had to admit that I had actually preferred it when she was gone. Of course, I felt justified in having casual affairs with several women on the set in her absence. Looking back, I can see how hypocritical it was of me to be so angry with her when I had been unfaithful countless times. But back then, I was ill equipped to look deeper at the reasons behind any of my actions.

Our production moved to another filming location, where there were no hotels nearby. The studio set up tents for us. It was great fun, camping out and barbecuing burgers at night. Early in the morning, Sidney and I set out to take a long walk on the beach. We made it about a hundred yards before a loud, booming voice came over a megaphone, ordering us to return immediately. When we got back, one of our assistant directors told us that we were only about a quarter of a mile from the Albanian border. If we had gone any closer, we would have been shot!

"I'm glad we didn't get shot," I said. "I can just see the headlines now: 'Sidney Poitier and another actor shot on location in Yugoslavia.'"

We laughed about it, but we were a little more careful going forward.

After four long months, we finally said goodbye to Yugoslavia. I had a big storm sequence to film, and Sidney also had a scene that needed to be shot in London, so we booked rooms at the same hotel. Sidney and I were very excited to be back in a civilized city and decided to go out for dinner together and order all the food we had been missing in Yugoslavia. So Sidney, Elizabeth, and I went to dinner at the White Elephant, which was considered to be the very best dining experience in London at the time—and also the most expensive. We didn't care. We had been collecting big cash per diems for months and months, with nothing to spend them on in Yugoslavia. My suit was stuffed with thousands of pounds, and I was determined to spoil Elizabeth and myself to no end. We ordered two bottles of Dom Pérignon champagne, a full tin of black Russian caviar, and some black truffles. That was just for starters. We went on to stuff ourselves with prime rib and lobster. When the three of us were gastronomically overstuffed, Sidney insisted on picking up the entire tab.

"No way!" I said. "My pockets are overflowing with British pounds. Plus, there are two of us, and so our portion of the bill is higher."

Sidney started to argue that his pockets were more overflowing than mine, until unexpectedly, the maître d' announced that the White Elephant was honored to have Sidney and us as their guests and wanted to treat us to the entire evening. Boy, did the waiter get a big tip that night! What a way to finish an incredible trip.

Little did I know, that would be my second-to-last big studio film—for a very long time.

—

By January 1964, my unhappiness was growing. Elizabeth and I had not been brought closer together when I had bought us a big, beautiful home in the Pacific Palisades with a balcony that overlooked the ocean. It felt excessive and empty. Our only friends in the Palisades were a gay couple, Richard and Jimmy, who owned a fancy gift shop that sold antiques and curios, such as imported glass animals. This all felt a little fussy and full of artifice for me, but it was in keeping with the European taste and sensibility with which Elizabeth had been raised, and our differences were feeling more pronounced than ever. She hit it off with them, and they came by our house often to drink champagne and play cards. They bought us lavish gifts, including a very expensive chandelier for Christmas one year. They were really Elizabeth's friends, and she ended up working for them in their store. Getting her out of the house was ideal for me, as it allowed me to have more freedom. It wasn't that I didn't like the guys, but I didn't feel like I fit in with them, and I looked elsewhere for fulfillment.

Yes, romping around film sets with the many work friends I had made over the years was mostly fun and even interesting at times. But when I wasn't filming, as I sat in my cavernous house, contemplating my existence, I began to sense an emptiness developing deep within me. My pleasure-seeking lifestyle was not fulfilling; it was shallow and superficial and had a lack of any moral or spiritual foundation. Increasingly, in those days, I felt like crying, but I couldn't.

I was uncomfortable but didn't have any idea how to make a change or what else I might possibly do with myself. Since I had jumped up on that stage in Inglewood, my life had been dancing and acting lessons and, soon enough, auditions and parts on stage and screen. Acting was all I had known since I was nine years old. Hollywood had been my playground and training ground, since my first part in *The Boy with the Green Hair*, which had come out when I was thirteen. Even if it wasn't fulfilling me anymore, I didn't know any existence outside of it, and I simply yearned for something deeper and more satisfying.

I had a lot of acquaintances, but I didn't have many real friends. I know I'm not the first actor to become isolated, due to our extremely nomadic lifestyle from set to set. Intense friendships and romances ignited in the close quarters of a project. But then, after a few months, everyone scattered to their next job. Sometimes we were reunited a few years later. Sometimes we never saw each other again.

When we were home in the Palisades, we often had people over for dinner parties. One of the draws of our house was a large game room downstairs with a built-in bar and a shuffleboard court in its solid wood floor. There was also an adjoining open room with a pool table, plus two bedrooms and two full bathrooms. Best of all, there was a full-length, soundproof bowling alley next to the big game room. Because an automatic pinsetter was prohibitively expensive, whenever we had a party, we would hire a kid from the neighborhood to do the pin setting for us.

It was definitely a house for entertaining, but I was beginning to find that the Hollywood lifestyle was not where I was at anymore, even if an alternative had yet to present itself to me. Several times, my former costar Jeff Richards, who had played one of my brothers a decade earlier in *Seven Brides for Seven Brothers*, came by the house. Jeff loved to hang out at the bar downstairs and drink . . . and drink . . . and drink. It got to the point where he wouldn't leave. Sometimes, he would stay for days in one of our spare bedrooms. Even though he was my longtime friend, I didn't know how to deal with him, and it finally got way out of hand. Eventually, he drank up all the booze in the house and wanted me to go out and buy some more.

"You know what, Jeff?" I said. "I think I'm going to stop drinking for a while, just to give my body a break."

He stood there, unsteadily, holding an empty bottle in his hand. "How about I give this a break?" he said. Then he smashed the bottle on the floor. Glass flew all over the place. That was it. I told him to get out of the house and not to come back until he was sober. He finally left, and we never saw each other again.

I had started smoking pot a few years earlier, and that was more where my head was at in those years—and where the counterculture was headed, although I didn't know it at the time. In my typical fashion, it wasn't something I had ever set out to try, but when it was offered to me back in the summer of 1957, I was game.

I could feel myself longing for a change, but I didn't yet know what it would be. Elizabeth and I really tried to make a go of married life. But from the beginning, Elizabeth had trouble whenever she got around alcohol, and I lacked the maturity to take my marriage vows seriously. As was my way before I was married to Elizabeth (and honestly, even afterward), I was always open to flirtations with the many pretty young women who came my way in my line of work. It was a very lonely time for me (as I'm sure it was for Elizabeth), but I had no idea what I would do if I didn't work as an actor anymore. And as unhappy as Elizabeth and I were, neither of us could bring ourselves to leave the marriage. So we just kept limping along.

Russ as a rebel assassin in *How the West Was Won* (1962) with George Peppard.

Claire Bloom, Russ, Julie Harris, and Richard Johnson outside the haunted manor Hill House in *The Haunting* (1963).

Sidney Poitier and Russ discuss the next scenes in *The Long Ships* (1964).

Human Highway
Collage by Russ Tamblyn

Created in 1977 for the poster for the film *Human Highway*.

PART 2

ESCAPE TO TOPANGA

CHAPTER 7

IN ONE EAR
AND OUT THE EYE

I was always happy when Henry Miller wanted to visit me in the Pacific Palisades. Although the shine was off Hollywood for me, like many, Henry remained very enamored of that world and enjoyed the glamour of hobnobbing with movie stars (especially the pretty female ones) at my home. In fact, he liked it so much that he ended up buying a big house near mine, with a swimming pool and everything. I was suffocating in this nice, upscale neighborhood, and I couldn't have been more surprised that this artistic lion I admired so much felt comfortable here. If you're familiar with Henry's work, you'll know that a home with a swimming pool in the Palisades was the last place you would ever expect him to end up, but there he was. I was too excited to have him as my new neighbor to seriously question his decision.

Soon after Henry had moved to the Palisades, I offered to host a welcome party for him. He liked that idea very much, especially if I would have a few Hollywood celebrities in attendance. So we picked a date, and I did the inviting. I was thrilled by the chance to host one of my heroes and provide him with an evening he would enjoy, and I anticipated a fun night in the game room. I even hired a bartender and two neighborhood kids to set up the bowling pins.

In the lead-up to the big event, I drove into Hollywood on an errand

and ran into Dean Stockwell. I almost didn't recognize him. I hadn't seen him since our MGM days together, and he looked different. His hair was longer, and he was thinner. He was driving a Porsche, and I thought he looked a lot like James Dean. We talked for quite a while, catching up, and I mentioned I was throwing a party for Henry and invited him to come.

A couple of days later, Dean called and asked if he could bring Alice and Shelley Berman with him. I said, "Of course!" Berman was one of my favorite comedians in the late 1950s. He did a neurotic telephone routine that was a killer. I told Elizabeth how thrilled I was that he was coming and how I couldn't wait to meet him.

The night of the party, Dean came to the front door, but he wasn't with Alice and Shelley Berman. Instead he was with *Wallace* and *Shirley* Berman. Clearly, I had misheard him. I was so let down it was all I could do to greet my old friend Dean and smile politely as he introduced us.

Wallace was thin, his hair was long, and he had a distinctive profile, with a distinguished nose and shaggy beard. I had no clue that he had already earned a counterculture following as an assemblage artist and West Coast Beat. Or that he would go on to be considered ground zero of the Semina Culture art movement, so named for his publication *Semina*, a Latin word meaning "to plant or sow," which was an idea Wallace loved. He was especially known for his collages of Verifax mimeographs, his poetry, and his black-and-white photos, often with Shirley as his muse. His demeanor that evening, however, did nothing to enlighten me about his artistic genius or standing. He and Shirley sat very quietly in the big game room—Wallace was as silent as a ghost—while the other guests laughed and drank and played pool around them.

This was a far cry from the comedic entertainment I had been expecting, and I was very disappointed. Wallace and Shirley just didn't fit in with my old Hollywood crowd and seemed completely out of place, as if he were a shaman who had wandered into the noisy celebration.

It wasn't that I cared about Hollywood celebrities, per se. That was just who I knew, and Henry had specifically requested movie stars, so I had done my best to oblige him. In addition to Dean, other actors in attendance included Paula Prentiss, who had starred opposite me in *Follow the Boys*. The party was a success. Henry was in his element as the king of the evening, and I was thrilled that he'd had such a good time.

Several days later, I was surprised to receive a package in the mail from Wallace, thanking me for a "pleasant evening" and inviting me to come by his house "anytime." I held his hand-printed book of loose poems and photographs, which fit into a paper slot on the inside of a thick cardboard cover and was emblazoned with the title *Semina*. I couldn't reconcile this provocative and arresting piece of artwork with the shy man I had met and barely spoken to at my house. Yes, I had been intrigued by his presence, which was so different from that of the young Hollywood actors I knew, but I hadn't had any idea he was capable of this level of artistry. Or that my friend Dean was either—as I found out years later, Dean had designed this *Semina* cover.

I had never seen anything quite like it, but I was immediately drawn to its raw immediacy. The cover photo was a black-and-white image of a young man being booked at a police station. He was obviously out of it. His head rested on a desk, while a police officer forced him to sign something. A small photo tucked into the slot on the inside was of a hand giving the middle finger. Beneath it was a poem by Jerry Katz:

> i am that noise which
> must against their
> common paraphrase
> charge deceit. here,
> in this first and
> final place, with the
> impeccable and mad,
> i thrust my only blossom.

My life would never be the same again.

With the impeccable and mad! Yes, that was me—or at least I wanted it to be, even if I wasn't sure what that meant. As I read Jerry's poem, a feeling of recognition had risen within me. Although I didn't know it yet, my need to dance on the edge was again pushing me in the direction I was meant to go—and into a new way of being that would change everything.

Wallace had written his phone number inside the cover of *Semina*. I was intrigued by the publication itself and even more so by the man who had created it. The next day I called him and was pleased when he seemed glad to hear from me. We arranged for me to stop by for a visit later that afternoon.

As I drove out of my neighborhood of spacious, well-tended lots with their jewel box homes, I was buzzing with curiosity and excitement. I crossed Sunset Boulevard, my car climbing into the hills above Hollywood. Wallace lived at the end of Crater Lane, a small dead-end street off Beverly Glen. I had to park below, on Beverly Glen, and walk up a very steep incline. My intrigue grew with every precarious step. When I reached the top, a dirt path led to Wallace's tiny house, which was more of a shack. Not only was it small and ramshackle, but it was also precariously balanced on the side of the hill, like a cottage from a fairy tale.

Wallace came to the door to greet me, and I was again struck by his presence. He had a beautiful aura and a magnetism that made you want to hear what he was going to say next. As I would soon learn when we became friends, I wasn't the only person who felt this way. Although I was the celebrity who should have been recognized, people used to stop us on the street to ask Wallace, "Excuse me, but who are you? You're somebody." I never minded, as I thought Wallace was somebody, too! When Allen Ginsberg spent time at Wallace's house, he would literally sit at Wallace's feet, absorbing every word. The same was true of Keith Richards and Brian Jones from the Rolling Stones. I've often thought that the reason Jesus surprised and resonated with his disciples as he did must have been that he was a master of one-liners, even if there's no record of it. Wallace did much the same thing, often with humor but also with the freshness of his perspective. Even though Wallace was such a serious artist, his pieces contained a lot of irony.

When he led me into his house, the first thing I noticed was ivy growing down through a hole in the ceiling. Once again, I had never seen anything like it. "What do you do when it rains?" I asked.

"I just watch it," he replied.

I laughed a little and nodded. In some ways it was a ridiculous thing to say, and yet it made total sense. I had been struck by the original and vivid work Wallace had gifted me. Now I was witnessing the original and vivid vision that had created it and how he used that vision to approach all aspects and moments of his life as art. Sure, I had been getting more into the counterculture, through the books I was reading and the pot I was smoking, and I enjoyed working on my paintings. But I'd spent years on film sets, where the "art" happened between when the directors called "action" and when they said "cut." Even my most celebrated film roles, in *West Side Story* and *Peyton Place*, for which I had been nominated for a Best Supporting Actor Academy Award in 1958, were limited by the parameters of the characters I had been playing and the scripts from which I had performed. I could instantly tell this was a different way of, well, everything—making art, living, even being. I felt like, thanks to Wallace, my eyes were opened wider than they had ever been—I was soaking it all in and loving it.

Wallace's wife, Shirley, and their son, Tosh, weren't home, but photos Wallace had taken of them covered the walls. As I had noticed at my party, Shirley was a beautiful woman with a delicate neck and big dark eyes that seemed to look right through you. But my attention was captured by a picture of Tosh, and I couldn't pull my focus away. In it, he couldn't have been more than ten years old, and he held a big black gun in his hand, gazing intently at the viewer. It was a disturbing image, and I thought to myself, *Boy, this kid is going to be a real troublemaker.* Later, I would learn from Shirley that it was quite the opposite; Tosh was a sensitive, inquisitive kid. Again, my old way of thinking was being challenged at every turn, and my mind was expanding by the minute.

Wallace wanted to show me an eight-millimeter film he was working on. He didn't have a screen on which to project it, but he did have a blank white wall, and in his improvisational way, he made do. He indicated for me to sit on the floor, which I did as he moved around me. "My movie is going to be in twenty-two parts," he said. "Each section starts with a letter from the Kabbalah."

I had no idea what he was talking about, but I nodded and pretended I did. The last thing I wanted was to admit my ignorance and get kicked out of this paradise I had found.

"I haven't finished all of the parts yet, but I wanted to show you what I've done so far," he continued. Approaching a turntable and a stack of records, he selected one of his jazz albums. He dropped the needle onto the vinyl, and as the music started, he began projecting "Aleph."

The images jumped out of the projector in rapid succession, bursting forth on the wall like a series of embryonic breaths that came and went before they were fully realized. I had spent the better part of my life making movies that were all about telling a straightforward, narrative story, captivating the audience, and drawing them into a magical, self-contained world. Compared to popular cinema—well, by any standards, really—this film seemed incomprehensible. It jumped and danced in a collage of abstract imagery. Making it even more impenetrable, Wallace had scratched and painted on many of the single film frames with acetate ink; on others, he'd applied Letraset, which was preprinted sheets of transferable lettering that could be rubbed onto artwork.

I was sitting cross-legged on the bare wooden floor, but I felt myself expanding beyond the confines of my body, the room, my known experience. The film was disturbing because it was so foreign to me, but it was acting on me in a positive way that no Hollywood offering ever had.

A tremendous emotional charge ran through me, and I felt as if an artistic bombshell were detonating in my head, blowing up all the old rules. I could barely keep it together. As half-formed thoughts and confused feelings swirled within me, I was beyond words. I let out a whimper. Hearing me, Wallace looked away from the projection and over to my face, but he seemed to think I was merely yawning or having a much more mundane response. He chuckled and turned off the projector. Looking back at me, he opened his mouth to speak. I was waiting eagerly, almost leaning toward him in anticipation—what would this creative maestro say about this strange, unsettling masterwork he had just exploded all over me?

"How about a fried-egg sandwich?" he asked.

I laughed, feeling the tension within me release. "Sure," I said.

How could I resist? And so began one of the most profound and significant relationships in my life and a huge shift in my creative journey. Wallace and I started hanging out together all the time. We enjoyed each other's company, but Wallace wasn't just my friend. He had really struck a note in my heart, and he became my artistic mentor. I bought an eight-millimeter camera and began shooting my own film. Wallace would drive me around for hours while I held my camera out the car window, capturing whatever looked interesting—leaves trembling in the wind, the sky full of cloud patterns and moon shadows—sometimes shooting through a colored glass ashtray. Usually, the images were of something I was attracted to or found humor in, like a shot that started on a sign that read, *No Parking*, and then panned over to capture the long row of cars parked all the way down the street. Or still photos I took at the Santa Monica Pier: One sign that read, *Stop*. And ten feet away, another that read, *No Stopping*. Talk about mixed messages.

Much of the footage I shot was double exposure, for which I filmed one set of images and then ran the negative backward in the camera, filming over it a second time. Rather than trying to plan how the layered pictures would line up, I acted on instinct, letting the randomness of the universe work its magic. What amazed me was how many times a double-exposed image would look like it was planned exactly as it had ended up. This was an example of the wonderful mysteries that could be found all around us, or as Wallace always said, "First-class hokeypokey!"

Mind melding with Wallace was like falling through the looking glass into an all-new universe. Through him, I moved into a constellation of talented writers and artists, including my old friends Dean Stockwell and Billy Gray (from *Father Knows Best*). Poets Michael McClure, David Meltzer, and Jack Hirschman and artist and avant-garde filmmaker Bruce Conner became my new heroes. Artist George Herms blew me away with the variety and inventiveness of his artwork in all mediums, including his "Love Press" books, so called because they were made with the handpress he dubbed with that name—they were the most remarkable, unique colored-ink prints I had ever seen—and he became a lifelong friend. These artists were sometimes interested in beauty, yes. But more than that, they favored pure representation and surprising juxtapositions, sometimes even with ugliness or death thrown into the mix—like a flattened dead cat, which was included not for the shock value but simply as a curiosity. Or artist Ben Talbot's erotic Christmas cards, which broke free of societal norms.

Although my longtime creative idol Henry Miller had bought a house near me in the Palisades, I didn't spend as much time with him as I would have previously expected. To me, the world he was immersed in felt very materialistic, with him now earning a lot of money from his *Tropic of Cancer* and *Tropic of Capricorn* books and articles for *Playboy* and seeking entrée to parties with marquee idols and pretty, young starlets. I felt like he had changed—that he'd lost his bohemian edge—and whether or not this was true, I was changing too. I was infinitely more intrigued by Wallace and his freethinking crew, who were inspired by what seemed a purer form of self-expression. Of course, what I didn't understand at the time was how much older Henry was. He had just turned eighty, and he was in a much different place in life. One time when he visited me, we were sitting downstairs in the playroom, talking together. It was a nice day, and I had the doors to the swimming pool open a little bit, to let in the sun and fresh air.

"Do you mind shutting the door?" Henry asked me. "I'm getting chilly."

On other visits, he wanted to sit in the sun because he was always cold. Being in my late twenties myself, I had no conception of what he was going through. I could see how things were changing for Henry, and for me too; we were in different places in our lives. He was moving into Pacific Palisades, and I was moving out. I was drifting away from him, and I felt more intrigued by Wallace. I did once try to bridge the two worlds by giving one of Wallace's books to Henry at Wallace's request. "Oh, I don't do anything this dark anymore," Henry said, flipping through the pages. In the moment, I felt disappointed, but really, he was setting me free. And I've always appreciated that Henry was the one who opened the door through which I was exposed to a new way of expressing my creativity—after all, it was his "welcome to the Pacific Palisades" party where I met Wallace in the first place.

———

In the performing arts, which had dominated my life since I was a boy, you do whatever you can to make the audience's head spin. In fine art, you do whatever you can to make your own head spin. My head was finally spinning. But learning a whole new way of thinking and articulating myself didn't happen overnight. On more than one occasion, while making a piece of art, I had a thought along the lines of: *Oh boy, so-and-so would really like this.* But then I would quickly think: *Wait a minute. Am I doing this for so-and-so? No.* Then I would alter it, complicate it.

I was still on the cusp of any major life-changing decisions, but my day-to-day existence had shifted radically from my very first visit to Wallace's house. Just take the day when he accepted my return invitation and visited me at my place. We went downstairs to the game room to play pool. After we had knocked the balls around for a while, Wallace turned to the dartboard on the far wall.

"Okay if I shoot darts for a few minutes?" he asked.

"Sure," I said.

So he took the darts in one hand and started hitting bull's-eye after bull's-eye (as with every other sport I ever saw him try, he was a natural). Next to the dartboard was a gigantic poster of El Cordobés, who was known as the Marlon Brando of bullfighting. I had been so struck by the stories of how he was confident enough to turn his back on bulls that I had bought this eight-foot image of him and had it sent back from Spain. It was an expensive poster that I had taken some trouble to ship, and at the time, I was quite fond of it. Well, Wallace coolly threw a dart at the poster and hit El Cordobés right in the eye.

I was stunned. While he was essentially defacing my poster, Wallace exuded this radiant positivity. He wasn't mean spirited about it, as that just wasn't his personality. But he was very calculated, alternating between tossing darts at the board and throwing them at the poster.

Comprehension began to dawn on me, but I didn't fully get his meaning until I thought about it later—he had a love for wordplay, and he was cleverly alternating a bull's-eye with a bullfighter's eye. Also, it was as if he were asking me why there wasn't any art on my walls. And he was showing me that he didn't have much respect for this huge commercial poster, and yet, with just a few darts, he could transform it into art. This was one of the first lessons Wallace would give me. There was no going back—my mind was banging open, and all these wonderful new ideas were crashing into my consciousness.

My primary drive altered from chasing success, celebrityhood, and the next big starring film role—or even just a paycheck—to digging deeper into myself through whatever means were available. I had suddenly found myself in a fertile community of artists, and the cross-pollination between us was constant. Michael McClure's book *Ghost Tantras* contains a poem with a line that struck me deeply then and still resonates for me now: *Live not for others but affect thyself* . . . That was the point exactly.

I was consumed with my new passion for creating modern art. In addition to my eight-millimeter films, which were constantly spooling out of me like messages from my subconscious, I got heavily into collage, cutting up pieces of paper and gluing them onto cardboard, creating images that weren't meant to tell a story, to entice, or to do anything, really. I arranged them as I was inspired to do, simply because they turned me on. Sometimes there ended up being a message in my work, and sometimes there didn't, but I never started out with a particular communication in mind. Rather, I chose the images that called to me, and the art emerged from my subconscious in this way. Occasionally, a poem was included, but not always, and there were no rules as to where or when it was. It was just something that would strike me. And if the viewer got something out of it, that would be cool, but it wasn't necessary to make the piece a success. I'm reminded of that old story about someone asking musician Louis Armstrong if he could explain jazz so people could understand it, to which he replied, "If you have to ask what jazz is, you'll never know." I felt that deeply about art, and I still do.

Art became a twenty-four-seven proposition. I reached the point where I even found myself moving lettuce leaves around on my salad plate just to see what kind of visual impact I could create. Small-time experimental filmmaking was my daily obsession, and my little eight-millimeter camera went everywhere with me, always at the ready, as most people use their cell phones today. I had never experienced such freedom of expression before. Viewing the world through my camera lens was like discovering everything for the first time. Before long, I began seeing things anew—both literally and metaphorically—and my camera became my paintbrush, replacing my longtime passion for painting. This footage was not meant as entertainment or even representation; it was intended to become experimental art films.

I had spent so many years in front of thirty-five-millimeter cameras, which were as slow and lumbering as dinosaurs. When making a big commercial film—or even a small commercial film—it could take a whole day to capture a single shot. With everything measured and set up in advance, hours were spent perfecting the lighting and tracking. That was just one of the thousands of intricate, interlocking steps that went into making a feature film. Now, suddenly, I could shoot from the hip, literally, grabbing footage whenever I wanted, then edit it myself and project my creations.

Suddenly, my spacious mansion in the Palisades had a whole new value. It was the perfect setting for lengthy gatherings that had the mood of impromptu art festivals, as my new compatriots ranged in and out of the house. Having picked up an improvisational approach to living from Wallace, I repurposed my bowling alley into an ad hoc cinema by setting up a screen in front of the pins. Bruce Conner brought his early short films to project there, and Wallace and I both showed our works in progress. Sitting in front of the long wooden lanes, transfixed by the kaleidoscope of images unspooling across the far wall, I felt entirely different than I had at the more formal parties I'd once hosted there with cocktails and Hollywood insiders.

Now, instead of bringing a bottle of booze or flowers for Elizabeth, as past guests had done, attendees often showed up with books—their own, of course, and titles by other writers who had challenged and inspired them. The flow of interesting new ideas and forms of expression into my house—and existence—shook me awake from my long slumber. The vague dissatisfaction I had been feeling for the last few years—all those days I had felt like crying and been unable to—finally came into focus. Although the studio system and its films had been my whole world since childhood, it wasn't enough of a life for me anymore. I leaned into the fresh energy and excitement I felt as I became more deeply immersed in the world of fine art.

It became difficult for me to pretend any enthusiasm for Hollywood, beyond the few true friendships I had maintained with other actors and filmmakers. In June 1964, when *The Long Ships* had its Hollywood premiere, I didn't attend. I was no longer under contract to MGM, so they couldn't influence my behavior in the way they once had. And I didn't think beyond what turned me on in the moment. I opted out of doing any press for the film, without realizing that this would lead the producers to become angry with me and informally blacklist me for not being a good team player. I didn't know at the time and probably wouldn't have cared if I had.

Not that I was totally unaware of the consequences of outgrowing the wholesome image of a child actor. I had recently made friends with Billy Gray, also a former young star best known for his role on *Father Knows Best*, who constantly had fans stop him on the street and say, "Hey, Billy, does Father always know best?" To which he loved to reply, "No, you do." Around this time, he had gotten arrested for smoking marijuana. It undoubtedly hurt his career, because neither the producers nor the public was ready to see him as anything but a clean-cut kid. Years later, a leading film critic would accuse him of being a heroin addict, which was not true. He filed a libel suit and won a sizable settlement, but the reputational damage had been done. Hearing Billy recount his woes to me then didn't have the impact it should have, though. I was going through a rebellious phase and valued my freedom over what anyone beyond our merry little band of artists thought of me.

Elizabeth did not quite get the "art thing." It was not a passion of hers, although she did once help me by shooting Super 8 film of her mother riding on the back of my motorcycle. Elizabeth had no external passions aside from the culinary arts. She would cook incredible gourmet meals for everyone, and she always had advice and ideas about cooking for our friends. Having very much enjoyed her role as a film star's wife, with our frequent travel to Europe and the luxurious meals and exclusive parties we had access to, she would have been happy to live that way forever. While I changed my focus to fine art and more bohemian pursuits, she remained loyal to me in so many ways rather than questioning the direction our shared life was taking. But her drinking had escalated, and she now passed out every night. This gave me a great deal of freedom to devote my time to making art and carousing with Wallace, as well as indulging in my new friends and lifestyle. This was also very convenient for me, as I didn't know how to help her, and I didn't want to fight with her, so I avoided any serious conversations and simply did what I wanted. It wasn't an ideal marriage, but we were both doing the best we could, and for a while, it continued to be easier to go along than to stop and question it all.

At the weekly hangouts at our house in the Palisades, my guests and I would play pool and bang on our bongos. Wallace and I challenged each other to fiercely competitive matches on the badminton court. Although I wore the more traditional costume of white shorts and tennis shoes, while he clomped around in his big, heavy army boots, he still won every game.

Another way Wallace and I loved to spend time together was to cruise around Los Angeles on our motorcycles. I would hop on my brand-new Triumph 650 and tear up Sunset to Beverly Glen, where I would hook up with Wallace, who rode his old motorcycle. He had painted it OD green, and the gas tank was adorned with his trademark signature—a small aleph, which is the first letter of the Hebrew alphabet.

We would glide up to the top of Beverly Glen and wind along Mulholland Drive, catching views of the San Fernando Valley on one side and Beverly Hills on the other. We would often go to the beach, where

Wallace eventually created one of his large Kabbalah pieces on a rock, which I commemorated with a photograph. On our way back down Beverly Glen, halfway between Mulholland and Sunset, we stopped at a little café called the Four Oaks. This classic hamburger joint had a room with a pool table where the locals played.

One afternoon, we pulled up on our bikes and went in to have a beer and play a game of pool. The actor Robert Blake, who I had known since we had both been in the studio system since our days as child actors, also lived in the glen, and he was just finishing up a pool game with one of the local boys. Wallace put up change to play the winner, and then I slapped my quarter down right behind him. Blake was talking in a loud voice, mouthing off with his usual kind of "deez guys and doze guys" talk, as if he were from the mean streets of New York.

Bobby won the game, and Wallace stepped up for his turn at the table. He wore jeans, a plain shirt, and his big combat boots, with his long hair flowing over his shoulders. He was calm, beatific even, and he seemed detached from Bobby's barrage of insults, which was the language of pool hall culture—being obnoxious and loud, using sarcasm to throw off your opponent. Bobby was gifted at this technique. As Wallace racked the balls, Bobby yammered away, "Yer ass is mine, Berman. And havin' your disciple witcha ain't gonna help."

Wallace stood there, cue in hand, quietly listening to everything Bobby had to say.

"Watch this power." Bobby clamored for attention from anyone who might listen. Then he busted the balls so hard they nearly jumped off the table. A ball slid into one of the pockets, and he went on to knock in a few more while ranting insults. Finally, he missed. "Yer shot, Berman," he said with a smirk. "See if ya can get some of yer garbage off the table."

Wallace stood there with his pool cue between his legs, suggestively chalking its tip. He slowly scoped out the table, cool as could be. "You know what, Bobby?" he said, his reply accompanied by the *wham!* of drilling his first ball into the corner pocket. "The only garbage I'm aware of seems to be coming out of your mouth," he continued, as—*bam!*—he drove another ball into the side pocket. "You may be a good actor,

Bobby," he continued. *Smack!* In went another ball. "But you need to work on your manners."

Wallace proceeded to run the table down to the last ball. He called the side pocket, turned the pool cue around backward, and gently tapped the 8-ball in, winning the game.

"Garbage is gone," Wallace said, softly. "Can I buy you a beer, Bobby?"

Cut even the wise guys down with love—that was Wallace.

We played hours and hours of pool in those days. Wallace even created a trophy (called TROPHI, as he loved wordplay) that was passed around to whoever could win three games of 8-ball in a row. Billy Gray, Wallace, and Dean were fierce competitors, but I seemed to win the most games and ended up with the trophy most of the time. (Is it any wonder? I had a pool table! So I played more than everyone else combined.) When in my possession, the prize was often tossed on the pool table as a cool-looking piece of art. (Who would have guessed that TROPHI would later be loaned out to the Whitney Museum of American Art in New York City and the Armory Center for the Arts in Pasadena?)

My good friend Bobby Driscoll also lived in Pacific Palisades. One day, I picked him up, and we went to our pot connection's house up in Beverly Glen. Bobby was friends with Robert Blake, and after we got our pot, he suggested we drop by to see him. I was a little hesitant, but Bobby talked me into going. When we got there, Bobby Blake was playing table tennis with Dean Stockwell and Billy Gray, and he seemed to have forgotten our pool game at the Four Oaks. I was glad, as I didn't want any tension with him. As we stood around drinking beer, I thought, *How strange. Five ex–child actors, all hanging out together, while mentioning nothing about what we have in common.* (Years later, Bobby Blake and I were reminiscing about that day. He described us as "a bunch of little drowning puppies, going down the rapids, hanging on to a life raft together.")

———

Visiting anywhere with Wallace was always an introduction to something new, whether it was a way of seeing or a way of experiencing life as an artist. For the first time in years, with Wallace as my guide, I explored the streets of Hollywood. It was all new and exciting. One afternoon, Wallace wanted to take me to Ciro's on the Sunset Strip, a nightclub where I had once gone to see Sammy Davis Jr. and Frank Sinatra, but which had fallen on hard times. In an attempt to revive the space, the club owners were trying out a different format, and they had booked a new band, the Byrds, with Jim McGuinn. On a different afternoon, when Wallace took me to see another band that he thought I just had to check out, we ran into Dennis Hopper with Bruce Conner.

Also among the artists Wallace introduced me to during this time was James Elliott. Bruce Conner had turned him on to eight-millimeter filmmaking in the early 1960s. So we had a lot to talk about, even though when I met Jim, he'd stopped his own filmmaking. He had recently been named chief curator at the Los Angeles County Museum of Art, and that was keeping him plenty busy. I still loved spending time with him, discussing art and culture.

Plus, he lived in one of the most unusual apartments I had ever been in—or have been in since. It was on the second floor of a building on the Santa Monica Pier that has been listed on the National Register of Historic Places for decades now. On the bottom floor, it contained a carousel that was built in 1922. Right above this, on the second floor, was Jim's apartment. It had these little windows that looked down on the hand-carved horses as they pranced around the room in dizzying circles. In the summer, when the attraction was open to the public, the deafening calliope music blasted away at top volume, all day and into the evening. Quite frankly, it would have driven me nuts to live there, but just visiting was an extraordinary delight.

Jim threw great parties with fascinating guests such as Andy Warhol and contemporary Swedish-born American sculptor Claes Oldenburg. In fact, a few years later, in 1966, when Jim married his wife, Judith, everyone attending the ceremony at Jim's house received a large slice of a giant white plaster wedding cake, created for the occasion by Oldenburg. (To this day, my piece of cake sits on a shelf in the kitchen of my house. I just hope nobody tries to eat it!)

During 1964, the first year that Jim and I became friends, he hosted a three-day Fourth of July beach party in Malibu, way out past Zuma and Point Mugu, on a stretch of sand that allowed camping and firepits. It was quite an event. These gatherings of hippies (or "Happenings") had begun to erupt all across Los Angeles in the 1960s, like the legendary time a crowd of these long-haired free spirits piled onto the Griffith Park carousel and scared the nice respectable folks.

For this particular party, maybe a hundred or so artists, musicians, hippies, and assorted friends camped out in tents and sleeping bags. Flags were flapping everywhere, proudly adorned with all sorts of symbols and photos, including a skull and crossbones and a hand flipping the bird. I brought a big tent for Wallace, Shirley, Elizabeth, and me to live out of during the multiple-day event. While the ladies retired to the tent at night, Wallace and I slept just outside the canvas door flap like a couple of guard dogs.

The surf was pounding, the wine was flowing, and the fireworks were exploding over the Pacific Ocean. Over the three days of the party, good musicians played rhythmic Latin jazz, while drummers pounded on their congas and bongos, and hippies and artists danced barefoot in the sand around a huge bonfire that shot sparks into the vast sky.

One night, as I was filming the gathering on my Super 8 camera by the light of the bonfire, a thin flower child, also circling the flames to the music, caught my eye. She was a delicate beauty with a crown of flowers in her hair. Even though I was there with my wife, I felt a strong urge to meet her. Elizabeth and I were only growing further and further apart in those years, but neither of us was ready to admit it was over. While Elizabeth pursued her drinking, I felt free to pursue other women. And so, caught up in the weekend's festivities, I was glad to learn this beautiful young woman was friendly with Wallace, and she soon came over to say hello. Wallace introduced her as Betsy, and she would come to play a surprising and unconventional role in the next chapter of my life. But for now, I was simply dancing my way along the edge, day by day, not yet ready to make any moves that would lead to major or lasting changes.

Russ considers embarking on a new life (circa 1965). Photo by Larry Keenan.

Russ and Elizabeth in their final days at their Pacific Palisades home (1965).

New friends and artistic compatriots Wallace and Shirley Berman with son Tosh (1959).
Self-portrait by Wallace Berman.
Photo courtesy of the Wallace Berman Estate and the Michael Kohn Gallery.

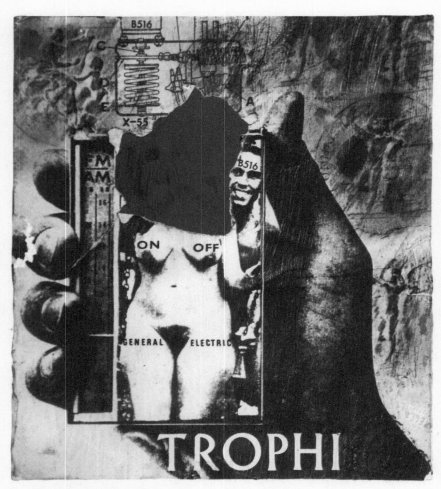

TROPHI
Collage by Wallace Berman (1964),
traded back and forth as the trophy for the winner of pool games in Topanga.

A day on the beach with Wallace as he turned a random rock into art with his signature Hebrew Letraset (1966). Photo by Russ.

Gift from Wallace Berman, *Semina* chapbook.

CHAPTER 8

Just Let It Grow

Although I had come up in the world of commercial filmmaking, I had experienced a profound perspective shift, and I was now stubbornly against making commercial artwork. I wanted to challenge viewers in the same way I was being challenged by my peers. And in these delightful days of near-constant exploration, it seemed like there was always something new to experience or learn.

One day in the fall of 1964, Wallace called me with a compelling proposition. "Are you interested in trying LSD with me?" he asked.

"Yes!" I immediately replied.

Neither of us had done it before, so we dedicated the next three or four days to preparing ourselves and learning as much as we could about this new mystical experience that was just gaining cultural significance. We went to a local bookstore and bought *The Psychedelic Experience: A Manual Based on the Tibetan Book of the Dead*. It had just come out, having been cowritten by Timothy Leary, Ralph Metzner, and Richard Alpert. But it was Leary (a Harvard University psychologist) who interested us the most. As we were well aware, he and Alpert had been experimenting with psychedelic drugs under the Harvard Psilocybin Project for quite some time before Harvard fired them due to the controversial nature of their research.

The Psychedelic Experience promised to take readers step by step through the stages of this transformational drug, and it was the perfect manual and guide for taking LSD. The book was dedicated to Aldous Huxley, who had written one of my favorite novels, *Brave New World*, as well as *The Doors of Perception*, the work that had inspired the dedication (and Jim Morrison to name his band the Doors). Huxley was known to be an ardent acid fan and famously asked to take it on his deathbed. Evidently, he did and went out of this world with a smile on his face.

After spending a day and a night relaxing and emptying my head, I drove to Wallace's early in the morning. We each dropped a tab of acid. Like a good student, I held Leary's hardcover manual, ready to open it to read chapter one. When I started to come on, I cracked the book, and there, filling the entire inside cover, was an astonishing, swirling, mandala-like artwork by Bruce Conner in black on red ink. That was the threshold. I didn't need to read any further. I turned my attention to the world around me, which was now liminal and electric.

I had heard stories of terrible trips, and I was a little nervous about how LSD would affect me. *Will I lose my mind and go a bit crazy? Will I end up doing something stupid that I'll be sorry for later?* These had been my underlying fears. However, as I relaxed into the trip, I was quite surprised by its impact. For me, everything became much clearer. I didn't have any scary hallucinations, and everything I saw was familiar. Only now, my vision, which was normally clouded with anticipation, thought, and knowledge, was fresh with a clear simplicity. That was good for a morning spent hanging out with my friend. But you certainly wouldn't want to do business on acid, or even read a book. Unless it was full of pictures! So Wallace and I decided to relax and go to the beach. The only question was: Could I drive? *We'll find out,* I thought.

Wallace and I walked to my car. It seemed like a boat as it glided down Beverly Glen, but driving was easy. I felt I could handle any situation that came up as I calmly piloted us along Sunset Boulevard toward Malibu. Luckily, nothing dramatic happened, so we didn't have to test whether my "doors of perception" were unhinged or not. The world was certainly beautiful to observe. The trees on the side of the road shimmered in the wind.

Soon, we were sitting on the beach, watching the waves pound the shore. Taking off my shoes and walking in the surf felt incredible and primal. The water wrapped around my feet, and the sand gave way a bit each time the water receded. It was a beautiful day, and the sun was a warm kiss on my face. I felt close to nature. When I returned to where Wallace was sitting on the sand, I was aware of how the earth was spinning around—it was a phenomenological experience.

After driving Wallace home, I headed back to the Palisades and sat under the lemon and orange trees in our little orchard. I felt the lawn with my hands and wondered, *Why is it so important to keep the grass cut short all the time? What would happen if I just let it grow?* That was the beginning of another big change in my lifestyle. I let the gardener go and allowed the lawn to fill in naturally. When it became tall, I loved lying in the luxuriant dell and discovering little white and yellow wildflowers popping up everywhere amid the vibrant green. It was not only more comfortable to lie down on; it was more beautiful to look at. I decided to start growing my beard and my hair long, thinking, *Maybe little flowers will start popping out of my head!*

At that time, very few men had long hair. As the look became more popular in the next few years, some of the more straitlaced guys started complaining that they couldn't tell the difference between men and women anymore. I had to laugh; maybe they were looking in the wrong places. I saw a big social change coming and was excited to be at the front end of it. But not everyone felt as happy about my new look. Having been a clean-cut movie star in my youth, I did face some backlash. At one point, a photo of my new shaggier self was printed in newspapers across the country with the caption *Can this be Russ Tamblyn?*

———

As 1964 drew to a close, even though film and TV offers were still coming in for me, I ignored them for the most part. I had enough money to get by on, and all I wanted to do was make art. Around this time, I was approached with the chance to star in a TV show that screenwriter and producer Sherwood Schwartz had created and was preparing to produce for CBS. Sherwood told me that he had written the show with me in mind and really hoped I would do it. But the plot sounded stupid to me: a silly bunch of unbelievable characters shipwrecked on an uncharted island somewhere in the Pacific Ocean. I could barely believe it, so I turned it down. Of course, that show was the long-running *Gilligan's Island*, which ended up going into syndication and airing forever. But there wasn't enough money in the world to make me spend my days working on such material.

After that, I was approached by Danny Thomas, who had moved on from being a successful nightclub comedian and the star of his own TV show for many years, to being the renowned producer of such TV classics as *The Andy Griffith Show* and *The Dick Van Dyke Show*. He offered me my own program, to be called *The Russ Tamblyn Show*. I declined. In that moment, it all seemed so irrelevant and boring. I would have felt guilty taking money for working on what I then considered to be mindless garbage. I was in the midst of a spiritual awakening, and that emptiness I had experienced for so many years had been filled up with a profound creative urge. I got so turned on shooting my own little movies that I had totally lost interest in performing in big commercial films or TV projects. As a matter of fact, I lost interest in the performing arts, *period*! I was into the fine arts now.

My two worlds—old Hollywood and the provocative contemporary art scene—almost lined up around this time when a new friend, poet Michael McClure, approached me about a play he had written entitled *The Beard*. He had experienced a vision of the flyer for a boxing match between Jean Harlow and Billy the Kid. This idea led him to write a play about their complicated attraction to each other during a conversation in heaven, culminating with a graphic scene of him performing oral sex on her. Michael wanted me to play Billy, and it was an interesting, well-written script. But I didn't have any interest in acting just then, so I passed. Michael got our mutual friend Dennis Hopper to play Billy and told me he wanted my old flame Tuesday Weld as Harlow. When I mentioned we went way back and I had recently done a TV show with her, he asked if I could introduce them. Right then and there, we got on my Triumph and drove down Pacific Coast Highway to Malibu, where Tuesday lived. We stopped and had a drink at just about every bar along the route. By the time we reached Tuesday's house, we were a little bombed and a lot raucous. We were probably incoherent but still thought we could convince her to take the role. She wouldn't answer the door, so we yelled up from beneath her second-story window. Finally, she opened the casement and stuck out her head. She did not look impressed when she saw us. We excitedly told her all about the play and her role as Jean Harlow.

"I'm not interested!" she yelled down.

That was how Tuesday was—very cocky and sure of herself—and of course, I didn't take it personally. We just laughed as she retreated inside, slamming the window after her. So that ended my brief foray into casting.

Not long after that, Dennis dropped out of *The Beard* because a producer gave him the money for his directorial debut, *Easy Rider*, which he would film several years later. Michael didn't give up on *The Beard*, and it eventually debuted in San Francisco in December 1965 with Richard Bright and Billie Dixon in the lead roles. A second performance occurred at the Fillmore for an audience of seven hundred in the summer of 1966. It was well received by the local creative community, but there was one major problem—the San Francisco Police Department arrested the actors for lewd conduct at the end of their fifth Bay Area performance. This was even though the stage lights faded to black during Billy's downward advance, so the sexual activity wasn't visible anywhere but in the audience members' imaginations.

The American Civil Liberties Union stepped in to represent *The Beard*, and many poets, artists, and other public figures came out in its defense to say it wasn't pornography—it was art. The ACLU called in famed personal injury attorney Melvin Belli, a colorful character who represented many celebrities over the years and took the case for free. Wallace was later inspired to pay tribute to Belli in one of his pieces, a poster that featured names that were significant to him, many of them spelled incorrectly, following Wallace's internal logic.

Michael won his case in San Francisco, but he was prohibited from performing the play there again. Andy Warhol got Michael's permission to film a seventy-minute version of the play, which apparently Michael thought was quite bad, but I've never seen it myself. Eventually, the play opened in Los Angeles, again with Billie Dixon and Richard Bright in the lead roles. Opening night was a big to-do, with a conservative politician having called up a film crew to capture him protesting the material outside with a microphone. When he saw me, he tried to draw me into the fray. "So, Russ, you came to see this pornography, right?" he asked.

I made a raspberry sound while flipping him the bird, which he was only too happy to film. He used this image of me in some kind of propaganda piece against Michael, or *The Beard*, or whatever it was that had him so scared. I think the studio executives got ahold of this and agreed among themselves: *Don't hire Russ anymore. He's a troublemaker.*

Michael and I found such uptight nonsense ridiculous, but the actors were again arrested after each performance—for fourteen nights in a row. Having attended the play, I can only laugh at how uptight the world once was. The controversial scene was beautiful, if ahead of its time. Now, most people wouldn't think twice about such a moment in a play. I guess that's the history of art, though; today's controversy is tomorrow's legacy.

This was the midsixties, and as you can tell, my friends were still considered pretty far out—even though there was love and positivity at the heart of their lives and artistic endeavors. This was especially true for my upscale neighborhood. Once their inspiration took hold of me, I became the rebel of the Pacific Palisades. That year at Christmastime, I put up lights on my garage door in the shape of a hand extending its middle finger. I thought it was hilarious. Two of my neighbors disagreed, leaving a signed letter on my front door that read, *We have children, please take down the lights.* I had meant it as a joke and certainly hadn't intended to offend anyone, but I knew they were right. As I removed the lights, I considered the possibility that the Palisades was no longer the place for me and that, actually, it hadn't been for a long time.

But I was torn. My spacious house allowed me to have my own art studio after I converted the old tool-and-garden room. I wasn't quite ready to leave my workspace behind. Creating experimental films and fine art had become my obsession. And I had finally set up my life in such a way that I could fully indulge in my passion. I bounced out of bed in the morning with a newfound sense of fulfillment and fresh excitement about what experiences the day would bring. I felt more alive than I had in years. I was moved to dance my way into the flow of the times. I experienced it as an exciting moment, with a door opening to life as I had never seen it before. I felt like a kid in a candy store, only the candy was nature, and the store was the earth.

A few months later, my perspective shifted further. I was finally ready to let go of my old way of living, which I had been holding on to, even though it hadn't made me happy in a very long time. It struck me that I needed to be somewhere that wasn't landscaped. And come to think of it, I didn't really need a five-bedroom house with a swimming pool. And I certainly didn't need a badminton court, or a bowling alley, or neighbors I didn't know who didn't get my sense of humor. I made up my mind to move to a new neighborhood. To commemorate this adventure on which I was about to embark, I wrote a poem:

> I'm stopping right where I am.
> no going forward or backward
> no more heights or depths
> watching opposites sneer at
> each other.
> I'm stopping right where I am.
> no more shrinking or growing
> no more twoness
> no more going
> no more stopping
> I'm stopped
> opening
> blossoming
> dying

I was sure I had to get the hell out of the Palisades, but where to next? George Herms was living in Topanga Canyon, a small mountain community, a little more than four miles up Topanga Canyon Boulevard from Pacific Coast Highway in Malibu. When Dean and his wonderful girlfriend at the time—choreographer and artist Toni Basil—moved up there too, close to our mutual friend Billy Gray, I thought I would go and check it out for myself. So in late 1965, I drove all around the snaking roads of Topanga, winding my way along Fernwood Pacific Drive for a mile or so, until I came upon an available house. High in the Santa Monica Mountains, it was the last property on a dead-end street, Sky Line Trail, which seemed to go straight up for about a hundred yards. Nestled in a grove of mighty oak trees, the house was perched on a rugged ridge that offered a majestic, 180-degree panoramic view of the mountain range across the canyon, all the way down to the Pacific Ocean. I fell in love with the locale right away. It was everything that I never knew I really wanted.

I sold my mansion and put a down payment on this two-bedroom house; here was the opposite of the life I had led in the conservative, prosaic Palisades. My decision to downsize to this much more modest and inspiring locale was the first in a series of choices that would create a domino effect of change throughout all areas of my life. I couldn't have been more ready for the winds of personal revolution to blow. As soon as my boxes arrived in January 1966 and I began to unpack my books, film, and art supplies, I finally exhaled a huge sigh of relief—letting go of the rigid restrictions and outmoded ideas of the place from which I had just fled.

When I moved to Topanga, all I wanted was to make art and swap inspiration with my friends, who were now my neighbors. At the time, I felt done with Hollywood, but I didn't realize how much I was giving up. Or even that I had to give up something—old ways of living, thinking, dressing, creating—to start something completely new. I followed my intuition, as I had always done, and shed the trappings of fame and success as if removing my costume at the end of a film shoot. I had just been born again, and I was already anticipating the adventures to come and the art to be made. Once again, I wasn't thinking about what I was doing or where it would lead me—I was following my instincts, which were telling me this was the direction that would allow me to dance on the edge in a new way, exploring my psyche and artistic vision in greater depth.

I didn't feel anything about what I was leaving behind, only curiosity and excitement about what I was moving toward, which was unknown, and I don't only mean for me personally. Of course, I had no idea this would be such a significant moment for me or for the contemporary California art scene. When I relocated to Topanga Canyon, I was at the forefront of the growing, rebellious population of artists that was gathering there. Little did I know at the time that I was a founding member of what would later be recognized as the California assemblage movement, which overlapped with the West Coast Beat movement. Or that our influence would begin to spread out into the neighborhood and beyond. But when I look back, I can see everything we couldn't grasp then because we were so close to it. Too young to be bohemians, which I associated with Henry Miller and the artists who had gone to Paris in the first half of the century, we admired their achievements but craved even more freedom in our self-expression and lives. And yet we weren't hippies—a term I hated being called, even though we often were, because it was still unusual enough for men to have long hair and dress in anything other than slacks or a pressed shirt. But really, it was a term I found meaningless— Charles Manson had been called a hippie, too, and although he also briefly lived in Topanga, I certainly didn't know him or feel any kinship to him.

In fact, he was so under the radar at the time that I didn't realize who he was when I picked up three or four girls hitchhiking along Topanga with a skinny, wild-eyed guy. They seemed a little weird to me, especially when they all piled into the back seat together. One of the girls said proudly to me, "Do you know who this is back here?"

"No, I have no idea."

"His name is Charlie Manson, and he's like the next Jesus."

Oh yeah, great, should I bow down? I thought. *Can't wait to drop him off.*

They asked me to drive them beyond my normal turnoff onto Sky Line Trail, up to a rocky area, where they were camping out. I agreed so they wouldn't have to walk the extra distance, but I was glad to see the last of them.

Manson was never taken seriously in the canyon, and the locals—especially the ladies of Topanga—thought of him as very creepy, so he moved away before long. Then he became the infamous person that everybody now knows.

My friends and I were forging a magical new canyon culture. Further west, our neighborhood was more natural and less culturally sanctioned than the simultaneous Laurel Canyon scene, which has been celebrated for the music of everyone from Frank Zappa to Joni Mitchell. I had friends who lived in Laurel Canyon, including Bobby Driscoll, who I bought my pot from. And I sometimes went to parties there. But when it came to living and creating, my compatriots and I sought out a destination that was everything we needed to support our art—cheap, wild, and isolated from mainstream culture. We turned ourselves inward, to our own little community of Canyonites and our mission to spin every aspect of our lives into a form of artistic expression. We didn't go in for labels or rules. We all shot from the hip when it came to our art, seeking each other out because we were inspired by each other's creative work and enjoyed each other's company. We joyfully cross-pollinated each other, all making some of the most ambitious work of our artistic careers while living in this fertile canyon.

For the first time in years, I felt like I was exactly where I was supposed to be, living exactly as I chose to live. Hollywood was only twenty-five miles away but felt distant. My old life as a Hollywood insider felt so far behind me that I threw my Academy Award nomination up on the roof, and then I forgot about it for the next few years. I was tired of going out on auditions and enduring that whole rigmarole for parts I didn't care about anymore. I had no interest in filling my brain with lines from scripts that seemed old fashioned and square. Since I was a kid, I had been expected to turn up at the studio on short notice, clean shaven and in tip-top shape. What a waste of time and energy that now seemed. I had stopped getting regular haircuts and let it grow wild and curly. I let my teeth go and only shaved if I felt like it—I was very scruffy, usually sporting a shaggy mustache and stubble, if not a full beard.

At first, even without trying, I still had connections to Hollywood—I had been in the business for too long for my reputation to evaporate overnight. But now, I only wanted to interact with the world of entertainment on my terms. The producer for *The Dean Martin Show* approached me to be a guest on an upcoming episode. I agreed, and I planned out this whole dance I was going to do in front of the camera—not like my shovel dance from *The Fastest Gun Alive* or my street-fighting choreography from *West Side Story*. I had something really far out planned, the likes of which the regular folks at home had never seen. But then the producer came back with a caveat: "You have to cut your hair down, so it looks normal," he said.

That pissed me off. "It is normal," I said. *Who isn't normal, at this moment in pop culture, is Dean Martin*, I added in my mind.

"But nobody knows you with long hair," he said.

"Yes, they do," I shot back. "One of my first movies for Cecil B. DeMille was *Samson and Delilah*, and I had long hair in that. So I've had long hair in movies before."

But my arguments did nothing to change his mind, and they decided to go with another guest star. The producer was well connected, and my hunch is that he warned his buddies that I was whacked out and nobody should hire me. Because after that, the sporadic offers I received for guest spots dried up. Not that anyone in Hollywood ever came out and said what was going on. They just gave me their favorite line: "We've decided to go in another direction."

Yeah, well, the feeling was mutual—I had definitely decided to go in a different direction myself. Not long after my move to Topanga, I made my break with Hollywood official. Until then, I'd had great representation, including agents Dick Clayton, who had repped James Dean, and Phil Gersh, who was also Robert Wise's agent. Since I now found fine art so much more satisfying than performing arts and didn't want to do any more auditions, I dropped them both.

At first, my life was grand. We had a two-bedroom house, and after many years of marriage, Elizabeth and I had no children and had resigned ourselves to the fact that we never would. So I turned the extra room into my studio and began creating artwork right away. Inspired by Wallace, I had painted the walls the same OD green—a flat, earthy color used by the army—he had painted his motorcycle. (I also did up my car this color, and I delighted in how it would blend into the verdant, sun-dappled canyon and seemingly disappear from view.)

Just above my garage was the main front room, in which I put a new full-size pool table so I could practice my game and play with friends who stopped by to visit. For a light over it, I repurposed an old toilet bowl, which funneled a muted circle of weak illumination down onto the green felt. Every time I walked in, I delighted in the unexpected visual absurdity of the upside-down commode suspended from the ceiling. I liked how the light was absorbed by the walls, making the room feel dim and restful. The main visual attraction was a window that overlooked the driveway that circled the house, beyond which were stunning views of the treetops and the canyon below. On mornings when the marine layer rolled in off the ocean, the mist would settle just under my house, and I felt like an eagle living on a cloud—it was eye opening, like finding myself in heaven. When storms rolled through, thunder exploded, echoing off the canyon walls like a volley of cannon shots fired by Mother Nature. Lightning flashes lit up my poolroom in a psychedelic ghost dance while I sat by the window, smoking a joint and taking it all in. Now, this was a fresh perspective from which to see the world, and when I was awaiting inspiration, I would often find myself dreamily staring out the window, watching hawks circle and swoop above the treetops that danced in the breeze just below my homestead.

I woke up in the morning thinking about art and went right into my studio, even before I had sipped my first cup of coffee, to dive back into the collage I had been piecing together late into the night. I spent many hours at my worktable there, happily piecing together the collages that were my primary medium at the time. For a midmorning break from creating, I took hikes off the road, down into the canyon, to watch the hippies skinny-dip and catch poison oak. I found a refuge in the woods and became a bit of a nature boy myself, making up my own trails. My favorite led up the side of a mountain to a flat clearing by a pond that was fed by a small waterfall. It was deep enough to cool off in the water, but mostly, I would sit next to it and meditate. Finding the space magical and inspiring, I always meant to include it in a series of photos I called *Secret Places* of all my favorite hidden gems in Topanga, but I never got around to it.

Most afternoons, I would settle in to work on whatever collage I had in progress. While I might have been an untrained, instinctual artist who was more about visual impact than making a single overt statement in my art, I was very precise in my techniques. I didn't learn this idea from any book or the advice of another artist—it was just what made visual sense to me. Collages are commonly quite bumpy and messy, with images overlapping each other, so the top picture is creased by the edge of the image below. This might seem like the smallest of inconsequential details, but such lines marred my vision for my pieces. I used trial and error to work out a method where I would trace the edge of the upper image along the bottom image and cut away any material that would be obscured by the top layer. The two pieces of found material fit like a puzzle, lining up seamlessly, no matter how discordant their pictures might be. I worked hard to pull off this visual witchcraft, which made my collages as smooth as possible, their surfaces often resembling photographs.

While I worked upstairs, Elizabeth spent most of her time down in the kitchen. There was really nothing for her to do in Topanga, and she didn't fit in—this kind of casual, artsy lifestyle wasn't what she was about. Her whole demeanor was very English, very proper—that was how she behaved most of the time. But she was loyal, and she didn't complain. We had already established the pattern of our marriage, and neither of us knew how to alter it. After Elizabeth's father died, her mother had moved in with us in the Pacific Palisades. Now, she found her own little house on Topanga Boulevard. It was quite a change for her, and she never quite adjusted. Whenever she walked down to the store, she would take all her money—nearly a thousand dollars in cash—and her jewelry in her purse. She was convinced that her house would be burglarized, no matter how many times I told her that the ethos of the neighborhood was all about giving, not taking, and that her handbag was actually the easiest thing to run off with.

Elizabeth spent some time with her mum, but her main outlet remained her cooking, and she could lay out a wonderful spread if we were having friends over, or just for the two of us. Most evenings, I took a break to eat whatever she had cooked. By then, she would be a few glasses in and well on her way to drinking herself to sleep. I used this as an excuse to pop back up to my studio for a few more hours and then go out with my artist friends whenever I wanted.

Sometimes, I was with other women—both casual flings and longer affairs. I was pleasantly surprised to reconnect with Betsy, who I had fallen for at the Fourth of July party in Malibu. I was drawn to her beautiful free spirit and innocence. We had a very casual affair—I was married, and we were both seeing other people—until she became pregnant. She came over to my house just before she gave birth and asked me to take a nude picture of her and her big naked belly, and I obliged. She never suggested the child might be mine. After that, I saw her around the canyon occasionally with her baby daughter, but we didn't really talk.

By this point, Elizabeth had endured several miscarriages, and she always blamed me, saying it was my fault that her pregnancies weren't viable. Both of my brothers had very large families, so I believed her. As someone who had been an acrobat for years, I figured I had shaken everything up and was infertile. Deep down, I suspected her heavy drinking probably contributed to our fertility issues, but I certainly never confronted her about it. We had married so quickly that it was only later we realized we had few points of real connection. It's not like we were in a good place to try to start a family anyhow. Alcoholism and infidelity—what a combination for marital disaster. But I didn't have the perspective to think about it that way at the time.

As I can see now, my womanizing only made my flimsy bond with Elizabeth more frayed. Because I got to do whatever I wanted, I felt no need to fight. Yes, her drinking made me sad sometimes, especially as it took its toll and she began to lose her vitality and wit. I loved companionship, which she provided, as dysfunctional as it was. We remained connected, if tenuously, through our sense of humor and our shared love of adventures, whether it was a picnic or a road trip. We had found a way to coexist together, and for many years, that's exactly what we did.

Russ's Topanga transformation, entering the world of counterculture (1966).

Russ's Skyline Press chapbook, *HNYC (Hirschman's New York City)*, in collaboration with poet Jack Hirschman.

Russ's first home on Sky Line Trail in Topanga. Photo saved from the fire.

CHAPTER 9

THE INCREDIBLE SHRINKING MAN

Rather than drawing creative impetus from the home front, I mostly found inspiration through spending time with my new cohort of artists—especially Wallace, Dean, George Herms, and poet Jack Hirschman, who also briefly lived in Topanga. I forged new friendships with a few other local artists, including James Gill and Ben Talbot, who made erotic art that was pretty outrageous.

In the spring of 1966, Dean generously bought Wallace and Shirley a house up in Topanga, after their little shack in Beverly Glen had slipped off its foundation during a heavy rainstorm, sliding down the hillside in a pile of mud. Luckily, no one had been home, but much of Wallace's artwork and their personal belongings were lost or damaged. Their new home was on a quiet road named Arteique. What a perfect place for Wallace Berman to live and create!

This story is a great example of how Dean was—a kind, creative soul who was like a loving brother to Wallace and me. In our little galaxy of artists, Dean was intelligent and intuitive, yet practical too. This allowed him to sometimes step in and take care of business for the rest of us who had gone a little further out there—even though Dean would go pretty far out there himself from time to time, he never turned his back on his career. A Hollywood lifer, he had already filmed a dozen movies by the time I met him on the set of *The Boy with Green Hair* when we were both teenagers. Even during the Topanga years, he never dropped out in the same way I did, and he always picked up fairly regular theater and TV work.

Now we were all in Topanga together—the Bermans, Dean and Toni, Louise and George Herms, Jack Hirschman, Billy Gray, Elizabeth, and me. I felt a strong creative surge taking hold of me, and I wasn't alone. We all worked hard and joyously inspired each other, having fun and making new pieces almost constantly.

Toni Basil, Dean's girlfriend in those years, was one female artist who ran around with us guys. A truly exceptional dancer and choreographer, she was the assistant to David Winters, who I knew as one of my fellow actors and dancers from *West Side Story*. In 1964, she had worked for him as he was choreographing the backup dancers for *T.A.M.I. Show*, which introduced James Brown and the Rolling Stones to an American television audience and also featured performances by the Beach Boys, among others. All vibrant, of-the-moment music, captured with incredible power and verve, making it one of the best chronicles of rock 'n' roll I have ever seen.

Toni was always making her own artwork, putting on dance recitals, and shooting short eight-millimeter films, including a great one of all of us Topanga boys playing baseball in the park there. One of her most famous film collaborations of this era was a dance she performed naked with rapid precision and beauty for a short movie by Bruce Conner. Toni was one of the gang, an artistic equal who was deeply involved in our creations.

Jack Hirschman was a native New Yorker, who looked and acted the part, dressing in a long black trench coat, endlessly pacing up and down the canyon, and darting into traffic to cross the street whenever he saw fit. Dean and I would go up to see Jack and take long rambles with him. He was tall and angular, with a big mustache and long flowing hair, and he swung his arms with gusto, making him an imposing figure. He didn't appear to belong in Topanga, and I found it funny whenever I came upon him out on a walk while I was driving.

More than just a poet, Jack lived his beliefs. A humanist and passionate communist in the true sense of the word (as in somebody who's
for the working man and for the commune), he was always advocating
for the voiceless. He knew all the unhoused people in every neighborhood where he lived. And wherever he was, if he saw someone on the
street, he would give them a dollar or two, even though he had little
money of his own.

My good friend George Herms and his wife, Louise, lived on the
tip-top of Topanga, about fifty yards up from the neighborhood's only
nightspot, the Corral. The scene at their homestead was wild and un-
tamed—the family's old wooden house and George's studio sprawled
across a dirt-covered hillside, overlooking the forested crags below. Their
living structure was ramshackle, with no glass in the windows. In the
winter months, they hung up blankets to keep out the chill and damp.
It might not have been much to look at, but it was a joyous spot, full of
life, creativity, and heart. Their two young daughters, Nalota and Lily,
could often be found with crowns of wildflowers in their long, tangled
hair, galloping around the property and playing on big rubber inner
tubes, repurposed into a kind of free-form jungle gym.

There was creativity in everything George and Louise did, and they
were both central to our little Topanga community. His work flourished
at the dawn of the assemblage movement, and along with Wallace, he
was a great inspiration to me when I began creating fine art—he still is.
He has always been a true master of painting, collage, sculpture, mixed
media, drawing, poetry, and performance art. One of his signature performance pieces was to blow into a garden hose that had been fitted
with a trumpet armature while flailing the rubber tubing around. Or
he might hold up a set of metal venetian blinds and shake them while
he danced around like a court jester, making an unbelievably cacoph-
onous noise. And then he would time it so that his pants dropped and
he'd stand there beaming in just his shorts. Among his signature looks
was an empty egg carton worn like a crown. He had this wonderful,
mischievous sense of humor, and everything he did was bursting with
amazing energy.

If there's a creative medium George hasn't participated in, I don't know what it is. In Topanga, he had his Love Press at hand, cranking out colored-ink prints. Over the decades, he has also created dozens of beautiful books of poetry. Another favorite form of expression for George was to print his own catchphrases onto small cards, which he handed out. Some of my favorites included:

Beauty is yr. duty.

Remember kids, it's not just second-hand smoke that kills you; it's second-hand thoughts.

Your lover is yr. best doctor.

There were dozens more—he was always coming up with something new. He didn't ever become too precious about making art—he created it and released it into the world right away.

Once a year, George would put on a raffle, playfully changing the name of the event each time, morphing it into a "Baffle" and then a "Waffle" and even an "Earful." The gathering was hyped up in advance to draw as big of a crowd as possible. Attendees would buy raffle tickets for five dollars or some other modest amount, and then the lucky winner could choose any of George's art pieces, which were major assemblages that should have sold for a thousand dollars or more at a gallery. George probably only made enough money from these gatherings to pay the rent and feed his family for a short time, but they were still major events in Topanga. I always attended these shindigs for the spectacle and the camaraderie, but I never entered the raffle myself. I was experiencing a downsizing of my Hollywood life, but the Herms were perpetually in a genuine financial struggle—there were more than a few days when they lived on coffee and popcorn. I bought pieces from George whenever I could afford to do so.

Louise made me beautiful shirts, which I wore on special occasions, as well as a few pairs of pants, such as jeans with ribbons decorating the sides and cuffs. I hadn't ever really been into fashion, and I didn't have money to spend on anything beyond the basics. But I was happy to be able to give Louise a little cash for her wonderful creations, which expressed my sensibility so much better than anything I could have found in a store. One of my favorite pieces, which I still have, was a handwoven sash of bold reds, pinks, and greens. Around this time, I took to wearing a white button-down shirt with formal cuffs, but instead of cuff links in the holes, I adorned them with fresh flowers. Art wasn't just something I made in my studio; it was woven into every aspect of my life.

———

Although I had left Hollywood behind, I had been a film actor for almost two decades, and I was still a household name with plenty of loyal admirers. One of the most striking of these was a man from Atlanta named Richard Newton, who we called "the Pear" because of his distinctive shape. He was sort of a nut, if a bighearted one.

Back when I had been drafted into the army in the late 1950s, MGM had forwarded my fan mail to me at Fort Sill in Oklahoma. One day, I received a giant wooden crate weighing hundreds of pounds. The base mail center told me to bring several pals to pick it up because it was about sixteen feet long and extremely heavy. So a bunch of us brought it back to the gym and opened it up on the basketball floor. There, inside the crate, was a long, rolled-up canvas. When we unfurled it, we all stood back in shock. It was a twenty-three-foot-long, fifteen-foot-high oil painting of Samson slaying the Philistines—all one thousand of 'em! The artist's name was Dean Chapman, and his style suggested his great admiration for Rembrandt. A note from Newton explained that he had commissioned Chapman to do the piece as an homage to my film *Samson and Delilah*. Well, after showing it to everyone in the gym and having a good laugh, we packed it up again and sent it back to him. I did leave a note in the crate thanking him but added, *Sorry, but it won't fit in my locker!* The monstrous painting eventually ended up on the wall of a bank in Scottsdale, Arizona.

Around the time I moved to Topanga, the Pear phoned from Atlanta. He told me that his father, who had been the head of the southeastern branch of General Motors, had passed away and left him a substantial inheritance. Wanting to share his financial windfall with me, the Pear offered me a brand-new Cadillac. I was hesitant about accepting such a substantial gift from a fan, especially a big white Cadillac, when I was consciously shedding the trappings of my old movie star life. But his timing was fortuitous—I had driven my little Austin-Healey for years, and it was falling apart. So I reluctantly agreed.

I had always loved nice cars and motorcycles, and when I had originally signed my seven-year contract with MGM, I celebrated by purchasing a deep-maroon 1952 Mercury convertible. It had a white top and a high, lustrous shine, thanks to its eighteen coats of lacquer. It was custom built, with no chrome anywhere, and lowered eighteen inches in the back. The car taillights were the wingtip lights from an airplane. To gain entrance, I used a foot lever under the driver's door to snap it open. It was gorgeous and extravagant, making me the student at my high school with the best wheels by far. I would cruise up to the Bob's Big Boy in the Valley, which was the gathering place for all the young studs with their ducktails and hot rods. I sure turned heads—I was the king!

Of course, I was in a very different frame of mind by the midsixties, and so, while I appreciated the elegance (and reliability) of my Cadillac, I also knew it looked surreally out of place in rustic Topanga. I remedied this by turning it into an art car, gluing feathers, paintings, and little photos on the dashboard and sticking a plastic hand in the air vents. I loved to cruise my neighborhood's winding hills with the window rolled down and my left arm draped out the driver's side window. I would pick up the many hitchhikers I passed as if I had my own far-out (and free) taxi company.

Once, during my on-again-off-again affair with Betsy, I drove down to visit her at her little cabin, one of several crammed together at the end of a long dirt road. On my way back up to the main drag, a big black sedan came out of nowhere. It stopped right in front of me, blocking the road. Two guys in black suits jumped out with their guns drawn. "Get out of the car with your hands up and don't move!" they yelled.

I lowered my window. "How can I get out of the car if I don't move?" I asked, like the smart-ass I was.

"Just get out of the car, wise guy!"

It quickly became clear they were undercover cops, hoping to make a major drug bust. Although they did their best to incriminate me by searching my car for a long time, they found nothing but a lot of artwork on the dashboard. Thankfully, and for no particular reason, I had left my pot at home.

I usually had a big stash of weed that I had bought from Bobby Driscoll, and my new car wasn't set up for such run-ins with the law. When I had my Austin-Healey, there was a hole in the floorboard, covered by the mat. So all I had to do was pull the mat back and drop the pot through the hole onto the ground. When the police pulled me over in that car, I made a point of slowing down to show I was cooperating. I'd drop my contraband through the hole onto the ground underneath and then pull a few feet forward so they wouldn't notice it. That way, when they searched me and my car, they could never find anything—because there was nothing to find *in* the car. Feeling pleased with myself, I couldn't help but give the officers a little attitude. And then, when they were out of sight, I'd back up and retrieve my stash.

While I had many other local adventures over the years, my most memorable ride in the Cadillac was a drive to San Francisco to visit Michael McClure. We had a glorious trip cruising up the coast in my fine automobile. Wallace rode shotgun, looking biblical with his long hair flowing, while our glamorous wives relaxed in the spacious back seat. When we arrived at Michael's apartment, he asked us if we wanted to meet Allen Ginsberg. Of course, this was an exciting prospect for me, as I thought he was brilliant and deeply admired the ferocity of his creative expression. Apparently meeting me was also an exciting prospect for Allen, for a slightly different reason.

When we entered the room where Allen was staying, he was sitting on the edge of his bed. I eased down next to him, as it was the only available seat. Because he was such a big intellectual hero of mine, I was filming our visit with my trusty eight-millimeter camera. Without a word, he proceeded to feel up my leg. This was a bit of a shock for me. Of course, I knew he was gay, but I wasn't expecting him to see me as an offering, gifted to him by our mutual friends. Calmly, I lifted his hand off my leg, and from there, we got to talking like old pals.

—

And then I found a way to merge my movie star past and my artistic present when I climbed onto my roof one day to fix the TV antenna. I came across my Academy Award nomination for *Peyton Place*, which I had thrown up there when I moved in. It was weather beaten, which made it more visually interesting to me. I took it into my studio and sat with it for a few days until inspiration struck; I added collage elements and used it as the basis for a new piece of artwork. Next, I remembered that I had several film stills I had brought home after completing my role in *The Wonderful World of the Brothers Grimm*. Now, I approached them with new interest—seeing these artifacts from my Hollywood past as emblematic of the fairy tales they literally portrayed and the fairy tale I had lived within their frames. I painted on them, completely transforming their symbolism and aesthetic. For Dean's birthday that year, I created a collage featuring the green hair and a page from a 1930s New York casting directory that had belonged to my father. Under the heading of *Juvenile Leading Men* was a listing of actors in alphabetical order: Harry Stockwell, Dean's father; and right under his name, Eddie Tamblyn, my father. What a coincidence, since Dean and I were like brothers throughout our lives.

I also found a new creative outlet around this time when I was gifted a small handpress by Bob Alexander of Temple of Man. This nonprofit beatnik collective in Venice Beach offered a gathering place for artists to enhance their creative endeavors and certified many of us, including myself, to officiate marriages (I only performed one over the years, but it has lasted, so my stats are good). Much like George's Love Press, my handpress was a really beautiful old-timey machine. I loved how it felt when the mechanism met the paper and I lifted it off to reveal an elegant line of prose. Doing one print after another was like a meditation; it got to a point where I was really sensitive to the workings of the machine, as we had become one, and it was a transcendent experience. I called my endeavor the Skyline Press, in homage to my home and studio on Sky Line Trail. I often printed my own poems, but my biggest venture was a limited-edition, hand-bound book of Jack Hirschman poems, *HNYC*, which stood for *Hirschman's New York City*. I gifted him a hundred copies and kept a hundred for myself, happily giving them out to everyone I knew.

Everywhere I looked, even back into my past, I now saw a source of potential art. My life began to feel more integrated as I merged its two major periods through the work I was making in my studio. Even if I was struggling financially, this was definitely the only existence for me. Now, I just had to come up with a way to afford my art supplies— not to mention food.

I was living a dream life of constant creativity and inspiration, but I had diminished myself from a wealthy movie star to a starving artist. My savings from my Hollywood career had been exhausted. I had no bank account, no money. I had dropped out completely. I felt like the incredible shrinking man, like I was going to disappear.

The truth was, I didn't really miss acting, but I missed being offered roles, and I hated feeling like my career was now completely out of my control. I needed to make some real money. I realized I couldn't do so by creating fine art, which took too long to complete. So I tried to resume my relationship with my former agent Phil Gersh. He told me, "Well, I'm not taking any more clients," which was his polite way of saying, *You blew it, buster.*

When I tried to get TV or movie work, it was very difficult. As I'd built up a major movie career as a studio player who was offered parts without having to audition, it was very humbling to now go to auditions with my proverbial hat in my hand. I knew I had to take whatever I could get, which often was nothing.

I could sense I had been blacklisted by producers who were afraid of me. Well, they probably should have been! I *was* a bit of a rebel at that point. I thought differently, and I probably couldn't have fit back into the studio system anyhow. I was all about authenticity, while they would never be honest about why they were no longer hiring me, no matter how many auditions I went on; they just stopped giving me roles. I was broke, and it was scary. If I wasn't the direction that Hollywood was going anymore, then I needed to find a direction of my own—one that also paid.

When I eventually made my way back in front of a film camera, the roles weren't quite what they had been. My last major Hollywood film had found me starring in *Son of a Gunfighter* (which Quentin Tarantino would later credit as one of his favorite movies). Now, I was offered the lead part in what I considered to be a terrible monster film, *War of the Gargantuas*. But I would get to travel to Japan for filming, and it paid $40,000. I certainly wasn't going to turn that down.

I was excited to visit Japan for the first time. During the height of our friendship, Henry Miller had sent me a postcard from there. On it, he had described his surprise at discovering how strong Japanese women were, as he had wrongly assumed they were subservient. And he told me, if I ever visited Ginza, the red-light district, I would find that 90 percent of the clubs were owned and run by women. Of course, I was curious to explore this myself, and I ended up taking many photographs and making a short film in Japan.

Thankfully, when I arrived on set, I found I was able to improvise, which was a favorite acting technique of mine. No one, including the director, spoke or understood English. With only one interpreter present, I was free to do (and say) pretty much whatever I wanted. The interpreter would give me my lines, and then I'd change them to suit the character. I figured I might as well have fun, since the script was pretty bad. I was at least adding humor, often coming up with replacement lines that were cleverer.

Plus, it would simply be a money project, and no one would see it. Little did I know that it would run on TV every night for several weeks. (Years later, at the eighty-fourth Academy Awards, actor Brad Pitt cited *War of the Gargantuas* as his inspiration for becoming an actor—he had to be kidding! Even Quentin has told me how much he enjoyed this movie—so I guess it just goes to show that it's impossible to tell which projects will have staying power.)

Not everyone was a fan of my work in the film, however. Its producer, Henry Saperstein, had gone from producing *The Famous Adventures of Mr. Magoo* to making Japanese monster movies, including 1965's *Invasion of Astro-Monster*, starring my old friend Nick Adams. Apparently, Henry was not amused by my improvisation. Years later, I read something he had written about working with me, in which he said I had been a real pain in the ass.

By then, I had mellowed out a great deal, and I didn't enjoy being taken down in print. But I could also see his point—because I was so passionate about fine art, I didn't really care about the movie at the time of filming. And I didn't care who knew it. So I wasn't the most cooperative guy on set. Of course, since Henry had put his own money into the film, this upset him. He thought I wasn't paying attention to the script and I was getting out of line. He didn't realize that my smart-ass repartee was of value, as it demonstrated an awareness of the inherent campiness of these types of films and therefore was more in line with youth culture. My spoken words were more alive than what had been written on the page, but my improv came off as cocky to the establishment, which Henry very much represented.

At the time, I was blissfully ignorant of any of this—I had enjoyed making the film and was thrilled to go back to Topanga with my paycheck. Having sorted out my financial problems, I threw myself back into my collages and eight-millimeter films.

—

After Wallace and his family moved to Topanga, we would often meet up in the evening and grab a beer together. The only nightclub in the neighborhood was the Topanga Corral. This venue, which would become quite famous, went through many iterations. The original Corral was a smaller joint, on the south side of the big bend on Topanga Canyon Boulevard. When I first moved to this mountain community, it was a small, unsophisticated country music bar. There was a neon desert scene with cacti on one wall, as well as a cow skull. The rest of the men who lived in

Topanga were cowboys and rednecks who spent their time riding horses and chasing girls, and we called them "the Boys." The residents wanted to keep the canyon rural and didn't favor paving the roads. I liked that. What I didn't particularly care for were the country bands that dominated the club. Once our gang of artists moved in, that began to shift.

One afternoon, before he was a local himself, Wallace called and asked if I wanted to go to the Corral to have a beer. It wasn't like him to drink in the afternoon, but he told me it was a special occasion.

"What's so special?" I asked.

"Two of the Rolling Stones are visiting," he said.

Now *that* was something special.

When I arrived at Wallace's house, he introduced me to Keith Richards and Brian Jones. Dean was there too. The two Stones were on their way to South America but had heard of Wallace and wanted to meet him. As we were getting to know each other, they showed us a hidden compartment in a briefcase where they kept their drugs. Having bonded, the five of us headed to the Corral for a drink.

The bar's manager, Johnny Desco, called out his usual greeting when he saw us: "Here come the hats!" That was his nickname for Wallace, Dean, and me because we often wore felt hats. Johnny, a big guy who was maybe a decade older than we were, had started out with short hair. By then, he had begun to grow it a bit in keeping with the times and the club's increasingly free-spirited clientele. He ran the bar and threw out the drunk-and-disorderlies. Johnny also liked rock 'n' roll and was thrilled to meet two of the Stones. The five of us sat down at a big table together while Keith checked out the jukebox. Suddenly, Keith came back to our table with a serious look on his face. "What's that shit on the jukebox?" he said.

Johnny laughed. "Have any good suggestions for changes?" he asked.

Keith paused for a moment. "Is a pig's ass pink?" he blurted out with a completely straight face. Keith promptly sat down at the table, and he and Brian made a list of hot tunes. That was the beginning of a musical change at the Corral, which never went back to how it had been. Johnny updated the jukebox, and with cooler music, the bar began to attract a hipper crowd. (My future wife, Bonnie, even hung out with her older sister Carrie at this iteration of the Corral when she was fifteen. Our paths would cross there, and sparks would fly, but not until many years later.)

It didn't take long for the live bands to transition from country music to more current offerings. The first band to play there was a crazy girl group called the GTOs (Girls Together Outrageously). These seven female musicians were first known as the Laurel Canyon Ballet Company and could be found playing wild music on the Sunset Strip, where they caught Frank Zappa's eye. He became their producer and financial backer and talked them into changing their name. They only recorded one album, *Permanent Damage*, but their hysterically funny songs like "The Eureka Springs Garbage Lady" and "Love on an Eleven Year Old Level" made for a spirited live show.

They had another supporter in Lowell George from Little Feat, who lived in Topanga and first booked them at the Corral. He also collaborated with Zappa and wrote material for the GTOs. Much like in the fine art world, everyone was hanging out together and turning each other on—creatively and otherwise. The GTOs performance was a big success, and many other great rock bands followed.

A few years later, a man named Ral Curren rebuilt at the north side of the same lot on the big bend in Topanga Canyon Boulevard. This version of the venue was a cool, dark, shotgun edifice, with a small stage at the far end. It featured a long bar that ran almost the length of the building and was covered with incredible photos of the hottest bands of the day, from the Rolling Stones and Janis Joplin to canyon locals like Taj Mahal and Little Feat, all covered in marine varnish as protection from the thousands of beers and shots consumed there over the years.

Now that Wallace and I were neighbors, we went out together frequently. Sometimes we went on longer road trips in my Cadillac, like one of our many drives up to San Francisco to see Michael McClure. At the filling station, as they were called back then, the young attendant looked in the car and surveyed Dean, Wallace, and me. "Are you guys in a band?" he asked.

Wallace, who always had a gift for great comebacks and one-liners, quickly answered, "Yeah, we are the Stone Statues."

"Yeah, we're the Stone Statues," we all agreed.

Mischievous and fun, Wallace was a great companion. Most nights around 11 p.m., Wallace had me pick him up down the street from his house because he didn't want Shirley to know he was going out on the town with me. We were scoundrels! As we strolled up to the Corral, talking about how our day's work had gone, we would greet Black Marie, a canyon local and the club's longtime doorperson. She checked IDs and collected a small cover charge. Locals like us never had to pay for entry.

Wallace and I would head for the dark wall next to the corner of the bar and lean against it. Peeking out from under our wide-brimmed hats, we would survey the room and watch the night's live music. The waitresses knew us and came over to hang out in between serving customers. When a band wasn't playing, music blasted from the jukebox. In 1967 one of the albums on the heaviest rotation was the Beatles' groundbreaking classic, *Sgt. Pepper's Lonely Hearts Club Band*. Among the five Grammys it won that year was the award for Best Album Cover, Graphic Arts, celebrating its instantly iconic collage art. The colorful image featured a who's who of celebrities from Oscar Wilde to Marilyn Monroe spread out behind the band. Wallace was among those pictured on the popular album, which made him a Topanga star.

Another favorite Beatles album at the Corral was *Magical Mystery Tour*, with its song "I Am the Walrus." Our friends used to love to kid us by saying, "How'd you get the Beatles to write a song for you guys, *Wall-Russ*?" I loved the Beatles! Even though the reference to our names was obviously accidental, we dealt in these kinds of puns and wordplay in our artwork all the time, and the cosmic coincidence made me feel important.

I had loved seeing the GTOs and Taj Mahal at the old Corral, and I was thrilled by the surge of incredible artists who followed them onto the new Corral's stage, including Little Feat, Canned Heat, Joni Mitchell, Spirit, Etta James, Emmylou Harris, Donovan, and of course Neil Young and Crazy Horse. It became a cool place to play and hang out, and many famous bands took part in this remarkable creative flowering in the canyon. Although the Doors never performed there, rumor has it that their song "Roadhouse Blues" is about the club.

I often played 8-ball on the Corral's pool table, and many nights I earned money hustling unsuspecting flatlanders who were mediocre players. I usually avoided pool sharks and could spot a potential mark. Watching my competition play someone else, I could tell if I would lose money to them. Once I challenged lesser players to a game, I knew how to win bets. Several times I played Janis Joplin. I think she was in Hollywood recording an album and had driven up to Topanga with a girlfriend. Janis was drunk and her pool playing was pretty pathetic, but I was in awe of her and didn't have the heart to hustle her for money. It was an honor just to have the chance to hang out with her for those few brief interludes.

The art and music worlds were smaller and more intimate then and often overlapped. Infamous record producer Phil Spector was a great fan and collector of Wallace's work. Around this time, at the height of Bob Dylan's popularity, Phil asked Wallace to pick up Bob at the airport. He figured the two geniuses would have a lot to discuss. Wallace later told me that when he arrived, he sensed Bob did not feel like talking. So they drove in silence to the Sunset Strip, where he dropped Bob at his hotel, with hardly a word spoken between the two icons.

The Corral was my main social outlet in those years until it burned down under mysterious circumstances (legend has it that the old-timey locals didn't appreciate the new culture and rowdy rock 'n' roll). I used it as a springboard for my artwork, which was never far from my mind. Usually, when the bar closed at two in the morning, I would head home and create until dawn. Some of my best pieces were born in those early-morning hours. But if I was doing a collage, I would wait until I was fresh to glue it down. When I woke up the next afternoon, even before coffee, I would race into the studio to appraise my creation. Most of the time, I didn't have to change a thing.

I was a canyon local who had formed many friendships in the community. Among these was Susan Acevedo, who lived about thirty yards down the hill from me, making her my only neighbor on Sky Line Trail. She ran a café, the Canyon Kitchen, in the small center of Topanga, which was also home to the market, the post office, and several shops. In late 1968, our little community of artists gained an inspired member when Susan began dating—and soon married—Neil Young, who was already gaining popularity for playing with psychedelic folk-rock band Buffalo Springfield. Neil moved into Susan's house, building a soundproof studio in the basement, where he recorded his new songs.

One day, Susan invited Elizabeth and me over for dinner. I had met Neil once before in Laurel Canyon, when he was living there with Buffalo Springfield. This time, over a long meal, I had a great opportunity to get to know him better, and Neil and I talked in depth about art and music. I found him to be intelligent and down to earth.

Not long after Neil moved in, he went on tour with Crosby, Stills, and Nash. While in Dallas, he got into some big disagreement with Stephen Stills and abruptly left the tour and came home to Topanga. When I saw him after his return, I felt bad for him. "What happened?" I asked.

"It just didn't work out," he said.

I nodded and didn't press him further. I was already learning that he was a lot like me—private and very independent—and he didn't seem to need or want any consolation. As Neil later told me, it was a combination of factors that caused him to leave the group—from the copious amounts of cocaine being consumed by some of the other members, which he began to find intolerable, to the fact that he was writing too many songs he wanted to record. With all of them contributing material, each member only had space to include one or two tunes on each album. As he would soon reveal, he certainly had enough material for a stellar solo album. This was a crossroads for Neil, as he changed his direction on so many levels, left CSNY, and struck out on his own.

As I got to know Neil better, I discovered him to be a truly complex and mercurial soul, and a devoted artist in whom I found a kindred spirit. We often had dinner together with our wives at one of our homes.

And he fell into the habit of walking up the hill and knocking on the door several times a week. Elizabeth led him to my art studio, where he poked in his head. "Is it okay to sit for a while?" he asked.

"Sure, but I'm pretty deeply involved in the work I'm doing, so I'm afraid I won't be much company."

"No problem," he said. "I promise not to interfere with your creative process."

During these studio visits, we hardly talked. Every once in a while, I would look over at him, and he would just be sitting there. Sometimes his deep-set dark eyes would be staring intensely into his journal. I figured he was writing song lyrics, but I never wanted to interrupt his thoughts to ask, just like he was always very respectful of my own space and process. We might not have talked much, but we forged a close friendship based on a deep artistic camaraderie.

Betsy, Russ's flower child lover, who he met during a gathering of rebel artists at Zuma Beach, California.
Photo by Ken Merril / Rory White Archive.

Russ: Topanga ennui.

Betsy's Topanga hideaway, where Russ often visited her.

Driving Topanga Canyon with
Wallace. Photo by Wallace Berman.

Flyer for production of *Man
with Bags* (circa 1980).
Design by Dean Stockwell,
art by Cooke.

Russ as Johnny Ketchum, outrunning the Ketchum gang, on location in Spain for
Son of a Gunfighter (1965).

CHAPTER 10

AFTER THE GOLD RUSH

Finally, I had what I guess you could call a breakthrough, but again, it was a mixed blessing. During the years I was doing the most important and fulfilling artwork of my life and hanging out with some of the greats in the contemporary art world, ironically I was making what I thought were some of the worst movies of my career. To support my life in Topanga, I found myself acting in several B movies. Not that I wouldn't have rather done A movies, but they weren't being offered to me anymore. Most of these low-budget projects I never even bothered to watch once my part in them was finished.

In the fall of 1968, however, I did get the chance to fulfill a longtime passion of mine. Ever since I'd seen Marlon Brando in *The Wild One*, I had dreamed of starring in a biker movie. Unfortunately, I had been out of town performing in a play when my friend Dennis Hopper made one of the most famous motorcycle movies of all time, *Easy Rider*. So while Wallace had enjoyed a cameo appearance as a seed sower at a hippie commune (his idea), I had missed out on the fun. When I got an offer to do Al Adamson's *Satan's Sadists*, I jumped at the chance. I knew it was a pretty bad script, but I didn't care. I figured I could make up most of my dialogue. And the thought of being the leader of a motorcycle gang, even just a pretend one, turned me on.

The experience did not in any way disappoint. One of the first scenes we filmed was out in the desert, with our whole gang cruising down the highway. It was a helicopter shot, so no one in the oncoming traffic knew we were making a movie. It's a powerful feeling to be riding down the highway with a gang of gnarly misfits behind you. Cars coming the other way would pull over to the side of the road until we roared by. Shooting from the helicopter high above was cinematographer Gary Graver, who ended up working with Orson Welles in the last days of both of their lives. He was a good cameraman, and he was really fast, and I liked him a lot. We did several B movies together, not only with Adamson but also with Fred Olen Ray, a beloved B-movie filmmaker. Fred became my friend, and I would later find out that he was the person who gave Quentin Tarantino his very first sixteen-millimeter camera, on which he shot his first movie, *My Best Friend's Birthday*.

My costar Regina Carrol was a voluptuous blond starlet and nightclub singer who was the serious girlfriend of our director, Al Adamson. He cast her in all his movies. She had a reputation for being courteous to her fans. She was also reportedly a very nice person who was a lot brighter than the characters she usually played, which I found to be true. Regina took a shine to me because I talked about art and joked around with her a great deal.

We were on location somewhere in the Mojave Desert, staying in a little motel. Al was off shooting somewhere else, and Regina wanted to go over her lines, so she came to my room. That was a *big* mistake! A short affair began, with us rendezvousing whenever Al wasn't around. Filling my dance card with this particular lady was risky business. I had a close call one day when Al came back from location early and knocked on my door looking for Regina. We were in bed together, so I stalled him by claiming I was in the shower. Regina jumped up, quickly dressed, and tried to dive through the small bathroom window head-first, but she became stuck until I pushed her through—barely. She ran down the narrow dirt path behind the motel. Perhaps I should have been a little more careful, given our director's penchant for blood-filled horror films with titles like *Brain of Blood, Five Bloody Graves, Horror of the Blood Monsters, Hell's Bloody Devils, Blood of Ghastly Horror,* and *Blood of Dracula's Castle.* Even *Satan's Sadists* was also known as *Nightmare Bloodbath!* (In an ironic and very sad twist of fate, Al's life ended like a plotline from one of his films when he was murdered in 1995 by his live-in contractor and buried beneath the concrete and tile where his hot tub had been.)

At the time, I wasn't the most honorable person when it came to extramarital affairs. I did feel quite guilty, but not enough to stop me from having my fun. I had a few rules, though—I never actively pursued somebody's girlfriend or wife, and I absolutely never pressured a woman into going to bed with me. But I hardly ever resisted if a woman was sexy and came on to me. And especially in the years when I was a young, cute movie star, women were constantly throwing themselves at me, often quite aggressively. And as has been widely documented in these pages and elsewhere, on-set romances felt almost inevitable—they were often an enjoyable part of the close camaraderie of working with my female costars, especially on location.

Looking back, I'm not proud of this behavior, and it's uncomfortable for me to face up to some of these stories, but it was as if I were still having my extended adolescence. Even though I had been married to Elizabeth for more than a decade at this point, I was often very impulsive and acted without thinking about the consequences or whether this was the kind of person I wanted to be. I still had a lot of growing up to do, and I hadn't yet found what would eventually inspire me to dig in and do the work.

Although *Satan's Sadists* was my first leading part in a feature film in two years, and I was having a blast doing many of my own stunts and improvising enough of the dialogue to get a cowriting credit on the finished film, I still had fine art on my mind. While on location in the Mojave Desert, I wandered around the sandy landscape, picking up old pieces of rusted metal, tin cans, and broken colored glass—whatever caught my eye. Later, back in Topanga, I made several pieces of junk art out of the treasures I found, even selling a few of them. During this time in my life, it was almost impossible for me *not* to make art.

Thankfully, my fling with Regina was short lived, and Al never found out about it. They went on to enjoy a twenty-year marriage. And he became my only source of work for the next few years. He cast me in two films, *The Female Bunch*, a campy romp about a gang of women who are disillusioned with society and men, and the low-budget horror film *Dracula vs. Frankenstein*. Both starred horror film legend Lon Chaney Jr., and *Dracula vs. Frankenstein* also included veteran character actor J. Carrol Naish. (To be honest, I never saw either film. And I am not eager to watch them now.) I did both projects because I needed the money. In *Dracula*, I had a scene with Lon Chaney Jr., who I had always wanted to meet. I didn't even know J. Carrol was involved until I showed up for my first day of shooting. I had worked with him years before on *Hit the Deck*, in which he played the boyfriend of Vic Damone's character's mother. It's funny to me that he should be remembered as a horror star, because I knew him as a comedy actor. I guess, like me, he worked wherever he could.

I didn't have to drive far to do the latter film. My scene with Lon took place under the Santa Monica Pier. It was a night shoot, and Gary Graver was once again the excellent cinematographer. I was so excited to meet Lon that night, but I found him to be drunk and having trouble with his lines. *This poor guy is on his last legs*, I thought. And sadly, I was right, as he only filmed one movie after that and died several years later, after struggling with alcohol and his failing health. At that time, I didn't think too much about it—I was just grateful to earn my check for a few thousand bucks and return to Topanga.

Looking back, though, I have a greater appreciation for B movies, as does the history of pop culture. They could be freewheeling and fun to film, and they were a sympathetic outlet for people (like me, in those years) who weren't able to find work elsewhere for a variety of reasons. I enjoyed doing B movies—they didn't have the big budgets and pretense I had come to dislike, and there was a small and lively circle of devotees working on them, almost like a family. They paid me well, and I felt validated as an actor because they were encouraging and appreciated my enthusiasm, even when the material wasn't great. I was often allowed to invent my own lines and even encouraged to throw in a bunch of punchy quips I never would have gotten away with in the more wholesome MGM fare I had once filmed. I felt like I had found my spot.

———

For several years, I had devoted myself, body, mind, and spirit, to my new existence in Topanga—and most importantly, I had devoted myself to my artistic output. When I finally had created enough pieces for an exhibition, I felt ready to share them. I drew inspiration from Wallace, who had organized a solo show of his work at the Topanga Community House in late February 1967. I thought maybe I could exhibit there too. My first public exhibition was, in fact, at the Community House in 1970.

As the date for my opening approached, I gathered together several dozen pieces—mostly collages. I had created all this output without any specific goal in mind because I loved making art, but it felt incredible to see such a clear manifestation of my commitment to creativity in the form of all the work I had done since leaving Hollywood. I wanted to have music playing in the background during the show, and I took Neil up on an offer he had made to help me set up big speakers in the venue. He even offered me the use of his music.

"Thank you," I said. "But I really wanted classical music as a soundtrack for the art." Neil was such a powerful songwriter and musician I was afraid his songs would eclipse the experience people had of my work. So I figured it was better to keep things light.

It was one of the most exciting nights of my artistic life, and it was a successful art show, thanks to Dennis Hopper. He bought more than half a dozen pieces, and Neil even bought a couple. But again, it had taken me a year to create all the artwork. I generally did not keep track of who bought work, as do most artists, especially those with gallery representation. I didn't feel territorial about my work; even though I loved it and was proud of it, I didn't care so much where it went. So although I've sold and gifted dozens of pieces in my fifty-plus years as a fine artist, I have no record of most of it. At the end of the night, I was feeling abuzz with the excitement of being surrounded by my work, among friends old and new. I totaled up my night's profits and received a rude awakening. I had earned about $2,000 for what was essentially a year's worth of work. I was used to earning that in one week!

I realized I would have to try harder to find acting work, even if it wasn't where my heart was anymore. That meant going on auditions. The problem was that I had always hated them, to the point where I thought the real work, when it came to acting, was auditioning. Once I had the part, all I had to do was show up. Then I could relax because being on set and acting was fun. In retrospect, I don't think I was very good at auditioning, which was probably why it was such agony for me. After my life-changing audition for Cecil B. DeMille when I was eleven, I had been in the enviable position of being a studio player and not really needing to audition anymore. I hadn't realized how fortunate I was until I tried to resume my acting career, now with a reputation as a troublemaker to overcome.

The only manager I could find to take me on wasn't at the same level of representation to which I had been accustomed, at least not at that stage in my career. I went out on more than a year's worth of auditions and didn't land a single part, which was extremely depressing after my past level of success and fame. And of course it was financially scary, as I still had a wife and household to support, even as modestly as we were living in those days. Finally, my manager was very excited when a part was actually offered to me. I wanted to work, but once again, I received a blow—my character only had two lines. I wasn't in a position to be choosy, so I took the role and tried to do my best, but it was disheartening.

Thankfully, the parts I'd landed in B movies were at least fun and creative. Looking back, I can see how these types of films were precursors to indie filmmaking. Moviemaking was changing to more of an independent, shoot-from-the-hip, cinema verité style, which was very much in keeping with my artistic leanings at the time. In that vein, Dean and I decided to make a movie together, and Dean wrote a script called *After the Gold Rush*. Neil wanted to write the music for it, and he got started right away. We had commitments from Janis Joplin, Canned Heat, and Taj Mahal. Dennis Hopper wanted to produce and act in it. Even Jack Nicholson was extremely interested in the lead role. I was going to play an over-the-hill rock star who had shacked up with a bunch of girls in a huge castle on a mountaintop on the other side of the canyon from where I really lived. Dean got producers from Universal Studios to come to Topanga, but the suits just didn't get it. Even though it was a very funny and inventive script, the studio was a little behind the times and scared to put money into it. So they passed. Unfortunately, Dean was so disappointed he decided not to take the script to any other studio and shelved it. Of course, we had a lot of great ideas in those days, but they weren't always easy to bring to fruition.

At least our concept wasn't a complete loss. The unfinished project inspired the title for Neil's beloved, classic album *After the Gold Rush*, much of which he wrote and recorded in Topanga—some of it in my studio, I'm sure. When it was completed, he held a listening party at his house. Elizabeth and I walked down and joined him and his manager, Elliot Roberts. Also in attendance were Dennis, Dean, and a few other close friends. Neil's wife, Susan, had sewn some patches on a pair of his old jeans, which he was wearing. None of us realized what a popular trend that would become. What we did realize, listening to these awesome songs, was that this album was something very special. The songs went right to my heart. I surmised the album would be a big success. Sure enough, it sold several million copies.

The only problem was, the record was such a huge hit that Neil became even more famous than he already had been. Fans found out where Neil lived and sat in front of his house, waiting for him to come outside to get his mail. We suddenly had a massive traffic problem. Driving from our narrow, one-lane street down the hill became difficult. This was exactly the craziness I had been trying to escape by moving to To- panga! But Neil remained so down to earth, and our life in the canyon was otherwise unchanged. So I tried to just laugh it off.

In the end, the change had a deeper impact on other areas of Neil's life. When he played concerts, Susan would hang out backstage afterward, and fans would charge right past her to get to Neil. I witnessed this on several occasions while sitting in his dressing room with both of them. It seemed perfectly natural to me, but it drove Susan crazy. She complained bitterly to him, and their relationship deteriorated, until he had finally had enough. They divorced, and he bought an enormous piece of forestland above Redwood City, near San Francisco. He came up to my house and told me about his big plans for building a recording studio on his new forest-laden ranch. He wanted it to be suspended off the ground, between four redwood trees, like a giant speaker in the sky. That never came to pass, but what a great idea! On his last day in Topanga, we said our goodbyes to each other, promising to stay in touch, and he moved up north, from Sky Line Trail to Skyline Drive.

—

Underground filmmaking was booming in the late 1960s and early 1970s, and I became a participant in this world, through the circumstances of my career, and also because these were the types of films my friends began making. Coming off the success of *Easy Rider*, Dennis Hopper got the money to write and direct a new film, *The Last Movie*. He wanted me to play a part. The film was going to be shot in Peru, and my Topanga neighbors Dean, Toni Basil, and Billy Gray would also be in the cast, as well as such luminaries as Peter Fonda, Michelle Phillips (from the Mamas and the Papas), Kris Kristofferson, and Sam Fuller. It sounded like a great adventure, and even though I had just started a new series of art pieces, I decided to take a break and do the film anyway.

Off to Cusco, Peru, we all flew in a commercial plane—and what a crazy flight it was. One of the cast members lit up a joint on the plane and began passing it around. The whole plane smelled like a marijuana den. The stewardess came running down the aisle and told our motley crew to put out the joint. Some of the passengers had complained. Apparently, cigarette smoke was okay, but not pot!

First, we landed in Lima, Peru's largest city and capital. Then we took a smaller plane high up into the Andes to Cusco, which has an elevation of 11,152 feet. That's where we stayed. But we worked in Chinchero, a town another 1,200 feet up in the Sacred Valley of the Incas, which many locals believed was the birthplace of the rainbow! The air was so thin that I took five steps and was out of breath. Many members of the cast were snorting cocaine, which was cheap there. Even cheaper were coca leaves—but what a price you paid with your mouth! Some of the local men were hooked on coca leaves, which they ate out of bags hanging from their necks. Before long, they had to eat them all day to get high, and eventually, their teeth turned black.

Fortunately, I'm allergic to cocaine. I'd end up with my head hanging over a bed, my nose dripping for half the night. For such a short high, it was too big of a price to pay. But I sure kept trying and spent far too many hours sprawled across a mattress. Some people never learn—and others just take a long time. (That's me: slow learner of what I should *not* be doing.)

Cusco, sometimes spelled Cuzco, was once recognized as the capital of the Inca Empire, and UNESCO even declared it a World Heritage Site in the early 1980s. It was quite fascinating and had incredible places to visit nearby, like Machu Picchu and the ruins of Saqsaywaman, which Dennis pronounced as "sexy woman."

One afternoon, while we were shooting in Chinchero, the mayor and chief of police came to the set from Lima. They carried a big book containing the history of Lima and lots of old black-and-white photos of the city. Pulling Dennis and Peter Fonda aside, they asked them if they would be interested in buying it for $5,000. "By the way, we heard you had some drug problems coming here on the plane," they said. "We certainly hope you can get through the movie here without being harassed and perhaps arrested by the government."

Suddenly, that book on the history of Lima started to look very attractive! Of course, Dennis knew what they were really saying and forked over the cash.

While Dennis was filming a sequence that didn't feature Dean, Billy, or me, we had three days off before the last of our location shoots. Dean and Billy decided to visit Machu Picchu and asked if I wanted to join them. I was coming down with a cold, but Billy and Dean and I took the train to Machu Picchu nonetheless.

Named one of the Seven Wonders of the World, it is located on a mountain ridge at almost eight thousand feet above sea level, high above the Urubamba River, and is considered by many to be a sacred site. Billy, who's always been a risk-taker, having raced motorcycles, separated from Dean and me. Then he decided to hike down to the Urubamba River. He crossed to the other side, got lost, and couldn't find his way back. Heavy rain expanded the river and made it even more treacherous. After he spent two nights on the bank, some local fishermen helped him across the river, and he hiked up the mountain and finally took the train back to Cusco. All that time, we had no idea where he was. He missed the filming of the final scenes, and we were extremely worried about him. When he finally showed up on the set, everyone applauded him for making it back alive, especially when we heard his wild stories about his near-death adventure.

Dennis worked tirelessly, shooting as much material as he possibly could. One scene I thought was amazing was the party at the end of the make-believe movie within the film. Dennis did a long, moving shot down the party house's exterior, revealing the action in six different rooms. In one, I was playing boogie-woogie on the piano. It was very effective. Dennis was extremely invested in directing his film, which was a passion project. He had so much responsibility that he even decreased his heavy drinking habit to a minimum to finish on schedule.

Finally, it was time to return home, and the Los Angeles cast flew back down to Lima. We had a three-hour layover before our flight, so Peter Fonda generously rented a room for us to wait out the delay. Dennis had stayed in Cusco to continue filming, and Peter wanted Dennis to know where we were, so he called him. We were laughing as someone told a funny story when Peter suddenly put down the phone. "Dennis said he just got word that all of us are going to be thoroughly searched when we go through customs in LA, so whoever has drugs, get rid of it!" he called out.

One of our actors, Richard Rust, had already been arrested on drug charges, so things were not looking good for us. The worst part of it was the headline that had appeared in a Peruvian newspaper: "Rust [*sic*] Tamblyn, actor and dancer, was arrested on drug charges in Cusco." *Damn!* I thought. *Maybe* The Last Movie *is going to be a prophecy for me.*

Thankfully, because I was allergic to cocaine, I only had to get rid of a little pot. Some of the guys had secretly packed away heavy doses of the white stuff. There was a copious amount of snorting, not to mention the near-constant white whirlpool going down the toilet. When it was time to leave, we headed for the airport, stoned but clean.

Arriving in LA, we were still nervous, but the customs officer waved us all through. No one was stopped, no one was questioned, and no one was searched. As we left the customs area, the only word I heard from one of my costars was "Shit!"

However, there *was* a problem with the film itself. Dennis rented a small theater and invited the whole cast to view the first, uncut version of *The Last Movie.* You had to pack a lunch because the film lasted for six or seven hours. Kris Kristofferson was constantly walking around between scenes, playing and singing "Me and Bobby McGee." After the screening, I swore I never wanted to hear that song again, ever. Even when Dennis finally whittled it down to a more manageable length, this ended up being another one of those movies that definitely fall into the cult-classic category. But it sure was fun to make!

—

Things got worse before they got better. One night in 1972, a fire started in the engine of my car in our garage. It quickly grew. By the time the fire department arrived, my whole front room above the garage was a blazing inferno. The rest of the house was charred, and the smoke made it an acrid mess. "How did a toilet bowl end up on top of the pool table?" the firemen asked me when they saw that my pool table had fallen through the floor and landed on my car. I tried to explain that it was a shitty light shade for the table, but they didn't get the joke, looking at me like I was crazy. Some beautiful pieces of art burned in the fire, including a special drawing and poem that Allen Ginsberg had done for me when he visited Topanga. I felt awful about losing those, as well as signed copies of poetry books by Michael McClure, Ginsberg, and others. Also, many boxes of memorabilia burned up in the garage, including magazine photos, framed awards, and priceless old scripts, which devastated me. But it was all gone, and there was nothing I could do to get it back, so I just tried to make the best of it.

I noticed the ceiling was scorched black where the flames had hit it and then gone out the side windows. Luckily, the roof stayed intact. I cut some of the charred boards out of the ceiling and sawed them into squares. The charcoal was easy to carve into, and I managed to create a series of art pieces I called *Fireworks*. It was too smelly in the house, so Elizabeth and I bought a tent and put it up in the front yard. We camped out there for almost a year, only using the kitchen and bathrooms. One of the things I found in the ashes was an RCA TV set that had gotten so hot the plastic casing and knob handle had melted. Being a curious artist, I wiped the soot off the screen and plugged it into a socket. To my astonishment, a blurry picture came onto the screen. I realized the aerial had melted too, so I stuck a wire coat hanger where it used to be. Lo and behold, a perfect black-and-white picture appeared. I had a great idea. I called my agent and suggested the set be used in a commercial for RCA. They could come to my half-burned house and film me turning on the TV that still worked. My agent agreed it was a good idea and said he would call RCA to see if they were interested. The next day, he called me and said they couldn't do it because they weren't allowed to use anything real. Union members would have to burn down a house and build a TV set that looked like it had been in a fire.

Later that year, I showed the TV, along with a melted phone and several burned objects, which I called *Fireworks*, at the Los Angeles Institute of Contemporary Art. Curated by Hal Glicksman, this show was the largest collage-and-assemblage exhibition ever put together. I was pretty excited to be exhibiting my work alongside such distinguished masters as Wallace Berman, Ed Moses, George Herms, Billy Al Bengston, Vija

Celmins, Ed Kienholz, Bruce Conner, Tony Berlant, and Llyn Foulkes. Also that year, I was included in another group exhibit at the Los Angeles County Museum of Art. These recognitions of my fine art were much more gratifying for me than any movie premiere.

Around this time, Dean called and asked if I'd be interested in reading for a film he was going to act in, *Another Day at the Races*. It was a comedy spoof and tribute to the Marx Brothers classic *A Day at the Races*, but the title was later changed to *Win, Place or Steal*. The film, based on a true story, was about three guys who steal a pari-mutuel printing press (the machine that prints betting tickets). They put it in a van just outside the track. One of them watches the race and waits for a winner. He then signals the winning horse's identity to the second guy, who is waiting on a motorcycle in the parking lot. He races the info to the van, and the third guy prints up a bunch of winning tickets. It was an independent production for the Picture Company, and the director, Richard Bailey, was a veteran of numerous TV commercials. It sounded like a funny movie, and I told Dean, "Yes, I most definitely will audition for it!"

The meeting took place at a small indie studio in Hollywood. I parked my car on a slight hill next to the studio and had to walk about two blocks, up the hill, to the entrance. Oddly enough, once I entered, I had to walk two blocks back down the hill to reach Richard Bailey's office. The first thing I noticed when Richard's secretary sent me in to meet him was the open window just behind his desk. My car was parked below, exactly in front of the window. The reading went well, and I seemed to really hit it off with Richard. When we finished, I was struck by an ingenious idea. "My car is parked just below your window," I said. "Would it be all right if I just climbed out to get to my car?"

He thought it was the funniest thing he'd ever heard and started laughing. "Please jump out the window," he said. "I won't tell my secretary. It'll drive her crazy, wondering where you went!"

Needless to say, I got the part, and filming was great fun, as the cast also included Alex Karras and Harry Dean Stanton. But when the movie was released in 1974, it got terrible reviews. The lighting was amateurish, and the film turned out way too dark, which is not good for a comedy. Not that I was worried about reviews in those days—I was just trying to enjoy myself and keep the lights on.

These low-budget B movies weren't filmed on the same prompt timeline that my MGM projects had been, and often, there was a delay of several years between when I shot my role and when the movie finally found an audience. Thankfully, I remained more interested in my artistic life than my acting career, so I didn't worry too much about the details, as long as I was at least getting by financially and enjoying enough free time to make new art pieces.

—

Elizabeth and I eventually moved to a funky ranch house just off Old Topanga Canyon Road. Set back in the woods, it was a vintage three-bedroom guesthouse on Eden Ranch, which spread out over twenty acres behind the Topanga Center. My house was by itself on the property.

It was lush and beautiful and quite isolated, with little traffic except for an occasional delivery truck. I would walk down to where the road forked, one way to the Topanga Riding Stables or to Old Topanga Canyon Road the other way. When I wanted to walk to the center, I made my own path down the middle of the fork, through the woods, over boulders, and across the creek. The oak and sycamore trees were massive, and the grass grew tall in the springtime.

The only drawback was that the Eden Ranch was a cattle ranch and attracted lots of mice. I got tired of killing them with mousetraps, so I built a "better mousetrap" that caught them alive. Then I would take them down to Topanga Creek and let them go.

I missed the eagle's-eye view I had cherished on Sky Line Trail, but the new vista was still stunning. My studio had sightlines down to Topanga Canyon Boulevard. I practically lived in there with a potbelly stove heating the room in the winter. I had my printing press and lots of shelves, and a huge table in the center of the room on which I created artwork. When company came over, we would sometimes sit in my studio and drink tequila and eat noshes Elizabeth had made. She remained a great hostess. Ben Talbot, Jack Hirschman, Michael Mc-Clure, George Herms, Dean, and of course Wallace often dropped by. We would sit and "chop it up" (as Wallace liked to say).

I also spent many hours looking out the window, emptying my head, and meditating. *Lighten up*—that was my mantra, and for me, it meant, *Stop thinking so much!* When you're young, you feel like you've seen and heard everything, from the glow of the moon and the sound of rain beating on the pavement to the smolder of a sunset. You start taking the wonder of all this beauty for granted. You stop truly listening and seeing. The mind is always thinking, and the problem with thought is that it's always in the past. The cool thing about art is that your eyes and ears become fresh again. You begin looking at things like a child would, constantly discovering the shape and originality of everything. That was my work now—to peel back the layers and become new again. As I always like to say, "I wish I didn't know yesterday what I don't know today."

———

In 1974, I got a call from Jimmie Rodgers, asking if I would be interested in appearing in a film he was directing, *The World through the Eyes of Children*. Jimmie had enjoyed a long career in show business since he had been a winner on the old *Arthur Godfrey's Talent Scouts* TV program in 1954. Having become the flagship artist for the new Roulette Records, he was a mainstay on the pop charts in the 1950s, with many hits like "Honeycomb" and "Kisses Sweeter than Wine." With a unique blend of country folk and pop, he had a slightly different sound from the normal mainstream fare. In 1958, we had sung together at the thirtieth Academy Awards ceremony, along with teen idol Tommy Sands, who was once married to Nancy Sinatra. Bob Hope introduced us, and we had a great time performing a silly song.

Jimmie had a big office in Santa Monica, and when I turned up there, he offered me $5,000 a week for a roughly six-week shoot.

That was all I needed to hear. "Yes, I'm very interested!" I said.

He told me I'd be playing the devil, who was trying to tempt children into doing evil. I was to wear red tights with a tail, Spock-like ears, and red face makeup. Jimmie was playing opposite me, as a sort of Pied Piper hero who kept the kids out of trouble.

Jimmie was a real sweetheart. Unfortunately, on set all the little kids were following me around instead of him. They liked playing with my tail. Besides, I made them laugh. I think he got a little jealous, as he asked me to stop being so funny in the scenes in which I appeared. "You're too likable to the children, and they're not supposed to like you," he said.

The filming began in Bryce Canyon National Park, Utah, which was beautiful. We then moved on to Cave City, Kentucky, which is a small tourist town with only a few thousand residents. They put me up on the second floor of a two-story motel, and I worked for about four weeks before they were able to pay me. When they finally did, I received $20,000—in cash! I certainly wasn't comfortable keeping that much money in my room. So I immediately went to a little bank in the next county with my earnings in a paper bag and had them changed into a cashier's check. I sent the check home to Elizabeth and then went back to the motel and took a long nap, satisfied the money was in a safe place. I guess I looked pretty grubby when I went into town, because I still had on some makeup, but I didn't really think about it.

When I woke up, I got dressed and went out the front door of my room to grab a bite to eat. To my surprise, I was met by nearly two dozen cops with their guns drawn, shouting through a bullhorn, "Put your hands above your head and don't move!"

I laughed when they told me to raise my hands, but I soon realized they weren't kidding. I explained that I was just a devilish actor. It took a few very tense minutes to straighten everything out. Eventually, they let me go, and I came to understand the whole incident wasn't as funny as I thought, and I could have been shot and killed. Unbeknownst to me, there had been a bank robbery in a nearby village a few days earlier, and when I showed up at the bank with all that cash, I had become a prime suspect. Once again, I was glad to have had the opportunity to work, but I was even happier to finish the film and head back to my home base in Topanga.

———

While my heart and home were in the canyon with my artistic cohort, I had spent so many years in Hollywood that I still had a toe in the industry. Having been an MGM player for more than a decade, I continued to be invited to their events, including the star-studded 1974 world premiere of *That's Entertainment*, which corresponded with MGM's fiftieth anniversary.

The night of the shindig, I invited Wallace over to take a photo of Elizabeth and me getting into the back seat of our limo, with the chauffeur holding the door open for us. We were dressed formally—me in a tux—but I was clutching a piece of my assemblage art in my right hand. The photo was very cool, and I was hoping to use it for a future art-show announcement.

At the theater, all the MGM stars were called out from the wings by the evening's hosts, Liza Minnelli and Sammy Davis Jr. Not content to simply stroll onto the stage, I made a grand entrance, leaping onto my hands and doing a mule kick. The audience howled, and Sammy gave me a high five. Then all fifty of us, including Lassie, posed for a photo onstage, which the studio printed and gave out as promo images with the tagline *More stars than there are in heaven*. While a large orchestra played show tunes, the stars and audience members stuffed themselves with gourmet food and vintage champagne. It might have been intimidating for these members of the audience to take the dance floor next to so many seasoned pros, but everyone seemed to dance and mingle together comfortably.

After dinner, Debbie Reynolds kept the mood light with several amusing comments and then invited up her *Singin' in the Rain* costar Donald O'Connor, followed by Gene Kelly.

Gene approached the microphone with his normal, easy grace. "Hey, it would only be fair if Fred was up here too."

So after a great deal of coaxing from the audience, Fred Astaire joined him. Fred and Gene proceeded to ad-lib a little soft shoe. Rushing back onto the stage, Debbie joined them.

"Before Fred leaves the stage," she said into the mic, "there's someone in the audience that would really make my night if she'd come up and have one last dance with Fred. Please, please, please, will you come up . . . Ginger Rogers?"

Ginger obviously did not want to perform, but the audience kept applauding and whistling and wouldn't take no for an answer. Finally, Ginger reluctantly joined Fred onstage. The orchestra eased into a slow number, and we all got to witness Fred Astaire and Ginger Rogers do a sweet little dance together for the last time.

At most of these big Hollywood events, the celebrities leave right away, but this night was different, special. It felt like old home week with so many of us who had appeared in countless movies together reconnecting and engaging in long conversations. I personally reminisced with Tony Martin and Vic Damone about our time together in *Hit the Deck*; caught up with Howard Keel, my big brother from *Seven Brides*; and received a huge hug from my old friend Glenn Ford, who still called me Rusty.

Finally, I headed back to my table. Fred Astaire came over, and after I introduced him to Elizabeth, he asked her if she would mind if he stole me away for a minute to come meet his sister, Adele. Evidently, she was a fan of mine. Fred held my arm and glided us across the wooden floor. I even managed to stay in step with him, and it felt like we were dancing.

It was the best time I had ever had at a Hollywood event, and I wished it would go on all night. As I later realized, it truly was the final celebration of the Golden Age of Hollywood. Of the fifty stars who were in attendance, there are now only four of us left: Margaret O'Brien, George Hamilton, Shirley MacLaine, and me.

———

I felt comfortable as both Hollywood insider and outsider artist, but I still earned some sneers from those who didn't understand the choices

I had made. My fellow child star and sometime pool opponent Robert Blake always seemed to have a chip on his shoulder. Speaking unkindly of others was a dishonest way of praising himself. He had become a big star with his TV show, *Baretta*, and was a frequent guest on *The Tonight Show*. He was always pretty cocky, and Johnny loved it when Bobby ragged on studio executives. Once Johnny asked how it felt having been a child star and now an adult star. "At least I'm not stoned, out living in a shack up in Topanga, like Billy Gray and Russ Tamblyn," he said. I laughed when I heard this, but I knew it was opinions like these that made it so difficult for me to find regular work in the movies.

Elizabeth and I had enjoyed that incredible MGM anniversary together, but unfortunately, she was drinking more than ever, and I dove into my collages like a junkie addicted to beauty. I really wanted to end our relationship, but I couldn't work up the nerve. So I continued avoiding the issue by throwing myself into my art, my friends, and my affairs, like I always did, and hoping everything would somehow work out.

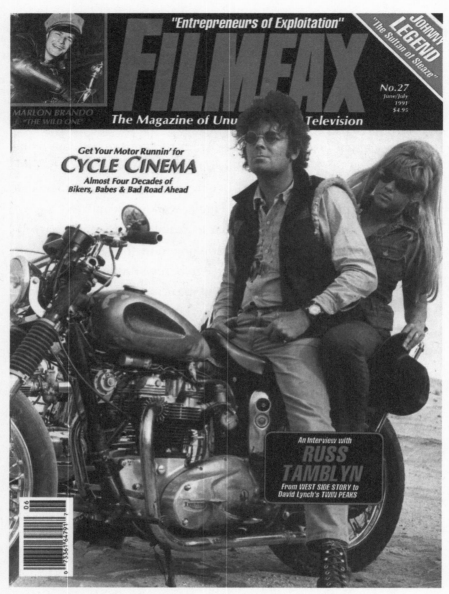

Russ as Anchor in the cult-classic movie *Satan's Sadists* (1969), with costar Regina Carrol. Cover of *Filmfax* magazine, June/July 1991 issue.

Collecting junk in the desertfor original art pieces during the shoot for *Satan's Sadists*. Photo by Heidi Dietz.

Russ and Elizabeth leaving for MGM's *That's Entertainment* premiere. Photo by Wallace Berman.

CHAPTER 11

HEARTBREAK IN MANY FORMS

During the more than a decade that I lived in Topanga Canyon, I saw a profound shift in the neighborhood and those who called it home. Even though the landscape itself remained wild and inspired, the locals changed quite a bit. By the early 1970s the original population of cowboys and blue-collar types had expanded to include more middle-class escapees from the city and a growing influx of artists and free spirits like me. But there still wasn't much to do, beyond having a beer and shooting a game of pool at the Corral. Such a sleepy community was good for making art but bad for people like Elizabeth, who favored more sophisticated diversions.

After Wallace relocated to Topanga, he did introduce me to one local outpost of culture that could still bring Elizabeth and me together—the Mermaid Tavern. Most weeks, Wallace, Shirley, Elizabeth, and I went to this remarkable space to listen to classical music. Built in 1930 at the northern end of the canyon, not far from the Corral, this limestone Spanish Revival mansion had an impressive interior with a grand fireplace in the 1,500-square-foot great room. Originally located on a piece of the Cheney Ranch, it had begun as the Sylvia Park Country Club. Then, during World War II, it took a turn for the seedier, reportedly becoming a gambling club and brothel run by Mickey Cohen and frequented by gangsters. Next, it had an unsuccessful stint as a dude ranch for kids, before becoming a Jewish boys' school and an American Legion Hall. In the 1960s, it was transformed by a former vice cop into a gay bar called the Canyon Club.

Now, this beautiful old relic was a private residence. It was owned by Ann and Mickey Nadel, a former double bassist for the Los Angeles Philharmonic, and was managed with help from their teenage daughter. Mickey had many friends who were top-of-the-line classical musicians, and on Sunday evenings, he had philharmonic players put on chamber music concerts featuring small ensemble groups. I tried not to miss a single performance. The music and atmosphere were stellar, and by this point in our marriage, it was a rare night of union for Elizabeth and me.

These were intimate, low-key affairs, with several house wines served to a crowd of fewer than a hundred people. We became friends with the Nadels, and one night when their busboy failed to turn up, I jumped in to lend a hand. As I was winding my way through the tables, lugging empty wine bottles back to the kitchen, I saw a female customer lean over and whisper something in her husband's ear. "Don't be ridiculous, darling," I heard him reply. "It couldn't be Russ Tamblyn. He would never be doing busboy work." Celebrities were not the norm, although a few other recognizable faces did sometimes turn up, including Burt Lancaster.

It was at the Mermaid Tavern that Elizabeth briefly recaptured some of the poise and performance acumen she'd possessed when we had first met more than a decade earlier. One evening, she delivered a dramatic recitation of Prokofiev's *Peter and the Wolf*. Appearing tall and beautiful in the room's low light and speaking with her strong English accent, she held the audience rapt with wonder. I was very pleased and impressed. Martin Bernheimer, then the main classical music critic for the *Los Angeles Times*, happened to be there that evening and gave her a glowing review the next day. Elizabeth reprised the monologue once more at the tavern, but it lacked the majesty she had previously achieved. There had been talk of an encore performance at the LA Philharmonic, but she got stage fright and didn't have the self-confidence to push herself into the spotlight. It was easier for her to go back to her love of gourmet cooking and her wine.

We had been living on next to nothing for years, and while I remained far from materialistic, earning the money to cover our basic needs was a constant concern. In the 1970s, Dean turned me on to a theatrical agent named Ben Pearson. In 1975, he helped me land a role in a summer stock musical, *Dames at Sea*, being staged at the University of Mississippi, with a cast of mostly college students. There was no getting around the fact that it was kind of a corny play about the threatened failure of a Broadway show during the Great Depression, set on Forty-Second Street in New York City. But I was grateful for the work, which meant a paycheck, and I was equally glad for the excuse to escape the pall of our dark and unhappy home for a few weeks.

In the fall of 1975, I decided to accept the role of famous early American song-and-dance man George M. Cohan in an Atlanta-based staging of the musical *George M!* The part had a nostalgic significance for me, as thirty years earlier I had sung Cohan's famous song "The Yankee Doodle Boy," during a war bond drive at my old school, Centinela Elementary. Several of my teachers had rolled a piano in and out of classrooms for my mother, who accompanied me. Dressed as Uncle Sam, I belted out the lyrics and did a waltz clog in the middle of the number.

Fast forward three decades. I needed the job, but I was out of shape, and the show included a great deal of tap dancing to Cohan's many upbeat tunes, from "You're a Grand Old Flag" to "Give My Regards to Broadway." I called my longtime choreographer friend Alex Romero and asked him if he would like to do some dance workouts with me if I rented a hall. He agreed. So I got my old tap shoes out of a box in the back of the closet and dusted them off, and we went to work. I had a month before I was to report for rehearsals in Fort Lauderdale. I threw myself into my preparation, practicing every day, losing about ten pounds, and getting fit for this challenging role. We prepared for nearly a month as a cast, leading up to the opening at the Peachtree Center's Midnight Sun Dinner Theater in downtown Atlanta.

I bought plane tickets and a car rental for Elizabeth and my mother, who had temporarily moved in with us, so they could attend the opening of the show. They planned to arrive the day before I flew in from Florida so they could settle in and pick me up when my flight landed. However, the next day, I found my mother waiting alone to greet me at the airport.

"Where's Elizabeth?" I asked, afraid I already knew the answer.

My mom rolled her eyes. "She's in the car. Drunk."

By this point in our marriage, I had witnessed Elizabeth intoxicated countless times, but my heart sank when I laid eyes on her. It had been a month since I had seen her, and she had deteriorated even further in that time. She was a real mess. Her face was bloated, and she looked unwell. We were way beyond having any kind of a real conversation about what was happening, so I did my best to get through the next few days. I was terribly embarrassed when I introduced her to the cast. All Elizabeth did during her brief stay was drink. Even on opening night, she got pretty wasted. With hindsight, I now have compassion for the dark drag of alcoholism that had taken her beauty and her spirit, but at the time, I was too exhausted to have much sympathy for her. I found her behavior pathetic and began to look forward to her flight back to Los Angeles. That was a turning point in our relationship. I finally accepted I needed to actually make a change.

However, it is no small thing to unwind two lives when they have been joined in matrimony for nearly two decades. And Elizabeth was past the point of being able to help herself. I kept putting off the conversation I knew we needed to have. But in early 1976, my marriage problems were eclipsed by one of the most shocking tragedies of my adult life. Before I had traveled to Atlanta for the play, Wallace had called and told me that he wanted to start taking his work out of the galleries where it was being shown. I never thought anything about it or asked him why. I simply knew he wanted all his artwork home, and that was good enough for me. Over a period of several weeks, we journeyed around Los Angeles, collecting all his pieces in his little pickup truck or my VW Dasher. Another thing that changed around this time was that he began signing much of his art, which he had never done before. Again, I didn't ask him why. I figured Wallace always had a good reason for everything.

Early on the morning of February 18, 1976, his wife, Shirley, called me with unbearable news. The previous night, around 10 or 11 p.m., Wallace had just finished drinking a cup of coffee at the Topanga Center, and he was headed up the canyon to their home. A drunk driver came from the opposite direction, zigzagged down Topanga Canyon Boulevard in his big three-quarter-ton pickup truck, swerved over the line, and hit Wallace head on. As we later learned, his name was Spike, and he was on probation for multiple drunk-driving infractions with a suspended driver's license, but he was behind the wheel anyway. Spike would go to prison for manslaughter, but it was no consolation for those of us who loved Wallace so dearly.

Wallace survived for only a few hours. He died early the next morning, on his fiftieth birthday. When Shirley told me all of this, I was speechless and stunned, frozen in despair. She could barely speak herself. When I finally mustered words, all I kept saying was, "No, no, no! That can't be true!"

I immediately took Elizabeth up to Shirley's house so she could do her best to comfort her. Both Shirley and her son, Tosh, were understandably overcome with grief. Elizabeth stayed all that day and night, but I couldn't handle being there and went home in a state of shock.

I had never in my life suffered such a loss. It was far greater than when my father died, also at age fifty, because his illness had been protracted, and his passing was rather expected. Wallace, who had been my near-daily companion for more than a decade, and who had felt like a real father to me, was gone overnight. To lose him, and so suddenly, was unfathomable.

When I got home from Shirley's, I tried to go back to sleep, hoping I would wake up from this terrible nightmare. But I only tossed and turned, feeling sick to my stomach, as the awful truth sank into my bones.

The next day, I sat under the big old oak tree that flanked our house. As the reality set in, I spent the whole day there just weeping. I isolated myself from everyone else in our little tribe, and I didn't even go to Wallace's funeral. I just couldn't bear it. (To be fair, I don't think Wallace would have gone either if he could have gotten out of it.) Shirley told me later that when Bob Alexander was speaking at Wallace's grave site on the side of a hill at the cemetery in Burbank, a big wind came up and knocked over the pulpit. The eulogy, written on several pages of paper, sailed through the sky like a flock of doves. Wallace would have loved the irreverent hand of nature stirring up the somber proceedings. That was the first time I had smiled in days!

Several weeks after Wallace's passing, George, Dean, and I decided it was time to go to Wallace's studio and begin organizing and cataloging his work. It was difficult to set foot in a sacred space where we had spent so many hours with Wallace, but we felt moved by the spirit of what he would have wanted. We even tore up his unfinished pieces. The process gave us all a sense of closure and completion, especially when we were able to set up his first retrospective in Los Angeles, which would be held at the Timothea Stewart Gallery in the summer of 1977.

—

Not long after Wallace's death, I was approached about a role in *The Quest*, which would launch a western series starring Kurt Russell and Tim Matheson as brothers searching for their long-lost sister. I would play the villain in the first episode, which sounded like a fun continuation of the darker parts I had recently taken on in B movies. Of course, I would have accepted any role; even though I didn't feel in any condition to work emotionally, I just couldn't afford to pass it up.

We soon began shooting at Warner Brothers Studio. One of the scenes involved a difficult portrayal of sexual assault, in which I was the attacker. Actress Susan Dey, best known as the oldest daughter on the popular TV series *The Partridge Family*, was to play the survivor. The producer had told both of us that he wanted it to be very graphic, and they would tone it down in the editing room. I had done many fight scenes in films over the years, and although none of them had involved sexual assaults, I knew how to choreograph an act of violence, and I thought that could be helpful in this situation. I was well aware that the more prepared we were, the better it would be, to make sure both that the scene looked believable and that Susan didn't accidentally get hurt during the filming.

But Susan wouldn't talk to me on the set and avoided me every time I came near her. Finally, it was Friday afternoon, and we were due to shoot the scene on Monday. I knew the topic was delicate, but I also knew that avoiding it would only make the experience harder. I approached Susan and brought up the inevitably uncomfortable moment that was looming for both of us. "Listen, Susan, we have to do a rape scene on Monday, and you keep avoiding me!"

"I know, I'm trying to stay in character because I'm supposed to hate you," she said.

"I understand, but this is a physically violent scene," I said. "It's similar in some ways to a fight scene, and if we want it to look authentic and don't want either of us to get hurt, we should talk about it and rehearse it."

She agreed we should work together to make it appear as real as possible. So we discussed the scene and choreographed the movement and action that would take place during the struggle, and it paid off. It was a powerful scene in which neither Susan nor I would be injured, physically or otherwise, while shooting. Our work together was successful, and Susan was well prepared to get through an extremely uncomfortable but hopefully believable performance.

Unfortunately, that weekend, she went to Palm Springs, lay out in the sun for too long, and got a bad sunburn on her chest. This would make the scene not only difficult but also physically painful for Susan, and I also felt uncomfortable and was concerned for her emotional well-being, which made it awkward when I had to tear open her shirt. Thankfully, Susan and I wrestled our way through this raw scene, and she was always a collaborative professional. I felt it went as well as it could have. But after all of that, as is typical when working with some producers, most of what we had tried so hard to get right ended up on the cutting room floor.

A far less intense scene was shot outdoors on the back lot of Warner Brothers. It was an extremely hot afternoon, and after eating lunch, I found an empty tent where I could stretch out and keep from burning up in the blistering sun. As I let my mind drift, I couldn't help but remember that Wallace was buried on the side of a hill at Forest Lawn Memorial Park, which was just across the LA River, close to where I was reclining. Compelled to search for some sign of my dearly missed friend, I looked out the front flap of the tent but could see no hint that his grave was so close by. And then my eyes drifted upward to the top of the Warner Brothers tower. I smiled. There were his initials: WB.

I missed Wallace terribly. I stopped going to the Corral. I stopped seeing friends. As I had found again and again, the only consolation available to me was art. Locked in my grief, I was very focused. I began creating circle collages that looked like mysterious planets, which I called *The Spheres Series*. I had already spent nearly a year collecting magazines that had very textured, abstract photos in both color and black and white. I now used the images out of context, as I was drawn to their visual tone. I was especially attracted to representations of microscopic diseases in scientific magazines and close-up photos of food. First, I snipped out the pages and collected them in piles. Then I cut out pieces and sorted them into individual palettes of varied colors, using them like a painter would employ tubes of different-colored paint. I can't recall how many Spheres I made overall—maybe one or two dozen. Some of the smaller ones I gave away as birthday cards and gifts. In those days, I didn't think it was important to keep track of my work. I labored tirelessly, sometimes without sleeping at all. Nothing seemed to slow me down.

One night, I was working late, and out of the corner of my eye, I caught a glimpse of the orange-and-turquoise sunrise outside my studio window. Suddenly, I was frozen in a blissful, naturally stoned state. I just sat there, looking out the window, mesmerized by the sky, watching the break of dawn. After months of raw, jagged pain, this moment of transcendent bliss was a sweet balm to my soul. In fact, many times when I was working creatively, I was left feeling high. Maybe it's because when you stare at a visual creation for a long time, you stop using your mind. You stop thinking at all! Your senses, including your sight, hearing, and touch, become more acute. The brain is always trying to name and categorize everything. When you can just look and not think, you see things like a child would—new and fresh. Clarity rules your head.

By 1977, I had created twenty-two Sphere pieces, which I gathered into my second solo show at my house. I displayed the work in the center bedroom, which adjoined my studio. Although I had broken away from my former Hollywood life more than a decade earlier, I still maintained a few close friendships there. My *West Side Story* director Robert Wise came and bought a large white Sphere, which he hung in his office. Iconic underground photographer Edmund Teske documented the show. We had a good turnout and the house buzzed with energy. But I once again ended the night disappointed. Even though I sold many pieces, I only charged three or four hundred bucks for each one, so I still only garnered a few thousand dollars for a year's work. Of course, I wasn't creating art for the money; I had the satisfaction of being deeply immersed in doing something I loved so much, especially during one of the darkest periods I had known.

But even with the handful of film and theater roles I had landed in the previous few years, I was always on the verge of total destitution. I wasn't sure how much longer I could hold out. In the meantime, I was contacted in mid-1977 about an artistic undertaking that would prove to be a deeply personal and healing experience for me. Stan and Elyse Grinstein were a wealthy couple living in Brentwood who were considered to be "the godparents of the LA art scene." They collected a massive amount of art and hosted lavish parties. One of the pieces they owned was a huge rock on which Wallace had created his Kabbalah. They kept it on the lawn in front of their grand house. After Wallace passed away, their sprinkler system damaged the Kabbalah, and the Grinsteins called me to see if I could repair it with some black paint.

Dean and I went to their house one afternoon to check it out, as we also wanted the piece for inclusion in the upcoming Wallace Berman Retrospective Art Exhibition. While we were there, we walked into the Grinsteins' library, and sitting in front of their fish tank was infamous

Beat writer William S. Burroughs. We introduced ourselves and sat down to chat with him. He was known for being among the edgiest of writers—a gay heroin addict who had once drunkenly killed his wife in a tragic accidental shooting and whose novel *Naked Lunch* was so controversial it had been banned in Boston and Los Angeles for a time. Nevertheless, we had a strikingly boring conversation with him. All he talked about for a full twenty or thirty minutes was the sex life of fish! We politely excused ourselves and headed back to Topanga.

Wallace's rock was moved from the Grinsteins' home to the Timothea Stewart Gallery for Wallace's first exhibition after his death. As I had been tasked with this important restoration, I wanted to do my best. It was soothing to feel close to Wallace as I crouched near his creation. With care, I applied black paint over each tattered Jewish Letraset letter. *Damn it, Wallace, if you had just painted these things, this would not have happened,* I thought to myself with deep affection for my lost friend. Wallace had even posed with a paintbrush in the series of pictures I took of him and his rocks at the beach. He was a trickster, that Wallace. George Herms's daughter, Lily, took a photo of me painstakingly making repairs. It was very satisfying to see the restored piece amid Wallace's remarkable breadth of work when his show opened in July.

———

One day in the spring of 1978, Neil Young showed up at my house with Dean and Larry Johnson, who was Neil's longtime collaborator and film producer. It was great to see my old friend again. He had moved out of Topanga almost a decade earlier and hadn't been back for a visit in a long time. He told me that his record company, Reprise, which is part of Warner Brothers, believed a video would be a good way to publicize his newest song. Neil, though, had come up with the bright idea of making a longer movie, like we had planned to do with Dean's script, *After the Gold Rush*. Of course, Dean's movie never got made because we couldn't find anyone to finance it. But Neil now had a small budget from Warner Brothers, and he was also willing to put up quite a bit of his own money to realize his vision. He aimed to create a kind of rock 'n' roll on-the-road film with Dean playing his manager, me as his best friend, and Dennis Hopper as a character we would visit in Taos, New Mexico.

It was as if no time had passed, and we instantly fell into an easy camaraderie. We were all sitting around the front room, joking and laughing, while Elizabeth fixed us something to eat in the kitchen. Every so often, she came out to kid with us; she had a good sense of humor when she hadn't been drinking heavily. At one point, she dropped a funny one-liner into the hubbub.

"Hey, do you mind?" Dean teased. "We're having a serious business meeting here!"

Well, there were about two dozen eggs in a basket on the kitchen counter. Elizabeth took one and smashed it on Dean's head. "Here's your serious business!" she said.

Neil laughed uproariously. So Dean got an egg out of the basket and crunched it on Neil's head. Next, Neil crowned me on the head. And then the whole room turned into an egg-demolishing battle, filled with a volley of explosions, until we terminated all the eggs and ran out of ammunition. It took hours to clean up, but it was worth it. We were in high spirits and full of slapdash, anything-goes energy. That was the first official meeting for *Human Highway*.

I ended up being the film's choreographer as well as the "cowriter," along with Neil, Dean, Jim Beshears, and associate producer Jeanne Field. I was thrilled! Of course, there was never any real script, per se, so most of us just made up our lines, flying by the seat of our improvisational pants. Then the script supervisor would transcribe what we had invented so we could deliver the same lines if we had to reshoot scenes. While he was in town, Neil had parked his tour bus, Pocahontas, on the Warner Brothers lot, so that's where we met to do casting, which included a few Topanga characters and some known actors. Neil would play himself.

Neil had a gig in a little club in San Francisco, so we began filming there. Over the course of several nights, we captured footage of him performing onstage and receiving guests in his dressing room. The idea was that we would use the best performances from each night for the film and edit them together to make it look like they were all taken from the same show. We documented everything for the movie and built the story around our footage.

The movie centered on Neil, but Dean and I had turned him on to a young new-wave band called Devo, which he also wanted to include. Neil brought them out from their hometown of Akron, Ohio. Their performance footage was shot at Mabuhay Gardens. It was one of San Francisco's most famous punk rock nightclubs, where bands like the Avengers and the Dead Kennedys got their start. Onstage, Devo sang and played their instruments while the young punk crowd danced wildly, bumping and banging into each other in the mosh pit. Glad I didn't have to be a part of this chaotic shoot, I leaned against the wall, mesmerized by the colorful swirl of kids seemingly gone mad. I found myself thinking how different this scene was from the dancing at the Topanga Corral, where everyone was laid back, usually under the influence of psychedelics, pot, or tranquilizers. These kids moved like they were on twenty uppers, spewing out their bodies' tension and tightness with the most extreme, spasmodic jerking. For the film, Neil had to walk toward the stage, holding a guitar high over his head. At one point, an out-of-control kid smashed into Neil's arm and bruised it. Thankfully, we got the footage we needed, so we didn't have to go back another night.

When we were done in San Francisco, our cinematographer, David Myers, filmed Dean, Neil, and me climbing aboard Pocahontas and heading toward Taos. Filming everything as we went, we filmed the crew that was following us too. Our entourage consisted of Neil's older tour bus, several vans, and a pickup truck with four of Neil's wooden cigar-store Indians standing up in the back. As we drove, we had another brilliant idea—with the cameras always rolling, we would stop at a restaurant. When we came out to resume our drive, we would discover that the four wooden Indians were gone. It would be hard to imagine who could have stolen such large items, and it would set up one of the most dynamic moments in the movie.

The crew had built a small platform on the front of the bus for the cameras, which allowed us to shoot from there onto the highway, as well as through the front window. Being a daredevil stunt guy, I got a bright idea. I suggested to Neil that I climb onto the platform to clean the windshield while he was driving the bus. "Great!" Neil said.

We shot the scene from the inside of the bus. The platform wasn't visible in the shot, so it looked like I was standing on air in front of the bus while we cruised down the road. Getting into my role, I sprayed some foamy cleaner on the window and started wiping away. Neil almost had a heart attack. Unable to see anything through the windshield, he laid on the horn. When he hit the brakes, I almost flew off the platform. Neil opened the bus door and yelled, "Bad idea!"

When we finally arrived in Taos, Neil performed a concert on the Santa Clara Pueblo Indian Reservation at the Puye Cliff Dwellings. Throughout my career, I had acted in many westerns, some of which included old-fashioned representations of Native American tribes, so I was absolutely thrilled to be working with Native Americans in a spirit of collaboration and creativity. Neil's crew had erected a huge sound system, and when he began to play, the music blasted across their pueblos and into the red sky. The tribe members were dressed to the hilt in beautiful, handcrafted leather-braided jackets, colorful turquoise and bone chokers, beaded moccasins, and feathers everywhere. They stood tall, emanating a regal power that underlined their identities as the original Americans. I could sense their powerful companionship deep in my heart and felt ashamed of how our ancestors had treated them in the early days of our violent settlement on this land we took from them, and how I had kept stereotypes alive in the films in which I had acted.

We all built a big bonfire in the center of the gathering place. As we had planned, a group of young Native men came out onto our concert site, carrying the four wooden cigar-store Indians. While they were valuable as art pieces, they were insulting because of their racist representations of Native Americans. The men rectified this wrong by throwing them onto the bonfire. Fed by the antique wood, the flames roared higher into the air. We all held hands and danced in a circle around the fire. It was one of the most powerful experiences of my life. When the fire burned low, we each leaped over the smoldering coals, celebrating a spiritual cleansing with our Native brothers and sisters as the smoke and ashes carried our intentions for a better way into the sky.

Since Dennis Hopper was living in Taos, he introduced us to some fabulous locations. We were on the hunt for footage for the film but also enjoying the fun of having our old band of friends back together. While we were there, we heard a local theater group was performing *West Side Story* at a small theater in town. Neil, Dennis, and Dean wanted to go, but when we arrived, it was sold out. Dean leaned over to the manager in a conspiratorial way, pointed at me, and said, "He was in the movie, you know."

The manager looked me up and down as if unconvinced and replied, "Well, there are no seats, but you guys can sit on the floor if you want."

It was the craziest version of *West Side Story* I have ever seen. None of the cast could sing or dance, so they spoke the song lyrics while walking around the stage. I didn't want to be mean spirited, but there was only so much of this I could stand. Finally, after what felt like forever, intermission arrived. "Let's get out of here!" I said. So we snuck out the front. As we ran to our car, our pent-up laughter burst into the air.

One of our more spectacular location shoots was at the Rio Grande Gorge Bridge. Nine or ten miles northwest of Taos, it's elevated more than five hundred feet above the Rio Grande, and the views on both sides are absolutely breathtaking, with winding orange, red, and yellow canyons embracing the snaking water. The scene we shot there was a wild good time and just the kind of crazy magic we wanted to create with our film.

In it, we pulled Pocahontas over to the middle of the bridge to aid the passengers in a broken-down old black Chrysler Coupe (from Neil's classic-car collection). While we were talking to the passengers in the car, who were members of a small San Francisco street band, the very large trunk popped open and out climbed the rest of their bandmates, including an old turbaned Sikh tap dancer, who tuned his taps with a screwdriver; a Japanese girl playing guitar; a hippie horn player; and a

Native American woman on tambourine. The Sikh danced and sang as they played "Boulevard of Broken Dreams" with Neil on the piano. (Where did the piano come from? Movie magic!) The rest of the cast joined in the dancing on the bridge, except for me. I danced on top of the bus, which was filmed in a spectacular long shot of the river, the bridge, the bus, and me.

The final scene found the entire cast floating down the Rio Grande on rubber life rafts. Did it make sense? Probably not. Was it inspired, irreverent joy? Yep. It was definitely the most fun I ever had on a movie set. I was collaborating with my closest friends, improvising, and choreographing, and I was totally engaged in every moment of the whole chaotic process. More than a professional film, it felt like the recording of an outlandishly extravagant home movie.

I returned to Topanga still riding our creative high and began the long wait for Neil to edit our many hours of footage into a film. In the meantime, I continued this antiestablishment period of my career by performing at a benefit play entitled *Showdown at Forked Tongue Canyon*. Given how magical our Topanga neighborhood was, I guess it was no surprise that we were under constant threat from developers. The latest batch of immoral capitalists wanted to fill in Topanga Creek and build a trailer park, even though they would need to rezone the canyon for commercial development to do so. We required a lawyer to stop this nightmare. So we decided to put on a benefit play. In it, I joined many of the locals, including George Herms, Billy Gray, Toni Basil, and Taj Mahal, as well as singer Spanky McFarlane from the group Spanky and Our Gang and actors Tisha Sterling, Lou Gossett Jr., and Jan-Michael Vincent. I played Sheriff Peter Pitchess, who was actually the local sheriff at the time. For my grand entrance, I climbed down onto the stage from a simulated helicopter. Only the noisy rotors could be heard. My first action was to swing a fake billy club at Elizabeth's mother, who was a good enough sport to take part in our protest play. "Who are you?" someone shouted.

"I'm Sheriff Peter Pitchess, but you can call me PP," was my reply.

The rest of the show went on in the same vein, earning us some big laughs. Many celebrities attended, including Jack Nicholson, who wrote a big check for our cause. There was so much demand to see the show that we were held over for two weekends. Then two more weekends were sold out. Shirley and Elizabeth handled the refreshments and served a lot of wine at intermission. Of course, Elizabeth drank quite a bit of it as well, but we still managed to make plenty of profit for our fund. In the end, we retained an excellent lawyer and stopped the greedy developers from accomplishing their nefarious plan.

In August 1978, I landed another musical-theater role that turned out to be one of my favorites. *Cabaret* originally starred Joel Grey on Broadway, and he won an Oscar for the film version. The Little Theatre on the Square wasn't Broadway, but it was a terrific venue in suburban Chicago. I played the part of the emcee, and not only did I get to sing and dance some pretty great numbers, but I also got to add plenty of my own creative ideas. For instance, the opening of the second act had me dressed in drag, as part of a girls' chorus line. I could kick higher than some of the dancers, and the audience took a few seconds to recognize me.

I so relished doing *Cabaret*. Of all the shows I had been in, it was my favorite theater experience, and the local reviews I received were outstanding (if you can stand me bragging a bit more). Much of the credit for my reception was due to the director, Richard Caspar, also a choreographer, who tailored the show to my abilities, despite having only one week to rehearse. There's something magical about working in the theater. When you walk onto that stage, you can actually feel the audience with you. I absolutely loved it. After five weeks of performing with all I had, you might have thought I would need a vacation, but I was exhilarated. I was in great shape and felt like I could go on forever. I would miss those energizing nights onstage, as well as the warm companionship of the cast members and staff, the beautiful two-bedroom house in which I stayed, and my early-morning swims in the lake on my days off. Now, I had to again face my dilemma at home, which I had yet to do anything to improve or end.

Returning from Chicago, I found Elizabeth had slipped even deeper into alcoholism. It was heartbreaking to come back to a depressed spouse, especially after the stimulating euphoria of my *Cabaret* experience. Some afternoons, she would return from the store and pass out in the parked car, with her legs sticking out. I knew I was partially to blame, but not completely. She'd had a drinking problem when I met her, and I was just too naive to recognize how serious it was.

Elizabeth's friends were well aware of her struggle, and so after finding a stash of her empty vodka bottles hidden in a kitchen cabinet, I talked to them about rallying around her. We met and decided to have an intervention that would include Louise Herms; Elizabeth's goddaughters, Rocket and Susie; their mother, Jeanne; and at least two other friends. I told Elizabeth that I thought I could get help for her through the Screen Actors Guild. We all really tried, but it just didn't work. First of all, we weren't mental health professionals, and we had no idea how to fix the situation, other than to beg her to get help, which she stubbornly refused. She argued that we also drank a lot, and she was no different. While it's true that we were social drinkers who liked to party sometimes, she drank heavily, every day, until she passed out. It felt hopeless. But I still loved her in a strange way, and I resigned myself to sticking it out longer, not yet ready to give up. I can see now I had this bad habit of looking the other way when things got tough. Or maybe I couldn't bear to face another divorce; the first one had been too painful.

Around April 1979, neither Dean nor I was working. We wanted to do something creative together, and Dean suggested an absurdist play, *Man with Bags*, by Romanian playwright Eugène Ionesco. The work was based on a translation by Ionesco's only child, Marie-France Ionesco, and had been adapted by Israel Horovitz.

The play was a dreamlike comedy, similar to Samuel Beckett's existential *Waiting for Godot*. Dean wanted to direct, with me starring and choreographing a tap-dancing number for the whole cast as the play's finale, and Mark Mothersbaugh, the lead singer and musical genius from Devo, composing the music. So all we needed was some financial backing. We were hoping to get Neil to help with the production costs, but he had already spent more than $2 million on *Human Highway* and didn't want to cough up any more money on our crazy idea. However, we did get Robert Wise and Jack Nicholson to each donate a thousand dollars. With this, we were able to start rehearsal at the Pilot Theater, a small, inexpensive spot in Hollywood.

Rehearsals went smoothly, except for one day during a run-through of the tap-dance number, when Elizabeth staggered in and interrupted the actors. She was festooned in a big hat with lots of feathers and a drapey scarf. She had obviously been drinking. "It's okay, everybody. I'm Mr. T's old lady!" she shouted with the flair of Isadora Duncan.

I was embarrassed (once again) but managed to explain to her that I was in the middle of rehearsing and needed her to sit down and behave herself.

We opened on May 25, and unbelievably, Ionesco just happened to be in town doing a lecture at UCLA. We somehow found out where he was staying and invited him to come to the performance. When he arrived with his interpreter, I was very pleased to introduce him to Robert Wise, who really wanted to meet him. However, Dean and I were not so pleased when Ionesco told us the play was too long. Somehow, the adaptation into English had lengthened it into two and a half hours, and Ionesco had written his play to only last one hour and twenty minutes.

The next day, we cut about forty-five minutes out of the play, but it was too late—the reviews had already come out, and they weren't very good. They said the play was too long and not that funny. The critics thought the tongue-in-cheek humor was both slapstick and leaden (not a good combo). I didn't think it was that bad, but who knows? Maybe it was!

This was a low point for me. I had little money and no work in sight. I was collecting unemployment and thinking, like many actors do, that I would never work again. Despite this, I continued to have fond memories of my exhilarating work on *Human Highway*, and I couldn't wait for its release, or even to see a cut. But a year went by and still no film. However, there was a song with the same title on Neil's album *Comes a Time*, which he released in October 1978. The album sold well, although the rumor was that Neil had bought up 200,000 copies himself because he didn't like the way the album sounded after it had been mixed. Neil got pulled away from his work on *Human Highway*, as the record label wanted him to tour in support of the album. So he embarked on the twenty-four-city tour Rust Never Sleeps. He filmed the final performance at the Cow Palace in Daly City and began work on this new concert movie.

Russ dubs this photo by Dennis Hopper *The Stone Statues*. Featured from left to right: Wallace Berman, Russ, and Dean Stockwell.

Russ with an artwork from
his *Spheres Series*.
Photo by Edmund Teske.

Russ repairs the Letraset
on Wallace's big rock,
Topanga Seed.
Photo by Lily Belle Herms.

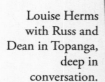

Louise Herms
with Russ and
Dean in Topanga,
deep in
conversation.

Best pals Dean Stockwell and Russ on the set of *Win, Place or Steal* (1974).

Russ at Neil Young's ranch, starting the filming for *Human Highway* (1982).
Photo by Bruce Conner.

Crystal Rose
Collage by Russ Tamblyn
(1980)

PART 3

REBIRTH

CHAPTER 12

FAIT ACCOMPLI

Whenever I asked any of our mutual friends about the progress on *Human Highway*, all I heard was that Neil was doing a lot of editing. Boy, did he ever. Finally, in 1979, Neil called me. "Sorry," he said. "I cut the film down to about ten or fifteen minutes!"

Well, I nearly blew a gasket. But Neil had a plan, as he always did.

"I wanna turn the portion I kept into a dream sequence and shoot a whole new beginning and end."

Thrilled to dive back into the playful world of creative freedom in which we had filmed the original segments, I was eager to hear what he had in mind. For starters, instead of filming on the road, we shot in Los Angeles at Raleigh Studios, which was a blast! Everyone in our crew was really into it. Neil and I had a lot of scenes together, and often, instead of eating lunch in the commissary, we would sneak out and drive to Pink's on La Brea. We loved their chili dogs, so much so that sometimes we would each consume two! The walls at Pink's are full of celebrity photos, mainly of actors and musicians. It always surprised me that there was no picture of Neil among them. Here was an icon, sitting right in their midst, and they never knew it. Of course, when he wanted to, Neil had that quality of being able to look like everyone else in the room.

In the new version of *Human Highway*, Neil and I played two dorks (he was Lionel, and I was Fred Kelly), who were riding our bicycles to a diner made from an old train car with an adjacent filling station. Dennis was the crazy cook, and Dean was the greedy owner. A cartoonish set of a small diner with one of Neil's miniature trains running on a track behind it was built on one of the Raleigh stages, in accordance with Neil's specifications. This is where we shot most of the new beginning and end of *Human Highway*. And true to the plan—the plan was to have no plan.

The basic story is that Lionel and Fred both get jobs at the filling station, but the waitresses at the diner, played by Sally Kirkland, Charlotte Stewart, and Geraldine Baron, will have nothing to do with them. Of course, Dennis was drunk most of the time we were shooting. And he was playing his part while waving a knife around. At one point, Sally Kirkland grabbed for it. When she did, Dennis pulled it away quickly and cut a tendon in her hand. We rushed her to the hospital, and she would go on to sue Neil, Dennis, and the company but lost the court case.

In a later scene, while Lionel is beneath a limo changing the oil, a wrench falls on his head, knocking him out and launching his dream. Among the surreal happenings is a crazy scene, directed by Beat artist Bruce Conner, of Neil rocking out with Booji Boy (a Devo invention) in a baby crib, playing "Out of the Blue and into the Black" on a keyboard. This footage had been shot in San Francisco, which meant it was now two years old, but it still fit in perfectly with our new vision for the film. It is wild and loud. "Hey hey, my my, rock 'n' roll can never die."

From there, the dream includes more footage from our trip to San Francisco, as well as Taos. Then Lionel wakes up. As I shake him into consciousness, all the characters from the diner gather around us. "I think he's got a conclusion!" I tell them, always loving my wordplay.

The nuclear power plant explodes; rockets go off, triggering the end of the world; and we all sing and dance with shovels while Devo's Mark Mothersbaugh leads us in performing "It Takes a Worried Man."

Filming the dance number was certainly one of the highlights of my involvement with *Human Highway*. In all my Hollywood musicals, I always contributed a great deal of my own steps, moves, and acrobatics, but this was the first time I was asked to choreograph a whole number by myself. And if you think teaching Neil Young, Dean Stockwell, and Dennis Hopper dance steps was easy, you're sadly mistaken. In fact, most of the whole cast had never danced choreographed moves before, so I created steps that were fairly easy. But even easy steps were difficult for Dennis. He just didn't know his right from his left. I had to keep saying, "Your other left, Dennis! Your other left!" However, it was especially fun giving Neil dance instruction. He's very independent and told me that no one ever gives him directions. But I did, and he loved it.

To get everyone in the frame, I had to set the camera way back. All you could see was a long, horizontal row of more than twenty cast members with a great deal of space in front of them and behind them. I quickly broke us up into three lines with Neil, Dean, and myself at the front. From the camera crane, about fifteen feet off the ground, the frame was filled nicely.

Our final shoot was at Culver Studios, where independent filmmakers from David O. Selznick to Orson Welles made their monumental film classics. An exorbitant, sky-high staircase was built on one of the stages so we could all climb up and go to heaven.

Then the world ended, as did the film.

When the Hollywood filming began, Neil had wanted Dean and me to stay in the city, so he put us up for a few weeks at the Sunset Marquis, which is a legendary rock 'n' roll hotel. Elizabeth hadn't traveled with me on location in years, and she stayed at home in Topanga.

During this time, Elizabeth and I attended a small dinner party at Robert Wise's luxurious beach house in Malibu. He was screening *The Haunting* for a few guests, including my favorite choreographer, Michael Kidd from *Seven Brides for Seven Brothers*. It was such a great surprise to see Michael and his wife, Shelah. Also attending was one of my favorite actresses, Patricia Neal, who had won a Best Actress Academy Award for her smart performance in *Hud*. We were all having a wonderful conversation about acting and dancing, but Elizabeth kept refilling her glass. I'm sure I should have paid more attention to her, but I was lost in the conversation. By the time Robert began screening the film, Elizabeth was snoring on the floor. I shook her, but it didn't do any good. She would sit up briefly and then pass out again. I was so embarrassed I could hardly see straight. When the film ended, Bob pulled me aside and asked, "Would Elizabeth like to lie down in one of the guest rooms? I think she's had a little too much to drink."

"Thank you for your kind offer, but I think it's best if I just take her home," I said.

During our drive back to Topanga, I couldn't keep quiet about Elizabeth's drinking, but the more I told her how much she needed help, the more she argued. It blew up into a big argument. But it didn't take me long to realize it was useless trying to talk to her when she was in such a drunken stupor, so I gave up. Suddenly, there was a long period of silence, which was an improvement, but the drive home was still very solemn. When I looked over at Elizabeth in the passenger seat, she had passed out again against the window. She looked bedraggled, and I felt very sorry for her. I could feel my heart breaking. When we first met, she had been cultured, well traveled, and a great wit. We had fun together. Once she'd had vitality and presence; she had turned men's heads whenever she walked into a room. In Las Vegas, she strutted across the Dunes stage looking like Sophia Loren. Now, it was as if she only lived to drink, and everything from her body to her spirit was paying the price.

I had vowed to leave before. This time, I knew it was different. But for now, I had to get her home and make sure she stumbled up the front porch steps without tripping over the flowerpots. Once I had walked her into the house and put her to bed, I roamed the living room, looking at the artwork on the walls of our home, remembering the amazing meals she had cooked in her kitchen and the laughter we had shared with our dearest friends in these rooms. I stared at the big oak tree outside my studio window, reminiscing about our nineteen years together. It was sad, but it was over. I knew I would finally say goodbye in the morning.

I awoke to a morning that was gloomy and dismal. A billowy mass of gray fog drifted in off the ocean and covered the Eden Ranch like a shroud. It didn't take me long to pack up. One suitcase did the trick. I figured I could come back at some point and retrieve the rest of my stuff.

When I had my bag in hand, I faced Elizabeth for our final goodbye. "I'm only coming back to get the rest of my things," I said.

"Oh, you'll come crawling back," she said. "The question is, will I let you stay?"

Responses flashed across my mind, but I knew there was no point. And Dean was waiting for me outside. He was truly like a brother to me, especially during this difficult and disorienting transition in my life. He drove me into town, listening to me as I unspooled my anxiety about leaving Elizabeth in such a state. Finally, I had nothing left to say about her or the end of our marriage, and I grew silent.

"Fait accompli," he said.

I had never heard the term before. "What does it mean?"

"It's over. Finished. Just cut the cord."

That made total sense. After nineteen years, it really was over. But there were practical matters to be considered. We had a few more scenes to film for *Human Highway*, which meant I had my room at the Sunset Marquis for a little while longer. When the shoot wrapped, I would have to find a place to live. I confided in Dean that I had no idea where I should go next.

"Well, I've been thinking of moving out of Topanga when the film ends, so how about we get a place in town together?" Dean said.

"Perfect," I replied. "You've got yourself a roommate."

The plan was for Dean, Dennis, and me to rent a house in Hollywood. Dean loved Laurel Canyon. He'd once had a house there, and I had always enjoyed driving over to visit him and other friends, such as Bobby Driscoll. So this idea sounded cool to me. Honestly, at that moment in my life, I was not a happy camper, and I was kind of lost. I would have lived anywhere.

Dennis landed a part and went back East to film, so Dean rented a small house in Laurel Canyon for the two of us. He gave me a tiny room that only fit a single bed. But I was glad to have that. Thank God Dennis didn't end up living with us. I think it would have been disastrous! The three of us together were pretty wild. We drank and partied a lot. At this point in his life, Dennis was a full-blown alcoholic. I had never met anyone who consumed more alcohol than he did. Dennis was also a big cocaine user, and when he wanted some, I was always the one who was sent out to score. They knew I would come back with all of it because I was allergic to the stuff.

Dean also rented a storage space in Hollywood for his excess furniture from Topanga. He invited me to keep things there too, so I had to go back to Topanga and face Elizabeth. She was a mess. She had a squatter living with her, and they had managed to get into my studio and break up some of my artwork. I was past caring too much, though. I just wanted to collect whatever belongings I really needed and get the hell out of there. Elizabeth and her drinking friend left the house, and while they were gone, I took a piece of chalk and wrote a long goodbye letter to her on the dark-green studio wall. My words were spontaneous and from my heart. I wished her well and hoped her future would be better than her life currently seemed to be. She acted like it didn't bother her that I had instigated our divorce, but I know it did. It's hard enough to leave someone, especially after two decades together, but I know it's even harder to be left.

Once we became roommates, Dean and I hung out a lot together. We often drove down to the store. One day, Dean was driving, and I was sitting in the passenger seat. At a red light, a car pulled up. The driver was a teenager with bright-green hair. I nudged Dean. "Look!" I said.

We were both staring at the kid when he rolled down his window and yelled, "What's the matter? You've never seen green hair before?"

Retorts ricocheted through my mind. I wish I had yelled through the window, *Yes, as a matter of fact, there was a movie made in 1948, before you were born, called* The Boy with Green Hair. *That boy, now a man, is sitting here next to me, and as far as I know, he is the first boy to ever have bright-green hair!* But instead, the light changed, and we drove away.

———

In July 1980, I got an offer to perform in the musical *Bye Bye Birdie*, which would open at the Starlight Theater in Kansas City and also travel to the Muny in Saint Louis. I couldn't have been happier. Not only did the show give me the opportunity to sing and dance opposite a longtime friend, the incredibly talented Chita Rivera, but also it was a fun musical with lots of classic songs. Chita had opened the show on Broadway in 1960 opposite Dick Van Dyke. Tony Mordente, her then husband, had been one of my Jets in *West Side Story*, and Chita and I now reminisced about the happy times we had spent together when I was in New York filming the movie. Back then, I never would have dreamed I would one day play a part originated by the great Dick Van Dyke and have the chance to sing amazing tunes like "Put on a Happy Face." Of course, Chita had played Anita in *West Side Story* on Broadway, so we also enjoyed sharing memories about the stage show and film version. She was a down-to-earth lady with a vivacious personality and sense of humor (as long as you didn't mention Rita Moreno—sometimes she was pretty bitter that she didn't get to play Anita in the film, which I understood).

The Starlight Theater was a beautiful eight-thousand-seat outdoor amphitheater. The only downside, which I learned very quickly, had to do with performing outside in the summer. The bright stage lights attracted lots of moths. One night, I was singing "Put on a Happy Face," and a moth flew right into my mouth! I choked and spit it out, with a not-so-happy face. To make the job even better, I was earning $7,500 a week, which was big money compared to earning a few thousand dollars a year from my fine art. I actually had enough cash to pay Dean for rent and buy us groceries. I felt flush, and I was starting to emerge from the dark valley of my marriage woes.

Dean was seeing Valerie Venet, an actress from the TV show *The Monkees* and the wife of music producer Nick Venet, who produced Linda Ronstadt and the Beach Boys. Valerie invited Dean and me to the Troubadour to see her friend singer-songwriter Bonnie Murray, who was going to record an album with Nick. We stopped and had a few drinks first. When we finally arrived, we had missed Bonnie's set, but Valerie introduced us. Bonnie and I sat up in the club's balcony and chatted. I felt an intuitive physical and emotional connection, as if I had known

Bonnie all my life. Without realizing quite what was happening, I was falling in love again. I was starting over.

There was just one problem: Bonnie was married to her manager, Johnny Palazzotto, and I was technically still married to Elizabeth. But Johnny was away in New Orleans for long spells with acts he managed. Bonnie had just lost her mother after a long battle with cancer and was feeling vulnerable and in need of a friend. It turned out I had made an impression on her. After having Dean ask Valerie for Bonnie's phone number, I called her, and it turned out she was about to perform at the Topanga Corral of all places! I told her I would see her there and that I looked forward to finally hearing her sing with her Flying A Band.

That weekend—on the night of October 16, 1980—I drove back to Topanga to see Bonnie play. This time, I wasn't late. Her band rocked the Corral with her powerful singing and performance. Now I knew I was hooked. Many of her songs were stories from her stint as a waitress at the Ranch House Café, a truck stop located on Highway 395 in the High Sierra. Bonnie had lived there for a time when she ran away with a cowboy and was writing music and playing in honky-tonks. Everyone at the Corral was on the dance floor, including me. When the set ended, I couldn't wait to talk to her again. "I loved your singing so much," I said.

"I loved watching you dance with your girls on the floor," she teased me.

"I want to teach you to dance," I said, offering the best line I could think of in the moment. Billy Gray was hanging out at the Corral that night, and the three of us strolled out to the parking lot together. Billy mentioned he had several pieces of my art on display at his house.

"Would you like to come see them?" I asked Bonnie.

She nodded with a big smile. So we climbed into Billy's little Volkswagen, with Billy driving and Bonnie and me sitting in the back. We talked and laughed all the way down the canyon to Billy's. At one point, I couldn't contain myself any longer, and I leaned over and stole a kiss from Bonnie. Once again, my life was changed in an instant.

Almost two months later, on December 11, Bonnie and I had our first official date—a double date with Dean and Valerie. That afternoon, we set off on an adventure to explore the Bradbury Building in downtown Los Angeles, which had been designated a National Historic Landmark in 1977. We thought it would be a fun place to visit. The interior has two open cage elevators with beautiful French-made ironwork and a glass ceiling that lights up the whole atrium in the daytime. Upon entering the building, we climbed a flight of gorgeous marble stairs. On the way back down, I thought I would show off for Bonnie. So I did a stunt in which I crouched down and leaped backward, clicking my shoes on six or seven of the stairs before landing at the bottom. I'm not sure if I impressed her or if she thought I was crazy! Afterward, we drove to Little Tokyo for sushi. Bonnie made me an origami bird out of a napkin, and I still have it, even forty years later. There was no question about it; we were mesmerized by each other.

Several days later, I was having my car repaired, so I asked Bonnie if she would come pick me up. She arrived at the mechanic shop in a huge 1955 DeSoto Fireflite. It was pink with a black top and was as uniquely beautiful as she was. I climbed in next to her on the wide, dark-pink front seat, which had no center console to divide us. As she drove, I was transfixed by her long honey-colored hair, blowing in the wind, and her long white legs, peeking out from her thin wraparound skirt. Instinct beckoned me to slide over and put my hand on her leg.

She sighed and then said, "Russ, I'm driving!"

"Yes," I replied. "You're driving me crazy!"

She smiled, but I knew she was right. As difficult as it was, I controlled myself.

Bonnie felt very guilty. She was still married to Johnny, and if there are two qualities she exemplifies, they are honesty and loyalty. She told me that she couldn't go on with our relationship without first letting Johnny know that their marriage was over. She flew to Louisiana to spend Christmas with him and his family. She didn't come back until January, and when we were reunited, she told me it was one of the most difficult things she'd ever had to do. Johnny, who was a real southern gentleman, was heartbroken but understood as best he could. Johnny remained a good friend to Bonnie, and eventually to me.

We were overjoyed to be able to be together. However, not long after that, Bonnie booked a gig to sing up in the High Sierra at a little club in June Lake. Even though we talked on the phone every night, I really missed her, but I also understood her passion for her music ran as deep as my passion for my art. She explained to me how beautiful it was in June Lake and that she hoped I could make it up there sometime. Her father had built a big cabin on Silver Lake, which is part of the June Lake Loop. I, too, wished to see it with her soon.

The longer I knew Bonnie, the more I learned of her strong reputation as a singer-songwriter and how she could charm audiences with her affectionate smile, passionate guitar playing, and fascinating songs about endangered Alaskan wolves, the cycles of the moon, and the charm of forgotten Flying A gas stations. In her long and storied career, Bonnie has written hundreds of songs. The country music singer Dottsy recorded Bonnie's track "I Hope You Understand When I'm Gone" for RCA Records, landing on the *Billboard* charts. Bonnie has also opened for artists including Jimmy Buffett, Three Dog Night, Fleetwood Mac, Dave Mason, Little Feat, Leo Kottke, Jesse Winchester, and the Flying Burrito Brothers. In a review, one California critic complimented Bonnie by writing that her voice is deep and rich, and she seems to float through every note like a warm wind.

Many of Bonnie's compositions were drawn from her observations of the people she met during her journeys in the High Sierra. She had dropped out of college, taking off on her own to explore a different culture—the wild world of honky-tonks and cowboys. She broke her father's heart. Alex Murray disapproved of her lifestyle and was distraught that she hadn't continued her classical studies on the cello. He was a first-call violinist and session player in Hollywood, and for a time, he was concertmaster at Republic Pictures. His solo violin can be heard in the John Wayne film *The Searchers* and many other Republic movies. When Bonnie told me about her father during our courtship, I thought back to when I was twelve years old and had climbed over the wall at Republic, looking for Roy Rogers. That was the same year Bonnie was born. A little later, when I knew how our love story would turn out,

I had a good laugh as I fantasized about running into her father that day and saying, "Excuse me, Mr. Murray, you're about to become the father of a baby girl, and guess what? I'm going to marry her someday and father your granddaughter!" Well, he probably would have been so shocked he might have hit me over the head with his violin and broken a very expensive instrument. So it's a good thing I didn't run into him that day—or know my future!

A little time passed before I saw Bonnie again. Although we had obvious chemistry, our relationship was not without its complications. Just take our second date, which was almost our last. An old friend from *Human Highway*, Danny Tucker, who was also a friend of Neil Young's, invited Bonnie and me to Topanga. He had just opened a new restaurant called the Gold Rush after Neil's album. While confirming we would make it in for dinner, I hoped I wouldn't run into Elizabeth, but I didn't tell Bonnie anything about my ex-wife. While Bonnie and I were having a drink at the bar, Danny came over and warned me that Elizabeth had arrived. So he quickly ushered us to a nice corner table. When Elizabeth heard I was there, she came rushing into the dining room to confront us, wearing a wide-brimmed feathered hat and thick makeup. "I need to talk to you about our taxes!" she slurred. As she stood there with her hands on her hips and extreme hostility in her eyes, I knew taxes were the last thing on her mind.

"Elizabeth, this is not the time or place—" I said.

"This is a perfect time! So if you'll just get rid of this cunt for a while, we can talk!"

Out of the corner of my eye, I could see Bonnie taking out her earrings, preparing for a physical fight. Fortunately, two of Danny's bouncers showed up and dragged Elizabeth off; she screamed bloody murder all the way out the front door. Everyone in the restaurant was staring. Once again, it was an embarrassing situation brought on by Elizabeth and my inability to get through to her, but Bonnie had no knowledge of our uncomfortable run-ins.

"Do you still want to stay for dinner?" I asked her.

"I'd rather not, if you don't mind," she said.

As we started driving down the canyon, we saw poor Elizabeth staggering along the side of the road. She looked lost in the cold night. I glanced over at Bonnie, putting her earrings back in, and feared this would be as far as our romance went. "I'm sorry I didn't warn you that we might run into Elizabeth, and that I didn't tell you more about our decaying relationship," I said.

"I understand. I'm just glad I wasn't forced to have a fight in the middle of a restaurant."

We laughed a little at this, relieved as the tension began to ease.

"Elizabeth truly seems like a troubled soul," Bonnie continued. "You should have some empathy for her and, maybe, try to help her— if that's possible."

I nodded, feeling grateful that Bonnie was so understanding and compassionate. We drove to another restaurant down by the ocean and enjoyed a peaceful meal. Then we strolled along the beach and had a long talk. Bonnie asked many questions about my marriage and my life. Even though we had only known each other for such a short time, I began to confess to her about my past casual affairs and how I felt that I was partly to blame for Elizabeth's condition. Bonnie was a good listener. I knew I had finally found someone very special.

Bonnie began a recording session for several of her songs, "Dirty Job" and "Leda." Her producer, Nick Venet, warned her that she should stay away from Dean, Dennis, and me. "They're a bunch of over-the-hill, alcoholic losers who should just face the fact that their careers are over and they're on their way to the grave!" he said.

Thankfully, Bonnie wasn't the type to listen to gossip, but I was still living at Dean's, and that meant she had some run-ins with Dennis that could have made her question the whole lot of us. Dennis was still drinking very heavily in these days, and he was extremely manic, as in he would never stop talking. I would take Bonnie into the minuscule bedroom that barely fit my bed so we could have a little privacy. But the room had an open transom above it, so we could still hear Dennis ranting outside. On the door, I had hung one of Wallace's posters that contained a picture of marijuana and the words *Love Weed*. Incensed at having been left alone, Dennis started throwing quarters over the door-frame into my room and yelling, "Come out, love weed! Come out of there, love weed!"

Bonnie later confessed that she sometimes wondered what she was getting herself into.

—

I wanted to steal Bonnie away somewhere special for a few days, so I rented a condo in Palm Springs. I gave the phone number to Dean and asked him to get in touch if anything important came up. Sure enough, after only one night, Dean called and said, "Neil wants you to call him."

When I did, Neil said he needed me up at his Broken Arrow Ranch in the hills of Woodside, just south of San Francisco, to do some voice dubbing for *Human Highway*.

"Well, I'd love to, but I'm in Palm Springs, having sort of a honeymoon."

"That's great, Russ. I'll fly you both up," Neil said.

I asked Bonnie if she would like to go to Neil's house.

Her eyes lit up. "Of course!" she said.

When we flew in, Neil's producer, Larry Johnson, picked us up and drove us to his ranch just above Redwood City. After driving down Bear Gulch Road, where Larry used the combination to open Neil's big wooden gate, we drove onto the property, passing rustic sculptures, a small herd of buffalo roaming behind a long wooden fence, and a small lake. After winding down the narrow, twisting road, we arrived at Neil's extraordinary house, all multilevel wood and stained glass, surrounded by a magnificent grove of redwoods. We stopped in to say hello and have a beer. Neil was pleased to meet Bonnie and asked her to do one of the voices for the film. She readily agreed. I was pleased that she could jump into the fun with my friends and me.

Larry drove us farther along the property, several miles to the guest-house, past various structures and barns dedicated to Neil's passions for music, trains, and classic cars. We rode through a dark tunnel of redwoods so thick and tall they blocked out the sun, then over a bridge and a fast-running river, and finally arrived at an opening that looked down on a large white guesthouse. No one else was staying there at the time, so we had free rein over the whole six-bedroom place and its well-stocked refrigerator and bar. Bonnie and I found ourselves ensconced in a lush forest that was a private paradise. On the backside of the property was a long deck that overlooked the rushing river, racing down to the coast and Half Moon Bay. For the film, Bonnie recorded the high-pitched voice of a girl in the crowd saying, "Hi, Lionel." And I did a few voice-overs for my part. Then, having happily reconnected with my old friend and our ongoing passion project, I flew back to Palm Springs with Bonnie, and we finished our little getaway.

Bonnie and I arrived back at Dean's to what sounded like good news. A message from Elizabeth indicated that she was ready to go into a rehab center for alcoholics and she wondered if I could possibly arrange it. When I called her back, she apologized for her outburst at the Gold Rush and said she really wanted to get her life in order.

I had found new love, and I always wished the best for Elizabeth. Since we were still legally married, I called the Screen Actors Guild and arranged for her to go to a good rehabilitation program for women on the outskirts of downtown Los Angeles. I drove her down there and checked her into the center, which was an old Victorian mansion. The minimum stay was thirty days, but if Elizabeth wanted to stay longer, she could. I wished her luck and hoped her recovery would be a success. Bonnie was happy I had made the effort to help Elizabeth. As the connection between Bonnie and me grew deeper, our old relationships began to fade away.

Dean met a woman named Joy Marchenko, and their feelings for each other also grew serious very quickly. He wanted her to move in with him, so it was imperative that I move out. Bonnie was living at her father's house in Nichols Canyon, but things were strained between them in the wake of her mother's death. So we decided to seek somewhere to live together. Until we could do so, we stayed at friends' houses. Eventually, we found ourselves an ideal spot. I secured a guesthouse north of

Malibu in Point Dume. It was on a handsome piece of cliffside property overlooking the ocean. The very eccentric owner, Hannah, lived
all alone in the main house.

Our little casita consisted of one big room with a small toilet and
a giant bathtub. We bought a coffee maker and a small bookshelf, on
which we stored our food and microwave. We didn't need much more
than that, especially as the house had its own Jacuzzi, nestled in a den
of trees and shrubs on a corner of the cliff's edge. With the crashing
waves below us and the night sky filled with glittering stars above us, we
would quietly soak with a glass of wine and full hearts. We were about
to be gifted with even more, but we didn't know it yet.

I landed a part in the farcical play *Here Lies Jeremy Troy*, which would
open in Odessa, Texas, and have a run in Midland. While I learned my
lines, I became Bonnie's roadie, carrying her equipment when she played
small LA venues like the Steak and Sirloin, a smoky bar that we jokingly
called the "Barf and Bag It." Right before I left for Texas, in early March
1981, I picked up Elizabeth from rehab. The staff gave her a thirty-day
AA sobriety chip, a red coin that symbolized a month of successful treatment. She said she was ready for a new start in life. I congratulated her
and took her to dinner in Chinatown. I made a point not to drink and
so did she. Since I was leaving for Texas in the morning, she asked to
borrow my car, and I agreed. So Elizabeth dropped me off at Dean's,
and I watched her take off with my little Datsun. I had a bad feeling
about it, but I hoped everything would be okay—for her and for my car.

I had arranged for Bonnie to come be with me in Texas once the
play got underway. I wanted to do something special to welcome her,
and I remembered a spectacular field of wildflowers on the outskirts of
town. The day Bonnie was due to arrive, I picked bunches and bunches
of flowers and took them back to the house where I had been put up by
the production. I placed them on the rafters and the wagon-wheel chandelier; I loaded up the bedside tables and even the top of the bed with a
profuse expression of my love. When I came back from the airport with
Bonnie, she stopped short and beamed at the beautiful room. "Aw, Russ,
they're beautiful, and that's such a sweet, welcoming gesture," she said.

I was pleased my inspiration had gone over so well and overjoyed to have her there with me. Later that night, Bonnie suddenly awoke from a deep sleep and sat up in bed. "Something's crawling in my hair!" she said.

Turning on the lights, we discovered a whole village of ants had hitched a ride on the flowers and were climbing all over the bed—and us! I was afraid I had made a mess of things, but Bonnie didn't seem to mind. She thought it was funny and we both just laughed.

When the play ended, we rented a car and took a road trip, stopping in Carlsbad Caverns, New Mexico, on our way to El Paso. I was very excited to revisit this beautiful locale with my new love. Watching her face was a joy as we traveled from chamber to sparkling chamber, deep in the caverns, marveling at Mother Nature's sculptures. Every direction we looked was another unbelievably miraculous creation. Of course, when you're in love, everything seems even more amazing and beautiful than normal. Bonnie and I were in a state of ecstasy, enjoying every moment of our newfound love, our soul connection, and the incredibly inspiring trip.

The last time I had been in El Paso was to film *Take the High Ground!* in 1953. Again, I felt like I was seeing it for the first time. I rented us a hotel room with a balcony that overlooked the whole city. Of course, we went out to a Mexican restaurant for dinner. Then we stopped in a liquor store and bought a special bottle of mezcal from Oaxaca. Mezcal is like tequila's smoky, earthy older brother and comes from the heart of the agave plant. My favorite part is the worm at the bottom, which many people believe is a rite of passage that will give you a bit of a psychedelic experience. I've eaten the worm before and experienced something I can't quite explain, so I talked Bonnie into partaking. It would be a celebration of our union.

We took a blanket and our magic bottle out to our balcony under a million stars.

"If the worm wasn't in the mezcal, it would have turned into a butterfly, so after you eat it, don't be surprised if you flutter a little," I told Bonnie.

"How am I supposed to eat it when it's at the bottom of the bottle?" she laughed.

"The trick is to hold the open bottle upside down in your mouth. It'll slowly float down."

She did as I instructed, and I watched the worm gracefully dance into her mouth. We stayed awake for hours, drinking mezcal and making love. What an unforgettable night; the deliciousness of everything was overwhelming. No doubt about it, we were in love!

I brought Bonnie over the border to Juárez for a visit and told her about the last time I was there, when the guys had taken me to a brothel and whispered to the prostitutes that I was a virgin.

"You're not taking me to a brothel, I hope?" she laughed.

"No! Maybe a boot store but not a brothel."

We walked around until I spotted a western boot store, where I bought her a pair of beautiful red cowboy boots. She loved them and still has them to this day; she even wears them occasionally. After re-crossing the border to the US, we headed for the El Paso airport. It was time to go home, reminisce about our journey, and contemplate our future lives together.

Back in Los Angeles, I learned that after Elizabeth dropped me off at Dean's, she had gone straight to a liquor store and bought a bottle of booze. She then drove drunk on the freeway and got into an accident. She totaled my car and was arrested on a DUI charge. Luckily, I had insurance, so all I had to pay for was the deductible. But that was finally the last straw. When her girlfriend called to tell me how very sorry Elizabeth was, I told her to please never call me again. Not only was I upset about being without a car when I needed one, but also I was done with Elizabeth's cycle of addiction, and it was clear that there was nothing about me being in her life that could help her. I started divorce proceedings, and Bonnie would soon follow suit. We were almost free to be together.

Russ as Fred Kelly in *Human Highway*. Photo by Joel Bernstein.

Poster for *Human Highway*, distributed by Shakey Pictures.

Russ as Fred Kelly and Neil Young as Lionel Switch: two dorks biking into Otto's Corner in *Human Highway*. Photo by Joel Bernstein.

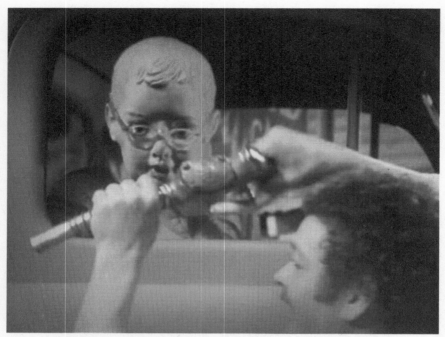

Human Highway: Fred Kelly fills up the truck as Booji Boy offers directions.

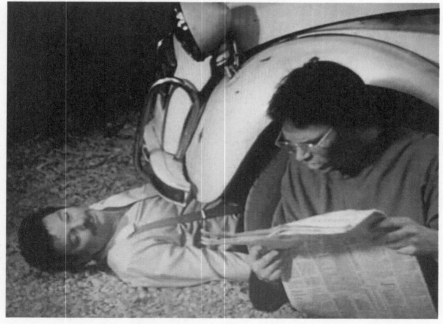

Lionel parks a car on top of Fred.

Final shovel dance in *Human Highway*. Left to right: Dennis Hopper, Russ, Neil Young, Elliot Roberts (in background), and Dean Stockwell. Photo courtesy of Jeanne Field.

Russ and Neil at the Boarding House in San Francisco, discussing scenes in the first version of *Human Highway*. Photo courtesy of Jeanne Field.

People magazine (June 1983):
Neil, Russ, and Dean at the
Human Highway premiere.
Photo by Paul Le Mar.

Celluloid fallout∧

To launch his anti-nuke film *Human Highway*, rocker Neil Young assembled a cast of partygoers in an underground L.A. parking lot. The film features '60s faces Russ (*West Side Story*) Tamblyn, center, and Dean (*Long Day's Journey Into Night*) Stockwell, right. "No one in the movie had a clue to what was going on," admits Tamblyn. Apparently neither did at least one critic, who dubbed it a bomb.

Russ meets singer-songwriter
Bonnie Murray as she performs at the
Topanga Corral (1980).

LOVEWEED

Poster by Wallace Berman on Russ's
bedroom door in Laurel Canyon.

Bonnie's promo shot. Photo by Donna Zweig.

CHAPTER 13

COMING OF AGE IN MIDLIFE

I was just starting to ease into my new life when fresh tragedy struck. In November 1981, I was shocked by the sudden drowning of Natalie Wood. We hadn't kept in close touch after I had dropped out of Hollywood, but she had remained like a sister to me since we had starred in *West Side Story* together. I couldn't help but think back to the time I had seen RJ Wagner lash out at her during our innocent game of "Truth," when she had chosen an Academy Award over their marriage in response to my theoretical question. I recalled how they had broken up not long after that and how melancholy she had been during our walk on the beach in the breakup's wake. I had tried to convince her that her personal problems would pass, but I don't think I got through. Clearly her issues were deeper and darker than I had known. I will always believe there is more to the story of what happened to her the night she drowned. I was no stranger to grief by this point, but my experience didn't make the loss any easier, and I was brought low for a time. Fortunately, the power of love continued to transform my life in miraculous ways.

That December, Dean married Joy, and not long afterward, he asked Bonnie and me to travel with them to visit Dennis at his new property near Vermilion Cliffs in Arizona. It was a small piece of land, but Dennis wanted to plant half a dozen trees there to cast some shade on an otherwise barren landscape. He had invited a bunch of his friends to make the journey to Arizona and help him work on his newly purchased acre.

When we finally rolled up in Dean's Cadillac, we discovered that Dennis's truck, with six baby trees in its bed, was high ended, stuck on some rocks up the hill. We tried getting it off by rocking it like a teeter-totter, but nothing worked. I walked back to the highway and managed to flag down a tractor driver, who pulled Dennis's truck off the rocks. This was not an auspicious start to our work, and it got worse from there, as Dennis was drunk most of the time, yelling and raving into the remote desert night. He screamed about how the FBI was watching him, and his paranoia was very uncomfortable to be around. We did manage to get the trees planted and watered, but of course, I learned they died not long after we got them in the ground.

As a break, we drove to Lake Powell and rented three large motorboats. Bonnie and I were happy not to be in Dennis's boat. He stood in the bow, looking like Napoleon with a bottle of tequila in his hand and ranting bombastically about nothing in particular. Things just got more surreal from there. We were accompanied by several actors, a jewelry salesman, and a drug dealer who had brought psychedelic magic mushrooms. I got stoned on the hallucinogenic drug and had a dreamlike walk in the desert with Bonnie. The impact was so strong that I became disoriented and thought I was having a seizure. We ended up back in our motel room, where I rested until I finally came back down to earth.

For Dennis, it was the alcohol, rather than anything stronger, that was proving to be a major problem. First, he got stopped by the highway patrol and was given a warning for driving erratically. We all ended up at a local bar, where Dennis continued his manic behavior. When he stomped on a scorpion, I was sure it was a bad omen. The next night, he was arrested for drunk driving. He was still in jail when we returned to Los Angeles.

———

We returned from the tumultuous adventure with Dennis and retreated to the Eastern High Sierra for some much-needed rest and solitude. On

July 6, we joined our friends Genie and Joseph Pawlick at their camp-site to watch a full eclipse of the moon. We were high up in the aspen forests at an elevation of about nine thousand feet. The camp trailer and tent were set up on a remote spot at the base of Mount Wood in Mono County. We had all the provisions and gear we needed to stay up there and watch an amazing display of nature, far from the city lights. Getting ready for the eclipse, we gathered deadwood for the firepit.

It was a clear night with a gentle summer breeze rustling the aspen leaves. When the shadow of the earth began to slowly cross the moon, I decided to stroll down the dirt road. After I'd been walking for about half a mile, the moon darkened and began to turn bloodred. Everything became so still; not even the night birds or coyotes were calling, as if they, too, were watching. I figured it was a good time to get back up the road to our camp. However, I could no longer see a thing in front of me. But I discovered that if I looked up while I was walking and fol-lowed the aspen treetops that lined either side of the road, I found an opening—a river of stars above me formed a path for me to follow. It was a fantastic experience, walking for a long distance, being guided by the only thing I could make out: the sky. I finally reached our campsite, where we all enjoyed the fire with a good bottle of tequila and the whole cosmos above us. As the moon crossed the sky and returned to its full brilliance, Bonnie and I snuggled into our sleeping bags. Upon returning to Point Dume, we found out that our lives would be forever changed. Bonnie was pregnant. Just like that, my world was turned upside down.

On September 12, 1982, my Topanga artist friend George Herms held a small party at his big studio in downtown Los Angeles. It's a date I remember well, for reasons you will soon understand. This gathering seemed like the perfect moment to introduce Bonnie to George. He immediately liked her, as did everyone else there. I took George aside and told him our joyous news. "I want to spend the rest of my life with Bonnie—and we're going to have a baby!"

George looked at me with his wise smile. "Well, you better tie the knot then," he said. He reminded me that he was an ordained minister from the Temple of Man in Venice. In fact, we both were.

Suddenly, inspiration struck me, and I proposed to Bonnie on the spot.

"But I'm still married!" she said.

"Well, we'll have a spiritual marriage. That's even better, and we'll make it legal later."

She smiled and whispered, "Okay."

George performed his crazy jazz wedding by blowing through a portion of garden hose that had the mouthpiece of a trumpet on one end and a funnel on the other. It sounded like a herd of elephants was celebrating our nuptials! Although his approach was somewhat unorthodox, it sealed the deal. Now, our union was official—well, sorta.

We still had some life details to iron out. That fall, there were terrible fires in the Santa Monica Mountains. We headed down the coast to check out the situation, and the Santa Ana winds were tearing flaming tumbleweeds from the cliffs and tossing them onto the highway. One narrowly missed our car. The highway was closed, so we drove on the wrong side of the road to get back home. Once there, we couldn't rest, though. We were afraid the flames would jump the Pacific Coast Highway and burn us out of our little love nest. It was time to leave!

Bonnie had a dear friend named Pamela London living in Santa Monica, who informed us that a vacant apartment was available in her building. I had no money, but I thought if I called the Screen Actors Guild, they might give me a loan. They invited me in for a meeting.

"How much money do you have in your bank account?" the interviewer asked me.

"I don't have a bank account," I answered sheepishly.

As I'd had such a successful movie career, it was embarrassing to try to explain how I had ended up being so broke. I had abandoned all my wealth and fame for the sake of art. I was feeling desperate, but the interviewer couldn't have been nicer. The guild came through for us, and he wrote me a check for $5,000. We were on our way! For the first time in years, I opened a bank account and actually had a little nest egg.

Even though I was mostly getting by on unemployment insurance and an occasional residual, Bonnie and I managed to live a pretty exciting life. We drove to San Francisco and visited Neil's ranch once again with Bonnie full of baby. Only this time, we stayed in a guest room in the big main house, tucked up in a loft with beautiful oak trees and redwoods all around. We visited and dined with Neil and his wife, Pegi, for several nights. They took us to the Mountain House restaurant, where some years later Neil shot the video for his hit song "Harvest Moon," which he wrote about Pegi. What great food and such a warm, cozy place to dine. Then we headed down to the city to see Jack Hirschman give a poetry reading. Jack took us on a tour of all the smoky bars, like Specs' on Columbus Avenue, and backstreet jazz joints. For me, poetry, art, and music are the languages of the soul. Bonnie loved the new vistas of contemporary art, jazz, philosophy, and politics that were opening up before her. Jack was an inspiration, and he and Bonnie had a grand time singing old commie songs together. Having sometimes been unsure about the crowd I hung around, Bonnie was relieved to meet Jack, who she instantly admired and adored. We also visited with Michael Mc-Clure and his wife, Amy, at their home in a beautiful, wooded area of Oakland. During every visit, his reading was music to our ears, and it was magic to be with this handsome and famed mystical poet.

—

The prospect of having a child was heartwarming and also overwhelming. I had spent so many years wandering and wondering whether I would ever be a father, especially at this late stage in my life. Nearing the age of fifty as I was, I had finally given up on the possibility.

But now, it was happening, and my adrenaline was running high. Our ob-gyn, Dr. Ross, gave Bonnie a prenatal sonogram, and we happily discovered our baby was a girl. I couldn't have been more jubilant.

Early on, I found a crib, started fixing up the nursery, and began thinking about implementing safeguards in our apartment. Friends who already had children gave us baby clothes. As if Bonnie weren't beautiful enough already, she was glowing now. For the first time ever, I was sensing something almost holy happening in my life, and it resonated deeply within me, like a sonorous bell gonging in my little brain. I was waking up, and I knew my reality was about to change. I was driven to follow my heart straight to the birth of our daughter.

My lucky number has always been four, and I couldn't have been more pleased when Amber Rose was born at 4:44 in the morning of May 14, 1983. Bonnie and I slept in the hospital room with Amber nestled in her mother's arms. As the sun was rising, I walked down to get some fresh air and have a smoke. When I stepped outside, I was paralyzed with wonder and could do nothing more than stare at the pink sky. I had just been at Bonnie's side for an all-natural, twenty-four-hour childbirth. My mother, Sally, and Bonnie's sister Andie helped us with the delivery. Bonnie was so strong and brave, but there was a struggle toward the end.

"The baby is in distress," Dr. Ross said. "And if she doesn't come out on this contraction, we'll have to do a C-section!"

"No way!" I said. "We've come too far." I had trained with Bonnie for the birth, and I had learned in our Lamaze classes that if we had Bonnie squat down, the gravity would help. So Andie got on one side and I got on the other. We lifted Bonnie up and into a squat, and out came Amber Rose Tamblyn into the world. I even got to cut the cord!

In the wake of this miracle, I was in a state of shock. "I'm a father—a father," I kept saying over and over.

When I ferried Bonnie and our newborn daughter home from the hospital, it was comical. I have a reputation for driving fast and furious, like the wild Mr. Toad, but suddenly I was as cautious as if my cargo were a sensitive bomb that might explode. Being responsible for our little family that I loved so much definitely matured me—and fast!

I wasn't the only one who experienced a profound maturation at this time. Shortly after Amber was born, I met up with Dennis and found him greatly changed. Speaking in a new calm, quiet tone, and with a humbled self-awareness, he shared the story of the crazy adventure that had caused him to undergo his dramatic transformation. He had gone down to Mexico to make a movie, gotten fired, and experienced a psychotic break, drunk and naked, in the streets of Mexico City.

He told me that he had planned to walk, naked, all the way back to the United States. However, residents of the city wrapped him in blankets and called the police. Eventually, when Dennis sobered up, he was brought to the US border and handed over to some medics. They took him to a Los Angeles hospital, where he spent many months in rehab. The new Dennis was pretty amazing. Bonnie and I, along with George and Louise Herms, took Dennis and his lady Ellen for a walk on the Venice Boardwalk next to the sandy beach and the majestic Pacific. He loved the "scene" and decided right then and there to move to Venice.

—

I spent the next few years adjusting to my role as a family man. As blissed out as Bonnie and I were with our beautiful daughter, we had more practical concerns, like how we were going to support ourselves. I was still receiving some residuals, but when Elizabeth and I divorced in 1983, I split them with her.

And then in 1988, I got a call about Elizabeth. She and her mother had ended up living in a trailer in Arizona, where Elizabeth was getting sicker and sicker. She had severe liver disease, and she was swelling up, but she wouldn't stop drinking. Finally, her mother called 911, and when she went to the door to let the paramedics in, Elizabeth locked her out. In the end, she just sat in her chair and drank herself to death. The official cause of death was cirrhosis of the liver. I was saddened but not shocked to hear the news.

Now busy with my new duties as a partner to Bonnie and father to Amber Rose, I couldn't help but reflect on how much my life had transformed. It was almost twenty years since I had walked away from Hollywood, and the industry had changed a great deal as well. Many of my old compatriots had retired or passed away, and tastes were different. Even the sporadic B-movie work and supporting roles on television shows I had managed to land in the past decade began to dry up. I continued to find theater work where I could, and I was still devoted to making fine art and communing with my creative compatriots, but I wasn't sure what was next for me in terms of performing. Thankfully, Bonnie deferred her music career. She was a terrific graphic artist and procured many jobs that kept us out of trouble.

In June 1983, *Human Highway* finally had its official premiere at a theater in Westwood Village in Los Angeles. Neil and Pegi flew down from San Francisco and invited Bonnie and me to celebrate the night with them. The four of us were to have dinner at Neil's hotel, L'Ermitage, but the power went off and the restaurant was closed, so we drove our stretch limo through McDonald's for cheeseburgers.

As I've said before, the plan for *Human Highway* was to have no plan, and apparently it showed. The previous year, Dean had flown up to San Francisco to see Neil's first cut. As he later told me, his first response was that the pace was "a little slow" and people might get bored. "Good, I like slow," Neil had replied. "Let them get bored."

When Dean called me to report all of this, he said, "We're in trouble."

The whole project was a farcical blend of fantasy, reality, and who knows what else. We thought we were fabulous, and we couldn't wait to see how it had all turned out. We, of course, loved it! My favorite review declared that *Human Highway* was like *The Wizard of Oz* on acid.

Over many years, Neil continued reworking the film, adding subtitles and a comedic radio-style voice-over, narrating a commentary on the not-so-linear life in Linear Valley.

It does have that unique Neil Young touch: humor, social commentary, fantasy, and rock 'n' roll.

Now it has become a cult classic and is much beloved by Neil's fans—including me!

—

Times were hard financially, and I had to take on whatever odd jobs I could find to support my family. Bonnie's dad, Alex, was close to the renowned luthier Hans Weisshaar, who was considered a master of stringed instruments. He had a studio in Hollywood where he built and repaired them, and he even wrote a book, *Violin Restoration: A Manual for Violin Makers.* Bonnie was the art director and graphic artist for the book. Through these relationships, I was hired to paint his decorative wrought-iron sign with gold leaf and red roses. I really needed the money and was glad to be working. While on a ladder, painting the flowers, I looked up the block and saw where the RKO studios had once been. I remembered doing my first movie there when I was just thirteen years old. *How ironic*, I thought to myself. *Look how far I've come: half a block.*

Around this same time, I got an offer to appear in the Stephen Sondheim musical *Follies* at the Pittsburgh Civic Light Opera. I was a little hesitant because the music in this show is extremely difficult and really requires a professional operatic singer to do it justice. But Bonnie said she would help me to prepare, and it paid well, so I took the gig.

Follies was fun. On show nights, Bonnie and Amber stayed backstage with me, in what was Amber's introduction to showbiz. When I had a number to perform, the showgirls would hold Amber so Bonnie could go out front and watch me. One night, we took Amber to a theater near the opera house where Joni Mitchell was performing. I had gotten to know her after she had visited us several times on the *Human Highway* set. So she said to come down and see her after her performance. Of course, she was incredible, and following the show we went backstage to say hello. She was blown away by Amber and tenderly held her on her lap and kissed her tiny feet.

During these years, I still saw Dean and Dennis often. In 1985, they both worked on David Lynch's film *Blue Velvet*. When the shoot wrapped, Dennis threw a birthday party for David in late January 1986, at his Venice home. I went with Dean. When David was opening birthday cards, one of them featured a picture of a guy surrounded by sexy women. It had some funny line printed under the photo, and we all laughed. I happened to be standing next to David. "Hey, Russ," he said in his high, quirky Boy Scout voice, "how'd you like to be this guy?"

I was beyond all that now, and so I said, "What I'd really like, David, is to work with you sometime."

"Okay, next project," he chuckled.

Of course, this kind of talk happens often in Hollywood—I knew better than to take it too seriously. What I didn't realize was that David Lynch is a man of his word, and he would propel me into one of the greatest adventures of my acting life. But before that, there would be another surprise coming my way.

—

Bonnie and I were settling into family life when I got a call in the spring of 1986 from my agent, Sharon DeBord. She told me that a man named Lou Rhodes was trying to get ahold of me concerning a girl I had known in Topanga. "He can't talk to you because he will be in court all day," Sharon said.

Uh-oh, I thought. *My past has caught up with me.*

But when I finally called him, I found out he was a tennis player and was *on the* court all day, not *in* court. Apparently, according to Lou, I had a daughter. Another one. When I told Bonnie I thought I had a second daughter out there, she got real with me. "You probably have *lots* of them out there!" she said.

I did have fond memories of the girl's mother, Betsy, who had been my lover in Topanga. It was the late 1960s, and she was a free-love spirit woman, and even though she had asked me to photograph her when she was pregnant, she never hinted the baby was mine. Later, I would find out that Betsy's reasons for not telling me about my role in her pregnancy were quite well founded. As she was aware, I was immature and a playboy, and knowing I would not be ready to step into the responsibilities of fatherhood, she had decided to raise our daughter on her own.

I invited Lou Rhodes over to our apartment to share the pertinent information. This new daughter, China Faye, had created a beautiful scrapbook to share with me with photos of her life from birth up to age seventeen. When I started going through the scrapbook, I immediately felt a deep sense of connection, and I could see right away that she was a Tamblyn. Her baby photos looked just like mine, and I had to hold back my tears. I talked with Bonnie to see if it would be okay to bring her to meet our family and her little sister, Amber Rose. Of course, being the understanding person she is, Bonnie wholeheartedly agreed.

I flew China down from Oakland and met her at the airport. I wanted to go by myself, and I took a single red rose to greet her. In those days, you could still meet people directly at the gate. As I was riding up the escalator, she was riding down. We locked eyes, and I knew right away she was mine. We hardly talked on the drive from the airport to our home. Amber was now three years old, and Bonnie welcomed China with open arms. Instead of being fifty and childless, I suddenly had two daughters. I hadn't even known I had been missing anything, but now my family was complete.

It wasn't long after China came into my life that I returned to my place in the public eye, thanks to my role as Dr. Jacoby on *Twin Peaks*. I was even featured on an episode of *Lifestyles of the Rich and Famous*, even though I wasn't at all rich and barely famous. What they were really interested in was the tale of my budding relationship with my secret daughter, China. She was a beautiful young woman of twenty who had become best buddies with six-year-old Amber. The producers filmed China with Amber in her lap on a swing at Amber's school. China's beautiful auburn curls floated through the air behind her, making her look like a Pre-Raphaelite nymph. I found the show's telling of the events, with the melodramatic narration of Robin Leach, mushy and a little silly, but I agreed it was an incredible story with a happy ending.

A few years later, I was offered the lead part of the sheriff (played by Burt Reynolds in the movie version) in a production of the musical *The Best Little Whorehouse in Texas*, which was to be staged in Portland, Oregon. So I asked China if she would like to join me, and she excitedly accepted. She was a very big help to me. In the morning, she made me healthy protein smoothies. On weekends, we took long hikes in the gorgeous canyons just outside the city. Sometimes we took days off and enjoyed the beach house that had been offered to us by the theater's producers. This was our first opportunity to be together for an extended period, and it was a great chance to share our life stories, talk for hours, and bond.

As the years went by, our family grew so much closer together. Mysteriously, China even looked like Bonnie, so everyone thought she was our daughter—and she kind of was. Over the years, China began to join in on more and more of our journeys and adventures. And we also grew close with her mom, Betsy, who we would frequently visit in San Francisco. For many summers, we would drive to Colorado to visit Bonnie's family, and Amber and China would sing Madonna songs in the back seat, all the way there and back. Those were happy days.

When they were older, my daughters gave me one of the most meaningful gifts of my life on a Father's Day we spent together in San Francisco. They said they had a Father's Day gift for me and wanted me to meet them at a sushi joint in the city, where we would have lunch and they would give me their present. When they kept ordering me glasses of sake, I sensed they were trying to get me drunk but couldn't figure out why. Finally, they seemed to feel like I was ready. "Come with us," they said.

I had no idea what they were up to, other than that their secret was something to do with my Father's Day present. I followed them across the street, staggering a little from the sake, and they led me into a tattoo parlor. I had sworn up and down that I would never get a tattoo, but they had already prearranged for all three of us to get the same tattoo on our arms: a mark I had created back in the 1960s and still use as a signature on art pieces and special stationery. I was so moved that my two daughters would want to bond our hearts with my mark in this way, and it was one of the best gifts ever—right up there with the arrival of my two daughters in my life.

First rendezvous in Odessa, Texas.

First family Christmas photo with Bonnie, Russ, and Amber. Photo by Donna Zweig.

Russ and Amber Rose at Big Sur (1983). Photo by Bonnie.

Dennis Hopper, on the left, with Bonnie and Russ on the Venice Boardwalk.

Dad and Mom with brand-new baby Amber.   George Herms and Dennis Hopper.

Friends-and-family reunion in Venice with Dennis Hopper, his girlfriend Ellen Archuleta (left), Bonnie, Louise, and George Herms (1983).

China Faye with her mama, Betsy: Topanga Canyon (1969).

Russ's mom, Sally, meets her new granddaughter, China Faye. Baby sister Amber is delighted.

Russ with his family of girls—Amber Rose, Bonnie, and China Faye—at the twentieth Woodstock anniversary (1989).

Russ and China in the
Twin Peaks era (1991).
Photo © Wayne Williams.

Russ, China, and Bonnie with Amber in Santa Monica (1991).
Photo © Wayne Williams.

China and Russ in Telluride: their first trip to Colorado.

CHAPTER 14

THE OWLS ARE NOT WHAT THEY SEEM

These years contained some of the happiest and most rewarding moments of my life as I learned to approach fatherhood and matrimony with a new, deeper consciousness I had never before possessed. But it was also extremely challenging. Real personal growth doesn't just happen on its own, and I often found myself struggling to handle my emotions. I was used to being able to do as I pleased and come and go as I liked. As thrilled as I was by how beautifully my life had blossomed with all these new connections and responsibilities, it wasn't entirely natural for me to take on such roles. And so I was trying to develop the tools to do so in real time.

On top of that, we were constantly stretching ourselves to make our financial life work, and there were many professional near misses and disappointments, which it was hard not to take personally. For years, I had pinned my hopes on the release of *Human Highway*, not only because it was a passion project but also because I hoped it would receive popular and critical acclaim and launch me back into mainstream pop culture. That most certainly did not happen. So in the mideighties, when I was in my early fifties, I found myself auditioning again, and as I undeniably aged further from my days as a fresh-faced matinee idol, this grew even more disheartening. I can't tell you how many times I went in to meet with casting directors who raved about how much they had loved my earlier work and then didn't give me the part. One time I even read for a role that was described in the script as "an older Russ Tamblyn," and I still didn't get the part because they told me I wasn't quite right. What can you even do with that?

We were able to cobble together a living from Bonnie's graphic design work, my unemployment benefits and residuals, the regional musicals I was cast in about once a year, and the few roles I landed in B movies like *Necromancer* and guest spots on TV shows. But even these weren't guaranteed. For years, it was understood in Hollywood that pretty much any former star could find work on the long-running TV show *The Love Boat*. But I couldn't even get cast there! I was at peace with my life's choices, but these rejections did bring me down.

Thankfully, during these challenging seasons for our family, Bonnie had reason to gain some support that ultimately benefited us both. Initially, she sought out an art therapist to work through some old wounds from her childhood and the death of her mother, and to learn to cope with and support her father's mourning after that devastating loss. He and Bonnie had a loving relationship, which could turn very turbulent at times. Bonnie enjoyed such a positive bond with her therapist, Judy Leventhal, that when the subject of our marriage came up in their sessions, I agreed to meet with Judy, thinking I would be helping Bonnie. Of course, I soon gleaned from Judy that my contribution to our marital tensions—my problems with impatience and rage—had probably been learned from growing up with my own father, also a man prone to uncontrollable anger. Once I saw this through line, it was obvious. Even better, I learned that by working on my own personal development, I could handle my emotions in more constructive ways. Consequently, our family dynamics improved. It also allowed me to heal wounds from my past, and I was able to forgive my ex-wife Venetia, who was now a producer, for divorcing me when I wasn't ready. She and I even spent a few months in early 1987 developing a film project about troubled former star and good friend Bobby Driscoll, who had died under mysterious circumstances in March 1968.

So much had changed. I was now married to my third and final wife and had two daughters, and my life was rich with love and fulfillment. The project with Venetia didn't work out because we had creative differences—she felt that Bobby's emotional trouble had started because his small size had made him feel inferior, while my recent therapy had helped me to understand the impact of family dynamics, and I believed his parents had caused him deep emotional damage. Since we couldn't agree on how to present Bobby's character development, the project soon fizzled, but not before Venetia and I had a profound moment. One day, Bonnie and I went to Venetia's house for a meeting, during which I told Venetia I was now happy in my life. I remembered that when she broke up with me, she had said that someday I would thank her. I looked deep into her eyes. "You know what, Venetia?" I said. "You were right. Thank you."

Becoming more self-aware also helped me to internalize the teachings of the theological philosopher J. Krishnamurti, who has influenced my thinking hugely throughout my lifetime, since I was first turned on to him through my friendship with Wallace.

In 1972, when Krishnamurti gave a legendary four-day talk at the Santa Monica Auditorium, Wallace, George, and I were in attendance. George fell asleep (this was understandable, given the guru's slow and hypnotic delivery), but I was entranced. One of the central ideas of his teachings, which really got through to me, was this: If you want to know God, don't look for God. Instead, look for everything that isn't God, and you can't help but find what you seek. Or to put it another way: if you're looking for happiness or peace, that means you don't have it, and by training your focus on your search, you're putting your focus on what you don't have, which is not exactly a means for bringing more of something into your life.

Now as I revisited these teachings, I wasn't learning anything new as much as I was thinking about the same old questions with a fresh perspective, which made a big difference for me. All of this helped my life immensely—or probably more accurately, it helped the lives of those around me immensely. Except for times of profound grief, such as after my first divorce and the death of Wallace, I had always been a fairly happy-go-lucky guy. But the trick was to not always put myself and my artistry first, as I couldn't anymore, and to still be happy, which I was more and more. Although I was not immersing myself in my creative pursuits with the same devotion as I had during my Topanga years, I had learned to think like an artist and trust my gut, and those guiding principles never left me.

Sometimes my intuition showed up in surprising ways, like on an extremely hot August day in 1987. With the sun beating down and the temperatures in triple digits, our refrigerator broke. Before our food could spoil, I raced to pick up a bag of ice in our 1965 Mustang. It was a very special car because it had belonged to Bonnie's mother, and after she passed away, it became Bonnie's car. The license plate was *Moo 5*, her mother's nickname and a nod to her five grandchildren.

The freezer containing the ice was right inside the store's front door. I parked maybe twenty feet from the entrance, hurried inside, and paid quickly. In a matter of seconds, I returned to my parking spot to find the car gone! Like a dummy, I had left the keys in the ignition, and someone stole it. I called the police, who picked me up and drove me to the station, where I filled out a report. Then I walked home, holding what was now a bag of water.

When I told Bonnie what happened, she began to cry. "You left the keys in the car?" she said. "How could you?"

I was so upset and ashamed of myself that I headed back to the store in our second car, a Volvo, determined to find the Mustang. Pulling into the same parking space, I tried to tap into some kind of intuitive feeling of where the thief might have gone. Finally, without any idea of what direction I should go, I pulled onto the street. In a liminal, Zen-like state, almost as if someone else were driving the car, I kept moving forward. After several turns, there to my astonishment and wonder was the yellow Mustang, sitting in front of a little corner house. I wrote down the address, quickly drove to a phone booth, and called the police.

Back at the thief's house, while I waited for the cops, a short young man strode outside, carrying a small black canvas tote bag. He threw it in the back seat of the Mustang and drove off. My heart was pounding as I followed, trying not to lose him, unsure what I would do next.

Eventually, he parked near the beach. After walking up to the beachfront path, he began talking to several guys while pointing to the Mustang. Finally, a big truck passed slowly between us. With his view blocked, I ran up to see if he had left the keys in the car. Of course, he hadn't. But I grabbed his tote bag and threw it in my Volvo. Then I ran into a barbershop and asked if I could borrow his phone to call the police. Once again, I waited in vain.

The thief started to walk back to the car. I knew I had to do something! When he drew up next to the Mustang, I seized my chance, adrenaline pumping.

"Hey, man, you better stay away from that car," I yelled at him. "It's mine, and someone stole it. I'm just waiting for the police!"

This startled him, and he hurried away. When the police finally showed up, I gave them the tote bag, which contained the guy's ID with his address. Back at home, I told Bonnie everything, and thank God, I was in her good graces again, with an amazing story to tell. Now that was some first-class hokeypokey of which Wallace would have surely approved.

———

As I've already pointed out, the roles I've been most associated with in my career did not require me to audition, and the same again became true in the late 1980s. Almost a year after David Lynch's birthday party, when I'd expressed my wish to work with him, I got a call from my agent, Sharon DeBord. She had just received word from David Lynch's office that he wanted to see me about a new project called "Northwest Passage" he was working on with his cocreator, Mark Frost. This was a pilot for a TV show that would hopefully turn into a series.

When I went to see David, he told me, "The part I want you to play is a very eccentric psychiatrist named Dr. Jacoby."

As I headed home, I was already allowing myself to get excited as

I thought, *He didn't say "the part I'm considering you for." He said "the part I want you to* play*"!* I couldn't wait to tell Bonnie.

David kept his word and cast me. Having not done any significant acting work in years, I had to get used to the idea that I had landed a place for myself on a wonderfully strange and demented television pilot. I was a big fan of David Lynch and Mark Frost, but even as I pored over this unique and inventive script, I had no idea of the important role the show would go on to have in my own life, or in pop culture more broadly.

As I prepared to travel to Seattle to shoot the pilot, I began to consider my part and what I could bring to it. With only one scene to do, I was determined to make the most of it. I decided my character, Laura Palmer's nutty shrink, Dr. Jacoby, was really a loner pervert who didn't like listening to other peoples' problems when he was out of the office. I was talking this concept over with Dean one day, and he suggested that Jacoby should stuff cotton in his ears as a way to communicate the nuttiness of the character. I loved this idea, as it would add to my portrayal of him as silently slinking around in his sardonic, stoner-like bliss. So I packed some cotton balls in my suitcase, as well as a swimsuit and some new leather Pivetta hiking boots for walking in the woods on my days off.

While flying over Washington's beautiful landscape, I gazed out the window at the vast acres of timberland below. I couldn't help but think about infamous hijacker D. B. Cooper, who had parachuted out of a commercial jet with a large bag of stolen cash in 1971 and touched down somewhere in the Washington woods, never to be found by the FBI or seen again.

After landing at Seattle International Airport, I climbed into the car that had been sent for me, which I hoped was driving me to the Salish Lodge & Spa, just thirty miles from Seattle. This is the lodge near Snoqualmie Falls, where white water tumbles nearly three hundred feet over granite cliffs into the emerald river canyon below. It is this waterfall that graces the opening titles of every *Twin Peaks* episode. I had the whole weekend ahead of me to swim and relax before filming began on Monday. But hold on! The car pulled into a motel next to a freeway. There was no waterfall, no woods—not even a swimming pool. The motel was located in a grim industrial area without even a shopping mall or restaurant nearby. After checking into my room, I walked outside to look for a tree, but there were only lanes of fast-moving traffic. I couldn't afford to rent a car, and it wouldn't have done me much good anyhow. It began to rain, and it rained all weekend. At least I was rested when it came time to shoot.

Early Monday morning, I was driven to an abandoned hospital a few miles away, where I was due to film a scene in an elevator with my costar Kyle MacLachlan. I had heard so much about David's directing style from Dean and expected a wild man, but he welcomed me to the set with his distinctive, high-pitched voice and his great, wholesome enthusiasm, like a Boy Scout leader on a camping trip. "How are you today?" he asked.

"Fine," I said.

"Well, that's just swell," he said.

I explained to David why I had brought cotton for my ears.

"Swell," he said, again using what I would learn was one of his favorite words. "But I think earplugs would be more fitting for a doctor."

"That'll work," I said.

While rehearsing the scene, when Kyle introduced himself as Agent Cooper, I told David that I'd had the inspiration to take one earplug out and ask, "Did you say D. B. Cooper?"

David loved the idea but didn't think enough people would remember who D. B. Cooper was, so we settled on Gary Cooper. The scene seemed to go well. David is an actor's director; he doesn't stand back by the camera. He was right down there with the actors during our scenes and was enthusiastic about improvising on the set, which I had always loved. I was so happy to finally be working again on a project where my collaboration was encouraged—and even better, the project was something that felt like it had legs. Now, I just had to have patience and hope the show would get picked up, which is never a sure thing in Hollywood.

We also did some filming of the pilot in Los Angeles, and one day, I came home from the set around noon. Our front window was ajar, the screen off. Bonnie was out, so I knew something was wrong. Inside, I came upon a tall skinny guy in an old sailor hat. Our eyes met briefly, and then he disappeared into the back bedroom. Fearing he might emerge with a gun, I dashed outside and down into the parking lot. He ran out from the alley next to our building and kept going when he saw me. I jumped back in my car to search for him. After driving through Santa Monica and Venice, I finally had to accept he had gotten away. Back at home, I called the police and filed a report. They asked for his description and what he had stolen. That was when I noticed my favorite vintage bracelet, of old peso silver and rare turquoise, was missing. I was sad, but I must have arrived home just in time, because he didn't get away with anything else.

It had felt like a major violation to have this thief in our home, and it became my mission to find him. Weeks passed. Then, one day, as I left our parking lot and glanced in the rearview mirror, I saw a tall skinny guy in a sailor hat walking the other way. It was him! Turning around, I followed him as he knocked on several front doors. When someone answered, he said something and continued walking. I drove by him nonchalantly and recognized his short goatee. Now, I was quite sure he was the thief. After several blocks, he knocked on a door that no one answered and soon disappeared. I knew he must have broken into the house, and I memorized the address. Just before I arrived home to call the police, I saw my neighbor Armand and gave him the address, asking him to call the station and tell the officers I would meet them by the house.

The man was finally caught, hiding under a basket of laundry. I later learned he was a forty-one-year-old transient who had been on drugs when he broke into our apartment. He claimed he'd buried my bracelet in a nearby park, but even with a metal detector, I could find no trace of it.

Sometime later, his trial was held at the Santa Monica Courthouse. The prosecuting attorney brought me up to the witness box and had me go through my whole story in great detail. When he finally concluded and sat down, the public defender rose to question me. I was very nervous, thinking he was going to try to trip me up somehow. He looked at his paperwork and then gazed up at me. "Mr. Tamblyn, I only have one question to ask you," he said. "Was the arresting officer's name Krupke?" Of course, this was a reference to a song I sang in *WSS*, and I almost fell out of the witness chair! Some of the courtroom attendees let out a little chuckle.

"How do you spell that?" the judge asked.

"*K-R-U-P-K-E*," I answered as another round of laughter rose up.

That was it, and the serial burglar got nine years in jail!

———

It took nearly a year for us to learn the fate of the *Twin Peaks* pilot. During that time, we had a major reversal of fortune when Bonnie's father, Alex, passed away. When her inheritance came through, we went from being more than $10,000 in debt to being able to pay everything down and buy our condo in Santa Monica and a car. Not only was the loss of her father difficult for Bonnie, but it was bittersweet for me. He had always feared I would lead Bonnie into poverty, and he died just a few months before my career underwent a major resurgence. Still, we were grateful for all that he did for our little family through the generosity of his will.

While we were waiting to hear about *Twin Peaks*, I kept in touch with my old crew. For Dennis this meant attending his fourth wedding to ballet dancer, choreographer, and actress Katherine LaNasa. And in Dean's case, it meant visiting him on the set of the new hit television show *Quantum Leap*, in which he played a starring role. Dean told the producers I was one of the greatest talents in this town and they should hire me for *Quantum Leap*. It was the kind of exuberant pitch that only a real friend would do. After years of going out on hundreds of auditions and getting nothing, I couldn't believe it when they offered me a part in one episode on the spot.

Twin Peaks would, in fact, be made into a television series by ABC. That whole time, the character of Dr. Jacoby took on a life of his own in the corners of my subconscious. Since I knew from the script that he favored dressing in Hawaiian shirts, I figured some colored sunglasses would be the perfect accessory. So I strolled down the famous Venice Beach Boardwalk, checking out hundreds of pairs as I popped in and out of tourist stands. Finally, I narrowed my choice down to a pair with red lenses and a pair with blue lenses. I held both up to my face, trying to choose the best pair. Then the light bulb turned on in my head. "Of course," I said to myself. "One from each!" So I had a pair custom-made with one red lens and one blue lens.

When it was time to begin filming, I explained to David how the two different lens colors affected the bicameral brain. The red lens on the right eye added passion to the left hemisphere of the brain, which is analytical and better at reading, writing, and computations. The blue lens on the left eye cooled down the more wild and creative right hemisphere of the brain. David was thrilled by the idea of the glasses, but he had just one line of direction for me. "Let's not tell anyone why you're wearing them," he said. That's David Lynch for you. He loves a good secret.

On our first day of filming, I couldn't believe it when I entered a warehouse in the San Fernando Valley and—with its wood paneling, unpainted beams, and bearskins on the wall—it had been transformed into the interior world of Twin Peaks. It was as if we had been transported to the great Northwest. Meanwhile, a second unit traveled to Washington to film exteriors. I was absolutely thrilled to be working again, especially now that it finally felt like all aspects of my life—from the personal to the creative—were lining up to be fulfilling and enjoyable.

I had been out of the business for so long that some of the younger actors didn't know who I was. It took some time, but soon enough, the ensemble became tight. The show was such fun to make, and I was thrilled that my daughter China got to visit the set, meet everyone, and feel like a part of the series. What a talented cast! I was reunited with Richard Beymer, my long-ago castmate from *West Side Story*. Only he was different now—he seemed much more comfortable, and he really came into his own and was incredibly good in the role of Benjamin Horne. It was such a joy to work with him again, especially during a scene in an episode directed by Diane Keaton, when I as Dr. Jacoby try to cure his neurosis.

The future began to look bright for a fifty-six-year-old guy who had begun to fear he would never act again. Although at the time we had no idea what kind of a cultural phenomenon the show would become, it was clearly very special. Many talented creatives wanted to be involved, including guest stars David Bowie and Kiefer Sutherland. But for me, nothing was more exciting or creatively fulfilling than working with David Lynch himself. He gave me one of the best directions I have ever received. This was in a scene that occurs after my character has been conked on the head, had a heart attack, and landed in the hospital. Agent Cooper, played by Kyle MacLachlan, visits me in my bed and asks what happened. In a half-conscious state, I deliver this long speech. After filming it a couple of times, David leaned in close and said, "Try it once more, Russ, only this time forget about the lines, just ramble, and think about ghosts."

Closing my eyes, I remembered the brick of ice on the back of my neck in the graveyard twenty-six years earlier while I'd been shooting *The Haunting*. I opened them and began my speech.

One of my favorite moments occurred when several different chapters of my life overlapped while we were filming. Neil Young performed a concert in Los Angeles, and his manager, Elliot Roberts, reserved some tickets for me, Dean, and Dennis. I invited Kyle MacLachlan, and he came to my house before we left for the venue. At one point, Amber, who was eight or nine at the time and was a big fan of *Twin Peaks*, came running out of her bedroom. When she saw Kyle sitting there, her jaw dropped down to her knees and her eyes almost popped out of her head—Agent Cooper was in her living room!

Twin Peaks first aired on April 8, 1990, to critical and popular raves and jump-started my career again. Because my character wasn't in every episode and many of the other actors didn't enjoy doing publicity, I became the de facto spokesperson for the show. I often wore my Dr. Jacoby glasses, which were a big hit. My press junkets included a trip to New York City with the very intelligent and glamorous actress Joan Chen to appear on *The Joan Rivers Show*. Suddenly, I was doing talk shows again, from *Good Morning America* and *Live with Regis and*

Kathie Lee to *Entertainment Tonight* and *Late Night with David Letterman*. David asked me about where I had been, prompting me to tell him how I had dropped out to pursue fine art in Topanga. As I said, "It was during that time when everyone was reading books on how to meditate, and I was trying to find one that taught you how to stop meditating." To which David laughed and replied, "How to break the trance." Yep, that sounded like the story of my life.

Back home between press appearances, I threw myself into fundraising for the school Amber was attending, Santa Monica Alternative School House (a.k.a. SMASH). I had the inspiration to hold a *Twin Peaks*–themed auction. David's production company was kind enough to donate memorabilia, including T-shirts and Laura Palmer diaries, for us to sell. Kyle MacLachlan attended the event, and it was a huge success, raising $20,000 for the school.

There were lots of magazine stories and newspaper interviews with me and other members of the cast, and there were even photos of Bonnie, China, little seven-year-old Amber, and me in *People* magazine, as well as press all across the country. I also traveled to cities around the US and Europe. During the summer of 1990, I was the grand marshal of the annual Independence Day parade in Atlanta. That October, I flew to London for yet another *Twin Peaks* junket and then on to Madrid, where King Juan Carlos invited me to his palace. A huge *Twin Peaks* fan, he gave me a beautiful gift, a very elegant Pasha de Cartier fountain pen with an eighteen-karat-gold nib. Needless to say, I was overwhelmed!

I didn't think it could get any better, but 1990 ended on a high note when my old friend Debbie Reynolds asked me to perform at a benefit for her charity, the Thalians. The event was held at the Century Plaza Hotel in LA, and the producers had Debbie, Tony Martin, and me recreate "Hallelujah!," a musical number we had performed together in *Hit the Deck*. It was wonderful to see Debbie again after so many years. She was still as energetic as ever, a bubbly delight and a true entertainer who had us all in stitches most of the time.

The finale of *Twin Peaks'* second and final season was aired on June 10, 1991. We were all devastated and shocked when it was canceled after only a year and two months. Not only was it beloved by critics, but it also received fourteen Emmy nominations. However, when we attended the Emmys and our composer, Angelo Badalamenti, did not win for best music, we knew it was all over. And we did not win a single Emmy. It was a huge cult phenomenon, especially with college kids, who did not have Nielsen rating machines in their dorms. There was a big movement to keep it going. College kids would cram into their dorm rooms on Thursday nights and have cherry-pie viewing parties, in homage to Agent Cooper's favorite indulgence on the show. But sadly, the end had come. It was simply too out there for the time. Yet so many people have told me over the years what an important television breakthrough it was.

The night of the wrap party, I was up on the roof with some of the cast members when I spied the head of ABC, Robert Iger. I walked over and asked him, "Why are you canceling *Twin Peaks*? Don't the suits realize how popular it really is?"

"Yes, of course, we know that," he said. "But the advertisers don't."

And as I was well aware, advertisers are the ones who foot the bill.

—

Later that year, Dennis Hopper's wife, Katherine LaNasa, staged a solo dance concert at a small theater in the Venice neighborhood with the help of George Herms. Bonnie and I were asked to attend the invitation-only performance, and we enjoyed her inventive choreography, including imaginative dancing on a wooden A-frame ladder that had been decorated by George. Among the few guests in attendance was Madonna. She was in disguise, with her hair dark, but I knew who she was. Being a dancer myself, I wanted to tell her how much I admired her dancing. So I walked over and introduced myself. She looked up at me for a long moment. "Well, you're sure bold!" she said.

"Excuse me," I said, "I certainly didn't mean to bother you."

After the performance, a small group of us walked several blocks from the theater to a restaurant on Main Street. Aside from Bonnie and me, Dennis and Katherine, and George, Madonna was with a date who looked like a young model. We all sat down at a table and ordered drinks and food. Everyone entered into conversation except Madonna, who was preoccupied with her boy. At one point, a couple of people came over to our table and asked Dennis and me for autographs. No one asked Madonna. She was totally unrecognizable, distant from everyone at the table, and, quite frankly, a bore.

—

I was on a high in the wake of *Twin Peaks'* success. I had loved acting regularly again, but unfortunately all the positive press during the show's run had not led to an influx of new work as I had hoped. And most days after it had been canceled weren't so triumphant. After yet another run of lackluster auditions, I read for Quentin Tarantino, who had just written the script for his debut feature film, *Reservoir Dogs*, and was looking to cast it. It was a terrible audition, and Quentin was very dismissive. "Whatever happened to you, Russ?" he asked.

I went home and had a couple of stiff drinks. That lessened the initial sting, but I couldn't get his words out of my mind. Even after a few days, his condescension affected me so strongly that I decided to retire. I was sick of going on auditions and not getting anything. Quentin's audition was the last straw. I just couldn't force myself to endure the humiliation of open casting calls any longer.

I asked my agent and manager to only contact me when I was offered a role and severed my other connections to the entertainment industry, except for those people in the business who were close personal colleagues and friends.

Russ plays Dr. Jacoby in the first season of *Twin Peaks* (1990).
© Twin Peaks Productions Inc.

Twin Peaks tarot card, designed and illustrated by Benjamin Mackey.

THE HANGED MAN.

Russ and David Lynch celebrate at the wrap party. Photo by Bonnie.

Spin magazine publicity shot with Lara Flynn Boyle, David Duchovny, and Russ (1990).

People magazine: Russ with Amber Rose and Bonnie (June 1990).

STAR TRACKS

▲ *Twin Peaks*'s Russ Tamblyn, 55, with wife Bonnie, 44, and daughter Amber Rose, 7, went to an L.A. benefit for Project Angel Food, which delivers a great piece of pie and other eats to AIDS patients.

Cover for *Twin Peaks* fundraiser for Santa Monica Alternative School House. Art by Bonnie.

Russ and Bonnie at the kitchen table surrounded by art. Left: David Lynch.
Middle top: Russ. Below: Dean Stockwell. Upper right: Wallace Berman.
Lower right: George Herms. Photo © Wayne Williams.

Russ in his studio in Santa Monica. Photo © Wayne Williams.

CHAPTER 15

Passing the Baton

Despite the disappointments, returning to acting was a thrill, but my passion for the fine arts had never waned, and so I was always gratified to receive recognition in this area as well. I had exhibited at the Los Angeles Institute of Contemporary Art in 1972 and then at the Los Angeles County Museum of Art in 1975. I also had a solo show at the Mizuno Gallery on La Cienega Boulevard in LA and sold some work there. That felt good! But it had been several decades since my last show.

So in 1992, I was excited to be invited to participate in a group show at Les Célébrités restaurant in New York's newly restored Essex House hotel. Bonnie and I were flown to New York City for the opening, and we were thrilled to be in attendance with the other artists. Actress Elke Sommer curated the show, which consisted of artwork by many celebrities, including James Dean, Anthony Quinn, Henry Fonda, and Red Skelton. But no one's work was more prominently displayed than Elke's, who had several of her own pieces hung in the central dining room.

The night of the opening reception, dressed in my tuxedo and ready for an elegant affair, I went to see where Elke had hung my artwork, but I couldn't find it anywhere. Finally, I asked a hotel employee about my piece, and I was led to a dimly lit room next to the main gallery. There, behind some coatracks, was my art piece. Elke's work was hanging in the main room, but my piece was literally impossible to see unless you moved some coats out of the way. I was furious. I immediately took down my piece and carried it up to my hotel room. Then I confronted Elke about this insult.

"We ran out of space," she said.

Go fuck yourself! I wanted to say.

Instead, the next morning, I packed my art in a pillowcase, and we flew home.

—

In 1993, I landed a fun role as a half Viking–half shark in Tim Burton's cult comedy *Cabin Boy*, directed by Adam Resnick and starring Chris Elliott. Around this time, two of my Jets from *West Side Story* took me to lunch and asked me what I was working on. I told them I was playing a shark, and they both stood up and walked away from the table. When they turned around, they said the Jets wanted nothing to do with Sharks! We laughed heartily.

Even though I had no lines and the film didn't get very good reviews, I absolutely loved doing it. I had to be specially made up like a merman, which was very uncomfortable. Once my ten-foot shark tail was attached to my body, I couldn't pee again until the end of the day. I accomplished this feat by not having coffee in the morning and drinking very little water. The crew carried me around everywhere and even built a special chair that allowed my tail to stick out. When I first got in front of the camera for a wardrobe test, I remembered my song from *West Side Story* and started to sing, "When you're a Shark, you're a Shark all the way!" It was a good joke, and everyone on the set laughed.

My part was shot in Long Beach in a gigantic water tank. I was in terrific shape because I had been working out at the gym and felt very comfortable going topless for this strange part. I could swim very fast by barely wiggling my tail, and that was incredible fun.

And then, suddenly, I wasn't the only actor in the family. That same year Amber landed the lead role in a school production of *Pippi*

Longstocking. I had never wanted Amber to follow in my footsteps, but when I went to see her on opening night, it was undeniable how talented she was—not just performing the lines with panache but seeming to embody the character completely. My longtime agent, Sharon DeBord, also attended the show and was equally impressed, to the point where she encouraged me to let Amber pursue what was obviously a natural calling for her. I was still wary of the industry and wanted to protect my young daughter from all the things I had experienced, but I agreed to let her go on a few auditions to see what might happen.

Although I had officially retired, I still took parts when they seemed enjoyable or involved people I liked. My old friend from Devo, Mark Mothersbaugh, had gone on to become the composer of many film and TV soundtracks. His wife, actress Nancye Ferguson, was about to act in a play with the strange title *Zastrozzi.* They invited me to take part in this very black comedy, which was also to feature actor David L. Lander, who had played Squiggy on *Laverne & Shirley.* Jonathan Penner played the title role. He was an excellent actor who went on to appear many times on the reality TV show *Survivor.* He was in great physical shape, and our scene together was very confrontational, with him climbing a rope while delivering his lines. I sat in a chair, patiently waiting for him to finish before doing my big speech. I felt like I needed to do something physical too, so one day in rehearsal, I put one hand on the back of the chair and the other hand on the front of the seat. Then I began to hoist my body through my arms and up into a handstand while performing my lines. When it came time for my last sentence, I lowered my body back through my arms, casually crossing my legs and sitting back down. It seemed to be very effective, and on opening night, the audience even burst into applause. The *LA Times* theater review by Richard Stayton included a mention of my move: "There is something undeniably hypnotic about watching Russ Tamblyn deliver dialogue while doing a handstand on a chair."

The performance ran for several weeks, and I enjoyed my part in it immensely. I hadn't really wanted to retire, and it felt good to be working again. I even received a Drama-Logue Award for Best Actor for my role in the play.

In 1994, my agent, Sharon DeBord, called with an offer to do a play, *Love Letters*, for one night. The salary was $7,500, and there were no lines to memorize. It was simply two lovers reading letters they had written to each other over many years. I couldn't believe it: $7,500 for one night of reading out loud. "I'll do it!" I shouted into the phone.

"Hold on," Sharon said. "There's a catch. The play is on a cruise ship, sailing around the world, and they would need you for three weeks. They'd fly both you and Bonnie first class to Nairobi, where you'd rent a car and drive to the port of Mombasa, Kenya. You'd spend a couple of nights there while waiting to board Holland America Line's *Statendam*." This was the largest cruise ship then in existence. "Then you'd sail up the east coast around the northeast end of Africa and on to the Red Sea."

Of course, we accepted, and from start to finish, it felt like we were on a paid vacation. I was to appear opposite former child star Margaret O'Brien, and I was very excited to work with her. When I was a kid, she had been in one of my favorite films, *The Secret Garden*, with my friend Dean Stockwell. She went on to star in many MGM films, including *Meet Me in St. Louis* and *Little Women*, but we had never before worked together.

We did our one performance in the exquisite Picasso Theater while our ship was traveling across the Red Sea, up the Gulf of Aqaba, to Jordan, for a trek to the most extraordinary ancient Roman city of Petra (where I was offered two camels for my beautiful wife). Then our journey took us through the Suez Canal, and we finished Greece. On our last night, we were joined by Vic Damone, another old friend and costar from my MGM days. The whole experience was wonderful.

Also that year, I was thrilled to be offered a solo show at a gallery on Main Street in Santa Monica. It had been years since I had exhibited so much of my work, and it felt gratifying to walk through the room and see pieces from every era of my fine art career. I was also pleased when, at the opening reception, Dennis Hopper showed up. I hadn't seen him in a few years, and it was wonderful to reconnect, especially because he was familiar with the way my art represented my long history in the city. It was October and the Santa Ana winds were blowing. There was also a large fire burning in Topanga Canyon. My RCA television that had been burned up in my house fire in Topanga was installed in the front window of the gallery. It was stuffed in a trash can full of old film strips and movie memorabilia. This gnarled, melted art piece, with a coat hanger for an antenna, actually still displayed a picture in black and white. I brought the moment full circle by tuning the TV to local news stations, broadcasting images of Topanga burning. It was a surreal scene: people gathered at the gallery window to watch the Topanga fire on a melted TV.

—

Much like my father was opposed to having me follow him into the family trade, I didn't really want my daughter Amber to be an actress. I knew how hard the industry was on kids. Since Amber was only eleven, I figured she would get burned out and give up on it soon enough. But it didn't take long for Amber to gain momentum. After landing a small part in an indie film starring Dana Delaney, Amber had the chance to appear in another independent film called *Biker Poet*. It was being produced by my friends Norbert Meisel and 1950s movie star Nancy Kwan, from a script written by her son, Bernie Pock, a budding young filmmaker who had been working on this passion project for years. Amber was thrilled to land the lead role and became very close to Bernie during the production. He passed away not long after filming, and Amber read a tearful tribute to him at his memorial service and would later dedicate a book of her poetry to him.

Next, in 1995, Amber was one of sixty young actresses to try out for a part on the long-running soap opera *General Hospital*. After several callbacks, it was down to Amber and one other actress, so Amber read a poem she had written and finally landed the role. Although she did not receive a contract right away, she was to regularly guest star as Emily Quartermaine. I was so proud of her and experienced a strange sense of déjà vu as I accompanied her to the set, now serving as the chaperone. This feeling was intensified early on when I was walking down the ABC Studios hallway with *GH*'s casting director, Mark Teschner, surveying cast member pictures on the wall as we talked. Noticing a large black-and-white photo of a distinguished-looking man, I stopped to look.

"That's John Beradino," Mark said. "He's been on this show for thirty years, since its inception."

"Oh, I know who he is—as a matter of fact, I helped him get started in show business."

Mark's jaw dropped. I explained how I had known John as the second baseman for the Cleveland Guardians, formerly the Cleveland Indians, when he auditioned for *The Kid from Cleveland* in 1949, and then how I had petitioned for him to land a part, helping to give him his start. Mark could hardly believe it. Not long after, I bumped into Johnny, who of course remembered me well for my role in his career. In fact, he insisted on giving me a VHS copy of the film because it had such significance.

At first Amber's role was to be only a ten-to-twelve-episode run, but the producers kept her on through the end of the year. This was a life changer for her. She had to adjust to a split education, partially attending her regular school while also taking classes on the set of *GH*. It was very different for her—instead of being in class with thirty other kids, she now had only one or two classmates.

Whenever Amber worked, she needed an adult on the set with her, and my mom, Sally, loved to take her to the studio and watch over her, just like she used to do for me when I was a kid. During this period, I went on so many auditions (too many), but even with my high-profile part in *Twin Peaks*, I couldn't seem to land anything. I organically found myself supporting Amber's career by stepping in as her manager.

Looking back, I feel fortunate that Amber's regular acting work meant we were both spending more time with my mother. She was seventy-nine, and her health had been declining. That September, we celebrated Labor Day as a family at my brother Larry's home. Mom delighted us by playing the piano, which she hadn't been able to do for several years. Only a few days later, she passed away, not quite making

it to her eightieth birthday. She had always supported me with her love
and her belief in my talent, and I'm so grateful she was able to do the
same for our daughter as well. After this, I took over as Amber's on-set
guardian. I have to admit it felt strange not being the main performer
in the family, but I was so proud of her success, and I quickly adjusted.
Amber had once been known as Russ Tamblyn's daughter, but suddenly, I was Amber Tamblyn's father! I felt like I was passing the baton
in a relay race, and I couldn't have been prouder. When soap operas are
filmed, there is no director on the set. Everything is directed from the
booth, and the actors have to work fast. When Amber was filming, I
would stand just behind the camera, and between takes, I would give
her some notes, or just a thumbs-up if she was right on, which she was
most of the time.

It was also fun for me to be on set again, even if not as a performer.
Hollywood was a remarkably small world, and I ran into many people
from my past, including Anna Lee, the mother of my first wife, Venetia
Stevenson, and the actor who had starred in *How Green Was My Valley*
and portrayed the matriarch Lila Quartermaine for a quarter century
on *General Hospital*. It was through Amber's long-running part on the
show that I was invited to Anna's eighty-seventh birthday party a few
years later. In attendance, of course, was her daughter, Venetia. Sadly,
Anna Lee was in poor health, and it would be the last time I saw her.

Amber did amazingly well as Emily Quartermaine. Although her
character had originally been written to only appear in a few episodes,
the producers were so impressed with her natural acting ability that they
kept her on the show for seven years. Twice, in 1999 and 2000, she won
the YoungStar Award for Best Young Actress in a Daytime TV Program.

In 1996, Amber took time off from *GH* to do a kids' fantasy film
called *Johnny Mysto: Boy Wizard*. In fact, Amber and I both landed
parts in the project, which was to be filmed in Romania of all places.
I jumped at the chance to do a film with my talented daughter, who
was now twelve. It was a pretty silly fantasy film, but we decided to do
it anyway because of the wonderful location and the money, and best
of all, I got to play an over-the-hill magician named Blackmoor. That

was right up my alley! I had loved magic as a kid, and I had even done some sleight of hand in *Twin Peaks*. Amber played a wild little character named Sprout who lived in a medieval time field. It was her first really good acting job, and she took to it like an old pro. She was animated and created a great accent and persona. Watching her do her scenes, I was thrilled by how terrific she was, and I felt so proud. I was also still her protective papa. A young actor named Toran Caudell played Johnny Mysto. Amber had a crush on him, but I watched her like a hawk and made sure she didn't get into any trouble.

We were given a few days off around the time of Amber's thirteenth birthday in May. We celebrated by taking a train up to Transylvania, which is north of Bucharest. The trip was pretty wild. We paid only ten bucks for a whole big train car all to ourselves and crawled up the Carpathian mountain range through wild virgin territory. We arrived in a green, forested valley known historically for its association with vampires and especially Vlad the Impaler.

When we returned to set, one of the strangest locations we worked in was a garlic forest outside Bucharest. First of all, it smelled awful, and second, it was filled with a million mosquitoes. Luckily, we had plenty of bug repellent. So we just kept spraying ourselves, but the poor locals who were hired as extras weren't given any, because the low-budget production couldn't afford it. Feeling sorry for them, we shared our spray with them as best we could, but most of the extras just had to suffer through getting bitten all day.

Amber learned a great deal about filmmaking on this project, from enduring the exhausting schedule and staying energized for late-night shoots that lasted until dawn, to becoming attached to the crew during our many intimate hours together and learning about another country. She also had a crash course in how exhilarating—and terrifying—stunts can be. Thankfully our special effects supervisor, Al Magliochetti, was very helpful to Amber and kept a close eye on her. In one scene, a group of soldiers was galloping through the woods on horseback, chasing Amber. She nearly got trampled, but Al pulled her to safety just in time. After several takes, one of the horsemen took an unintended and dramatic spill. As the horse crashed down in a heap, Amber screamed and fell to the ground, crying with fear that the horse had been injured. Al rushed over and consoled her. After I saw this display of his deep care, not only for his job but also for my daughter, we became fast friends. All these years later, we've remained in contact.

It was quite the adventure in a foreign land, but Bonnie helped with Amber's studies and kept everything on an even keel. Overall, it was a wonderful experience for our family.

———

Amber wasn't my only daughter whose life was blossoming during these years. Although China lived in the Bay Area and had her own life, we remained deeply connected. And in 1998, our family grew again when China became a mother to my first grandson, Dylan Roark.

Our family expanded even further when China fell in love with a wonderful guy, handsome rock musician and entrepreneur Elton Cunniffe, a seasoned musical recording engineer. He is of Hispanic heritage and speaks fluent Spanish, so in 2000, they were to be married on a Mexican beach in Zipolite, a tiny coastal pueblo in the southern state of Oaxaca. Bonnie, Amber, and I were in charge of decorating the little Volkswagen bug in which I drove China to the ceremony with bright paper flowers and streamers. Once there, I proudly walked her along the sand to join Elton.

The day after the wedding, we were recovering on the beach. Amber splashed in the surf, while Bonnie talked with Betsy, China's mom. I decided to go for a swim. I had always been a strong swimmer, and so I confidently swam out beyond the wild waves that were smashing against the shore. I reached the calmer sea, all right, but I couldn't get back! Big waves kept crashing over me. I couldn't move toward the shore at all. I realized I was probably stuck in a riptide and needed to swim sideways. I tried, but I couldn't get anywhere. It also dawned on me that I'd had a lot of mezcal the night before. I was becoming exhausted, and I could barely move my arms and felt like I couldn't swim anymore. All I could think was, *This is it. I'm gonna drown and ruin the wedding.* I tried yelling and waving to shore, but nobody noticed. Nothing was working. Finally, just as I gave up, a young local on a surfboard came out of nowhere and told me to hang on to a rubber tube. As I would later learn, he was aptly named Aguilar (taken from *águila*, meaning "eagle"). I was so wiped out I struggled to hold on, and he managed to swim me to the shore. When I got back to the beach, I flopped down on the sand. Bonnie came running over, terrified and relieved.

That night, a mariachi band played in the cabana. I drank tequila and sang and danced with family members and all the guests. I'd never felt so happy to be alive. We had more reason to rejoice when, nine months later, our grandbaby Vivian Racquel was born.

———

In 2000, Amber bid farewell to *General Hospital*, and I officially retired as an actor, having reached the point where I couldn't bring myself to go on one more fruitless audition. If someone approached me with a good part, of course I would consider it, but I was done putting myself out there.

As I contemplated the scope of my career, I felt proud. In 2001, we were due to celebrate the fortieth anniversary of *West Side Story*. I wish every actor could have at least one such epic stage or film production in their career—I am so grateful that this gem was mine. A special screening was to be held at Radio City Music Hall in New York City on October 6, 2001. And then, of course, it almost didn't happen. Those of us associated with the film had all been planning for this wonderful event for months when the September 11 attacks on the World Trade Center happened and everything turned into a nightmare. At first, we hoped things would calm down in the next month, but as the days passed, more disastrous information kept coming out, and the whole country was suffering along with New York City. It seemed like a terrible time to put all our focus on a movie. So Bob Wise, George Chakiris, Rita Moreno, and I decided to cancel our trip. But then Bob called back a few days later to tell us that Mayor Giuliani thought a *West Side Story* anniversary party was just what the emotionally trampled city needed, and the mayor had asked us to please not cancel our screening. How could we say no to that?

The mayor was right. Even though it had only been a month since 9/11, Radio City Music Hall sold out. In fact, crowds of people waited outside the theater and cheered us as we entered. After Bob, George, Rita, Richard Beymer, and I were introduced from the stage, the film began. We had all forgotten that the opening shot of *WSS* contains a panoramic view of the Manhattan skyline *without* the Twin Towers, because they weren't constructed until 1973. Well, the audience went nuts and started cheering what was a beautiful sight, even without the Twin Towers. It was very emotional to see and hear New Yorkers express their love for this tremendous city and for *WSS*. From then on, the movie was like a Broadway show; the audience applauded after every musical number. It was so touching to witness.

———

During the years I was celebrating the arc of my long and varied career, Amber was just launching the first chapter in her creative life, as a successful actor and writer. She published her first full-length book of poems with Simon & Schuster at the age of twenty and starred in such hit films as *The Ring* and *The Sisterhood of the Traveling Pants*. She received an Emmy nomination for the title role in the critically acclaimed TV series *Joan of Arcadia*. This was around the time I was stage directing, choreographing, and touring with Neil as part of his *Greendale* rock opera, and I became tight with Neil's bass player, Billy Talbot. We even wrote a song together on the road. Called "God and Me," it was about a young girl's relationship with God, and Neil played pump organ on the recording, and we hoped the producers of *Joan of Arcadia* would use it in the show. Ultimately, they didn't, but my chance to do a guest spot with Amber was gratifying enough, especially as my part was "God the dog walker."

"Maybe, now that I'm God, you'll listen to me!" I said.

"I doubt it!" she replied.

You can see why I love working with the next generation—we keep each other in line, and it gives me such deep pride and pleasure to watch them take up our work.

Joan of Arcadia sadly only lasted two seasons, but Amber continued to land good roles. In 2007, she played the title role in *Stephanie Daley*, a Sundance project. The movie was filmed in upstate New York, where Bonnie and I shared a beautiful old house with Amber during the shoot. We became friends with Amber's costar Tilda Swinton. She invited us to visit her sometime at her home in the north of Scotland. Being Scottish herself, Bonnie was thrilled by the invitation, and we vowed to take Tilda up on her kind offer as soon as we could. Amber gave a powerful performance and won the Best Actress award at the Locarno International Film Festival.

Mustang caper in Santa Monica *Outlook* (1987).

'West Side' actor nabs car rustler

By Susan Loux
STAFF WRITER

A jaunt to the grocery store Monday turned into a real-life detective drama for actor Russ Tamblyn, whose gut instincts and sly resourcefulness helped him nab a man who stole his prized 1966 Mustang.

Best known for his portrayal of Riff, the manipulative, street-smart Jets street gang leader in the classic 1960 musical "West

CAR/BACK PAGE

Car
FROM PAGE A1

Side Story," Tamblyn was drawn into a tightly spun game of cat and mouse with a thief who led him through the alleys and side streets of Venice before forfeiting his catch.

"It's one of the craziest things that's ever happened," Tamblyn said. "If this were made into a movie, nobody would believe it."

Earlier that day, he had inadvertently left his car keys in the ignition when he stopped at the Lucky supermarket on Lincoln Boulevard for a bag of ice. When he returned to the parking lot minutes later, his space was vacant.

"I was blown away," he said. "The car was gone, and I was left holding a bag of ice."

He called the Santa Monica Police Department, then called his wife, Bonnie. It was a call he dreaded making.

The couple had recently inherited the yellow coupe from his mother-in-law. She had been the car's original owner and had fawned over it until she died. It was even equiped with personalized license plates, "MOO 5", reflecting her playful nickname.

Having broken his wife's heart, Tamblyn opted to walk the mile or so back to their Santa Monica apartment, leaving a trail of water drippings from the melting ice behind him.

"I felt just terrible that I could be so thoughtless and careless," he said.

By the time he got home, he had become determined to find the missing Mustang himself. With the spirit of a true sleuth,

Riff gets his Mustang: Russ Tamblyn with his wife Bonnie before their prized 1966 Mustang.

ROBERT E. CLARK/STAFF PHOTOGRA...

he dashed off to the scene of the crime in the couple's Volvo.

"I drove around the store once, and I felt like I picked up on this guy's scent," he said. "I don't really know how to explain it, but it was like I was being led. From there it was all automatic."

Without any clues, Tamblyn wove his way down main avenues and side streets and located his car in the 600 block of Vernon within 15 minutes.

He called police, then rushed back to the site, discreetly staking it out from across the street.

About 15 minutes later, a young man with a duffel bag sauntered over to the car and drove off. "He was as cool as a cucumber," Tamblyn said.

With Tamblyn on his tail, the man headed to Venice Besch, pulling off of the road at Speedway near Westminister. Tamblyn parked about 20 feet away.

While the man joined some friends on Ocean Front Walk, the actor darted to a nearby barbershop and called the police once more, then returned to his Volvo for cover.

Later, he was able to run to the Mustang, reach in through an open window, grab the duffel bag from the passenger seat and hide it in the floor boards of the Volvo.

About 10 minutes later, as

the suspect approached the ... Tamblyn yelled to him, "... had better stay away from t... car, it's mine and it's been ... len, and the police are on ... way," Tamblyn said.

With that, the man dis... peared along Ocean Fr... Walk.

Inside the bag, police fou... the suspect's driver's lice... and an employee orientat... packet from the same Lu... supermarket where the car ... stolen.

Anthony Hill, 21, who is st... ing with relatives in Venice, ... arrested on charges of gr... theft auto, a Los Angeles Po... Department spokesman said.

Russ and Amber
on *General
Hospital* set for
a scene from the
Nurses' Ball
(1997).

On the set of
*Johnny Mysto:
Boy Wizard* in
Romania: Russ with
Ian Abercrombie
and Amber (1996).

China and her papa,
Russ: a happy man.
Photo by Scott Hoover.

China's wedding in Huatulco, Mexico, with baby Dylan, China, and mama Betsy.

Fortieth anniversary of *West Side Story* at the Hollywood Bowl (2001).
From left to right, Rita Hyde, Nobuko Miyamoto, Jaime Rogers, Yvonne Wilder, a friend,
George Chakiris, Walter Mirisch, Russ, Talia (*WSS* dancer), another friend,
Maria Henley, Carol D'Andrea, Gina Trikonis, and Bobby Banas. Photo by Larry Mirisch.

West Side Story fiftieth anniversary in New York. Old friends and castmates left to right:
Bobby Banas, Russ, David Bean, Bert Michaels, Eddie Verso, and Harvey Evans.
Photo by Larry Mirisch.

CHAPTER 16

PACIFIC STANDARD TIME

Even though we were getting older, my compatriots and I were not ready to stop creating. In 2003, I received a call from Neil. He was on tour in Paris and playing some new songs he had written for his rock opera, *Greendale*, which he had begun performing live with his band, Crazy Horse. He had already directed a small version of the show on sixteen-millimeter film—produced at his ranch in Woodside—but had decided to do a big stage production to take on tour. Knowing that I had performed in an extensive array of theatrical shows all over the US and had deep experience in this area, he asked me if I would like to direct and choreograph the show, which would play in ten- to twenty-thousand-seat amphitheaters. Handing off these duties to me would give him more time to concentrate on the music. Of course, I said yes, and that was the beginning of a wonderful collaboration, which culminated with a very long tour: three times across the United States, a concert in Canada, and a Pacific Rim tour, including three cities in Japan and three cities in Australia, plus one concert in Hong Kong.

Several weeks after our initial conversation, Neil returned to the States and reached out with a follow-up call. "I need a little vacation, but I really want to talk to you about *Greendale*," he said. "Would you be willing to come to my house in Hawaii?"

He flew me there and met me at the Kona airport, which is on the west side of the Big Island of Hawaii. As he drove us along the coast, I marveled at the lava rock everywhere. We finally came to a driveway heading down the promontory, which is a piece of land that juts out over the ocean. This was Neil's property. Suddenly, I had a view of a big old two-story white wooden house on thick green grass that overlooked the clear blue ocean. Surrounded on three sides by water, his home was completely private and totally enticing. I called it Point Neil.

Neil showed me to my guest room, and I took a nap right away. When I got up, he was ready for the adventure to begin, and so was I. His wife, Pegi, was not there with him, so it was just the two of us.

"Let's take a swim first and then talk about *Greendale*," he said.

We dropped into the transparent water just beyond his house and luxuriated next to some giant turtles who were flippering by us. It took me back to the days of swimming at my beach house in Malibu. I could have lived in that gorgeous moment for the rest of my life, but there was work to be done, so we sat down in the kitchen, ate a big pile of sashimi, and began dreaming up our plan for the staging of *Greendale*.

Neil explained his brilliant vision for a new kind of musical, which involved combining his rock music with actors and dancers for a vibrant show with a message. *Greendale* was about some serious subjects, including the politics of environmentalism, media capitalism (which promotes the selling of commodities, no matter the cost to humanity), and corrupt government officials. It was a completely original idea that only Neil would've dreamed up. Aside from being a musical icon, Neil is an environmental activist and a passionate and impactful supporter of human rights and universal freedoms. He's constantly thinking of how he can incorporate his strong beliefs into his music and life. For the show, he would sing the songs with Crazy Horse and backup singers and dancers. I would handle the staging and choreography and play one of the show's characters, Captain John Green. It was a huge challenge and responsibility, but one I approached excitedly. I came up with the idea of working with nonactors and hiring local hip-hop dancers in the cities along the tour.

"Great," he said. "You're in charge of everyone."

I was sad when it was time to leave the island paradise and fly back to the mainland. But I was also eager to get down to work and create something fresh and fabulous with Neil.

We began rehearsals in San Francisco, which was our first tour stop. All of those who worked on the scenes I needed to choreograph really gave it their all, and I was very grateful. But it was definitely a challenge. Theoretically, it was exciting to work with nonactors, and the concept lined up with Neil's democratic approach to music and art. But it's hard enough for trained professionals to project their parts in ten- to twenty-thousand-seat amphitheaters, where much of the audience is seated far from the stage. It was an even greater challenge with nonactors, many of whom didn't have much experience or confidence on the stage. If they didn't make their physical moves big and bold, no one would be able to see them or infer the emotions they were meant to express with their actions. And then, after working fast and furious for the big show, whenever we got a cast ready for prime time, we moved to another city.

We developed a routine. My talented assistant, Marcy Gensic, would call ahead to our next stop and arrange to have a dozen new dancers audition for the show. Marcy would teach them the choreography, and then I would come before the performance and give everyone a polish. I staged family members, dancers, and crew members behind Neil and Crazy Horse, and as Neil sang the songs, everyone else acted out and mouthed the words. It was like there was a play unfolding behind him, with everyone coming out to sing and dance the big finale number, "Be the Rain," an anthem to fire up environmental activism. At the end, the dancing wasn't choreographed; we all felt the drive of Neil's guitar and the soul of the message. Everyone boogied and jumped around the stage. The crowd went wild, rocking out with Neil and Crazy Horse. This was not like other stage productions I had been a part of but a wonderful new kind of adventure. Also, Neil had several great performers open for him during the tour—Elvis Costello, Emmylou Harris, and Lucinda Williams—who I loved watching from the wings.

When we played at the Farm Aid show, many of the performers parked their buses together and hung out backstage. Neil invited me to go with him to visit Willie Nelson's bus. It was well known that Willie loved his weed, so the grateful farmers he had helped with his benefit grew some for him as a small, separate section of their crops. He had a huge barrel of pot that came from his farmers. I don't think Willie has ever had to buy marijuana, and let me tell you, this was the good stuff. I got so stoned that day I barely made it back to Neil's bus.

While on the road, I originally traveled with Crazy Horse, but I had recently given up cigarettes, and I could no longer stand the smell of it. Because many members of the band and entourage smoked, the stink of it was heavy in the tight quarters of the bus (at least for me). I'd open the window next to my bunk and stick my head out to get fresh air, but all that did was suck the smoke out the window after it first blew across my face. Finally, I asked for a change. I ended up on Elliot Roberts's bus, which was way more comfortable. Its other passengers included Neil's producer, Larry Johnson, as well as Eric Johnson (no relation). Eric played a major role in the show. He was also the tour director, who booked our hotels and kept things running smoothly. Mainly, though, he took care of Neil's needs, like hauling his guitars and walking his dog. One night, during a heavy rainstorm, Neil's bus was driving in front of ours. Neil called and asked Eric to make him a grilled cheese sandwich. Eric prepared the snack on a George Foreman grill, which he used all the time. The caravan of buses pulled over while Eric dashed out in the pouring rain and took the sandwich to Neil's bus. The door swung open, and Neil stuck out his arm, grabbed the sandwich, and promptly shut the door. Eric came back, soaking wet but happy.

"Hey, Eric," I quipped. "Be the rain, hey?"

I was having a great time and enjoying my creative role, but there was definitely a learning curve for me when it came to acclimating to the rock 'n' roll lifestyle, which was very different from how movies were made. Of course, not everyone got along on set, but generally, there was an easygoing camaraderie and shared goodwill because of the common goal of making the best film we could with the time and budget we had.

Rock had a different energy. While the shows themselves were electric and exciting, the rest of the time on the road could be a drag. The drives between tour stops were often long and boring, and it was easy to get on each other's nerves. Sometimes there would be tension, teasing, and backbiting on the tour. Everyone had their own little clique of friends and stayed as separate as they could from other crew members.

Also, the culture was much different from what I was used to in the theater. Even the way reviews worked was different for a rock 'n' roll icon like Neil. In theater, the reviews don't just focus on the stars; the many contributors that go into the show are mentioned, including the director, choreographer, set designer, and playwright. In all the *Greendale* press coverage, only Neil was reviewed, and he received credit for all aspects of the production, even those that others had created. I was also used to the main people in a production getting credit in the program. Neil's show didn't do this, and when I made him aware of the issue, he directed his manager Elliot Roberts to fix it. So they had thousands of new programs printed up, with everyone in the crew receiving their credit, which we all appreciated. By the time we got to the Greek Theater in Los Angeles, my name appeared in the program as director and choreographer, credits that were especially important to me given all the work I had done to bring my friend's creative vision to life.

When we played the Greek, it was so much fun inviting all my friends to see the show. My good friend and neighbor Norm Basham, a huge Neil fan, stood right in the front row when the band played the second half, with just Neil and Crazy Horse. While *Greendale* was incredible and inspiring, there was nothing like watching Neil rip it up with his classic guitar riffs wailing into the night over raucous rock 'n' roll that still possessed the same fire it had thirty years earlier. I must say, I never got tired of hearing Neil and Crazy Horse play. After my work with *Greendale* was finished, I would stand backstage on the sideline and take it all in. They rocked so hard, and the crowd went mad. All powerful performers, they delivered to the huge audiences night after night. That was, truly, the best part of the whole experience for me.

Bonnie joined me on the last leg of the tour, and I couldn't have been happier to see her. Even better, there was an opportunity for Bonnie and Amber to join everyone onstage at Radio City Music Hall to perform in the *Greendale* finale, even though Amber was quite busy with her acting career at the time. Amber's show, *Joan of Arcadia*, had become a huge critical success, so much so that even my tour mates made jokes about it, revising the name tag on my dressing room door from *Russ Tamblyn* to *Amber Tamblyn's Dad*. I had a good laugh over that and told them to leave it that way.

Collaborating on *Greendale* and being there to support my dear friend Neil was one of the highlights of my life, but when the tour ended, I was glad to go home. I told Bonnie no more tours for me. It was too hard being on the road without her, and I missed my life back home, working on my art and taking walks around the neighborhood together.

I might have grown too old to be a road dog, but I always jumped at any opportunity to create magic with friends, especially Neil. Once, when he asked me to choreograph the video for his song "People on the Street," I was there. He flew me to his ranch in Woodside. We had dinner, spent the night, and in the morning drove up to the city and filmed all over San Francisco. We planned to have Neil look like he was dancing, but actually, it was me. Neil wore a tuxedo, and in certain sections of the number, he would dance. Except when the camera was on his legs, they were really my legs doing all the dancing. Then the camera would cut to him (from the waist up), and he would be flailing his arms like he was crazily doing all the steps. Good fun.

Some years later, Bonnie and I attended Neil's seventieth birthday at the Rainbow Bar and Grill on Sunset Boulevard, where we met his new love, actress Daryl Hannah, who would soon become his wife. A few years after that, we attended their secret wedding reception in an amazing one-hundred-year-old barn in California's wine country. When we arrived, we were greeted with a mariachi band, cocktails, and hors d'oeuvres. The space was decorated with flowers, candles, hay bales, comfy couches and chairs, and of course a stage where Neil sang for his bride. It was an incredible night of music and love. As we were leaving, we noticed an owl up in the rafters, watching over us. We walked out beneath the full summer moon in amazement. I have never seen Neil so happy or fulfilled, and I was infinitely happy myself for my friend.

Neil and I have shared a bond for almost five decades, a friendship that has truly stood the test of time. I have loved collaborating and reconnecting with him over the years, our separate lives dipping in and out of each other's in the most profoundly unexpected and wonderful ways. I have watched as so many of my old collaborators and friends have passed away in recent years, and Neil is one of the last who remain. We have been there for each other through so much: divorces, deaths, spiritual awakenings, creative revolutions, and, of course, adventure. Always, adventure.

———

Dennis Hopper lived in his Venice compound for the rest of his life. When he had first moved there, he tried to talk us into buying the property next to his, but it was a rough neighborhood back then, and Amber was a toddler, so it didn't seem like a good fit for our family. We spent time with him there on many occasions over the years, including one memorable visit when he shared with us his huge book of photos that had just been printed. In it was his picture of Dean, Wallace, and me, which we had always called *The Stone Statues*. I asked Dennis then if I could use it in my book, and he said yes.

In 2010, we heard that Dennis's prostate cancer had begun to weaken him, and we intuited that it was time to say our last goodbyes. Michael McClure came down from San Francisco, and Bonnie, Michael, and I had a final dinner with Dennis. His face was pale and gaunt, but he still had that wry smile and wicked chuckle. It was not long after that that he passed away. I was so glad we had that last special moment together and so sad he was gone. It was truly the beginning of the end of an era.

Amber continued to thrive as an actress, author, and political activist, and in 2009 she began seriously dating the very talented and funny comedian David Cross. Around this time David created, cowrote, coproduced, and starred in a TV series shot in London called *The*

Increasingly Poor Decisions of Todd Margaret, which garnered quite the cult following when it aired. When he asked me if I would play his father, I joyfully accepted. Now, I was the father of my future son-in-law. How cool is that? Bonnie and I flew to London to work on this long-titled, very funny show about Todd (David) constantly making incredibly bad decisions and ending up in serious trouble. Amber worked on the series too. While we were in the UK, we finally had the opportunity to accept Tilda Swinton's gracious invitation to visit her two-hundred-year-old stone manor in a small town called Nairn on the northern coast of Scotland. She cooked dinner for us, making us nettle soup from her own garden. While we ate, her two big hounds jumped in and out of her low-slung kitchen windows. We talked and drank wine for hours. Tilda was a fabulous hostess, as well as a brilliant woman, and she and Amber had become close friends after working together.

Sadly, while we were gone, I missed Dennis's memorial and funeral in Taos. His *Easy Rider* costars Jack Nicholson and Peter Fonda led friends and family to the historic San Francisco de Assisi church, where Dennis's wooden coffin was brought into the adobe chapel. Dean was there and, as he later told me, was deeply affected by the loss of our dear friend. I was saddened to not have been able to attend, but I didn't even know about the memorial and funeral until I got back to the United States. But thank God I had already said goodbye in my own way.

Not long after returning from Scotland, Tilda invited us to attend the Magnolia Pictures reception for the film *I Am Love*, which she was cohosting with Quentin Tarantino at the Sunset Tower in Hollywood. After a couple of drinks, I got up enough nerve to confront Quentin about that humiliating audition I'd had with him, which had made me retire from acting, at least for a little while. Of course, when I reminded him of his harsh words, he barely remembered the incident. "I'm so sorry, Russ," he said. "That was my first movie, and I was very nervous about getting it right."

I could certainly understand that and began to soften toward him.

"I'm a big fan of yours," he continued, which of course made me soften even more. And then he even started quoting my speeches from several different B movies, as well as what he said was one of his favorite films of mine, *Son of a Gunfighter*. Clearly, he knew and appreciated my work. Suddenly, I felt embarrassed and realized paranoia had gotten the best of me during a dark time when I had become very insecure about my acting and Hollywood career. Quentin and I connected, having a great conversation about movies, and I left the event feeling much better.

Amber became close friends with Quentin. When he asked her if there was anything he could do to make it up to me for our awful audition, she knew exactly what to say: "Hire him in your next film, and that'll make him happy."

And he did! His next project was *Django Unchained*, and the billing he gave me was pretty cool: *Son of a Gunfighter*. Amber, who also had a cameo in the film, was billed as *Daughter of a Son of a Gunfighter*. I only had one or two lines, but they were pretty outrageous. It was great to be back on set again, especially on a Tarantino film, and to work with Amber, if only briefly. Plus, the residuals that came in were gravy.

—

It's hard to believe how the time has gone by, and still, *West Side Story*, my costars, and the Mirisch family are all very much part of my contemporary life. In 2011, we celebrated the film's fiftieth anniversary, which created new interest in the film and my Hollywood legacy. It was a spectacular year of many stunning events. We started with a sold-out concert of nearly ten thousand people at the Hollywood Bowl in July, where they showed a newly remastered print of *WSS* on a giant screen above the stage. Working with the Leonard Bernstein office for over a year, audio engineers had managed to extract all the music from the film, leaving only the singing voices and dialogue. Magically, David Newman conducted the Los Angeles Philharmonic onstage, playing the entire score to the film live. Once again, the audience applauded after every musical number. Many of the Jets and Sharks were present to enjoy this world premiere.

Then in September, the New York Philharmonic performed the same show at Avery Fisher Hall at Lincoln Center. Bonnie and I, along with George Chakiris, Walter Mirisch, his son Larry, and Marni Nixon (who sang for Natalie in the film), attended this concert. The experience had greater significance than the Bowl because Lincoln Center was where it had all started. This was the exact spot where we had danced in the film's opening number. We all looked down from our box seats on the packed house, while David Newman conducted almost one hundred musicians as they played Bernstein's incredible score. Right after intermission, Walter and Marni were introduced, and then I was. I don't remember ever receiving a standing ovation like that before. I was stunned and humbled by the honor! Saving the best for last, David Newman introduced George, who also received a standing O.

I must say, this was one of the best times I've ever had in New York! This began my close bond and friendship with Larry and George, and of course, I was in awe of Mr. Walter Mirisch, who, along with his brothers, Marvin and Harold, produced some of the greatest movies in Hollywood history, including *The Magnificent Seven*, *In the Heat of the Night*, *Some Like It Hot*, and *The Pink Panther*, to name just a few. During our New York adventure, we enjoyed meals together and did interviews. I heard many of Walter's stories for the first time. Like how he had to call Jerry Robbins into his office and fire him, after which Jerry never talked to Walter again. "It was one of the saddest moments of my life," Walter confessed.

As if we hadn't celebrated enough, the official fiftieth anniversary of *West Side Story* was marked with a screening at the historic Grauman's Chinese Theatre in Hollywood on November 15, 2011, in conjunction with the release of the Blu-ray DVD. That morning, George, Rita, and I were honored by having our hand- and footprints pressed into the cement in front of the theater. That evening, after the screening, a party was held on the roof garden of the Madame Tussauds wax museum, which is right next door to Grauman's. Lots of people attended, many dear friends and castmates—Jets and Sharks—but most importantly, Bonnie and my two beautiful daughters, China and Amber Rose, as well as Amber's future husband, comedian David Cross. My two grandkids,

Dylan and Vivian, walked the red carpet with me for a good thirty minutes. Telling the same story over and over again to different news stations from around the country has never been my favorite, but the kids made it fun by participating in the interviews. Vivian got up on her toes to make sure she was on camera, and handsome Dylan charmed everyone. That was my favorite part of the night!

George and I have continued to get together whenever we can. We have done many personal appearances together. By this point, my legs are pretty well shot from all those backflips over the years. When I travel by plane, I need a wheelchair to take me to the gate. A few years ago, George and I did a *WSS* event in Chicago. We met at LAX to fly out together, along with Bonnie. George had injured his knee. So picture this: the leader of the Sharks and the leader of the Jets, being pushed in wheelchairs, side by side, down the airport concourse toward the departure gate. As we snapped our fingers, Bonnie sang from behind us: "The Jets are gonna have their day toni . . . ight . . . The Sharks are gonna have their way toni . . . ight!"

The young man pushing George in his wheelchair asked: "What song is that?"

"It's the 'Tonight Quintet' from *West Side Story*," Bonnie said.

George and I had a good laugh. We don't rumble anymore—we ramble!

We got to see Walter a few last times at his son Larry's beautiful home in Westwood for movie nights, where old Hollywood cronies meet and "chop it up." Sadly, Walter is gone now. I am eternally grateful to have had the chance to be a part of his masterpiece—the highlight of my life in motion pictures. Of the dozens of films that I've starred in during my seventy-year career, none has ever had the same camaraderie or staying power of *WSS*.

—

I received recognition of another kind that meant so much to me when my eight-millimeter films were screened at the Getty in 2012, alongside work by my old friends Wallace Berman and Bruce Conner, among others. The films were contained in their exhibition, *Pacific Standard Time*, which celebrated the post–World War II art scene in Los Angeles. It was incredibly gratifying to be recognized as a member of the West Coast Beat movement and to have my work shown, along with those of my peers who had been my compatriots during some of the most creatively fulfilling times of my life. While I had attended many film premieres over the years, I don't think I was ever as proud as I was the night of the Getty screening. It solidified for me the truth that I was both an artist *and* an actor, not just one or the other, and had something valuable to say in both of these mediums.

In October 2012, our family had a more personal reason to celebrate. Amber married David at a beautiful wedding in upstate New York, amid the gorgeous fall foliage. It was the biggest party I have ever seen. A hundred guests attended, including my old pal Jack Hirschman, who was Amber's lifelong mentor. Amber and David rented a Jewish sleepaway camp, where most of the guests stayed. It was raining for days, and we feared the celebration would be washed out. Instead of walking Amber down the aisle, I paddled her to the ceremony, down the gorgeous Delaware River, in a red canoe. Sure enough, the sun came out right on cue.

China and her husband, Elton, pulled the canoe up to shore. Both Amber and I were barefoot and walked through the sand to her waiting husband-to-be. As the poet Derrick Brown performed the ceremony, the rays of sunshine beamed down on all of us, and it was an epic moment of joy and light! Jack read a beautiful poem he had written especially for Amber and David, and the whole event was quite spectacular. We celebrated for three days. Our joy grew when, five years later, our granddaughter Marlow Alice was born.

More than twenty-five years after *Twin Peaks* aired on ABC, David Lynch and Mark Frost decided to have another go at it. Only this time, the series would be produced by Showtime. We eagerly anticipated that they would get to pull out all the stops creatively because censorship would not be an issue this time around. The reboot was titled *Twin Peaks: The Return*, with David and Mark writing all the episodes and

David directing. The actors were only allowed to see their own parts of the script, and the storylines were strictly confidential. We all had to sign a nondisclosure agreement, and mum was the word—always and forever. David loves his secrets.

Jumping back into the skin of Dr. Jacoby was intoxicating. I had to dig deep in my memorabilia to find my special red-and-blue-lensed glasses. A quarter century had passed, so with a new prescription and point of view, I got to explore a new Jacoby. Now, "Dr. J." had turned into scruffy, irascible "Dr. Amp." No more Hawaiian shirts. I was to wear overalls and an old sea captain's hat. He was a recluse, living far out in the woods, selling gold shovels to people who wanted to dig themselves out of the shit they were in. This was very relevant to the political climate in 2017. On my character's podcast, I ranted and raved these wild monologues about the state of affairs to whoever would listen to my antiestablishment screeds, lambasting crooked politicians, greedy millionaires, self-serving pharmaceutical companies, and manufacturers of unhealthy food. "The fucks are at it again," Dr. Amp would snarl at the camera. I was thrilled and honored to take part and to bring this character back to life on screen, but I was now in my early eighties and no longer accustomed to the extreme rigors of TV production. David and Mark had composed long monologues for my character, and I was worried about mastering all those lines in time for our shoot. The anxiety I felt about going back to work was almost overwhelming.

Luckily, before we began shooting, Bonnie and I drove to Durango, Colorado, to visit Bonnie's sister, Tin-Tin, and her brother-in-law, Rudy. I drove while Bonnie helped me to learn my lines. With hours of open road and inspiring scenery, I was able to focus and master the material. We stayed in Durango for a few days and then drove to the rugged but enchanting mountainous town of Telluride, where Rudy and Tin-Tin had a second home. It was a great visit and certainly helped to calm me down and make me feel more centered before I went back in front of the camera.

I couldn't wait to return to Washington. It had been almost thirty years since we made the original series, and stepping back onto the set felt like a homecoming. The production company flew both Bonnie and me to Seattle. I learned that my scenes would be the very first ones shot for this long-anticipated project. What an honor. The location was just south of North Bend, in a remote part of the Mount Baker–Snoqualmie National Forest. It was late summer, and the wind whipped through the giant ponderosa pines and silver fir. The aromas of the forest were intoxicating. There, in the dense woods, was Dr. Amp's hideaway, where his character recorded his antiestablishment podcast. These scenes were shot inside the cramped quarters of an old thirty-five-foot trailer. David is an intimate director, and he sat maybe two feet away from me, quietly giving me direction about how he wanted me to rant and rave about the government ripping us all off. He urged me to go over the top. Now, that was exactly the kind of direction I loved.

"More!" he would say, leaning in. "Lose yourself!"

David's direction was amazing. I was thankful I had studied my lines so thoroughly. I was able to race through them, losing myself in a dizzying diatribe of blustering anger. It was super emotional content, and at one point, I had to catch my breath and wipe my forehead to have the fortitude to reach the end. When I finally finished the scene and walked out of the trailer, I was surprised and thrilled that the entire crew gathered and gave me a standing ovation. *Still got it*, I told myself. *Still got it*.

We also worked in the town where we had originally filmed, now known as Twin Peaks. I had scenes with Wendy Robie, who played the character Nadine, always recognizable with her black eye patch. It was like a homecoming to be with her again and the entire cast, really, with all of us sharing so many wonderful memories from the original show. At age eighty-two, I couldn't think of a better project to finish off my long career. But once again, life had other plans for me.

———

In 2017, I received a call from director Mike Flanagan. He was getting ready to helm a ten-episode TV series, *The Haunting of Hill House*. It was based on the same Shirley Jackson book as the film *The Haunting*, which I had made for MGM fifty-five years earlier. This time, Steven Spielberg's Amblin Entertainment would be producing the show for Netflix. Mike told me he was a big fan of the movie and wondered if I would do a cameo in the first episode. In it, a new young actress, Victoria Pedretti, would star as Nell, played in the original film by Julie Harris. Mike wanted me to play the role of Nell's therapist. He sent me a copy of the scene, and it was well written. Then he agreed to fly Bonnie and me, first class, to Atlanta, where the series was being filmed. He also said the whole company was extremely excited that I might be in the first episode. So how could I resist? But always a pro, I wanted to make sure it was a great experience for all of us. Now eighty-three, I explained to Mike that my memory wasn't what it used to be, and he would have to help me by shortening the shots of each scene or putting what I would call a "dummy board" next to the camera from which I could read my lines.

"No problem," he said. "We'll find a way to make it as easy as possible for you."

So Bonnie and I flew to Atlanta. Early the next morning, we went to the studio, which was a huge complex several miles outside the city. Mike gave me a tour of the Hill House set, and it was very impressive. I know Robert Wise would have admired it too. All the rooms were authentically gothic and, of course, creepy. It was amazing to see how they could film in one room and still have sightlines down a hallway into another room—very realistic!

As promised, Mike gave me a clipboard containing a printout of my lines, and I kept it on my lap while I filmed my scenes with Victoria. For the most part, I had everything memorized. When I finished my last shot, the crew cheered and applauded, and I gave Mike and Victoria signed photos of the original cast of *The Haunting*. On Victoria's photo I wrote, *To the new Nellie.* When she saw it, she cried. It was very moving. The series streamed on Netflix on Halloween 2018. All the reviews were extraordinary, and even though I'd had such a small part, my friends were hooked and watched all ten episodes. I couldn't have been more pleased by my last turn in front of the camera.

In early 2021, I was invited to come to the set of the *West Side Story* reboot, directed by Steven Spielberg. Steven invited me himself, through his producers, who had been in contact with my daughter Amber. We visited the soundstage in Brooklyn, and Steven gave me a personal tour of the sets on which they were filming the number "I Feel Pretty." I met some of the cast there, including the wonderful actresses Rachel Zegler, who was playing the new Maria, and Ariana DeBose, who later won an Academy Award for her portrayal of Anita.

At the end of the year, I was invited to the world premiere of *West Side Story* in New York City. Of course, I was accompanied by Bonnie, Amber, and David, which made it extra special. I thought Steven did a brilliant job of reimagining this tale that is so close to my heart. It was an honor to be in attendance, and to see a couple of my old Jet pals there, too—David Bean and Bert Michaels. Steven introduced us all from our seats amid the audience. Stephen Sondheim, who was greatly involved in this new and beautiful production, had recently passed away, and his absence was felt by all, most especially me, who had worked with him not only in the original *West Side Story* but also in my brief turn as Buddy in Stephen's *Follies*, which was one of my most challenging and wonderful stage roles ever.

I loved witnessing the joy and enthusiasm of the talented young new actors of Steven's *WSS*, all dressed to the nines, as they gleefully awaited the screening of their film, for which they had danced and sung their hearts out. I knew exactly how they felt. It was a bittersweet and beautiful evening, and I once again felt proud to be passing the baton to a new generation of artists in their prime.

Over the years, I always remained close to my longtime poet/artist comrades Jack Hirschman, George Herms, and Michael McClure. They were all intellectual heavyweights who produced masterpieces of art and poetry. Their works have been a tremendous influence on me. But when we were together, we would talk about what all aging friends do—our growing-old pains, our loving spouses, and how time has given us a better understanding and appreciation of life. Most of all, we developed a good sense of humor, as anyone who has aged knows you must. We sometimes talked gibberish and constantly laughed at each other's silliness. And of course, we reached a point where we were comfortable to sit in silence with each other. They were like brothers to me for decades.

Bonnie and I would often visit San Francisco to see China, Elton, and the grandkids, plus Jack and Michael. One day Bonnie suggested that we had better all get together for a photo shoot to preserve the legacy of our creative cohort. Bonnie's childhood friend and coconspirator for many of our creative endeavors, Katherine Michiels, who also lives in San Francisco, sponsored an epic photo shoot at the famous City Lights Bookstore. It was yet another day of mischievous and affectionate collaboration, and I am so grateful to have those photos now.

Michael had a stroke in the spring of 2020. This was a hard blow. We always loved our visits with him and his beautiful wife, Amy, in Oakland. She kept us in touch after his stroke, and after a long stay in the hospital, he was finally able to go home. We called him late one night, and Amy held the phone to his ear. I was able to tell him that I loved him. He passed away a few hours later. I wept when Amy sent a photo of him lying serenely on his bed in their front room, holding an art piece that George Herms had made for him next to his heart.

No loss was more difficult, though, than losing Dean in 2021. Although he was younger, he had always been like a big brother to me, and we had known each other for seventy years. In many ways, he changed my life—he introduced me to Wallace Berman, to David Lynch, and to Bonnie. And I've detailed the many kindnesses he showed me over the years.

Sadly, along with our many good times, I also watched Dean struggle with alcoholism. He drank a lot to hide his demons and traumatic memories from his childhood. Dean and Dennis were pickle partners, and wild drunken episodes would ensue when they were together. Over the years, Dean's wife, Joy, tried to get him to stop drinking, especially for the sake of their two kids. Eventually they separated, and Dean moved to Taos, to be closer to Dennis. There, he made beautiful pieces of art and tried to create a new life for himself, but the bottle won out.

We visited him once in Taos, and by the afternoon, he was passed out in his big leather chair. After Dennis's death, things went downhill for him in Taos, as unsavory characters moved in and took advantage of him. Tragically, he had a massive stroke and lost his memory. I called him while he was still in Santa Fe, in rehabilitation, but I am sure he didn't know who I was. Nothing would ever be the same again. Eventually, Joy and their kids were able to move him to New Zealand, where they could look after him.

Joy called us one morning in early November 2021, telling us Dean had passed away quietly in his sleep the night before while living with his daughter. Dean was my lifelong friend, but in my heart, I felt I had lost him already, many years before. I will remember him for all the good times we had together, all he did for me, and his brilliance as an actor and fine artist.

Jack Hirschman remained one of my closest soulmates until his death in the summer of 2021. We both had bad knees, and when we walked down the streets of San Francisco, our spouses, Bonnie and Aggie, laughed from behind. They said we looked like a couple of old penguins! Our conversations were always uplifting and meaningful. Bonnie and I especially loved our Wednesday-night visits with him at the storied bar Specs' in North Beach, "where we used to raise a glass or two," with his joyous booming voice singing the old proletariat songs. "Those were the days, my friend," he used to sing. Boy, were they ever. It was a huge blow to us all to lose him.

As for George Herms, he and I have a special relationship. We jive and we jab. I tell him he's a "lazy good-for-nothing." To which he replies, "I thought I told you to not call me anymore." Of course, underneath our silly jive, we love each other like brothers. Thank God he has Sue to take good care of him and keep him in line.

———

As I reach the end of my book, I can't help but think of my family and friends, who are so close to me, and how much my life has changed since my wild days in Hollywood and Topanga. The older I grow, the more I appreciate being alive. My golden years are surely golden. I've discovered I love my family and friends more than ever, and I feel so grateful for the ways they continue to delight me and make my life an adventure.

I never thought I would still be living in the same place after more than forty years. Our home is small yet comfortable, located close to the beach, in a cozy seaside community. When Amber was born, we brought her home here. China and Elton come down often from San Francisco, and we have enjoyed many visits and family celebrations with the grandkids, too. We have a wonderful community at our apartment building. They don't see me on the red carpets at Hollywood events. They see me on the red bricks in our communal courtyard, cleaning the fountain or watering the plants. For years, I always decorated for the holidays, climbing the trees to string little twinkling lights in the central area. Often, we have barbecues that sprawl across the patio. We share potluck meals with our neighbors, who have also lived here for decades. We all have our own separate lives, but when we get together, it's like a big family. We talk about what's going on in our lives, our neighborhood, our country, and the world. Often, Bonnie brings out her guitar and sings a song or two. I've been known to play along on my djembe drum, and the whole courtyard joins in to sing along. Full of life and spirits, we've often been a rowdy bunch. More than once, the cops have come to shut us down, smiling all the while to see a bunch of old folks ripping it up. On special occasions, we walk together to the local club where Bonnie performs with her band, Blue Heaven, and continue to party there.

My daughters and grandchildren bring meaning to my life. There is the joy of having built an enduring relationship with China, admiring her artistry with metalwork and sculptures and how she holds the reins for Light Rail Studios in San Francisco, which she and her husband created through their determination and vision. And of seeing Amber, now a respected and successful actress and writer, as well as a wife and dedicated mother, continuing the Tamblyn story with our youngest granddaughter, Marlow Alice. My sons-in-law, Elton and David, supply many adventures with visits to pubs and tequila tastings, filled with laughter and brisk political discussions and banter. Now I am also blessed with three wonderfully talented grandchildren who will carry on the Tamblyn legacy.

I've always been proud of my younger brother, Larry. He and I had similar career trajectories in our youth—me as a movie star, and him with his successful 1960s garage band and its megahit "Dirty Water." The Standells broke up, but many years later, Larry got his group back together and started playing concerts again. His devoted and steadfast wife, actress Glenda Chism-Tamblyn, supported him throughout the Standells' revival. She is a beloved part of our family. As an accomplished composer, he also writes musical scores for independent films.

Bonnie has long been my rock. Anyone who knows her knows that she has deep understanding and compassion for everyone. In fact, you don't even have to know her; you can see it in her eyes when you meet her. She is educated in the arts, and as a singer-songwriter, she has a knack for storytelling herself. As a teacher and a mentor, at the deepest level, she is openhearted and has a good sense of humor about the complications of life itself. She holds us all in her "circle," as she calls it. In our decades together, I have found it wise to take her advice. These days, I walk the neighborhood with her, and we stop at a sunny little wall by the school, where we sit and talk while she massages my poor old legs. As the evenings close, she sings to me before I sleep.

For many years now, I've been complaining to Bonnie that I'll be happy when I finish this damn book. I confess I was hesitant to write it from the very beginning, and I am amazed by how long it has taken. Dennis was still alive when I started. So were Michael, Jack, and Dean! Not only did I have to weather their losses, but I had to stay the course during difficult memories and the hard work of trying to make sense of everything. So I turned to my own unique philosophy. I had once adhered to Norman Vincent Peale's book *The Power of Positive Thinking*, but then I bumped up against its limitations: if I thought a role or event was going to be great and it didn't live up to my expectation, I was disappointed. So I became a rebel and switched my approach to "The Positive Power of Negative Thinking." If I thought a role or event was going to be awful and it turned out to be nice, I was pleasantly surprised. And so, too, it is with this book.

Now, my philosophy has finally evolved even further, to "The Positive Power of No Thinking." There is always another anecdote to tell, but I am finished telling them. I feel a kind of good emptiness, even though I wish in a way that I could just keep writing as my life rolls on. But like they say, everything must come to an end, including this story, *Dancing on the Edge*, the most exciting, intense, and difficult dance I have ever been driven to do.

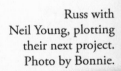

Russ with
Neil Young, plotting
their next project.
Photo by Bonnie.

Cover for *Greendale*
program.
Art by
James Mazzeo.

Neil Young with his
band Crazy Horse.
Left to right:
Ralph Molina,
Billy Talbot, Neil, and
Frank (Poncho) Sampedro.
Photo by Bonnie.

Russ directs *Greendale* actors and dancers at the back of the stage. Photo by Bonnie.

Russ with his arm around associate producer Marcy Gensic with the *Greendale* dancers. Photo by Bonnie.

Quentin Tarantino and
Russ celebrating *Once Upon
a Time in Hollywood*
at Musso & Frank in
Hollywood.
Photo by Bonnie.

Amber and
Russ in costume for
Django Unchained (2012).

Amber and Russ at David Lynch's Festival of Disruption in Hollywood (2018).
Photo by Agu Maru.

An outing with Amber in Santa Monica's Palisades Park. Photo by Vern Evans.

Amber and Dad paddling down the Delaware River to her wedding (2012). Photo by Matt Wignall.

China and her family at the legacy shoot at City Lights Bookstore in San Francisco. Left to right: grandson Dylan, Russ, China, husband and dad Elton Cunniffe, and granddaughter Vivian. Photo by Justin Buehl.

Russ with his creative cohort and lifelong friends at City Lights Bookstore in San Francisco; Amber with her godfathers. Left to right: Jack Hirschman, Russ, Amber, Michael McClure, and George Herms.
Photo by Justin Buehl.

George Chakiris, Rita Moreno, and Russ memorialize their feet and hands in cement at the famous Grauman's Chinese Theater in Hollywood. Photo by Larry Mirisch.

George Chakiris and *West Side Story* producer Walter Mirisch with Russ in New York, celebrating the fiftieth anniversary of *West Side Story*. Photo by Larry Mirisch.

Bernardo and Riff, *West Side Story* rivals; George and Russ, best of friends for more than sixty years. Photo by Mark J. Gross.

Russ calls the limo for an outing to Club Nokia for the Dizzy Feet Foundation Gala. Photo by Lillian Soderman.

Friends Nancy Levens, Larry Mirisch, Bonnie, and Russ ready for the Dizzy Feet event. Photo by Lillian Soderman.

A last visit with Sidney Poitier at the home of Larry Mirisch, where he screened Russ and Sidney's movie, *The Long Ships*. Photo by Larry Mirisch.

Russ as Dr. Amp on the set
for *Twin Peaks: The Return*, in
front of the old trailer where
he delivered his rants (2017).
Photo by Bonnie.

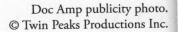

Doc Amp publicity photo.
© Twin Peaks Productions Inc.

Russ studies lines for his last
performance in the TV series
The Haunting of Hill House
(2018), shot at the EUE/Screen
Gems studios in Atlanta.
Photo by Bonnie.

Bonnie with her band Blue Heaven. Left to right: Rick Huhnke, Bonz, Davey Chegwidden, and Johnny Albert. Photo by Lauri Reimer.

Brothers Russ and
Larry Tamblyn at a
Standells performance.
Photo by
Glenda Chism-Tamblyn.

Russ with son-in-law David Cross, together for David's sitcom
The Increasingly Poor Decisions of Todd Margaret. Photo by Amber.

Happy holidays in New York with
Russ and his ladies, Bonnie and
Katherine Anne Michiels.
Photo by Amber.

An evening of Irish music at Hartley's
in Brooklyn with granddaughter
Marlow Alice: taking it in.
Photo by Lillian Soderman.

Russ visits with
Steven Spielberg on the
new *West Side Story*
set in New York.
Photo by Amber.

Still Riff after all these years! (2019)
Photo by Amber.

Russ greets a few of the newest Jets. Left to right: Kyle Allen, Russ, Julian Elia,
Steven Spielberg, and Mike Faist (Riff). Photo by Bonnie.

Ben Mankiewicz celebrates with Russ at the 2022 TCM Classic Festival in Hollywood. Photo by Carol Summers.

Walking the picket line with friend Antonia Bogdanovich (2023). Photo by Bonnie.

Sphere
Collage by Russ Tamblyn
(1977)

AFTERWORD

One more story for the road, I promise.

Over the past decade, I have been certain many times that I had reached the end of this book, but then there was always another event that needed to be marked, or a lost friend who needed to be honored, or another story that needed to be told. When you've written something for so long—in the case of this book, since the 1990s—it feels like you can just keep writing forever, that the work will never truly be done, as long as your life isn't. But I know better. I learned from Wallace that a work of art will tell you when it's ready to be done, when there's nothing more that needs to be added, fine-tuned, or changed, and when it's finally ready to let the world see it. A book can tell you the same thing if you let it. All you have to do is listen from the heart. Mine finally did this for me in the happiest of ways on the occasion of my eighty-eighth birthday, back on December 30, 2022.

Normally I don't do much to mark my birthday, but something felt different that year. I had spent the past eighteen months immersed in the process of bringing this book to life, working from the original manuscript with my cowriter, Sarah Tomlinson. Sarah helped me organize these existing stories and excavate the ones never before told, gathering together in written form what it's felt like to find myself dancing on the edge for almost a century. What it feels like to grow or be outgrown, to break a heart or have your own broken. To create art, children, and community. To be rich as hell and miserable, and broke as heaven and thriving. To say the most thrilling hellos and most tender goodbyes. Together, Sarah and I, along with Bonnie, painstakingly pasted it all together to create the full picture of all that I have been: the grand collage of my lifetime.

Reflecting on this work, I told Bonnie that this year I wanted to celebrate. Bonnie loves to bring people together, so we planned a dinner with close friends at my favorite restaurant in Santa Monica. That's how I found myself seated at the head of a long table laden with food and drinks, laughing and growing teary with emotion as I surveyed representatives in attendance from every chapter of my life. There were our neighbors, Tom Nolan and his wife, Peggy O'Brien, who had been at the heart of our Santa Monica community and raised their children alongside Amber. There was also Larry Mirisch and his partner, Nancy Levens, who represented the heyday of my Hollywood career; Larry is himself a successful producer, as well as the son of legendary *WSS* producer Walter Mirisch, who literally changed my life by casting me in that film. Across from them was seated Wallace Berman's son, Tosh Berman, all grown up now, with his wife, artist Lun*na Menoh, representing all the ways the baton is passed in art and life. At my right hand were my longtime friend and artistic compatriot Neil Young and his wife, Daryl Hannah. And of course, my cowriter, Sarah, and my beloved wife and coheart of forty years, Bonnie.

When it came time to give a toast, I raised my glass and said, "Here's to the women." A hearty cheer went up, and we all clinked our glasses, and I thought about how far I had come. I thought about Venetia, who had taught me how to become a man; about Elizabeth, who had taught me how to be brave; about my daughters, Amber Rose and China Faye, who taught me the meaning of true love; and of course, most of all, about Bonnie, who changed my life forever.

As I looked around that table, full of the faces of people who had been by my side for so many years, and thought of the ones who are gone now but remain in spirit, I couldn't help but notice that the conversation turned to the future just as much as it looked back to the past. I was surrounded by the living embodiment of my stories, my legacy.

Bonnie brought out a cake with candles blazing, and she launched into singing "Happy Birthday." Everyone began to sing, even Neil, like a whole chorus of my memories come to life. And although I can't tell you what I wished for when I blew out my candle (you know why), let's just say everything I ever wanted, and everything I never knew I needed, has come true.

I closed my eyes and inhaled, surrounded by the sounds of my friends and family singing joyously around me. As I blew out the candles, I heard the lyrics of one of Bonnie's songs play through my head:

> The winter wind is calling me home.
> The leaves have all fallen, and the birds have flown,
> and if I never see you again . . .
> I send you my love on the winter wind.

The eighty-eighth birthday!
Top row, left to right: Nancy Levens, Larry Mirisch, Richard Stein, Sarah Tomlinson, Tosh Berman, Lun*na Menoh, Bonnie, and Tom Nolan. Bottom row: Russ, Peggy O'Brien, Neil Young, and Daryl Hannah.

ACKNOWLEDGMENTS

How can I condense a quarter century's worth of gratitude into just a few pages of acknowledgments of all the support, generosity, and encouragement friends and family have given me during the writing, rewriting, and re-rewriting of this book? Let me try and go back to the beginning, to trace a record of appreciation for all the people, both past and present, who were there with me on this journey.

Thank you to Dr. David Soren for first putting this wild idea into my head, and to his wife, Noelle, who supported and edited the very first draft. I am forever grateful to my friend and neighbor Susan Cope, who encouraged me to then rewrite it in my own voice, propelling me into uncharted territory. Thanks to author and counterculture historian Pat Thomas, who was instrumental in the beginning stages of bringing this book to life, and to our dear friend Jeanne Field, who gave me invaluable thoughts and insights on an early draft and came back in to see the project over the finish line, helping us to secure *Human Highway* photos. Thank you to our neighbor and friend Joy Bertwell for yet another read and spit and polish. Thank you to my pal Norm Basham, who early on, as I was first writing, would come into my office and listen to my stories; he encouraged me with his enthusiasm. Thank you to Bill Jonas for his early inspiration for the book's cover. To Jerry Katz for the use of his beautiful poem. To Tosh Berman for valuable information about the Topanga years and his generous sharing of his contacts and resources. To Karl Puchik and the Kohn Gallery for helping us secure photos of the Berman family. To my new friend and neighbor Antonia Bogdanovich, who gave me some good advice about publishing and has been an incredible help in everything to do with the production of the book's images. And to photographer Carol Summers, a very good and helpful friend, for her archival prowess and Photoshop magic. Of course, a huge part of this story is about my MGM years, and I am grateful for the assistance from our friend Maggie Adams, head of MGM archives, and Shannon Muchow, both valuable resources in how to approach the complicated task of licensing. And to the general goodwill ambassadors: Larry Mirisch, Nancy Levens, and George Chakiris from the *West Side Story* family. Also, thank you to Larry McCallister at Paramount for his support. And to our friends Dori Stegman and Ben Mankiewicz of Turner Classic Movies, who keep the spotlight on the importance of classic film and my legacy within it. Womb to tomb, all of you.

I'd also like to extend my gratitude to Anthony Mattero at Creative Artists Agency for connecting me with David Dunton, my great literary agent, and the whole team at Harvey Klinger Inc. David, you've been a champion, a sounding board filled with great insight and advice, and a strong protector and advocate for this book. Thank you for all of it.

Thank you to the team at Blackstone: Rick Bleiweiss for bringing me on board; our editorial director, Josie Woodbridge, who deftly guided us through the publishing hoops and barrels; the awesome editors Holly Rubino and Riam Griswold; and to the art department: Alenka Linaschke for the beautiful cover design, Art Director Stephanie Stanton, and Amy Craig, for bringing my stories to life with the many photos and images.

Thank you to the creatives, the beating hearts of my lifetime: author Janet Fitch, who gave encouragement and support; poet Brendan Constantine; and Julia Ingalls, all of whom led me to meeting the great Sarah Tomlinson, extraordinary cowriter of this book. Thank you, Vicky Wilson, for cheering me on. Thank you, Derrick C. Brown, for the encouragement with publishing and more puns than any man should be forced to endure. Thank you, Rose Eichenbaum, for your superb photography. I am forever grateful to David Lynch and Mark Frost for bringing me back to the screen in the most memorable way. To David's assistant and our friend Sabrina Sutherland for her encouragement and for securing the rights to the *Twin Peaks* photos. To Neil Young, thank you for our creative works together and for your enduring friendship. To Joel Bernstein for his help with the photos he took on the set of *Human Highway*. And also to Bonnie Levitan and Frank Geronda at Lookout Management for their help with *Human Highway* photos. Thank you to my forever friend and sparring partner, George Herms, and my late brothers Jack Hirschman and Michael McClure, for inspiring not just the artist in me but the writer.

And one more shout-out to my ace, Sarah Tomlinson, whose name must be mentioned twice in these acknowledgments. Sarah, you've been a friend, a confidant, and a beloved collaborator in the process of unpacking more than seven decades' worth of my stories onto the page. I am honored to share this book with you.

And to the women who shaped so much of my early life: Venetia, Elizabeth, and Betsy. Thank you for showing me the way. My experiences with you made me a better man.

Much appreciation to my incredible family and their love along the way: My brother Larry and his wife, Glenda Chism-Tamblyn, for all their support and good company. My wild and woolly sons-in-law: thank you, Elton Cunniffe, for the camaraderie over a good bottle of tequila, and thank you, David Cross, for your never-ending humor, keeping my head from getting too serious. To my daughter China Faye, who is the bright light and happiest surprise from those Topanga days. And to my fiercest editor, my daughter Amber Rose, who helped me shape these stories with contemporary sensibilities.

I can't say enough about how much my beautiful wife, Bonnie, inspired me to keep writing when I thought I could not go on. She tirelessly kept track of my memories and all my archives and worked in partnership with Sarah, me, and the whole Blackstone team. And a salute to her family who supported her for all these years, including her sisters, Carrie and Andie (Tin-Tin), and brother, Rudy (thanks for the high-country Jeep adventures!) And most of all I must say thank you to all the doctors who kept me tickin' well into my eighties and hopefully beyond.

Love to my grandchildren, Dylan Roark, Vivian Raquel, and Marlow Alice, who keep me young at heart.

Finally, my heartfelt thanks to everyone who supported me all through the years on this incredible journey, some of whose names I may have forgotten to mention individually, but I couldn't have done it without you.

Book of Romans:

Bible Studies

Books by Paul J. Bucknell

Allowing the Bible to speak to our lives today!

- Overcoming Anxiety: Finding Peace, Discovering God
- Reaching Beyond Mediocrity: Being an Overcomer
- The Life Core: Discovering the Heart of Great Training
- The Godly Man: When God Touches a Man's Life
- Redemption Through the Scriptures
- Godly Beginnings for the Family
- Principles and Practices of Biblical Parenting
- Building a Great Marriage
- Christian Premarital Counseling Manual for Counselors
- Relational Discipleship: Cross Training
- Running the Race: Overcoming Lusts
- Genesis: The Book of Foundations
- Book of Romans: The Living Commentary
- Book of Romans: Bible Studies
- Book of Ephesians: Bible Studies
- Walking with Jesus: Abiding in Christ
- Inductive Bible Studies in Titus
- 1 Peter Bible Study Questions: Living in a Fallen World.
- Take Your Next Step into Ministry
- Training Leaders for Ministry
- Study Guide for Jonah: Understanding God's Heart

   Check out these valuable resources at
   www.foundationsforfreedom.net

Book of Romans:

Bible Studies

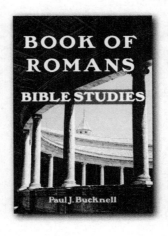

Paul J. Bucknell

With basic and advanced questions!

Book of Romans: Bible Studies

Copyright ©2015 Paul J. Bucknell

ISBN-10: 1619930447

ISBN-13: 978-1-61993-044-5

Digital e-Book:

ISBN-10: 1619930455

ISBN-13: 978-1-61993-045-2

www.foundationsforfreedom.net

Pittsburgh, PA 15212

Introduction

Our Challenge

Think of a Bible study as a lake or ocean. You can be superficial and just get your feet wet, or you can wade in deeper and deeper until you are surrounded by the water swirling about your head. God's Word was designed to escort you into the deeps of spiritual intimacy with God. We have designed these Bible study questions in such a way that whether you are a beginner or advanced swimmer, these questions can be of great benefit for you in your knowing God through Romans. These studies are also great to accompany a seminary, church or youth class.

How have we done this? We have provided two sets of study questions on the same passage, basic and advanced. The first set of questions seeks to provide a good Bible study for those not very familiar with God's Word. Except for a few application questions, most of the answers are straightforward and can be found in the Bible text. The second set of questions, the advanced study questions, enable the student of God's Word to wade in deeper and through meditation on God's Word be able to see how the text at hand is related to societal and theological issues. Our approach is discussed further below.

General approach to Bible study questions

The Book of Romans is separated into teaching or study sections. For each teaching section there are two sets of questions. Our assumptions underlying all of these studies are:

- God's Word is fully trustworthy and given to us to grow as His people, both in our character and service but also in our relationship with Him.

- Believers are blessed when we meditate on God's Word (Jos 1:6). The more God's Word enters our lives and thoughts, the more we are transformed by Him.

- It is easy to only 'understand' a passage but not see how it applies to our lives. This simple 'knowledge' approach leads to a dead spiritual life and must be avoided at all costs.

- Good study questions lead us to understand what is being said as well as the applications (implications) of those truths to our lives.

This series of questions are designed to lead us into the discovery and application of the scripture's teaching to our lives. The NASB is used but other translations can be used alongside the questions. A good study Bible is suggested (NASB, ESV, KJV, etc.) rather than paraphrases (Living Bible, Good News for Modern Man, etc.).

The basic set of questions

The basic study questions have three parts. Most of the time the answers to these questions will be found right in the Bible passage. This is the reason the verse numbers (5:8) are attached to the question. These questions will encourage one to ask, "What does the scripture passage actually say?" The NASB text is provided so feel free to keep your version nearby for further comparison. We suggest using your own notebook or writing program. For example, by opening these questions in your Word Processor (like *Word*) enables you to make more space between the questions by adjusting the style 'after paragraph' spacing. It is easy to add, delete or modify questions!

We sprinkle a few application questions throughout the Basic Study Questions but concentrate them towards the end and conclusion. These questions will encourage one to ask, "What does the passage mean to me?" These answers are meant to be personal and have to do with one's own life.

This new edition has added the NASB Bible text, outlines, an introduction and summary as well as a starter question which introduces the general topic in a more interesting way. The outline is for your use but can be ignored. It serves to break up longer texts into shorter sections, which of course, can become smaller studies depending on one's time and purpose. Our Roman's Commentary can help one dig deeper.

Sometimes, a few deeper questions are added to the Basic Set of Study Questions which help us ponder and reflect, fostering the spirit of biblical meditation.

Generally, the questions progress along with the text—verse 1, 2, 3 and so forth. Please feel free to skip over irrelevant or unclear questions. During small group Bible studies, for example, some answers are too obvious or the answer has already been stated. Skip these questions! And please add your own questions or modify these. These questions just get you going in your own study.

The advanced set of questions

The advanced set of questions is noticeably different from the basic set. The advanced set of questions has several purposes:

(1) The small group leaders should familiarize themselves with these advanced questions so that they will not get caught off guard from various discussion points that might pop up.

(2) The small group leader should take some of these questions and mix them into the basic set of questions while leading. I personally find each Bible study to be led by the Spirit of God. We generally know where He will lead us with the text but need to be careful to have a good conclusion highlighting the particular emphasis the Spirit brings. One or two

advanced questions are great to help lead the study into further thought and application.

(3) Those engaged in a deeper personal study or preparation of preaching and teaching the Book of Romans can greatly profit from these questions. Advanced students of God's Word have been trained in other parts of the scriptures and should see how the one passage applies to other Bible passages or issues. Some of these passages are so rich and deep that a simple Bible study cannot capture the many truths therein. The scriptures, like a broad river, divides into many smaller streams. These questions tend to be more applicative both in a practical and theological sense. They are designed to have God's Word reshape our thoughts and decisions. In the basic set of questions the focus is on what is stated in the text while in the advanced set of study questions, a deep analysis of certain verses or the whole is developed. Do not quickly rush to the answer but ponder the depth of God's truths in His holy presence. Learn to 'swim' in God's presence as our thoughts meditate on the riches and glory of God and His ways in Christ.

Expanded and revised in 2015.

Paul J. Bucknell

Table of Contents

#1 Romans 1:1-17 Study Questions

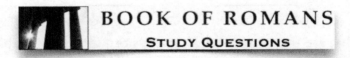

BOOK OF ROMANS
STUDY QUESTIONS

THE PROCLAMATION OF THE GOSPEL

What is the gospel? Many people have heard this term but are not clear what it means. The study on Romans 1:1-17 gives a better understanding of what the gospel is and how it can affect our lives.

- **Starter:** Briefly describe what first comes to your mind when you hear the word 'Gospel'.

A) The Gospel's Message (Rom 1:1-7)

1:1 Paul, a bond-servant of Christ Jesus, called as an apostle, set apart for the gospel of God, 2 which He promised beforehand through His prophets in the holy Scriptures, 3 concerning His Son, who was born of a descendant of David according to the flesh, 4 who was declared the Son of God with power by the resurrection from the dead, according to the Spirit of holiness, Jesus Christ our Lord, 5 through whom we have received grace and apostleship to bring about the obedience of faith among all the Gentiles, for His name's sake, 6 among whom you also are the called of Jesus Christ; 7 to all who are beloved of God in Rome, called as saints: Grace to you and peace from God our Father and the Lord Jesus Christ.

1. What term did Paul use to describe his relationship to Jesus Christ (1:1)?

2. What was promised beforehand through the prophets (1-2)?

3. List at least 4 key characteristics of the gospel of Jesus Christ (3-5).

4. What are the two special ways the Lord spiritually enable Paul and others to carry out the ministry (5)?

5. What was God's purpose for calling apostles (5)?

6. What do we know about whom Paul was writing to (7)? List at least three things about the recipients of this letter.

7. What two ways did the Lord especially helps the Roman believers (and us all) (7)? Explain each term.

B) The Gospel's Mission (Rom 1:8-15)

[8] First, I thank my God through Jesus Christ for you all, because your faith is being proclaimed throughout the whole world. [9] For God, whom I serve in my spirit in the preaching of the gospel of His Son, is my witness as to how unceasingly I make mention of you, [10] always in my prayers making request, if perhaps now at last by the will of God I may succeed in coming to you. [11] For I long to see you in order that I may impart some spiritual gift to you, that you may be established; [12] that is, that I may be encouraged together with you while among you, each of us by the other's faith, both yours and mine. [13] And I do not want you to be unaware, brethren, that often I have planned to come to you (and have been prevented thus far) in order that I might obtain some fruit among

you also, even as among the rest of the Gentiles. ^{14} I am under
obligation both to Greeks and to barbarians, both to the wise and
to the foolish. ^{15} Thus, for my part, I am eager to preach the gospel
to you also who are in Rome.

8. Scan through verses 1:8-9 and describe Paul's attitude toward
    the Roman Christians.

9. What was Paul's request in verse 10?

10. Why did he yearn and long to see these church members
    (11)?

11. What did he expect to receive from them (12)? Have you ever
    shared this expectation when you hope to meet some beloved
    Christian believers? Explain.

12. Why didn't Paul come right away to see the church members
    at Rome (1:13; 15:22, 23)?

13. What one word could we replace for the different people
    mentioned in verse 14?

14. How are we to feel concerning our obligation to present the
    Word of God to everyone (15)?

C) The Gospel's Power (Rom 1:16-17)

¹⁶ For I am not ashamed of the gospel, for it is the power of God for salvation to everyone who believes, to the Jew first and also to the Greek. ¹⁷ For in it the righteousness of God is revealed from faith to faith; as it is written, "BUT THE RIGHTEOUS man SHALL LIVE BY FAITH."

15. Why shouldn't we be ashamed of the Gospel (16)?

16. What is revealed in the Gospel (17)?

17. What is the only way people can gain God's righteousness (17)?

Summary

The gospel is the core of the Bible's saving message as well as the theme of the Book of Romans. It is exciting to see how the apostle and the church at Rome had been positively affected by the gospel, the power of God unto salvation.

18. What truth about the Christian faith and life have you been deeply blessed? Any you wrestle with?

19. Do you likewise see yourself as God's specially gifted servant carrying out God's greater purposes? Explain.

20. What has God called you for? How has He specially gifted you for this purpose? What are you doing about it?

21. What are some reasons that we do not share the gospel?

Romans 1:1-17 Advanced Discussion Questions

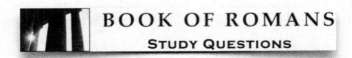

BOOK OF ROMANS
STUDY QUESTIONS

1. Who is the author of Romans? Include a description of his background from Acts with a map describing his birth place and places of ministry.

2. Carefully think through Acts 9:1-19 where Paul's conversion is recorded. How does this help you better understand verse 1?

3. How does the usage or reference of the word 'Son' differ in verses 1:3-4? What do they intimate about the nature of Jesus Christ?

4. In what ways does Jesus' death, resurrection and Lordship affect your life? How important is this to you?

5. Would you say Paul shows a spirit of superiority? If not, use three adjectives that describe Paul's relationship with the Roman Christians. What best describes your attitudes towards other believers around you?

6. What obligation does Paul strongly sense (1:14)? Where did he get that? Why do we use the word 'call' to describe God's special purposes that He reveals to His children?

7. Does Paul speak about not being ashamed of the gospel or sharing it (16)? Do you think there is a difference to him?

8. Why do you think Paul adds that phrase 'power of God' to verse 16? What does it mean?

9. Are there any areas in which I think God's grace is insufficient to accomplish His plans for my life? Discuss.

#2 Romans 1:18-32 Study Questions

BOOK OF ROMANS
STUDY QUESTIONS

THE EVIDENT GUILT OF MANKIND

A longstanding argument has been that since man has difficulty understanding truth, then he is not responsible for his sin. In this case, man pleads "ignorance then innocent" of knowing an invisible God and His standards. Most typically, they will refer to some remote tribe in an obscure part of the world, but usually they are developing their own excuse.

- **Starter:** From your contacts and conversations, do you think everyone knows about God's presence (even though they differently define Him)?

A) Rejection of God (Rom 1:18-23)

[18] For the wrath of God is revealed from heaven against all ungodliness and unrighteousness of men, who suppress the truth in unrighteousness, [19] because that which is known about God is evident within them; for God made it evident to them. [20] For since the creation of the world His invisible attributes, His eternal power and divine nature, have been clearly seen, being understood through what has been made, so that they are without excuse. [21] For even though they knew God, they did not honor Him as God, or give thanks; but they became futile in their speculations, and their foolish heart was darkened. [22] Professing to be wise, they became fools, [23] and exchanged the glory of the incorruptible God for an

image in the form of corruptible man and of birds and four-footed animals and crawling creatures.

1. What is revealed from heaven against the unrighteousness of men (1:18)? How so?

2. Instead of responding positively to the truth, how do people treat the truth (18-19)?

3. What three aspects of God have been clearly seen since the creation of the world (20)?

   •

   •

   •

4. What are two ways human beings need to respond to God considering who He is (21)?

5. What did man trade for images in the form of man, birds, animals or crawling creatures (23)?

B) Rejection of God's Righteousness (Rom 1:24-32)

24 Therefore God gave them over in the lusts of their hearts to impurity, that their bodies might be dishonored among them. 25 For they exchanged the truth of God for a lie, and worshiped and

served the creature rather than the Creator, who is blessed forever. Amen. [26] For this reason God gave them over to degrading passions; for their women exchanged the natural function for that which is unnatural, [27] and in the same way also the men abandoned the natural function of the woman and burned in their desire toward one another, men with men committing indecent acts and receiving in their own persons the due penalty of their error. [28] And just as they did not see fit to acknowledge God any longer, God gave them over to a depraved mind, to do those things which are not proper, [29] being filled with all unrighteousness, wickedness, greed, evil; full of envy, murder, strife, deceit, malice; they are gossips, [30] slanderers, haters of God, insolent, arrogant, boastful, inventors of evil, disobedient to parents, [31] without understanding, untrustworthy, unloving, unmerciful; [32] and, although they know the ordinance of God, that those who practice such things are worthy of death, they not only do the same, but also give hearty approval to those who practice them.

6. What three sinful tendencies does God allow to dominate men who reject the truth (see 24, 26, 28)?

   • v. 24

   • v. 26

   • v. 28

7. What happens when man does the impure things that he wants to do (24)?

8. What is a clear sign of a decadent and self-worshiping society (26-27)?

9. How does God judge them (26-27)? What does this refer to?

10. If God does not preserve and restrain mankind, what kinds of evil deeds and attitudes will people be filled with (29-31)?

11. List the 21 evil deeds mentioned in verses 29-31. Do you find anything unexpected in the list? Why so?

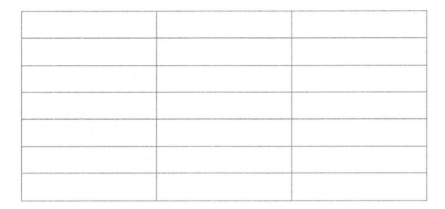

12. What are the two things these people know (32)?

13. How does this knowledge affect their behavior (32)?

Summary

A society's evil often gets increasingly worse. Paul links this waywardness in mankind to their rejection of God. If we were not restrained by God's grace, we too would get worse and worse.

14. Is God just or unjust when He manifests His wrath (18-23)? Do you think you have strong enough reasons to defend the Lord when people say He is unfair in judging people and sending them to hell?

15. Is man naturally innocent or ungodly? (24-32) How does God's wrath depict this? Use Bible verses to backup your answer.

16. List at least two changes you desire to take place in your life because of these verses:

•

•

Romans 1:18-32 Advanced Discussion Questions

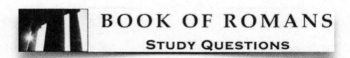

1. Many believe God to be loving. How is it, then, that God's wrath is being displayed here in the New Testament? Do you believe that God is fiercely angry with the ungodly?

2. Why does there need to be judgment? How does God judge people during their life on earth?

3. Mankind's depravity is not looked upon as a one time decision but as a process. Discover the three steps to this process and identify where God has extended His patience.

4. From this passage how should we view men who reject God? In evangelism, we often stress the love of God. Is the subject of God's wrath taboo? Is it necessary?

5. Does the passage state whether homosexuality is a sin (26-27)? Explain. What truths have they rejected?

6. Paul first speaks of sexual sins and later provides a long list of
    other wicked acts. If God deals with people this way, how are
    we to respond to them? (e.g. HIV positive, divorced, rebellious
    son, prideful leader, etc.)

#3 Romans 2:1-11 Study Questions

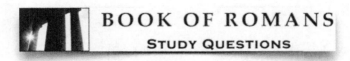

JUDGMENT BY THE FACTS

If we are not careful, we will miss Paul's point. He continues to reveal the great void of righteousness among all peoples, Gentiles and Jews. All men need the righteousness of Jesus Christ. Even the self-righteous and religious are liable for their sins before God and need Jesus.

- **Starter:** Is it easy for you to confess your wrong? Name your favorite excuse that hides your sinfulness.

A) Everyone will be prosecuted (Rom 2:1-4)

2:1 You, therefore, have no excuse, you who pass judgment on someone else, for at whatever point you judge the other, you are condemning yourself, because you who pass judgment do the same things. 2 Now we know that God's judgment against those who do such things is based on truth. 3 So when you, a mere man, pass judgment on them and yet do the same things, do you think you will escape God's judgment? 4 Or do you show contempt for the riches of his kindness, tolerance and patience, not realising that God's kindness leads you towards repentance? (NIV)

1. Who is Paul talking about in 1:18-32? What pronoun is used?

2. Beginning in chapter 2 what pronoun is used? Who does this pronoun refer to?

3. What are these people doing (2:1)?

4. How does a man condemn himself (1-3)?

5. What happens to a person who acknowledges (literally: judges) another person's wrongdoing and then does it himself (3)?

6. What is the proper response to God's kindness and patience (4)?

7. How do some people wrongly respond to God's kindness, forbearance and patience (4)?

B) Everyone will be justly prosecuted (Rom 2:5-11)

[5] But because of your stubbornness and unrepentant heart you are storing up wrath for yourself in the day of wrath and revelation of the righteous judgment of God, [6] who WILL RENDER TO EVERY MAN ACCORDING TO HIS DEEDS: [7] to those who by perseverance in doing good seek for glory and honor and immortality, eternal life; [8] but to those who are selfishly ambitious and do not obey the truth, but obey unrighteousness, wrath and indignation. [9] There will be tribulation and distress for every soul of man who does evil, of the Jew first and also of the Greek [10] but glory and honor and peace to every man who does good, to the

Jew first and also to the Greek. ¹¹ For there is no partiality with
God.

8. What are the stubborn and unrepentant people storing up
    (5)?

9. How is the Day of Judgment <u>described</u> in verse 5? What is the
    significance of each of the terms used?

10. Please write verse 6 down. It is the standard of justice among
    God and man.

11. What will those doing good and seeking immortality receive
    (7)? Would you say that you are good enough to receive
    eternal life?

12. What will those who are selfishly ambitious and do not obey
    the truth obtain (8)?

13. Does God, as Judge, treat people differently due to their
    background, color, sex, religion, etc., (9-11)?

Summary

Paul approaches our lives this way to uncover any roots of self-
righteousness. The apostle had deep insight into this area because
of his own past life. He pushes everyone into a situation where
they need to evaluate their lives according to their moral
behavior. In the end, people have miserably failed and only in Jesus

Christ can we find the needed righteousness to avoid God's wrath.

14. The Roman church had these 'hypocrites' (1-4). Do you think our churches have them too?

15. What can you say to a person who says he stays out of church because hypocrites go there?

16. Considering 5-11, is Paul more concerned with what one says or how one lives? How do you think God will deal with those who do what they condemn in others in the church?

17. Paul in 6-7 is clearly catching those who have confidence in their good works. Find and state some verses from Romans that affirm that there are no righteous people and that the Law exposes our sin.

18. Does a man need to hear the gospel before He can be condemned?

19. List at least two changes you desire to take place in your life because of these verses.

    •

    •

Romans 2:1-11 Advanced Discussion Questions

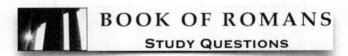

1. What kind of judging is being exposed and condemned (2:3)?
   Is all judging wrong? (Compare with James 4:11-12.)

2. Paul gives one or two ways these men might think about God.
   Name them (3-4).

3. Do you tend to look at other people's sins with condemnation
   thinking, "I am not like them"? Can you think of any
   illustrations of yourself doing this?

4. Memorize 2:6. Name three truths that come from this verse.

5. Many commentators, unfortunately, have neglected to carefully
   observe the context when understanding verses 6-7. List two
   verses that affirm there are no righteous people. As time
   allows, read up on the commentators and group them
   according to their view on this passage.

6. List two verses that state how a person can only gain righteousness through Christ.

7. Can anyone because of a special relationship with God or degree of virtue escape these blessings or curses? Why or why not?

#4 Romans 2:12-29 Study Questions

BOOK OF ROMANS
STUDY QUESTIONS

EXPOSING THREE EXCUSES OF THE SELF-RIGHTEOUS

Paul confronts three false confidences of the self-righteous Jew. Their 'good' deeds were wrongly used by the Jews to justify themselves before God, just as many religious Christians do today.

• **Starter:** Briefly share what you think will happen to those people who have never heard the gospel?

A) Not Through the Law (Rom 2:12-16)

[12] For all who have sinned without the Law will also perish without the Law; and all who have sinned under the Law will be judged by the Law; [13] for not the hearers of the Law are just before God, but the doers of the Law will be justified. [14] For when Gentiles who do not have the Law do instinctively the things of the Law, these, not having the Law, are a law to themselves, [15] in that they show the work of the Law written in their hearts, their conscience bearing witness, and their thoughts alternately accusing or else defending them, [16] on the day when, according to my gospel, God will judge the secrets of men through Christ Jesus.

1. How will those who sinned without knowing about God's Law (as revealed to the Jewish people) be judged (2:12)?

2. How will those who have sinned under the Jewish Law be judged 12)?

3. How do we know those who have not heard of the Jewish Law have the work of the Law written on their hearts (14-15)?

4. Is it possible to sin and perish with a knowledge of the Law (i.e. God's truth) (15)?

5. What is it that God will one day judge through Jesus Christ (16)? What might that include?

6. Some suggest that the Gentiles do not know what was expected of them and therefore couldn't be held accountable for their actions. This sounds good, but Paul says that they are accountable. Why?

B) Not Through One's Heritage (Rom 2:17-24)

17 But if you bear the name "Jew," and rely upon the Law, and boast in God, 18 and know His will, and approve the things that are essential, being instructed out of the Law, 19 and are confident that you yourself are a guide to the blind, a light to those who are in darkness, 20 a corrector of the foolish, a teacher of the immature, having in the Law the embodiment of knowledge and of the truth, 21 you, therefore, who teach another, do you not teach yourself? You who preach that one should not steal, do you steal? 22 You who say that one should not commit adultery, do you commit adultery? You who abhor idols, do you rob temples? 23 You who boast in the Law, through your breaking the Law, do you dishonor God? 24 For

"THE NAME OF GOD IS BLASPHEMED AMONG THE GENTILES BECAUSE OF YOU," just as it is written.

7. Write down some general characteristics of the Jews described in verses 17-18.

8. In verses 19-20 how does Paul describe the negative traits of some Jews?

9. Write down the specific problems some of the Jews had mentioned in 21-24?

C) Not through special rites (Rom 2:25-29)

25 For indeed circumcision is of value, if you practice the Law; but if you are a transgressor of the Law, your circumcision has become uncircumcision. 26 If therefore the uncircumcised man keeps the requirements of the Law, will not his uncircumcision be regarded as circumcision? 27 And will not he who is physically uncircumcised, if he keeps the Law, will he not judge you who though having the letter of the Law and circumcision are a transgressor of the Law? 28 For he is not a Jew who is one outwardly; neither is circumcision that which is outward in the flesh. 29 But he is a Jew who is one inwardly; and circumcision is that which is of the heart, by the Spirit, not by the letter; and his praise is not from men, but from God.

10. What is the significance of circumcision (Genesis 17:11)?

11. What does that last phrase in 25, "your circumcision has become uncircumcision" mean?

12. Is keeping the law or being physically circumcised more important (25-26)?

13. What does not necessarily make a person a Jew (27-28)?

14. How does Paul positively redefine a Jew in 2:29?

15. Christians also have religious rites like baptism. What makes a person a true Christian?

Summary

Any religion, or denomination, that points to good works for acceptance cannot save, whether they base their good works on the Old Testament or even New Testament—like many religious Christians do. If one perfectly acted out the Law as Jesus, then indeed there would be no problem, but since no one (except for Christ) has done that, then we all have failed and need salvation provided by Christ. We need a Savior which God has graciously provided.

16. Summarize the three ways Jews have excused themselves of God's judgment (12,17, 25). How does this dangerously parallel Christian perspectives causing many to be deceived?

17. Does baptism save? Explain. Does worship attendance save? Explain again.

18. List at least two changes you desire to take place in your life
because of these verses.

•

•

Romans 2:12-29 Advanced Discussion Questions

BOOK OF ROMANS
STUDY QUESTIONS

1. These Jews thought they were good religious people. How could they do these evil things in good conscience?

2. What is the conscience and how does it serve God's purposes? Is the conscience perfect?

3. Where do these truths from this passage leave the Japanese Buddhist and the tribal leader?

4. Read Genesis 17:9-14 to discover the origin of circumcision in Judaism? Who started it?

5. According to Paul what distinguishes a "real Jew" from those commonly called a Jew? Can you make the same distinction for a Christian? Is he a 'real' Christian?" What is the primary difference if any? Where do you think "circumcision of the heart" might have gotten its meaning?

6. How does one become a spiritual Jew? Look in 2:29. Are you a spiritual Jew? Explain.

7. Religious people call themselves Christians because they were baptized and go to church and yet do evil works. From the last two verses, how should we think of and approach these religious people (2:28-29)?

#5 Romans 3:1-20 Study Questions

BOOK OF ROMANS
STUDY QUESTIONS

CONNECTING GUILT WITH OUR SIN

Without a proper understanding of our sinfulness, we will overlook the need for grace and become weak Christians. Paul systematically eliminates any excuses a person, either Jew or Gentile, might depend upon to disguise their depravity.

- **Starter:** Are there really such a thing as 'good' people? Can people be accepted before God as righteous without Jesus?

A) The Grand Excuses (Rom 3:1-8)

3:1 Then what advantage has the Jew? Or what is the benefit of circumcision? 2 Great in every respect. First of all, that they were entrusted with the oracles of God. 3 What then? If some did not believe, their unbelief will not nullify the faithfulness of God, will it? 4 May it never be! Rather, let God be found true, though every man be found a liar, as it is written, "THAT THOU MIGHTEST BE JUSTIFIED IN THY WORDS, AND MIGHTEST PREVAIL WHEN THOU ART JUDGED." 5 But if our unrighteousness demonstrates the righteousness of God, what shall we say? The God who inflicts wrath is not unrighteous, is He? (I am speaking in human terms.) 6 May it never be! For otherwise how will God judge the world? 7 But if through my lie the truth of God abounded to His glory, why am I also still being judged as a sinner? 8 And why not say (as we are slanderously reported and as some affirm that we say), "Let us do evil that good may come"? Their condemnation is just.

1. List the advantages mentioned in 3:1-2 that the Jews have over the Gentiles (non-Jews). What does this mean?

2. Even though the Jews had the Word of God, some of them didn't actually believe God and obey Him (3).

3. What is the opposite to belief in God's Word? Do Christians have the same problem today? Explain.

4. Would it be correct to state that God is always right, even though man thinks he is right correcting God (3-4)?

5. Although every man might have to be called a liar, God will always "be found _____" (4).

6. What arguments do some non-Christians use to cover up their sin (7)? Have you ever heard a professing believer say something like that?

7. Some people twist Paul's words, suggesting that God can be equally glorified through our sin and our righteous lives. What is Paul's response to this (8)?

B) The Fair Assessment (Rom 3:9-20)

⁹ What then? Are we Jews any better off? No, not at all. For we have already charged that all, both Jews and Greeks, are under sin, ¹⁰ as it is written: "None is righteous, no, not one; ¹¹ no one understands; no one seeks for God. ¹² All have turned aside; together they have become worthless; no one does good, not even one. ¹³ Their throat is an open grave; they use their tongues to deceive. The venom of asps is under their lips. ¹⁴ Their mouth is full of curses and bitterness. ¹⁵ Their feet are swift to shed blood; ¹⁶ in their paths are ruin and misery, ¹⁷ and the way of peace they have not known. ¹⁸ There is no fear of God before their eyes." ¹⁹ Now we know that whatever the law says it speaks to those who are under the law, so that every mouth may be stopped, and the whole world may be held accountable to God. ²⁰ For by works of the law no human being will be justified in his sight, since through the law comes knowledge of sin. (ESV)

8. Are the Jews, who have God's Word, better off than those who do not have the Bible (9)? Why so?

9. About what percentage of people in this world are righteous or seek for God (10-12)? Circle the closest appropriate answer below.

    0%   25%   50%   75%   100%

10. Go through the verses 10-18 (all quotes from the OT) and list all the descriptions of these people. How many do you find?

11. What surprises you most from the statements in the above question? Why?

12. Who is Paul describing in verses 10-18 (9)? Does that include us? Explain.

13. What is it that all these people do not have (18)? Describe what that means? How does the possession of it change our lifestyles?

14. What is one major function of the Law for those who live under it (19)?

15. Will the people who really try hard to obey the Law (live a righteous life) be justified in God's sight (20)?

Summary

We tend to overestimate the value of our lives and virtue which in turn diminishes the power of our guilt and sin to properly accuse us. Paul undermines all our attempts to prop ourselves up by verse 20, "For by works of the law no human being will be justified in his sight" (ESV).

16. How do you reconcile verses 10-12 with people who are sincerely seeking for the truth? Rephrase these verses in your own words.

17. Do you believe these verses apply to your own life? Explain.

18. List at least two changes you desire to take place in your life because of these verses.

Romans 3:1-20 Advanced Discussion Questions

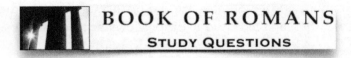

BOOK OF ROMANS
STUDY QUESTIONS

1. Disbelief in God's Word strips away the greatest privilege we have growing up in a Christian home. Share how disbelief in the authority of God's Word regarding the institution of marriage has caused confusion even among professing believers.

2. Unbelief in God's authoritative Word largely began with the rise of humanism when scholars assumed the Christian scriptures were on par with other religious scriptures and philosophies—believing all were manmade. How would you counter this argument?

3. How has liberalism within Christianity expressed its unbelief in God's Word?

4. What about Neo-orthodoxy? How have they conceptualized their unbelief in God's Word? (Some extra study might be required for answering this.)

5. What is the foundation of righteous courts (5-6)? Does the character of the judge make a difference? What difference

does it make, for example, if a judge thinks sexual immorality is
not evil?

6. Go through 3:10-18 and find the original sources of these Old
    Testament quotes. Summarize the picture of sin from these
    verses, then add about four other views people have towards
    sin.

7. What does the teaching of total depravity say? Are we as bad
    as we can be or is each part of us (total) corrupted? What are
    the parts of a person that are affected by depravity?

8. The depth of our understanding of grace is dependent upon a
    proper realization of our sin. Here are several parts of our
    Christian life that get messed up because of false views of our
    sinfulness. Explain how.

    •   Our salvation

    •   Our acceptance

    •   Our sanctification

    •   Our burden for evangelism

    •   Our commitment to God

#6 Romans 3:21-31 Study Questions

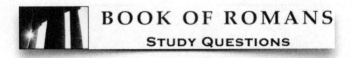

SALVATION BY FAITH

Paul has just about finished demonstrating that all men have sinned–there is not one human being who has a completely righteous character (except Jesus). Paul now teaches us how God in His graciousness provided a way to obtain this righteousness to find peace with Him.

- **Starter:** When did you first believe in Jesus Christ? How did it come about?

A) The fact of justification declared (Rom 3:21-26)

[21] But now apart from the Law the righteousness of God has been manifested, being witnessed by the Law and the Prophets, [22] even the righteousness of God through faith in Jesus Christ for all those who believe; for there is no distinction; [23] for all have sinned and fall short of the glory of God, [24] being justified as a gift by His grace through the redemption which is in Christ Jesus; [25] whom God displayed publicly as a propitiation in His blood through faith. [25b] This was to demonstrate His righteousness, because in the forbearance of God He passed over the sins previously committed; [26] for the demonstration, I say, of His righteousness at the present time, that He might be just and the justifier of the one who has faith in Jesus.

1. If righteousness does not come through the Law, how can we hope to obtain righteousness (3:21-22)?

2. How is this method different or like the way it is revealed in 1:16-17? Explain.

3. For this method of being justified by faith (literally declared to be righteous) to be effective, does it matter to which race or background one belongs (3:22)? Why?

4. Why is it that one's background does not influence how one is saved (23)?

5. What does it mean "fall short of the glory of God" in verse 23? What is God's standard? Where does it come from?

6. Why does Paul describe salvation as a "gift by His grace" (24)? How can this help us share the truth of the gospel?

7. What does propitiation mean (25)? What then does it mean by, "...Christ Jesus; whom God displayed publicly as a propitiation"?

8. Since we aren't justified in God's sight by perfectly completing the law, how is it possible to attain the righteousness of God (21-22)?

9. Why did God put up with all our sins, animal sacrifices that could never forgive anyone, along with our religions, rather than judge everyone right on the spot (25b-26)?

B) The results of justification (Rom 3:27-31)

[27] Where then is boasting? It is excluded. By what kind of law? Of works? No, but by a law of faith. [28] For we maintain that a man is justified by faith apart from works of the Law. [29] Or is God the God of Jews only? Is He not the God of Gentiles also? Yes, of Gentiles also, [30] since indeed God who will justify the circumcised by faith and the uncircumcised through faith is one. [31] Do we then nullify the Law through faith? May it never be! On the contrary, we establish the Law.

10. What cripples a man's attempt to boast before God about his righteous works (3:28)?

11. Is the Jew (circumcised) and the Gentile (not circumcised) justified and saved in the same way or in different ways (29-30)? Explain.

12. It is now clear that the laws in the Old Testament can't save us. What, then, should our attitude be toward the Law and the Old Testament (31)?

13. What does Paul mean that we "establish the Law" (31)?

Summary

The cross gives evidence of both God's standard of righteousness, and God's full satisfaction of righteousness for those who believe in Christ Jesus.

14. Why do you suppose so many people think they can earn their way to heaven? Seek to share the gospel with one such person this coming week.

15. Does it matter how wicked or bad someone has been in the past whether he or she can still be saved? Why?

16. List at least two changes you desire to take place in your life because of these verses.

•

•

Romans 3:21-31 Advanced Discussion Questions

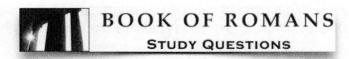

BOOK OF ROMANS
STUDY QUESTIONS

1. There are many religions out there. Would you agree that the basis of salvation starts in the character of God? Why and how does 3:23 with "fall short of the glory of God" assume that?

2. From verse 3:23b, how might you tell someone what sin is? (Hint: Look up the word for 'sin' in the original Greek language.)

3. There are numerous Christian theological terms used in this section. What does redemption literally mean (24)? How is it applied to the area of Christian salvation?

4. Where else is the word 'propitiation' used in the scripture? Why is this word used rather than sacrifice?

5. What does Jesus' crucifixion demonstrate about God?

6. Here is an often repeated question, "What about the sins of the people before Jesus' time?" Why did Jesus not come earlier?

7. Does any man naturally possess a righteousness acceptable to God? Can any man earn this necessary righteousness? Explain.

8. Circle the times a variation of the word 'justify' is used in this section. Define justify in a biblical sense (24,26,28,30) and relate it to the other theological terms used nearby: redemption, propitiation, faith, etc.

9. Is there more than one way by which a man may be justified? Explain and defend your answer from this passage.

#7 Romans 4:1-12 Study Questions

ILLUSTRATIONS OF FAITH'S POWER

Paul, deep in a theological discussion in chapter 3, suddenly jumps to using Old Testament stories, strengthening his argument by pointing out how these famous individuals affirm those truths.

- **Starter:** Which story of the Old Testament do you like best and why?

A) A Look at Abraham's Life (Rom 4:1-5)

4:1 What then shall we say that Abraham, our forefather according to the flesh, has found? 2 For if Abraham was justified by works, he has something to boast about; but not before God. 3 For what does the Scripture say? "AND ABRAHAM BELIEVED GOD, AND IT WAS RECKONED TO HIM AS RIGHTEOUSNESS." 4 Now to the one who works, his wage is not reckoned as a favor, but as what is due. 5 But to the one who does not work, but believes in Him who justifies the ungodly, his faith is reckoned as righteousness.

1. Which forefather of the Jews is mentioned in verse 1? List five facts from the Old Testament that you know about this character.

2. Write down and memorize Genesis 15:6, the Old Testament passage quoted here in verse 3.

3. Finish this statement (4): When one works, his wage is considered _____.

4. What kind of people does God justify (5)? (Note: 'Justify' here means to declare righteous as in contrast to make righteous.)

5. Give an example of some works, rites and ceremonies that people do to build up their sense of goodness. Do you have this tendency to emphasize your contribution to cover over your fault? Explain.

B) A Look at David's Life (Rom 4:6-8)

[6] Just as David also speaks of the blessing upon the man to whom God reckons righteousness apart from works: [7] "BLESSED ARE THOSE WHOSE LAWLESS DEEDS HAVE BEEN FORGIVEN, AND WHOSE SINS HAVE BEEN COVERED. [8] "BLESSED IS THE MAN WHOSE SIN THE LORD WILL NOT TAKE INTO ACCOUNT."

6. What famous Jewish ancestor is mentioned in verse 6? List five significant facts about his life.

7. What kind of person is it said that God greatly blesses (6)? Does this surprise you? Why or why not?

8. What word did David use to describe the benefit of receiving forgiveness of sin (4:6-8)?

9. Describe some sins of David connected to Bathsheba (cf. 2 Sam 11).

10. Do you think it is right for God to forgive such sinners? Why or why not?

11. Do you think it right for God to bless such great sinners? Again, why or why not?

12. Would you want God to forgive and bless you—no matter what your sin?

C) A Look at Old Testament Truths (Rom 4:9-12)

Paul did not stop with the above two cases but strengthened these arguments to take one more bold step.

> [9] Is this blessing then upon the circumcised, or upon the uncircumcised also? For we say, "FAITH WAS RECKONED TO ABRAHAM AS RIGHTEOUSNESS." [10] How then was it reckoned? While he was circumcised, or uncircumcised? Not while circumcised, but while uncircumcised; [11] and he received the sign of circumcision, a seal of the righteousness of the faith which he had while uncircumcised, that he might be the father of all who believe without being circumcised, that righteousness might be reckoned to them, [12] and the father of circumcision to those who not only are of the circumcision, but who also follow in the steps of the faith of our father Abraham which he had while uncircumcised.

13. Was Abraham considered or declared righteous before or after he was circumcised (10)?

14. What is circumcision? (Look up circumcision if you do not understand this ceremony.)

15. What is circumcision a wonderful sign of (11a)?

16. What does God's treatment of sinners show about God?

17. What kind of people does Abraham become the father of because of their faith in Jesus?

   • Verse 11:

   • Verse 12:

Summary

Salvation can be gained by all of us, no matter our nationality or the evil nature of our sin. Faith in the promise of God leads to forgiveness. As believers, we need to be careful to avoid emphasizing our works but rather renew one's thankfulness by contemplating our unworthiness and Christ's great work of love on the cross for us.

18. What do you answer those who say, "Salvation by faith is too easy. It should cost something"?

19. Do you think God is obligated to save mankind or you? Why or why not?

20. List at least two changes you desire to take place in your life because of these verses.

-

-

Romans 4:1-12 Advanced Discussion Questions

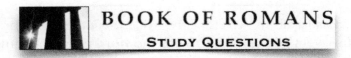

BOOK OF ROMANS
STUDY QUESTIONS

1. Read the Genesis passages (Gen 12-26) associated with Abraham. List the major events in order as Abraham experienced them. Which was the most significant and why?

2. Genesis 15:6 is called the gospel of the Old Testament. Why is this? On what basis does Paul or others suggest that this should be true of us as Christian believers too?

3. This passage stresses the need for our faith but not what we are to put our faith in. What are some examples of what people around the world put their trust in? Does it matter? What did Abraham believe?

4. What should we believe to be saved? Why is this important?

5. Read Psalm 32 in light of David's sin associated with Bathsheba. Should the grossest sinner be able to be forgiven? Why or why not? Give support for your answer? How should this apply to our penal system and the death sentence?

6. Some people believe baptism serves as a sign of salvation for the New Covenant as circumcision does for the Old Covenant. Is this discussed here? In what way may this be true or not true? Does faith come before or after baptism? Explain.

7. What is legalism? What are the evidences of legalism for unbelievers and believers? Does the word mean the same thing in both cases?

8. Is Paul basing theology upon experience in this chapter? Is this not dangerous? Explain.

9. This passage reminds us of the importance of faith. When God asks you to do something, do it! List something you need faith to obey.

10. How are the sins of Abraham and David different? Are you more like Abraham or David? Why so?

11. How can you share the gospel with someone who trusts in his good behavior, works or ceremony?

12. Many churches, Catholic, Orthodox and Protestant, have deserted the gospel by stressing good works as a means to acceptance before God. What are some signs that a church has a faulty view?

#8 Romans 4:13-25 Study Questions

THE NATURE OF SAVING FAITH

Paul might have convinced them that both Gentiles and Jews were sinners and required salvation, but the Jews needed convincing that salvation was also for the Gentiles.

- **Starter:** Give an example of where you exercised your faith and saw God work in a special way.

A) The Treachery of the Law (Rom 4:13-15)

^{13} For the promise to Abraham or to his descendants that he would be heir of the world was not through the Law, but through the righteousness of faith. ^{14} For if those who are of the Law are heirs, faith is made void and the promise is nullified; ^{15} for the Law brings about wrath, but where there is no law, neither is there violation.

1. What was the promise to Abraham and his descendants (4:13)?

2. What does the Law do (4:15)? How so?

B) The Character of Faith (Rom 4:16-22)

16 For this reason it is by faith, that it might be in accordance with grace, in order that the promise may be certain to all the descendants, not only to those who are of the Law, but also to those who are of the faith of Abraham, who is the father of us all, 17 (as it is written, "A FATHER OF MANY NATIONS HAVE I MADE YOU") in the sight of Him whom he believed, even God, who gives life to the dead and calls into being that which does not exist. 18 In hope against hope he believed, in order that he might become a father of many nations, according to that which had been spoken, "SO SHALL YOUR DESCENDANTS BE." 19 And without becoming weak in faith he contemplated his own body, now as good as dead since he was about a hundred years old, and the deadness of Sarah's womb; 20 yet, with respect to the promise of God, he did not waver in unbelief, but grew strong in faith, giving glory to God, 21 and being fully assured that what He had promised, He was able also to perform. 22 Therefore also IT WAS RECKONED TO HIM AS RIGHTEOUSNESS.

3. For what reason was salvation secured by faith rather than by Law (4:16)?

4. What are the several ways that God, the Giver of promises, is described in verse 17?

5. What was the promise given to Abraham, or at least the portion quoted here (4:18)?

6. What does it mean when describing Abraham's faith as "in hope against hope" (18-19)?

7. Describe the steps of Abraham's faith during the crisis time
    (spaces provided below) (4:19-21)?

    • Step #1 (4:19)

    • Step #2 (4:20)

    • Step #3 (4:21)

8. To what degree was Abraham sure that God would accomplish
    what He had promised (4:21)? (Circle the right answer.)

    not sure   a bit sure   fully assured

9. What was the result of this kind of faith (4:22)?

C) The Promise of Faith (Rom 4:23-25)

23 Now not for his sake only was it written, that it was reckoned to
him, 24 but for our sake also, to whom it will be reckoned, as those
who believe in Him who raised Jesus our Lord from the dead, 25 He
who was delivered up because of our transgressions, and was
raised because of our justification.

10. For whom was the OT phrase written, "It was reckoned to
    him" as righteousness (4:23-24)?

11. What do they need to believe in to gain this salvation (4:24)?

12. Jesus' death and resurrection reveal two aspects of our
    salvation (4:25): What profit did Jesus' death bring us? How did
    His resurrection help us?

Summary

Paul showed them how a person can, through faith, become Abraham's child. This faith becomes saving because it does two things: brings forgiveness of past wrongs and presents us as righteous in Christ! If we have the same type of faith as Abraham, we are Abraham's children.

13. Do you consider yourself Abraham's descendant? Why or why not?

14. We often hear, "It doesn't matter what you believe, just so you believe." Does it matter what you believe in? Explain your answer from these verses.

15. Many traditional Christians understand faith as an intellectual assent of knowledge. Is this the same as saving faith? Explain this using Abraham.

16. List at least two changes you desire to take place in your life because of these verses.

    •

    •

Romans 4:13-25 Advanced Discussion Questions

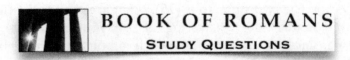

BOOK OF ROMANS
STUDY QUESTIONS

1. Why is the Law unable to help a person become a child of Abraham?

2. Describe the activity of Abraham's faith (or belief) from these phrases. Give examples of how your faith has grown stronger or weaker over time.

3. How does certain aspects of our faith differ or parallel with Abraham's faith 4:18-19, 24?

4. What does the usage of 'contemplated' (4:19) bring into this discussion? Why is this important?

5. Some people believe Jesus never died on the cross. Did Paul the apostle believe Jesus ever died? Describe the place Jesus' death has in saving His people.

6. Did you ever meet a person who said that they would believe
   if they first saw a miracle? How might you use Abraham's life
   and faith to answer such a question?

7. Salvation has two sides to it (25). What are they, and why is
   each essential? After answering this, use your answers to
   answer another question, "Why is it important that we believe
   in Jesus rather than in another person?"

#9 Romans 5:1-11 Study Questions

THE JOY OF OUR SALVATION

In the former sections, Paul spent much time describing the nature of salvation—how we believe, but here he introduces the blessings that salvation brings. How should salvation change our day-to-day lives?

• **Starter:** What are some things that make you happy? Why?

A) Confidence in God's Acceptance (Rom 5:1-2)

5:1 Therefore having been justified by faith, we have peace with God through our Lord Jesus Christ, 2 through whom also we have obtained our introduction by faith into this grace in which we stand; and we exult in hope of the glory of God.

1. What two results came into your life because you are justified by faith (5:1-2a)? (The word 'justification' means declared and accepted as righteous before God.)

    •

    •

2. Who enabled us to receive these privileges (5:1-2)?

B) Confidence of God's Purpose of Hardship (Rom 5:3-5)

³ And not only this, but we also exult in our tribulations, knowing that tribulation brings about perseverance; ⁴ and perseverance, proven character; and proven character, hope; ⁵ and hope does not disappoint, because the love of God has been poured out within our hearts through the Holy Spirit who was given to us.

3. Rewrite the short phrase "we exult in our tribulations" from verse 3 with your own words.

4. What special qualities should we expect God to be developing in our lives during difficult times (5:3-4)?

5. Who fills our hearts with the love of God (5:5)?

6. Complete this sentence with verse 5 (choose one). As a Christian, the Holy Spirit:

    •   has been given to us in the past.

    •   is being given to us in the present.

    •   will be given to us in the future.

C) Confidence in God's Risen Son (Rom 5:6-11)

⁶ For while we were still helpless, at the right time Christ died for the ungodly. ⁷ For one will hardly die for a righteous man; though perhaps for the good man someone would dare even to die. ⁸ But God demonstrates His own love toward us, in that while we were yet sinners, Christ died for us. ⁹ Much more then, having now been justified by His blood, we shall be saved from the wrath of God

through Him. [10] For if while we were enemies, we were reconciled to God through the death of His Son, much more, having been reconciled, we shall be saved by His life. [11] And not only this, but we also exult in God through our Lord Jesus Christ, through whom we have now received the reconciliation.

7. Fill in the blank. "At the _____ time Christ died for the ungodly" (5:6).

8. What kind of people did Christ die for (5:6-8)? {Please circle the right answer).

    • the unrighteous   the ungodly   people in sin

    • the righteous   the godly   good people

9. How did God show His love to us (8)?

10. What will we be saved from (5:9)?

11. Read verses 5:1 and 5:9 and please fill in the blanks.

    • "having been justified _____ " (5:1).

    • "having been justified _____ " (5:9).

12. What was our relationship with God like at the time we were reconciled with God (5:10)? (Reconciliation is the restoration of a relationship.)

13. How does Jesus make sure we will not suffer harm on Judgment Day (Rom 5:10; Mt 25:31-34)?

14. From verses 2, 3, 11 of chapter 5, please finish the phrases: {NIV uses "rejoice in" not "exult"}

   - 5:2 "we exult in _____"

   - 5:3 "we also exult in _____"

   - 5:11 "we also exult in _____"

Summary

Paul's spirit of joy clearly rings through these verses. God proves He has accepted us by not only objectively declaring us righteous but treating us righteous! This is the reason Christianity is signified by the word 'grace'.

15. Those who get sad or disheartened often drink or take a pill. Does that solve their problems? Explain.

16. What was Paul's joy based on?

17. Is your joy stable? Why or why not? Draw a line graph of your joy in your life as a believer. What caused it to be this way?

18. List at least two changes you desire to take place in your life because of these verses:

   •

   •

Romans 5:1-11 Advanced Discussion Questions

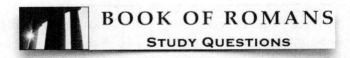

BOOK OF ROMANS
STUDY QUESTIONS

1. Can joy be found and maintained even through difficult times? Why or why not? Use Romans 5:1-11 to answer.

2. Doesn't man have peace with God anyway? How are we at war? What are some things man attempts to do so God will be at peace with him?

3. What does 'justified' means (5:1)? What does the 'by faith' mean (5:1)? Why only by faith can one be saved (relate to former section)?

4. Many people have trouble understanding suffering. How could you use this passage to explain suffering to believers and nonbelievers? Try to relate it to the discussion of evil.

5. What does this passage teach regarding Christian spiritual growth? How does it happen? How is spiritual growth affected by our life experiences?

6. Why is it that Christian believers question God's love even though it has been clearly demonstrated through Christ's death on the cross for us (5:8)?

7. All across the world people speak of self-esteem. How are we to integrate Paul's description of our persons as ungodly, sinners and enemies with this idea of self-esteem? Is self-esteem biblical? What would be a biblical self-perspective like?

8. Has our praise risen from exulting in hope to "exulting in God" (2)?

#10 Romans 5:12-21 Study Questions

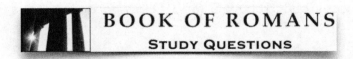

THE EXCELLENCE AND EFFECTIVENESS OF GRACE

People greatly influence the lives of others for good and bad. Adam introduced sin into the human race, but Jesus introduced righteousness. So how can we escape Adam's influence and gain Jesus' righteousness?

- **Starter:** What was one person that greatly influenced you? How so?

A) Worldwide Stain of Sin and Death (Rom 5:12-14)

5:12 Therefore, just as through one man sin entered into the world, and death through sin, and so death spread to all men, because all sinned— 13 for until the Law sin was in the world; but sin is not imputed when there is no law. 14 Nevertheless death reigned from Adam until Moses, even over those who had not sinned in the likeness of the offense of Adam, who is a type of Him who was to come.

1. Who is responsible for bringing sin into the world (5:12)? (See also Genesis chapters 2 and 3.)

2. What sign or evidence is there that everyone has sinned (5:12)?

3. Was there sin before the Old Testament Law was given by Moses around 2000 B.C. (5:13)? How do we know this (5:14)?

4. Who is Adam said to be a type for (5:14c)?

B) Adam and Christ Contrasted (Rom 5:15-17)

¹⁵ But the free gift is not like the transgression. For if by the transgression of the one the many died, much more did the grace of God and the gift by the grace of the one Man, Jesus Christ, abound to the many. ¹⁶ And the gift is not like that which came through the one who sinned; for on the one hand the judgment arose from one transgression resulting in condemnation, but on the other hand the free gift arose from many transgressions resulting in justification. ¹⁷ For if by the transgression of the one, death reigned through the one, much more those who receive the abundance of grace and of the gift of righteousness will reign in life through the One, Jesus Christ.

5. How is the gift of God different from the result of the one man's sin (5:15)?

6. The word 'gift' is used four times in 15-17. What is a gift? Who gave this gift? What was the gift?

7. Explain this part of verse 16 in your own words, "The free gift arose from many transgressions resulting in justification."

8. What is the transgression referred to in verse 17? Who transgressed? What happened as a result?

C) Adam and Christ Compared (Rom 5:18-19)

[18] So then as through one transgression there resulted condemnation to all men, even so through one act of righteousness there resulted justification of life to all men. [19] For as through the one man's disobedience the many were made sinners, even so through the obedience of the One the many will be made righteous.

9. How did one transgression affect so many people (18)?

10. What resulted through Jesus' act of righteousness (18)? How did this happen?

11. From Romans 5:19 write down the effect one man has had (Adam & Jesus) upon the world.

- 19a) Through the disobedience of the one man

  _____.

- 19b) Through the obedience of the one man

  _____ .

D) The Purpose of God (Rom 5:20-21)

[20] And the Law came in that the transgression might increase; but where sin increased, grace abounded all the more, [21] that, as sin reigned in death, even so grace might reign through righteousness to eternal life through Jesus Christ our Lord.

12. What increased as the Law was introduced (20)?
    What increased when sin increased?

13. If we know sin is all around us by the presence of death, what
    then is the mark or sign of God's grace in a Christian's life
    (5:21)?

Summary

People's minds, clouded with a modern glasses, have a difficulty
understanding and accepting how Adam's sin can implicate us even
though though the evidence is everywhere around us. But without
this truth, none of us would be saved. Like Adam, it is the headship
that allows the righteousness of Christ to be applied to our lives.

14. What is the difference between life and death?

15. Do you believe you are more influenced by the first Adam or
    the second Adam, Jesus? Explain.

16. Who do you influence? How do you influence them? What
    step can you take to better influence them?

17. List at least two changes you desire to take place in your life
    because of these verses:

    •

    •

Romans 5:12-21 Advanced Discussion Questions

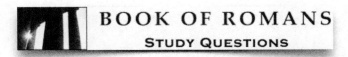

1. This representative nature of one over many, such as in Adam and Jesus, is called 'federal headship.' What do you think about one person representing so many people? Is it fair? Is it democratic? Does it need to be?

2. What does modern man believe about such things? Why?

3. What would happen if Jesus could not represent all those who believed in Him?

4. How come we suffer because of another person's sin? Do you want to be blessed by another person's (i.e. Jesus) obedience. Explain.

5. Will those who do not know the Jewish Law going to suffer judgment? How do we know?

6. Christ's death and resurrection can really help people across cultures and time. How can it help them?

7. How many times is the phrase 'the many' used in Romans
   5:12-21? What is the significance of this? Please refer to Isaiah
   53:1-12 (especially 10-12).

#11 Romans 6:1-14 Study Questions

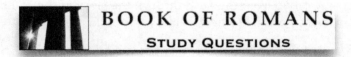

DOES JUSTIFICATION MEAN WE CAN SIN?

Romans 6 often confuses Christians because it refers to the ceremony of baptism but doesn't mention water. The baptism discussed here is not talking about the form or ceremony of baptism but the meaning and symbolism of baptism.

- **Starter:** Have you been baptized? When and what was it like?

A) The Question To Get Started (Rom 6:1)

6:1 What shall we say then? Are we to continue in sin that grace might increase?

1. Rephrase verse 6:1 loosely into your own words. Have you ever heard anyone ask this before?

2. Examine verses 5:20-21. Note any possible connection these verses have with chapter 6?

B) The Definition of Baptism (Rom 6:2-4)

^{2} May it never be! How shall we who died to sin still live in it? ^{3} Or do you not know that all of us who have been baptized into Christ Jesus have been baptized into His death? ^{4} Therefore we have been buried with Him through baptism into death, in order that as Christ was raised from the dead through the glory of the Father, so we too might walk in newness of life.

3. What answer does Paul give to the question he raises in verse 1 (see verse 2)?

4. What does Paul assume that all Christians should know (see verse 3)? What does it mean?

5. For what reason have we been buried with Christ through baptism into death (4)?

C) The Explanation of Baptism (Rom 6:5-11)

^{5} For if we have become united with Him in the likeness of His death, certainly we shall be also in the likeness of His resurrection, ^{6} knowing this, that our old self was crucified with Him, that our body of sin might be done away with, that we should no longer be slaves to sin; ^{7} for he who has died is freed from sin. ^{8} Now if we have died with Christ, we believe that we shall also live with Him, ^{9} knowing that Christ, having been raised from the dead, is never to die again; death no longer is master over Him. ^{10} For the death that He died, He died to sin, once for all; but the life that He lives, He lives to God. ^{11} Even so consider yourselves to be dead to sin, but alive to God in Christ Jesus.

6. Fill in the blanks. "If we have become united with Him

    in the likeness of His _____ , certainly we

shall be also in the likeness of His _____ " (5).

7. List two or three ways Paul describes us before we became Christians (6).

8. What happened to that "old" person (6, 8)? What does that mean?

9. Death used to be our master. Who is our master now (8-10)? What does that practically mean in our Christian lives?

10. Write down and memorize verse 11.

D) The Practical Meaning of Baptism (Rom 6:12-14)

[12] Therefore do not let sin reign in your mortal body that you should obey its lusts, [13] and do not go on presenting the members of your body to sin as instruments of unrighteousness; but present yourselves to God as those alive from the dead, and your members as instruments of righteousness to God. [14] For sin shall not be master over you, for you are not under law, but under grace.

11. What does verse 12 suggest the practical outworking of this spiritual experience and exchange of masters in our Christian lives?

12. Name three ways that we might present our members of our body to sin (13).

13. List several ways how we can present ourselves to God (13).

14. Why does he say that sin shall not be master over us (14)?

Summary

Don't be afraid of the implications of being joined to Christ for it is not only here we are saved, but it also the secret to a powerful life with Christ. Join Him and see what you can do with Him as He leads you!

15. What does it mean to be under grace rather than law?

16. What does this chapter teach about baptism?

17. How do these teachings of baptism relate to our ideas of baptism? List one practical step you can take to apply this lesson to your life.

18. List at least two changes you desire to take place in your life because of these verses:

    •

    •

Romans 6:1-14 Advanced Discussion Questions

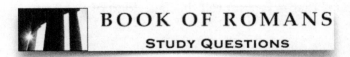

BOOK OF ROMANS
STUDY QUESTIONS

1. What is similar to the way Paul introduces each of these four wrong conclusions of justification by faith in chapters 6-7 (6:1, 15; 7:7, 13)?

2. The first of four different arguments in chapters 6-7 is dealt with in 6:1-14. What is the wrong conclusion these people made?

3. What is Paul's argument presented here in this section?

4. How would you use the above summary to speak to the professing believer who says, "Oh, I can do whatever I want now? I am free from sin under grace. God even gives more grace when I sin."

5. What other passages speak about the meaning of baptism? How does baptism relate to: a) justification by faith, and b) sanctification (i.e. Christian growth)?

6. Do any groups or individuals share this thinking as indicated in verse 1-2, in part or whole? Discuss.

7. For an advanced study, go through church history to find groups that have adopted this false kind of thinking.

8. Are believers free to do whatever they want? Use this passage to explain.

#12 Romans 6:15-23 Study Questions

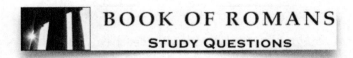

BOOK OF ROMANS
STUDY QUESTIONS

SERVING ONLY ONE MASTER

The Law's power over us is gone, and we have gained a new Master! Living under grace means that we have transferred to a new and better Master, the Lord Jesus Christ.

- **Starter:** Share an experience where you had to do something that you didn't like. How does that compare to doing something you do like?

A) Choice of a Master (Rom 6:15-16)

6:15 What then? Shall we sin because we are not under law but under grace? May it never be! 16 Do you not know that when you present yourselves to someone as slaves for obedience, you are slaves of the one whom you obey, either of sin resulting in death, or of obedience resulting in righteousness?

1. Rewrite the question found in verse 15 in your own words.

2. How does Paul answer that question in verse 15?

3. What happens when you become someone's slave (16)? Is it okay to change masters?

4. Paul gives examples of two kinds of slaves. Please fill in the
   outcome of each as verse 16 says.

   • If you give yourself to sin, then you will receive

     _____.

   • If you give yourself to obedience, then you will

     receive _____.

B) Change of Masters (Rom 6:17-18)

[17] But thanks be to God that though you were slaves of sin, you
became obedient from the heart to that form of teaching to which
you were committed, [18] and having been freed from sin, you
became slaves of righteousness.

5. From verse 17 what do we know about every Christian?

6. Describe what happens externally to a person who becomes a
   believer in Christ (see 17).

7. Following the former question, what happens internally (17)?

C) Two Different Masters (Rom 6:19-23)

[19] I am speaking in human terms because of the weakness of your
flesh. For just as you presented your members as slaves to impurity
and to lawlessness, resulting in further lawlessness, so now present
your members as slaves to righteousness, resulting in sanctification.
[20] For when you were slaves of sin, you were free in regard to
righteousness. [21] Therefore what benefit were you then deriving

from the things of which you are now ashamed? For the outcome of those things is death. [22] But now having been freed from sin and enslaved to God, you derive your benefit, resulting in sanctification, and the outcome, eternal life. [23] For the wages of sin is death, but the free gift of God is eternal life in Christ Jesus our Lord.

8. Some believers feel like it won't make a difference if they sin more. Paul disagrees. What does he say that happens when we sin (19)?

9. How then can we become a slave of righteousness (6:19)? (Key: notice the 'just as') Give an example of what this practically means.

10. What does Paul mean that we were free "in regard to righteousness" (20)?

11. What good came from the time before we were Christians (21)?

12. What should our attitude be to those still caught in sin (21)?

13. What good comes from being bound to serve God (22)? How are the two different from each other?

14. What is the difference between 'wages' and 'gift' (21)?

15. How important is it that one is actually a Christian (23)?
    Answer by observing the results. Circle one below:

    •   Not important   About the same   Important   Crucial

Summary

Unless we understand the way sin horribly affects our lives, we will never understand the delights of the way the Lord leads us in His grace and love. Now you have a new Master. Follow Him!

16. What is Paul's major point speaking about being a slave to sin and a slave to righteousness?

17. Can you personally identify with what Paul says about our spiritual lives here?

18. List at least two changes you desire to take place in your life because of these verses:

    •

    •

Romans 6:15-23 Advanced Discussion Questions

BOOK OF ROMANS
STUDY QUESTIONS

1. From this passage how would you respond to the person who says, "Wow! I don't have to live by the law anymore. I'm free. I can do whatever I feel like doing"?

2. If Christ fulfilled the law, why is it that we must go by it? Or do we?

3. Explain how the choices we make reflect what we end up with (6:1-2). How can you make your commitment to serve righteousness more clear?

4. Some Christians think they are neutral or not enslaved to anyone anymore (free, independent). How does this relate to verse 22, "But now having been freed from sin and enslaved to God"?

5. Explain why "free to serve God" more accurate describes the Christian life than just stating "free"? How should this biblical idea affect our society?

#13 Romans 7:1-12 Study Questions

FREED FROM SIN AND ENSLAVED TO GOD

This illustration of a married couple to show the power of the Law over our lives seems totally out of touch until we understand the heart of marriage.

- **Starter:** What are three great things about being married.

A) Illustration of Binding Power (Rom 7:1-3)

7:1 Or do you not know, brethren (for I am speaking to those who know the law), that the law has jurisdiction over a person as long as he lives? 2 For the married woman is bound by law to her husband while he is living; but if her husband dies, she is released from the law concerning the husband. 3 So then if, while her husband is living, she is joined to another man, she shall be called an adulteress; but if her husband dies, she is free from the law, so that she is not an adulteress, though she is joined to another man.

1. Paul begins chapter 7 by diving into some legal principles. What principle is stated in verse 1?

2. What example does he give in verse 2?

3. What two cases does Paul give to amplify the illustration in verse 2 (see verse 3)?

4. Why is adultery always wrong?

B) Dead to the Law (Rom 7:4-6)

[4] Therefore, my brethren, you also were made to die to the Law through the body of Christ, that you might be joined to another, to Him who was raised from the dead, that we might bear fruit for God. [5] For while we were in the flesh, the sinful passions, which were aroused by the Law, were at work in the members of our body to bear fruit for death. [6] But now we have been released from the Law, having died to that by which we were bound, so that we serve in newness of the Spirit and not in oldness of the letter.

5. How does he apply this second case, found in verse 3, to our Christian lives (see verse 4)?

6. We become free from the power of the Law but then in that process become bound to another. Who is that (4)?

7. What result does that new relationship have upon our lives (4)? What are the implications of that?

8. What was the result or fruit of that old relationship to the Law (5)?

9. Why did that old relationship to the law cause such terrible effects on their lives (5)?

10. Go back to verses 7:1-2 and review the proper way to be released from the legal contract. Fill in the wonderful consequences of believing in Christ and being freed from the Law (6).

- "... so that we serve in _____."

- "...and not (serve) in_____."

11. Do we as Christians still have this problem of sin even if we were not part of the Old Covenant Law? How so?

C) The Problem of Me (Rom 7:7-12)

7 What shall we say then? Is the Law sin? May it never be! On the contrary, I would not have come to know sin except through the Law; for I would not have known about coveting if the Law had not said, "YOU SHALL NOT COVET." 8 But sin, taking opportunity through the commandment, produced in me coveting of every kind; for apart from the Law sin is dead. 9 And I was once alive apart from the Law; but when the commandment came, sin became alive, and I died; 10 and this commandment, which was to result in life, proved to result in death for me; 11 for sin, taking opportunity through the commandment, deceived me, and through it killed me. 12 So then, the Law is holy, and the commandment is holy and righteous and good.

12. After looking at verses 1-6, would you say that the Law is sinful (7)?

13. What example does Paul give to show us that the Law is not sin (7)? What is the real problem, then?

14. Read Exodus 20:1-17. What are these laws specially called?
    Define coveting.

15. What does Romans 7:8 mean by "coveting of every kind"?

16. Is it a sinful heart or the commandment (the Law) <u>that</u>
    produces covetousness (8)?

17. Is it true during part of our lives that Paul and ourselves are
    free from the Law (9)? What does Paul refer to here?

18. What is the intent of the commandment of God (10)?

19. What instead happened because of God's commandment (11)?
    Why?

20. Write down the adjectives describing the Law and
    commandment in verse 12.

Summary

People, including many Christians, simply do not understand the
way we are bound to our fleshly nature. The only way out is
through death, much like a marriage. This is why we celebrate a
marriage union with Christ.

21. Coveting is a modern sin. Advertisements are everywhere fostering a spirit of discontent. See if you can remember the last few commercials you have seen or listened to.

22. In what ways are you suspicious of rules from authorities like parents, God or church? How are laws good and helpful? For example, think of the rules a toddler receives not to touch dangerous things.

23. List at least two changes you desire to take place in your life because of these verses.

   •

   •

Romans 7:1-12 Advanced Discussion Questions

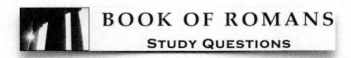

BOOK OF ROMANS
STUDY QUESTIONS

1. What is the Law mentioned here that has power over us? Is it God's Law, the Old Covenant, a moral law or something else? Use other verses to back up your opinion.

2. How does the power of the Law relate to all believers and not just Jewish ones, or does it?

3. What forms or breaks a marriage? Who says so? Explain the tension and misunderstandings between religious and civil laws of marriage, divorce and remarriage.

4. Examine the way modern philosophers and the world are denigrating the law's place in our society. What do they deep down believe about the Law? Is it good or bad? Why?

5. It is our sinful self that sins but how is it that the Law actually intensifies the sin?

6. Does verse 9 teach us anything regarding the teaching of an age of accountability? This teaching asserts one is not accountable for his sins until a certain age usually around 12. Is it really possible that Paul or other children are not aware of the Law until age of accountability? What might this verse refer to?

7. Reflect on your struggles with sin. Which sins do you struggle with most? How does the Law or the Word of God make you more aware of your wrong? Does the Law make you sin more?

8. How is it that we are to positively use our special relationship with Christ to live above the reach of sin? Can we be sinless? Why or why not?

9. How easy is it for your to humble yourself and admit your sin? What is one difficult sin to confess?

#14 Romans 7:13-25 Study Questions

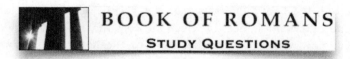

BOOK OF ROMANS
STUDY QUESTIONS

THE POWER OF OUR TWO NATURES

By exposing his own struggles, the apostle reveals the ugly work of the flesh dragging us into sin, clearly countering the work of the Spirit through the inner man. He exposes why we are judged for our sin and how the moral principles behind the law are good and to be loved.

- **Starter:** Name a misunderstanding someone had about you. Was it hard to deal with?

A) The Crucial Misunderstanding (Rom 7:13)

7:13 Therefore did that which is good become a cause of death for me? May it never be! Rather it was sin, in order that it might be shown to be sin by effecting my death through that which is good, that through the commandment sin might become utterly sinful.

1. What does the phrase "that which is good" refer to (13)? (Look at previous verses as needed.)

2. Can the law become the cause of spiritual or eternal death (13)? Why?

B) The Proper Understanding (Rom 7:14-25)

[14] For we know that the Law is spiritual; but I am of flesh, sold into bondage to sin. [15] For that which I am doing, I do not understand; for I am not practicing what I would like to do, but I am doing the very thing I hate. [16] But if I do the very thing I do not wish to do, I agree with the Law, confessing that it is good. [17] So now, no longer am I the one doing it, but sin which indwells me. [18] For I know that nothing good dwells in me, that is, in my flesh; for the wishing is present in me, but the doing of the good is not. [19] For the good that I wish, I do not do; but I practice the very evil that I do not wish.

[20] But if I am doing the very thing I do not wish, I am no longer the one doing it, but sin which dwells in me. [21] I find then the principle that evil is present in me, the one who wishes to do good. [22] For I joyfully concur with the law of God in the inner man, [23] but I see a different law in the members of my body, waging war against the law of my mind, and making me a prisoner of the law of sin which is in my members. [24] Wretched man that I am! Who will set me free from the body of this death? [25] Thanks be to God through Jesus Christ our Lord! So then, on the one hand I myself with my mind am serving the law of God, but on the other, with my flesh the law of sin.

3. How does Paul describe the Law in verse 14?

4. How does Paul here describe himself (14)? Would you describe yourself in this way? Why or why not?

5. Rewrite verse 15 in your own words? Do you sense this tension too? When?

6. Can sinful activity come from our spiritual nature (17-18)?

7. What does he want to do in verse 19? Does he do it?

8. What does he not desire to do (19)? Does he do it?

9. What conclusion does he make about his wrong deeds (20)? Do you think Paul is saying that he is not responsible for his sin? Why?

10. Please finish this quote from verse 21:"I find then the principle that evil is present in me, the one who _____."

11. "The inner man" or "inner being" is only used in Paul's writing (22). Does it refer to his spiritual or his fleshly nature? Why might he use this term?

12. Paul equates his inner nature with the law of his mind. What is this law of his mind waging war against (23)? Why does he use the term 'war'?

13. How does Paul the apostle describe himself in verse 24? Is this a question people should think about themselves? Why so?

14. What is the desperate question he raises in verse 24? Memorize this question.

15. His answer is split into three parts (25).

   • Who can set him free?

   • What part of him serves the law of God?

   • What part of him serves the law of sin?

Summary

If you haven't discovered it, the Christian life is a fight between our two natures. Yes, we are victors through Christ but do you still give into the flesh through temptation? Let's walk more wary so that we can please our kind Lord.

16. How can a believer still sin even when he has a new spiritual nature?

17. Do you believe God always has the best intentions in what He does for His people, including the giving of the Law? Explain.

18. Have you ever found delivery from this inner strife? How did Paul find it?

19. List at least two changes you desire to take place in your life because of these verses:

   •

   •

Romans 7:13-25 Advanced Discussion Questions

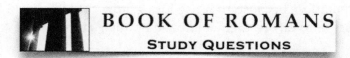

BOOK OF ROMANS
STUDY QUESTIONS

1. Compare the 'misunderstandings' people have toward righteous living in Romans 6 and 7. How does 7:13 differ from or is similar to the other three: 6:1, 6:15 and 7:7?

2. Does this section act as a fourth misunderstanding or is it used distinctively from the former? Explain. (This question is the same as how should chapters 6 and 7 be broken down in an outline.)

3. If we cannot expect anything good from the fleshly nature, are there any "good" non-Christians? Explain your answer.

4. Do you ever feel discouraged with the way you give into sin? How does this passage encourage you?

5. There is a huge difference in how people interpret this passage. We look at it as an ongoing spiritual struggle to live uprightly. Paul has a flesh and it is constantly fighting against him. How do others treat this passage? Why? (This question might take some research!)

6. Did you ever try to reason with an unbeliever on why he or she should do what is good and right?

7. If a brother (or sister) came up to you on how to fight temptation–because they are losing, how could you use this passage to advise them and build up their faith?

#15 Romans 8:1-11 Study Questions

BOOK OF ROMANS
STUDY QUESTIONS

FREED BY THE SPIRIT

In Romans 5:1-11 Paul shared the personal inner joy and peace stemming from becoming a Christian. The changes don't stop there! In 8:1-11 we learn what happens on the inside of the Christian that makes such a key difference in one's life.

- **Starter:** What image comes to your mind when you hear the phrase "set free"?

A.) Freed From Condemnation (Rom 8:1)

8:1 There is therefore now no condemnation for those who are in Christ Jesus.

1. What does Paul say regarding those who are in Christ Jesus (i.e., Christians) (1)?

2. Define "condemnation" (1). Use a dictionary as necessary.

3. What does it mean to be "in Christ Jesus"?

4. Although not mentioned here, what happens to those who are not in Christ Jesus?

B.) Freed By the Spirit (Rom 8:2-8)

[2] For the law of the Spirit of life in Christ Jesus has set you free from the law of sin and of death. [3] For what the Law could not do, weak as it was through the flesh, God did: sending His own Son in the likeness of sinful flesh and as an offering for sin, He condemned sin in the flesh, [4] in order that the requirement of the Law might be fulfilled in us, who do not walk according to the flesh, but according to the Spirit. [5] For those who are according to the flesh set their minds on the things of the flesh, but those who are according to the Spirit, the things of the Spirit. [6] For the mind set on the flesh is death, but the mind set on the Spirit is life and peace, [7] because the mind set on the flesh is hostile toward God; for it does not subject itself to the law of God, for it is not even able to do so; [8] and those who are in the flesh cannot please God.

5. Some translations use "you" in 8:2; others use "me." This does not matter since he is referring to Christians. What has set you free from the law of sin and death (2)?

6. What things could the Law not do (8:3; see 7:7-12)?

7. Who does the "His own Son'" refer to (3)?

8. What did "His own Son" do (3)?

9. For what reason did the "Son" accomplish these things (4)?

10. For whom does the "Son" accomplish these things (4)?

11. What two kinds of people are referred to in verse 5?

  • #1

  • #2

12. What is the difference between the minds of these two kinds of people (6)?

13. List the four statements that are made regarding the "mind set on the flesh" in verses 7-8?

  • 1)

  • 2)

  • 3)

  • 4)

C.) Freed for the Spirit (Rom 8:9-11)

[9] However, you are not in the flesh but in the Spirit, if indeed the Spirit of God dwells in you. But if anyone does not have the Spirit of Christ, he does not belong to Him. [10] And if Christ is in you, though the body is dead because of sin, yet the spirit is alive because of righteousness. [11] But if the Spirit of Him who raised Jesus from the dead dwells in you, He who raised Christ Jesus from the dead will also give life to your mortal bodies through His Spirit who indwells you.

14. What is the overriding characteristic of those who are controlled by the Spirit (9)?

15. Can anyone be a genuine Christian and not have the Holy Spirit (9)?

16. When he refers to the Christian's body as being "dead" (10), do you think he is talking about Christians who are physically dead or Christians who are living but as far as they are concerned, they are no longer living under the control of their bodies (i.e., flesh)? Explain.

Summary

Our evil nature is not just a little bad. Get convinced! Our sinful nature will always betray us. Don't trust it a bit. But the Spirit of God? Yes, trust Him always. God is eager to teach you how to live in harmony with Him just as Jesus did.

17. What does this passage say that Jesus did for you?

18. Think through the life of Jesus. What might it mean to have the Spirit of Jesus Christ in you?

19. Give an instance when you carried out something in the flesh (like getting angry or impatient). How did it help or hurt you and others? What would be the difference if you let the Spirit of Christ resolve that situation? What might happen?

20. List at least two changes you desire to take place in your life because of these verses

  •

  •

Romans 8:1-11 Advanced Discussion Questions

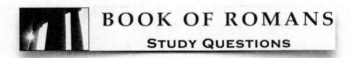

BOOK OF ROMANS
STUDY QUESTIONS

1. Read through chapter 8. Do all Christians have the Spirit? Is there any hint that the Spirit comes in greater and greater portions or stages?

2. All Christians have the Spirit of God but what if, as a believer, I don't feel like I have the Spirit?

3. Is the leading of the Spirit of Christ your delight or do you fear His complete leadership?

4. Do you find yourself making decisions in conflict with what you really want?

5. Think through the life of Jesus. What might it mean to have the Spirit of Jesus Christ in you?

6. Do we have to sin? Explain.

7. Verse 9 speaks of the "Spirit of God dwells in you" while verse 10 "Christ is in you." Are they the same? Why might Paul use different names?

8. How should we deal with our feelings and emotions when they go contrary to the will of God?

9. What are your experiences with your old nature? Do you still think the flesh can do any good or at any time can be relied upon? Explain.

10. Non-Christians and even some Christians are often surprised that God expects human beings to be perfect. Does it appear from Romans 8:4 that people are expected to fulfill the Law of God?

11. From verse 9 we learned the Spirit of God dwells in every Christian. How will that Spirit affect our present lives and bodies (11)? Connect your reflections with the idea of a temple (1 Cor 3:16-17; 6:19; Eph 2:21).

#16 Romans 8:12-25 Study Questions

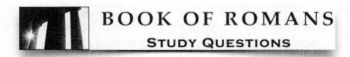

BOOK OF ROMANS
STUDY QUESTIONS

LIVING BY THE SPIRIT

Having escaped the clutches of the flesh, we are now led by the Spirit of God as the children of God. We are not free to simply do anything, but are committed to living for Jesus.

- **Starter:** Share one experience where you sensed God's closeness to you.

A) Not under obligation to the flesh (Rom 8:12-13)

8:12 So then, brethren, we are under obligation, not to the flesh, to live according to the flesh—13 for if you are living according to the flesh, you must die; but if by the Spirit you are putting to death the deeds of the body, you will live.

1. What are Christians obligated not to do (12)? State that in your own words.

2. What is the result for a person who lives under the principles and power of the flesh (13)?

3. What happens when one lives by the Spirit (13)? What does that practically mean?

B) Being led by the Spirit (Rom 8:14-17)

¹⁴ For all who are being led by the Spirit of God, these are sons of God. ¹⁵ For you have not received a spirit of slavery leading to fear again, but you have received a spirit of adoption as sons by which we cry out, "Abba! Father!" ¹⁶ The Spirit Himself bears witness with our spirit that we are children of God, ¹⁷ and if children, heirs also, heirs of God and fellow heirs with Christ, if indeed we suffer with Him in order that we may also be glorified with Him.

4. Please complete: Christians not only have the Spirit of God (9) but also are "_____" (14).

5. What happens when people are driven by a spirit of slavery (15)? Explain how this happens.

6. What happens when people are driven by a spirit of sonship (15)? Again explain why this happens.

7. From verse 16 share what the Spirit does in the hearts of Christians? Why is this important?

8. What happens as a result of being spiritually adopted in God's family (17)?

9. What pattern of Christian living is mentioned in the latter part of verse 17?

C) Being cared for by the Spirit (Rom 8:18-25)

[18] For I consider that the sufferings of this present time are not worthy to be compared with the glory that is to be revealed to us. [19] For the anxious longing of the creation waits eagerly for the revealing of the sons of God. [20] For the creation was subjected to futility, not of its own will, but because of Him who subjected it, in hope [21] that the creation itself also will be set free from its slavery to corruption into the freedom of the glory of the children of God. [22] For we know that the whole creation groans and suffers the pains of childbirth together until now. [23] And not only this, but also we ourselves, having the first fruits of the Spirit, even we ourselves groan within ourselves, waiting eagerly for our adoption as sons, the redemption of our body. [24] For in hope we have been saved, but hope that is seen is not hope; for why does one also hope for what he sees? [25] But if we hope for what we do not see, with perseverance we wait eagerly for it.

10. What are the two things that Paul compares in verse 18?

11. What is waiting for the sons of God to be revealed (19)?

12. Why is it so expectantly waiting (20)?

13. Like the end of a beautiful novel, share how this world's story will end (21)?

14. How does verse 22 amplify the phrase in verse 20: "creation was subjected to futility"? What are some signs of this that you see in the creation around you?

15. Who else besides the creation is groaning and anticipating the coming liberation (23)? Why so?

16. What is the "redemption of the body" (23)?

17. Why does "hope" accurately characterize a Christian's life on earth (24-25)?

18. Will we have hope in heaven (24-25)? Explain.

Summary

People around us sound so confident that they understand themselves (i.e. self-esteem) and the environment (i.e. green movement). Don't believe it for a second. Return to the scriptures! Note that when we adopt these truths revealed here for ourselves, our perspectives will follow reality, our lives stabilize so that God can start using us as we follow the Spirit's leading.

19. Have you learned to pause in prayer and in the Word to listen to the Spirit of God? How long is it before you get anxious and need to look at your text messages or computer screen? Do you need to do anything about it? What?

20. List at least two changes you desire to take place in your life because of these verses.

   •

   •

Romans 8:12-25 Advanced Discussion Questions

BOOK OF ROMANS
STUDY QUESTIONS

1. Some Christians assert that it is not important to make Jesus as 'Lord' of your life and obey Him. Is this consistent with 8:12-13? Explain.

2. Do you approach God as being uncaring and distant or near and personally caring for you? Explain from verse 15 which is the biblical perspective and why.

3. The Spirit of God is not an impersonal force but a person of the Godhead. What are some of the activities the Spirit is said to do in verses 8:12-17 that shows how He acts as a person?

4. Having been adopted as a child of God, we can call God "Daddy" (16). (The original word, *Abba*, is the informal use of Father.) Do you personally get close to God and call Him Daddy? Explain.

5. What are the presuppositions of environmentalists? What should be the Christian's perspective of these things (8:19-23)? Why did God subject the earth to futility? (cf. Gen 3).

6. In verses 20 and 22, Paul uses the word "creation". Does this make Paul a creationist in against evolutionist?

7. Go through 12-25 and mark all the promises and hopes for the Christian believer. Why is this hope in 23-25 so strongly emphasized?

#17 Romans 8:26-39 Study Questions

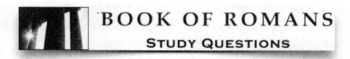

CONQUERORS THROUGH CHRIST

God wonderfully cares for His children, but questions about suffering tend to undermine that fact. By understanding how God's truth applies to questions of suffering, we can prepare ourselves for any suffering, distress or persecution. Counter the doubts that Satan subtly uses to lead us into despair and depression.

*   **Starter:** Share an incident where you suffered. (It can include things like sickness, abandonment, rejection, persecution, etc.)

A) Can I endure? (Rom 8:26-27)

8:26 And in the same way the Spirit also helps our weakness; for we do not know how to pray as we should, but the Spirit Himself intercedes for us with groanings too deep for words; 27 and He who searches the hearts knows what the mind of the Spirit is, because He intercedes for the saints according to the will of God.

1. What weakness does the Bible say Christians have (26)? Why might we have such weaknesses?

2. How does the Lord help us with this problem (26-27)?

B) Is God really in control? (Rom 8:28-30)

28 And we know that God causes all things to work together for good to those who love God, to those who are called according to His purpose. 29 For whom He foreknew, He also predestined to become conformed to the image of His Son, that He might be the first-born among many brethren; 30 and whom He predestined, these He also called; and whom He called, these He also justified; and whom He justified, these He also glorified.

3. Memorize Romans 8:28. What is so important about this verse so that Christians repeatedly quote this verse?

4. Discover the sequence in verses 29-30 that verify God's overriding purpose in our lives. The first of five is given to you! Define (or look up) each.

    • (1) For those God <u>foreknew</u>

    • (2) He also _____

    • (3) He also _____

    • (4) He also _____

    • (5) He also _____

5. Why is it important that God oversee our salvation from spiritual birth to glorification?

C) Does God really love me? (Rom 8:31-39)

31 What then shall we say to these things? If God is for us, who is against us? 32 He who did not spare His own Son, but delivered Him up for us all, how will He not also with Him freely give us all things? 33 Who will bring a charge against God's elect? God is the

one who justifies; ³⁴ who is the one who condemns? Christ Jesus is He who died, yes, rather who was raised, who is at the right hand of God, who also intercedes for us. ³⁵ Who shall separate us from the love of Christ? Shall tribulation, or distress, or persecution, or famine, or nakedness, or peril, or sword? ³⁶ Just as it is written, "FOR THY SAKE WE ARE BEING PUT TO DEATH ALL DAY LONG; WE WERE CONSIDERED AS SHEEP TO BE SLAUGHTERED." ³⁷ But in all these things we overwhelmingly conquer through Him who loved us. ³⁸ For I am convinced that neither death, nor life, nor angels, nor principalities, nor things present, nor things to come, nor powers, ³⁹ nor height, nor depth, nor any other created thing, shall be able to separate us from the love of God, which is in Christ Jesus our Lord.

6. Is God for us or against us (31)? What if it doesn't look like it, is He still for us? How do we know?

7. How does the Lord prove to us that He really is for us, that is, on our side (see verse 32)?

8. Why can't anyone bring a charge of incrimination against us (33-34)? Don't we really deserve judgment because of our sin?

9. Where in these verses does it <u>state</u> that the Lord loves us as His children (35-37)?

10. List those 7 troubles in verse 35 which Christians face at times.

    • (1) _____

    • (2) _____

- (3) _____

- (4) _____

- (5) _____

- (6) _____

- (7) _____

11. Even though we as Christians might face hardships, are we allowed to question God's love for us or another Christian (37)? What should our attitude be?

12. Where is the love of God to be found (39)? Why not somewhere else?

13. List the things that **cannot threaten** our loving relationship with the Lord (38-39). Many are given in pairs. Do you think Paul has tried to include everything here? Why or why not?

(1) _____   (2) _____

(3) _____   (4) _____

(5) _____   (6) _____

(7) _____

(8) _____   (9) _____

(10) _____

Summary

Satan has tricked many a believer so that they no longer trust God to lead them through life. The evil one has a long list of items to deceive us, but God, as our Father, carefully watches over us and would never lead us anywhere that He would not lead His own Son Jesus Christ. Isn't that wonderful?

14. What are one or two worries you face in life? Why do you worry? See what you doubt about God and His promises.

15. What would you share with a friend from these verses who might be going through a very difficult time?

16. Share at least two changes you desire to take place in your life because of these verses:

   •

   •

Romans 8:26-39 Advanced Discussion Questions

1. How is interceding connected to prayer (26-27)? Did you ever experience a situation which was too hard to pray for because of the pain or trouble involved but could only groan? Share.

2. Some people use this groaning (26-27) as speaking in other languages. Is this justified by the context here?

3. What does the word 'foreknow' mean? What words could you substitute for 'foreknew' here? "God _____ me". (Each time the word 'foreknew' is used in the Bible it refers not to things but people (Rom 8:29; 11:2; 1 Pet 1:20). (A.W. Pink's good observation.)

4. What does this sequence from foreknown to glorified (8:29-30) imply about God's care for our lives?

5. Why are people afraid of the word 'predestine' (31)? If God is sovereign, would it not be better to acknowledge it and embrace His work in our lives?

6. Some Christians are afraid of losing their salvation. Review
    verses **28-33** and try to think how you might explain to them
    that it is impossible for a genuine Christian to lose his
    salvation. How do professing believers (but not genuine) fit
    into this scheme?

7. Go through the two lists in verses **35-39** and think of the
    word or situation you fear the most. Share with the Lord your
    love for Him and willingness to trust Him even if you have to
    go through that particular situation.

#18 Romans 9:1-13 Study Questions

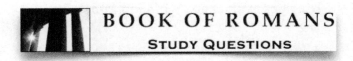

BOOK OF ROMANS
STUDY QUESTIONS

GOD'S PROMISES TO THE JEWS

Paul does not leave any loose arguments hanging nor does he give us the option of saying, "That is your interpretation," but forcibly presents two clear arguments in these 13 verses: God is just and faithful.

- **Starter:** Share a special concern and compassion that you have for someone, a family or group. How have you specially responded to this need?

A) God is Just (Rom 9:1-5)

9:1 I am telling the truth in Christ, I am not lying, my conscience bearing me witness in the Holy Spirit, 2 that I have great sorrow and unceasing grief in my heart. 3 For I could wish that I myself were accursed, separated from Christ for the sake of my brethren, my kinsmen according to the flesh, 4 who are Israelites, to whom belongs the adoption as sons and the glory and the covenants and the giving of the Law and the temple service and the promises, 5 whose are the fathers, and from whom is the Christ according to the flesh, who is over all, God blessed forever. Amen.

1. List the five phrases from 9:1-2 that describe Paul's sincerity and feelings. Why might he so excessively describe his feelings?

2. What is it that Paul wishes to happen (see verse 9:3)? Put it in your own words.

3. List all the ways Paul describes the special blessings that mark off the Israelites as the people of God (4-5)?

4. What does he mean by "Christ according to the flesh" (5; 1:3)?

5. Were you brought up in a Christian family? Name any special blessings you or others brought up in a Christian family received.

6. Restate the words from verse 5, "God blessed forever". What does Paul mean by them?

B) God is Faithful (Rom 9:6-13)

[6] But it is not as though the word of God has failed. For they are not all Israel who are descended from Israel; [7] neither are they all children because they are Abraham's descendants, but: "THROUGH ISAAC YOUR DESCENDANTS WILL BE NAMED." [8] That is, it is not the children of the flesh who are children of God, but the children of the promise are regarded as descendants. [9] For this is a word of promise: "AT THIS TIME I WILL COME, AND SARAH SHALL HAVE A SON." [10] And not only this, but there was Rebekah also, when she had conceived twins by one man, our father Isaac; [11] for though the twins were not yet born, and had not done anything good or bad, in order that God's purpose according to His choice might stand, not because of works, but because of Him who calls, [12]

it was said to her, "THE OLDER WILL SERVE THE YOUNGER. [13] Just as it is written, "JACOB I LOVED, BUT ESAU I HATED."

7.   Has God's word failed (6)?

8.   Why might people wrongly conclude that God's Word has failed (6)?

9.   What are some ways you or people around you think God's Word has failed or not brought the help needed?

10. Paul provides biblical proof for this conclusion (verse 6) by quoting and commenting on four Old Testament passages (6b-13). Write each verse down then go back and see what each quote proves.

     a. Romans 9:6b-7

     •   This proves:

     b. Romans 9:8-9

     •   This proves:

     c. Romans 9:10-12

     •   This proves:

     d. Romans 9:13

     (This is similar to the one in verses 10-12.)

11. Does Paul believe the Old Testament is important? How do you know?

12. So how would you answer the question, "Was God faithful to His promises to His people, the Jews?"

Summary

Paul emphasizes this choice of God by quoting Malachi 1:2, "Just as it is written, 'JACOB I LOVED, BUT ESAU I HATED'" (9:13). This should more deeply convince us that we are not chosen because of the good that we do but only because God's gracious choice. His choice of us should greatly humble us and cause us to delight in His awesome choice of us.

13. Take another look at verses 9:1-3 and reflect upon your desire for your friends and family to be saved. How has it changed in the last 5 years?

14. How important is God's faithfulness? Explain.

15. Do you think of people in the two groups: (1) Those that are loved and chosen of God and (2) those that are not chosen and left alone? Which group do you belong to? Why?

16. List at least one change you desire to take place in your life because of these verses.

Romans 9:1-13 Advanced Discussion Questions

BOOK OF ROMANS
STUDY QUESTIONS

1. Jesus was compassionate and caring. "And when He approached, He (Jesus) saw the city and wept over it" (Lu 19:41). Why do you think Jesus wept over the city? Should all of us should be so compassionate?

2. Look at 2 Timothy 3:16-17 and explain how Paul thought God's Word could be trusted. Examine your Christian discipline of studying God's Word each day. How does our confidence in its fidelity make a difference on your personal study habits?

3. Is there anything you now doubt about God or His promises? Think again through the verses in 8:31-39. Confess any doubts you have and ask for wisdom to understand His ways regarding that matter.

4. Has God been faithful to His promises to the Jewish people? After all you have read here, how would you summarize Paul's reasons?

5. Rewrite the phrase "they are not all Israel who are descended
    from Israel" (6) in your own words (not using the word
    'Israel'). What does Paul means here?

6. Many people, Christian and unbelievers, have problems
    understanding and accepting the phrase "Jacob I loved, but
    Esau I hated."

    •   Where does this verse come from? What is the original
        context?

    •   This topic will be discussed in the following verses in more
        depth, but for now, explain why people might have a
        problem with this verse. Do you?

    •   Did Paul have any doubts about the statement? How do
        you know?

    •   Describe Jacob and Esau's lives. Did either deserve God's
        favor? Explain.

7. One sign of a mature believer is the ability to announce God is
    blessed despite one's surrounding circumstances (3). Can you?
    What areas might you hold back on exclaiming God's
    extraordinary person and way? Why?

#19 Romans 9:14-23 Study Questions

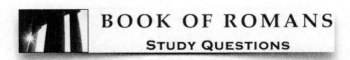

GOD'S ELECT

Questions about God's justice and fairness continue down to our present day. Paul faced them too. In one sense, this is fortunate for we have Paul's capable defense. Paul brings up the objection right from the start.

- **Starter:** Do you ever think about the issue of predestination, the teaching that speaks about God choosing ahead who would be saved? What is your impression of the whole issue?

A) God's Mercy and Justice (Rom 9:14-18)

[14] What shall we say then? There is no injustice with God, is there? May it never be! [15] For He says to Moses, "I WILL HAVE MERCY ON WHOM I HAVE MERCY, AND I WILL HAVE COMPASSION ON WHOM I HAVE COMPASSION." [16] So then it does not depend on the man who wills or the man who runs, but on God who has mercy. [17] For the Scripture says to Pharaoh, "FOR THIS VERY PURPOSE I RAISED YOU UP, TO DEMONSTRATE MY POWER IN YOU, AND THAT MY NAME MIGHT BE PROCLAIMED THROUGHOUT THE WHOLE EARTH." [18] So then He has mercy on whom He desires, and He hardens whom He desires.

1. What is the assumed question that Paul rebukes in 9:14?

2. How does Paul respond to his question (14)? (Notice he doesn't wait for anybody's answer!)

3. Write down the words God spoke to Moses (19) (see both Exodus 33:19 and Romans 9:15). Why did God say this (Ex 33:13)?

4. What conclusion does Paul draw from the quote just mentioned (16)? What does this mean?

5. What is one major reason God gave so much authority to Pharaoh (17)?

6. How does verse 18 differ from verse 15?

7. How does someone show mercy to another? Can you give a particular example where a person had mercy on you or you on another?

B) God's Choice (Rom 9:19-23)

[19] You will say to me then, "Why does He still find fault? For who resists His will?" [20] On the contrary, who are you, O man, who answers back to God? The thing molded will not say to the molder, "Why did you make me like this," will it? [21] Or does not the potter have a right over the clay, to make from the same lump one vessel

for honorable use, and another for common use? [22] What if God, although willing to demonstrate His wrath and to make His power known, endured with much patience vessels of wrath prepared for destruction? [23] And He did so in order that He might make known the riches of His glory upon vessels of mercy, which He prepared beforehand for glory,

8. What problem did Paul anticipate that people would have with his former conclusion (19)?

9. How does Paul answer those doubts (20-21)?

10. Have you ever been guilty of blaming God for what you have done wrong? If so, give an example.

11. What two kinds of objects (NIV) or vessels (NASB) do verses 22-23 mention?

    •   Verse 22:

    •   Verse 23:

12. Does God have to judge people right away (22)?

13. Name one reason God puts off judgment (22)?

14. Will God be glorified through the way He, as a righteous God, condemns the wicked (22)? Explain.

15. Explain how God will display his glory through His people (23)?

16. What might it mean that God "prepared them beforehand" (23)?

Summary

God has His clear purposes for salvation and judgment; His purposes do not often match our expectations. God is more interested in displaying various aspects of His majestic glory.

17. Why doesn't God save everyone?

18. Should God feel obligated to save everyone? Why or why not?

19. How do you want God to be glorified through your life? Why?

20. List at least two changes you desire to take place in your life because of these verses:

   •

   •

Romans 9:14-23 Advanced Discussion Questions

BOOK OF ROMANS
STUDY QUESTIONS

1. Give several examples of how people complain about God being unjust or unfair. Is it ever right to call or think God as being unjust? Why do people so quickly blame God for bad things?

2. What is the problem people have with predestination? (Those unfamiliar with this might need to look it up.) What do these verses teach on this topic?

3. A common question (and complaint against God) is, "Why did God create a world with so much evil and war? How would you answer this question to these two different people?

    • Those critical against God.

    • Those genuinely seeking answers for things they don't understand.

4. God's glory is often maligned, but it becomes one of the greatest reasons for God's creation of mankind. Explain how He manifests the different aspects of His glory through the lives of His people:

- Mercy

- Wrath

- Patience

- Power

5. Spend special time with the Lord and glorify Him for each of the above attributes. If you have time, read Arthur Pink's *The Attributes of God*."

#20 Romans 9:24-33 Study Questions

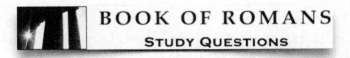

GRACE TO THE NATIONS

After establishing God's right to determine whom He calls to experience His grace, Paul addresses two major questions about these two groups that He selected.

- **Starter:** Do you ever get impatient with people? List two or three such situations and your reactions.

A) Calling by God's kind grace (Rom 9:23-24)

[22] What if God, although willing to demonstrate His wrath and to make His power known, endured with much patience vessels of wrath prepared for destruction? [23] And He did so in order that He might make known the riches of His glory upon vessels of mercy, which He prepared beforehand for glory, [24] even us, whom He also called, not from among Jews only, but also from among Gentiles.

1. Why did the Lord put up with lost sinners so long (22)? What about 'saint' sinners (23)?

2. Who does the "even us" of verse 24 refer to? Check out verses 22-23.

3. From what two groups were these special people comprised
   (24)?

   •

   •

4. What does it mean that these believers were 'called' (24)?
   What else do Christians mean by this word?

B) Calling not to be taken for granted (Rom 9:25-33)

[25] As He says also in Hosea, "I WILL CALL THOSE WHO WERE
NOT MY PEOPLE, 'MY PEOPLE,' AND HER WHO WAS NOT
BELOVED, 'BELOVED.'" [26] "AND IT SHALL BE THAT IN THE
PLACE WHERE IT WAS SAID TO THEM, 'YOU ARE NOT MY
PEOPLE,' THERE THEY SHALL BE CALLED SONS OF THE
LIVING GOD." [27] And Isaiah cries out concerning Israel,
"THOUGH THE NUMBER OF THE SONS OF ISRAEL BE AS THE
SAND OF THE SEA, IT IS THE REMNANT THAT WILL BE SAVED;
[28] FOR THE LORD WILL EXECUTE HIS WORD UPON THE
EARTH, THOROUGHLY AND QUICKLY." [29] And just as Isaiah
foretold, "EXCEPT THE LORD OF SABAOTH HAD LEFT TO US A
POSTERITY, WE WOULD HAVE BECOME AS SODOM, AND
WOULD HAVE RESEMBLED GOMORRAH." [30] What shall we say
then? That Gentiles, who did not pursue righteousness, attained
righteousness, even the righteousness which is by faith; [31] but
Israel, pursuing a law of righteousness, did not arrive at that law.
[32] Why? Because they did not pursue it by faith, but as though it
were by works. They stumbled over the stumbling stone, [33] just as
it is written, "BEHOLD, I LAY IN ZION A STONE OF STUMBLING
AND A ROCK OF OFFENSE, AND HE WHO BELIEVES IN HIM
WILL NOT BE DISAPPOINTED."

5. What book of the Bible does he quote verses from to prove
   his meaning (25)? Why does he do this?

6. List the three descriptions of God's people, before and after
    God dealt with them (25-26).

    •   Before   After

    •   Before   After

    •   Before   After

    •   Which means most to you? Why?

7. The Lord states two facts about the Israelites from verse 27.
    What is the second truth?

    •   First truth: The sons of Israel will be as many as the grains
        of sand of the sea.

    •   Second truth:

8. Are we sure these things will occur (28)? Why?

9. What does "Sabaoth" mean (29)? What about "Lord of
    Sabaoth" (29)?

10. What are the implications of verse 29? Do you think this is
    true of all of us?

11. Complete the two contrasts Paul makes in verses 30 & 31.
    Please circle the right answers and fill in the blank.

    •   The Gentiles (did/did not) pursue _____
        (have/have not) obtained it (30).

- The Israelites (did/did not) pursue _____ (have/have not) attained it (31).

12. What kind of righteousness did the Gentiles obtain (30)? Explain what this means.

13. Why is it that the Israelites were unsuccessful (32)?

14. What is a stumbling stone (32-33)? How does Paul spiritually use this thought?

15. Where is this stone or rock of offense to be found (33)? Where is that?

16. What promise is given both to the Jews and to the Gentiles (33)? How is this all related to Jesus?

Summary

Paul comes all the way around, starting with their election and calling, and then ending by focusing on their (our) responsibility to believe.

17. How would you answer someone that says, "How do I know if God predestined me?"

18. List at least one change you desire to take place in your life because of these verses.

Romans 9:23-33 Advanced Discussion Questions

BOOK OF ROMANS
STUDY QUESTIONS

1. Would you say from these verses that God has a bias either for the Jews or for the Gentiles? Explain.

2. Verse 29 is rephrased in the NIV with "Unless the Lord Almighty...". The original text literally translated from the Old Testament says, "Except the LORD of Sabaoth...." Why might the NIV translate it "Lord Almighty"?

3. It is sad that we so often become proud of our goodness. Meditate upon verse 29 again and write down what this verse teaches about God's grace. Complete the statement, "Unless the Lord had sent His grace into my life, I would have...."

4. Select one misunderstanding below that is commonly heard. Use this section of verses to state and defend the relevant truth.

   • God is unfair when He doesn't save everyone.

   • Everyone on earth is considered God's child.

   • God is specially indebted to certain kinds of people.

5. Comment on the way Paul uses these Old Testament verses in the New Testament. (Include Isaiah 8:14 and 28:16.)

6. The phrase "by faith" is used in this passage (11 times in Romans). How is this phrase related to the argument on saving pagan Gentiles and the exclusion of many Jews from "the people of God"?

7. Read the promise in 33, "He who believes in Him will not be disappointed" and examine your faith. Do you believe that you will never be disappointed if you believe in Christ? How does that work in real life? Give an instance.

#21 Romans 10:1-15 Study Questions

SHARING THE GOSPEL

With the emphasis on the sovereignty of God in the previous chapter, Paul now stresses a balanced understanding between the sovereignty of God and evangelism, revealing the urgent need to share God's Word with others.

- **Starter:** Do you share the Gospel? What keeps you from sharing the gospel more with others?

A) Compassion Displayed (Rom 10:1-5)

10:1 Brethren, my heart's desire and my prayer to God for them is for their salvation. 2 For I bear them witness that they have a zeal for God, but not in accordance with knowledge. 3 For not knowing about God's righteousness, and seeking to establish their own, they did not subject themselves to the righteousness of God. 4 For Christ is the end of the law for righteousness to everyone who believes. 5 For Moses writes that the man who practices the righteousness which is based on law shall live by that righteousness.

1. Who is Paul greatly concerned about at the beginning of this chapter (10:1; cf. 9:1-5)?

2. What are the two ways Paul sees his own concern for these people (10:1)?

3. Were they sincere in their religious beliefs (2)?

4. What was Paul's criticism of their belief (2)?

5. List the three obstacles that these people had in becoming saved (3).

6. What does it mean that "Christ is the end of the law for righteousness" (4)?

7. How does Moses describe the life based on the law (5)?

B) Faith Discovered (Rom 10:6-10)

[6] But the righteousness based on faith speaks thus, "DO NOT SAY IN YOUR HEART, 'WHO WILL ASCEND INTO HEAVEN?' (that is, to bring Christ down), [7] or 'WHO WILL DESCEND INTO THE ABYSS?' (that is, to bring Christ up from the dead)." [8] But what does it say? "THE WORD IS NEAR YOU, IN YOUR MOUTH AND IN YOUR HEART"--that is, the word of faith which we are preaching, [9] that if you confess with your mouth Jesus as Lord, and believe in your heart that God raised Him from the dead, you shall be saved; [10] for with the heart man believes, resulting in righteousness, and with the mouth he confesses, resulting in salvation.

8. The righteousness based on faith is also spoken of in the Old Testament. What two truths about Christ the Messiah are prophesied in these Old Testament verses (6-7)?

   - (6)

   - (7)

9. The confession stated in verse 9 and amplified in verse 10 is commonly spoken of. What is the connection between this confession and the quote in verse (8)?

10. What does it mean to you to "confess with your mouth Jesus as Lord"?

11. During different times of the Roman empire, stating "Jesus as Lord" would be considered a crime as only Caesar was Lord. Would you still be able to affirm this truth under such circumstances?

C) Faith Developed (Rom 10:11-15)

[11] For the Scripture says, "WHOEVER BELIEVES IN HIM WILL NOT BE DISAPPOINTED." [12] For there is no distinction between Jew and Greek; for the same Lord is Lord of all, abounding in riches for all who call upon Him; [13] for "WHOEVER WILL CALL UPON THE NAME OF THE LORD WILL BE SAVED." [14] How then shall they call upon Him in whom they have not believed? And how shall they believe in Him whom they have not heard? And how shall they hear without a preacher? [15] And how shall they preach unless they are sent? Just as it is written, "HOW BEAUTIFUL ARE THE FEET OF THOSE WHO BRING GLAD TIDINGS OF GOOD THINGS!"

12. Paul is sharing the gospel with the Jews in these verses. Please write down the quote that he uses to clinch his powerful gospel presentation in verse 11.

13. Paul was certain this message was not only for Jews but for Gentiles too. What other scripture does he give to them, showing that the riches of salvation are for whoever calls upon Him (12-13)?

14. Paul also uses Old Testament scripture to defend his missionary zeal (14-15). What are the four questions that Paul gives in these verses?

    •

    •

    •

    •

15. How would you answer the first and last question? What are the implications of each of these answers?

"HOW BEAUTIFUL FEET OF THOSE WHO BRING GOOD NEWS!"

Summary

Our conviction to share the gospel and participate in the worldwide mission movement is undergirded by our understanding on how evangelism and missions works under God's sovereign plan.

16. What scriptures are most pertinent to you on your participation in evangelism and missions?

17. If God elects the lost, why should we still evangelize and support missionaries?

18. Pray that the Lord of the harvest will send workers into the harvest.

19. List at least two changes you desire to take place in your life because of these verses.

    •

    •

Romans 10:1-15 Advanced Discussion Questions

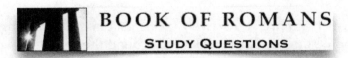

BOOK OF ROMANS
STUDY QUESTIONS

1. Use verses to share the major points of the gospel Paul brought up. What points would you include if someone asked you to clarify what the gospel meant?

2. Why does the teaching of election sometimes stifle the spreading of the gospel? What is your experience? What pointers did Paul make to keep a good balance between election and missions?

3. If God knows what He is going to do, why does He want us to pray? How does human responsibility mix with God's sovereign plan?

4. Paul proved Jesus was Christ by these two Old Testament scriptures (8). What aspect of Christ's life do they refer to?

    • "Do not say in your heart, 'Who will ascend into heaven?' (that is, to bring Christ down.)

    • 'Who will descend into the deep?' (that is, to bring Christ up from the dead)."

5. Why do people seem so slow to "call upon the name of the Lord" to be saved (13)? Use different words to explain this. How does this relate to those brought up in Christian families?

6. In what way are you actively taking part in the spreading of God's truth to those locally and around the world? Make sure you both have an evangelistic and mission involvement.

#22 Romans 10:16–11:10 Study Questions

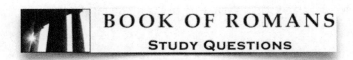

TROUBLE BELIEVING

If Israel was chosen, then what is the reason that they, who had God's Word, did not believe?

- **Starter:** Share a time where a parent had to deal with a disobedient child (maybe you!). What happened and why?

A) Israel's rejection of God's word (Rom 10:16-21)

10:16 However, they did not all heed the glad tidings; for Isaiah says, "LORD, WHO HAS BELIEVED OUR REPORT?" 17 So faith comes from hearing, and hearing by the word of Christ. 18 But I say, surely they have never heard, have they? Indeed they have; "THEIR VOICE HAS GONE OUT INTO ALL THE EARTH, AND THEIR WORDS TO THE ENDS OF THE WORLD." 19 But I say, surely Israel did not know, did they? At the first Moses says, "I WILL MAKE YOU JEALOUS BY THAT WHICH IS NOT A NATION, BY A NATION WITHOUT UNDERSTANDING WILL I ANGER YOU." 20 And Isaiah is very bold and says, "I WAS FOUND BY THOSE WHO SOUGHT ME NOT, I BECAME MANIFEST TO THOSE WHO DID NOT ASK FOR ME." 21 But as for Israel He says, "ALL THE DAY LONG I HAVE STRETCHED OUT MY HANDS TO A DISOBEDIENT AND OBSTINATE PEOPLE."

1. What do these 'glad tidings' ('message' in NIV) refer to (10:16)? How does this phrase relate to the word 'gospel'?

2. Did everyone believe the gospel who heard it (16)? How did Paul prove his point (16)?

3. Where does faith come from (17)? Does this mean people have to hear God's Word to become saved (17)?

4. Is the reason Israel did not believe in Christ because they had never heard the gospel (18)?

5. Verses 19-20 prove that Israel did hear but as a nation did not believe Christ. What did God say He would do if Israel turned away from the truth?

6. What parent-child image comes to your mind from God's treatment of disobedient Israel in 10:21?

7. Do you sense God is patient toward His people (10:21)? Do God's people sometimes misuse God's patience? Explain.

B) God's partial rejection of Israel (Rom 11:1-10)

11:1 I say then, God has not rejected His people, has He? May it never be! For I too am an Israelite, a descendant of Abraham, of the tribe of Benjamin. 2 God has not rejected His people whom He foreknew. Or do you not know what the Scripture says in the passage about Elijah, how he pleads with God against Israel? 3 "Lord, THEY HAVE KILLED THY PROPHETS, THEY HAVE TORN DOWN THINE ALTARS, AND I ALONE AM LEFT, AND THEY ARE SEEKING MY LIFE." 4 But what is the divine response to him? "I

HAVE KEPT for Myself SEVEN THOUSAND MEN WHO HAVE NOT BOWED THE KNEE TO BAAL." [5] In the same way then, there has also come to be at the present time a remnant according to God's gracious choice. [6] But if it is by grace, it is no longer on the basis of works, otherwise grace is no longer grace. [7] What then? That which Israel is seeking for, it has not obtained, but those who were chosen obtained it, and the rest were hardened; [8] just as it is written, "GOD GAVE THEM A SPIRIT OF STUPOR, EYES TO SEE NOT AND EARS TO HEAR NOT, DOWN TO THIS VERY DAY." [9] And David says, "LET THEIR TABLE BECOME A SNARE AND A TRAP, AND A STUMBLING BLOCK AND A RETRIBUTION TO THEM. [10] "LET THEIR EYES BE DARKENED TO SEE NOT, AND BEND THEIR BACKS FOREVER."

8. God hasn't totally rejected His people Israel. What example does Paul give to prove that in 11:1?

9. Which Israelites did the Lord not reject (11:2)?

10. What example does Paul give to prove that He has not rejected all Israelites (see 11:2-4)? As time permits, also read 1 Kings 18:17-19:18.

11. Paul described his own era as being, choose one: a) the same, b) better than or c) worse than the time of Elijah (11:5).

12. What are those chosen and reserved by God called in verse 5? In what everyday life situation is that word used? What does it mean and imply?

13. Explain the sentence, "If by grace, then it is no longer by works; if it were, grace would no longer be grace" (11:6).

14. Which of the two principles below did God use to save His people (see 11:7).

    • a) Those who work the hardest for Him are saved.

    • b) Those who had not really been seeking received salvation because they were chosen.

15. What does "hardened" mean (7)? Why does God harden them?

16. Describe the various ways Paul describes this hardening process or the results of it (11:8-10).

Summary

Without God's grace no one would be saved. We ought to celebrate God's grace extended to our lives.

17. Why is grace and the thought, "I deserve it" incompatible? Which way better describes your thinking?

18. Would you agree that a person's joy in salvation is related to the depth of his or her understanding of God's grace? Explain.

19. List at least one change you desire to take place in your life because of these verses.

Romans 10:16-11:10 Advanced Discussion Questions

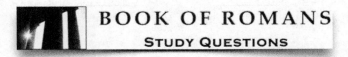

BOOK OF ROMANS
STUDY QUESTIONS

1. Is the Word of Christ (10:17) different from the Word of God? Explain your answer.

2. Compare this hardening of the Jews with the hardening or 'the letting go' of the pagans in chapter 1 (1:24,26,28). What similarities or differences do you see?

3. After again viewing this passage, answer the question, "Has God completely forgotten His people Israel?" Explain.

4. Name 2 or 3 things that the quotes from Elijah reveal about God. Does He still work the same way today?

5. How is faith different from knowledge? How many in our church know God's Word but do not respond in belief? Is there an area in your life you have knowledge but not belief?

6. Do you find that Christian church can experience the same
    problems that Israel suffered? Explain

7. There are two major ways this word 'foreknew' is interpreted
    (11:2). What are they? What is it that God foreknew: people or
    things? Study the places this word is used in the scripture then
    write your conclusion as to which understanding of 'foreknew'
    is best.

#23 Romans 11:11-24 Study Questions

A HOPE AND A WARNING

Until this point the apostle focused on spiritual Israel, composed of Jews and Gentiles–the church. In chapter 11, however, he selectively focuses on what happens to national Israel. What about all the promises about Israel? It reminds us of the question the apostles asked Jesus, "Lord, is it at this time You are restoring the kingdom to Israel?" (Acts 1:6). We get a few glimpses of God's plan for Israel here.

Starter: Share about something that you missed out on because you were late or uninterested.

A) Greater blessings coming (Rom 11:11-15)

^{11:11} I say then, they did not stumble so as to fall, did they? May it never be! But by their transgression salvation has come to the Gentiles, to make them jealous. ¹² Now if their transgression be riches for the world and their failure be riches for the Gentiles, how much more will their fulfillment be! ¹³ But I am speaking to you who are Gentiles. Inasmuch then as I am an apostle of Gentiles, I magnify my ministry, ¹⁴ if somehow I might move to jealousy my fellow countrymen and save some of them. ¹⁵ For if their rejection be the reconciliation of the world, what will their acceptance be but life from the dead?

1. Who is it that stumbled (11:11)?

2. What is the difference between stumbling and falling?

    •   Stumbling is when _____

    •   Falling is when   _____

3. So then, did Israel 'fall' (11)?

4. How is it that the Gentiles came to have opportunity to
    believe (11-12)?

5. What does the last phrase, "How much more will their
    fulfillment be" in verse 12 mean? Finish this statement:

    •   If God was to use Israel's sin and failures to bring blessings
        to the whole world, He will _____ when the
        Israelites obey.

6. Paul as the apostle to the Gentiles wanted his ministry to have
    an impact upon his fellow Israelites. How did he hope this
    might work out (13-14)?

7. What did Israel's rejection of the Messiah bring to the world
    (15)?

B) The Gentiles engrafted in (Rom 11:16-24)

16 And if the first piece of dough be holy, the lump is also; and if the
root be holy, the branches are too. 17 But if some of the branches
were broken off, and you, being a wild olive, were grafted in among
them and became partaker with them of the rich root of the olive
tree, 18 do not be arrogant toward the branches; but if you are

arrogant, remember that it is not you who supports the root, but the root supports you. [19] You will say then, "Branches were broken off so that I might be grafted in." [20] Quite right, they were broken off for their unbelief, but you stand by your faith. Do not be conceited, but fear; [21] for if God did not spare the natural branches, neither will He spare you. [22] Behold then the kindness and severity of God; to those who fell, severity, but to you, God's kindness, if you continue in His kindness; otherwise you also will be cut off. [23] And they also, if they do not continue in their unbelief, will be grafted in; for God is able to graft them in again. [24] For if you were cut off from what is by nature a wild olive tree, and were grafted contrary to nature into a cultivated olive tree, how much more shall these who are the natural branches be grafted into their own olive tree?

8. What are the two illustrations given in verse 16?

   •

   •

9. Explain the meaning of the two illustrations (16).

   •

   •

10. Paul takes the later illustration of verse 16 and enlarges upon it. Write down this illustration's literal meaning (17) and spiritual lesson (17-18).

   • Literal meaning (17):

   • Spiritual lesson (18):

11. Who is Paul warning in verse 18? What is the warning (18)?

12. Why is it that the Gentiles (the branches) might become prideful (19-21)?

13. List the two attributes of God stated in verse 22.

14. Who does God treat severely (22)?

15. Who does God treat kindly (22)?

16. Is God able to treat kindly those He has dealt severely with (23-24)? What illustration does He give to establish that fact?

Summary

God reveals His larger redemptive program. What appears like a failure to save the Israelites becomes God's special means of saving many more.

17. How should this passage shape our understanding of our own salvation?

18. Pray for the Jewish people that God would open their eyes. How should we pray for the non-Jewish people (i.e. Gentiles)?

19. List at least one change you desire to take place in your life because of these verses.

Romans 11:11-24 Advanced Discussion Questions

BOOK OF ROMANS
STUDY QUESTIONS

1. Is the church the true Israel? Explain using the illustration of the olive tree.

2. How can God be both severe and yet kind (11:22)? What are the ramifications of this for our lives?

3. Does this passage speak about losing one's salvation?

4. Religions and people tend to separate the two aspects of God's nature mentioned in verse 22. How has this affected different religions or attitudes of people that you are familiar with?

5. What warning from this section could we give a brother or sister that treat the preciousness of their faith lightly?

6. How does this passage help us understand our relationship with Jews along with other religions and philosophies? Describe God's larger program.

#24 Romans 11:25-36 Study Questions

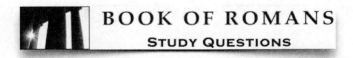

BOOK OF ROMANS

STUDY QUESTIONS

DON'T BE UNINFORMED!

What can we expect to happen before the Lord returns and how do the promises to Israel play part of God's overall plan? Everything is perfectly working out according to the Lord's wise plans which He hints at in this passage.

- **Starter:** At what point in your life did you think most about the Lord's return? Are you aware of any reason for this?

A) Three stages of mercy (Rom 11:25-32)

[11:25] For I do not want you, brethren, to be uninformed of this mystery, lest you be wise in your own estimation, that a partial hardening has happened to Israel until the fulness of the Gentiles has come in; [26] and thus all Israel will be saved; just as it is written, "THE DELIVERER WILL COME FROM ZION, HE WILL REMOVE UNGODLINESS FROM JACOB. [27] AND THIS IS MY COVENANT WITH THEM, WHEN I TAKE AWAY THEIR SINS." [28] From the standpoint of the gospel they are enemies for your sake, but from the standpoint of God's choice they are beloved for the sake of the fathers; [29] for the gifts and the calling of God are irrevocable. [30] For just as you once were disobedient to God, but now have been shown mercy because of their disobedience, [31] so these also now have been disobedient, in order that because of the mercy shown to you they also may now be shown mercy. [32] For God has shut up all in disobedience that He might show mercy to all.

1. Why doesn't Paul want us to be ignorant of the mystery (11:25)?

2. Read again Paul's explanation of this mystery in 11:25b-d and then restate it in your own words.

3. Will all or part of Israel be saved (26)?

4. How does Paul describe this salvation in verses 26-27 (this is quoted from Isaiah 59:20-21)?

5. Share the two different views of the Israelites expressed in verse 28. Whose two views are they?

   •

   •

6. Explain each of the two views above from verse 28.

7. What two things are irrevocable (29)? Explain how they differ.

8. The pronouns of verses 30-31 can be confusing. Please fill in below what each bold word <u>represents</u>. They are listed below. [30] For just as **you** once were disobedient to God, but now have been shown mercy because of **their** disobedience, [31] so **these** also now have been disobedient, in order that because of the mercy shown to **you they** also may now be shown mercy.

- you (30):

- their (30):

- these (31):

- you (31):

- they (31):

9. What does it mean in verse 32 when God "has shut up all in disobedience"?

10. Why has God bound all men in disobedience (32)?

B) Indescribable wisdom (Rom 11:33-36)

[33] Oh, the depth of the riches both of the wisdom and knowledge of God! How unsearchable are His judgments and unfathomable His ways! [34] For WHO HAS KNOWN THE MIND OF THE LORD, OR WHO BECAME HIS COUNSELOR? [35] Or WHO HAS FIRST GIVEN TO HIM THAT IT MIGHT BE PAID BACK TO HIM AGAIN? [36] For from Him and through Him and to Him are all things. To Him be the glory forever. Amen.

11. List at least five ways God is described in verses 33-35. Which impresses you most?

-

-

-

-

-

12. Verse 36 is an expressive, terse summary of God's power and being. Explain each of the given clauses below in your own words.

   • "from Him"

   • "through Him"

   • "to Him"

13. How does Paul close this message about election and salvation (36)?

Summary

God has given us special knowledge about His future dealings with the nation of Israel. Behind all of the Jewish resistance to the gospel is God's passion to bring the gospel to the ends of the world. Despite our points of confusion, we should see God's promises as the special way God carries out His great wise redemptive plan.

14. Share your view of the way God will work in Israel in the last days. How does this differ from other perspectives?

15. Check and see if you have a tendency to complain or argue with God about something you don't fully understand?

16. Why is there no problem too hard for the Lord to solve (33-36)?

17. Is it ever right to think that God owes us something (35)?
    Give an instance of when you had earlier thought this way.

18. List at least two changes you desire to take place in your life
    because of these verses.

    •

    •

Romans 11:25-36 Advanced Discussion Questions

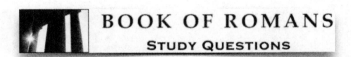

BOOK OF ROMANS
STUDY QUESTIONS

1. What does the phrase "until the fulness of the Gentiles has come in" (25) refer to? (Further study: Is 60:3, 66:19; Mic 4:1; Zec 8:22; Lu 21:24; Rev 7:9.)

2. What are the several ways to understand the phrase "so all Israel will be saved" (26)?

3. Are there situations that confound the Lord? Reflect on the implication of your answer.

4. Do you ever tend to criticize how God handles 'history' or the present world? Why so? How would you use verses 33-36 to rebuke these inferior perspectives?

5. Can we really understand God? Why or why not?

6. How is our Christian growth related to our knowledge of God? Can our Christian growth ever reach its fullest? Explain.

7. Look back over verses 33-36. What are some differences
   between God and yourself? Which difference stands out the
   most?

#25 Romans 12:1-8 Study Questions

GOD'S WILL FOR YOU!

God's Spirit now lives in us! This has an amazing impact on our lives. As we open our lives to the Spirit's guidance, God's will begins to be carried out right in our own lives.

- **Starter:** What are two things you like doing most for others?

A) Two kinds of commands (Rom 12:1-2)

^{12:1} I urge you therefore, brethren, by the mercies of God, to present your bodies a living and holy sacrifice, acceptable to God, which is your spiritual service of worship. ² And do not be conformed to this world, but be transformed by the renewing of your mind, that you may prove what the will of God is, that which is good and acceptable and perfect.

1. What does Paul urge his brothers and sisters to do (12:1)?

2. What do you think the difference is between a living and dead sacrifice (1)? Why does Paul use "living" here?

3. So how does Paul define "spiritual worship" in verse 1? Explain each term.

4. What are we **not** to pattern our lives after (2)? What does that practically mean?

5. How do we transform our lives (2)? What does that practically mean?

6. What happens as a result of our minds' transformation (2)?

7. What three ways does Paul describe God's will at the end of verse 2? Describe how each word differs from the other.

B) Properly ministering to each other (Rom 12:3-8)

3 For through the grace given to me I say to every man among you not to think more highly of himself than he ought to think; but to think so as to have sound judgment, as God has allotted to each a measure of faith. 4 For just as we have many members in one body and all the members do not have the same function, 5 so we, who are many, are one body in Christ, and individually members one of another. 6 And since we have gifts that differ according to the grace given to us, let each exercise them accordingly: if prophecy, according to the proportion of his faith; 7 if service, in his serving; or he who teaches, in his teaching; 8 or he who exhorts, in his exhortation; he who gives, with liberality; he who leads, with diligence; he who shows mercy, with cheerfulness.

8. How are we not to think of ourselves (3)?

9. How are we to think of ourselves (3)?

10. How should the truths stated in verses 4 and 5 affect the way
    we think of ourselves (3-5)?

11. Explain the analogy (illustration) of the church in verses 4-5?

12. In which way are the different gifts spread out among the
    members of the church (6)?

13. Does every believer have a spiritual gift (6)?

14. List the 7 different gifts mentioned in verses 6-8, and describe
    the way each is to be successfully used.

    •

    •

    •

    •

    •

    •

    •

Summary

Our spiritual lives should reflect God's purpose of service—in stark contrast to the self-serving flesh. Frustrations about God's will often arise when we focus on getting what we want more than how we can use our gifts for Him and others. It is easier to discover God's will when we seek how He wants us to serve others.

15. In what area do you sense you have been most shaped by the world?

16. Do you believe God's will is always "good and acceptable and perfect" (2)? Explain.

17. Do you know what spiritual gift is yours? Share. (This is not an exhaustive list.)

18. List at least two changes you desire to take place in your life because of these verses.

   •

   •

Romans 12:1-8 Advanced Discussion Questions

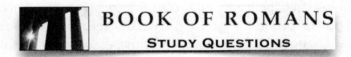

1. The world is seen both in day-to-day decisions as well as hidden philosophies. Pick an area like marriage, parenting, wealth, education, counseling and discover the world's philosophies which subtly but powerfully influence people's understanding of these larger areas of life. Relate this to Psalm 1:1 as time allows.

2. What does the scripture in 12:1-2 teach about the importance of dedication? Would you agree that the level of our dedication is reflected in our service? Identify a few people known for their service and observe the connection with their commitment to the Lord.

3. Seeking God's will is always an important topic among believers. What advice would you give regarding knowing and doing God's will from this passage?

4. What is the difference in the way Paul talks about our view toward ourselves (3-5) and the way the world or friends understand "self-esteem"?

5. Think through each of these spiritual gifts. Go through them
    and think about a person who seems to have such a gift.
    (Encourage them as appropriate.)

6. Paul instructs believers how they are to rightly appropriate the
    full power of these 7 gifts. Flip the counsel around and see
    what is one big danger for each of these gifts. An example is
    provided below.

    •   Example: #1 "Prophecy, <u>according to the proportion of his
        faith</u>." Flip: The danger is that a believer uses his/her gift to
        impress others and say things that he/she were not assured of in
        faith by God.

7. Identify which spiritual gift do you have? Where have you used
    it before? Is it something you like to do? Have you seen the
    advice help to you? Explain.

8. Think of what the church looks like from these verses. How
    does the individual relate to the whole (of the church)? How
    is individualism a threat to the welfare of the church? How is
    the Christian's corporate community so much more ideal?

#26 Romans 12:9-21 Study Questions

BOOK OF ROMANS
STUDY QUESTIONS

PRINCIPLES OF CHRISTIAN GROWTH

This passage provides more than twenty exhortations from the apostle Paul, each bringing a special insight on how to live out the successful Christian life. How exciting it is to have this specific advice to improve our life and service!

- **Starter**: What is the best advice that you ever heard and why?

A) General admonitions (Rom 12:9-18)

12:9 Let love be without hypocrisy. Abhor what is evil; cling to what is good. 10 Be devoted to one another in brotherly love; give preference to one another in honor; 11 not lagging behind in diligence, fervent in spirit, serving the Lord; 12 rejoicing in hope, persevering in tribulation, devoted to prayer, 13 contributing to the needs of the saints, practicing hospitality. 14 Bless those who persecute you; bless and curse not. 15 Rejoice with those who rejoice, and weep with those who weep. 16 Be of the same mind toward one another; do not be haughty in mind, but associate with the lowly. Do not be wise in your own estimation. 17 Never pay back evil for evil to anyone. Respect what is right in the sight of all men. 18 If possible, so far as it depends on you, be at peace with all men.

1. What does Paul say that our love toward others should look like (9a)? How does that work out practically?

2. What image comes to your mind when you think of "clinging"? What does "cling to what is good" in verse 9 mean?

3. What are the two ways Paul prescribes a Christian to love in verse 10?

4. List and explain in your own words the counsel Paul gives in verses 11-13 for our spiritual lives? Circle the ones that you consider to be 'difficult' to consistently carry out.

   - (11)

   - (11)

   - (11)

   - (12)

   - (12)

   - (12)

   - (13)

   - (13)

5. How are we to respond to those who persecute us (14)? Why do you think this instruction is given to us under those circumstances?

6. How do verses 15 and 16 complement each other?

7. Can we ever pay back evil for some wrong thing someone has done to us or another that we love (17)?

8. Paul's advice in verse 18 is brilliant. What does he there tell us to do? How does that work out if other people are not willing?

B) Admonitions on revenge (Rom 12:19-21)

[19] Never take your own revenge, beloved, but leave room for the wrath of God, for it is written, "VENGEANCE IS MINE, I WILL REPAY," says the Lord. [20] "BUT IF YOUR ENEMY IS HUNGRY, FEED HIM, AND IF HE IS THIRSTY, GIVE HIM A DRINK; FOR IN SO DOING YOU WILL HEAP BURNING COALS UPON HIS HEAD." [21] Do not be overcome by evil, but overcome evil with good.

9. List a few attitudes or thoughts we should have toward our desires to take our revenge (19-21). Give at least one for each verse.

    •   (19)

    •   (20)

    •   (21)

10. Why do believers need not be concerned with taking revenge (19)?

Summary

Wrestling with our feelings is one of the biggest challenges for us. One of the most basic principles to eliminate this tension is to live by obedience rather than feeling.

11. What is the difference between advice, suggestion, counsel and command? What are these in chapter 12?

12. Why do you think we need to hear the command "abhor what is evil" (9)? What evil do you need to hate more?

13. Pick out the two most outstanding commands from the above list, memorize them and apply them to your life. Identify what feelings or thoughts go contrary to each command.

14. List at least two changes you desire to take place in your life because of these verses.

    •

    •

Romans 12:9-21 Advanced Discussion Questions

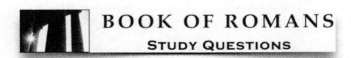

BOOK OF ROMANS
STUDY QUESTIONS

1. Do you always like advice? Explain how you best like to hear advice and why.

2. Go through each command in this section and identify which ones you have been obeying.

3. In the areas that you have not been complying, what are you doing or not doing which puts you in the wrong? What is keeping you from doing what is right?

4. What is legalism? Are these verses legalistic? Why or why not?

5. "Devoted to prayer" (12:12) forces to open our mind up to adopting a spiritual discipline of prayer. Devoted suggests consistency and repetition. What is your prayer life like? Do you pray regularly with others? Explain.

6. Many people secretly live in hope to take bitter revenge. Using the verses in this section, what could we say to them to urge

and encourage them to get rid of their bitterness? Do you
think they would listen? Why or why not?

#27 Romans 13:1-14 Study Questions

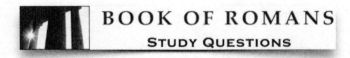

SUBMISSION TO GOVERNMENT & LOVE

From chapter 12 on to the end of Romans Paul carefully instructs the believer on godly Christian living. In this chapter he clearly focuses us on how to kindly treat others we meet up with in our daily affairs.

- **Starter:** Why is bitterness so bitter?

A) Living subject to authorities (Rom 13:1-7)

¹³:¹ Let every person be in subjection to the governing authorities. For there is no authority except from God, and those which exist are established by God. ² Therefore he who resists authority has opposed the ordinance of God; and they who have opposed will receive condemnation upon themselves. ³ For rulers are not a cause of fear for good behavior, but for evil. Do you want to have no fear of authority? Do what is good, and you will have praise from the same; ⁴ for it is a minister of God to you for good. But if you do what is evil, be afraid; for it does not bear the sword for nothing; for it is a minister of God, an avenger who brings wrath upon the one who practices evil. ⁵ Wherefore it is necessary to be in subjection, not only because of wrath, but also for conscience' sake. ⁶ For because of this you also pay taxes, for rulers are servants of God, devoting themselves to this very thing. ⁷ Render to all what is due them: tax to whom tax is due; custom to whom custom; fear to whom fear; honor to whom honor.

1. Who are we told to subject ourselves to (13:1)?

2. Why is it that we are to subject ourselves to them in this way (1)?

3. When a man rebels against authority, who else is he resisting (2)? What results from that (2)? Explain its meaning.

4. How does Paul instruct us to get rid of fear of governmental authorities (3)?

5. What are the governmental authorities called in verse 4? How is this possible?

6. What are the responsibility of governmental authorities (4)?

7. Besides fearing what the government might do to you if it catches you doing something wrong, what is the other reason we are to submit to the government (5)?

8. According to verse 6, what are taxes for?

9. What does Paul say about the preferential treatment the government or others might expect (7)?

B) Principles for Christian living (Rom 13:8-14)

[8] Owe nothing to anyone except to love one another; for he who loves his neighbor has fulfilled the law. [9] For this, "YOU SHALL NOT COMMIT ADULTERY, YOU SHALL NOT MURDER, YOU SHALL NOT STEAL, YOU SHALL NOT COVET," and if there is any other commandment, it is summed up in this saying, "YOU SHALL LOVE YOUR NEIGHBOR AS YOURSELF." [10] Love does no wrong to a neighbor; love therefore is the fulfillment of the law. [11] And this do, knowing the time, that it is already the hour for you to awaken from sleep; for now salvation is nearer to us than when we believed. [12] The night is almost gone, and the day is at hand. Let us therefore lay aside the deeds of darkness and put on the armor of light. [13] Let us behave properly as in the day, not in carousing and drunkenness, not in sexual promiscuity and sensuality, not in strife and jealousy. [14] But put on the Lord Jesus Christ, and make no provision for the flesh in regard to its lusts.

10. What does verse 8 say about debt?

11. What command summarizes most of the other commands from God (8,9)?

12. Complete this sentence, "Love is the _____ of the law" from verse 10.

13. According to verse 11, what are we to be doing now? Why?

14. What principles of spiritual warfare are stated or inferred from verse 12?

15. List the behaviors he tells us to avoid in verse 13.

16. What are we to put on (14)? What does that mean?

Summary

Christ is living His life through us! The way we live under the government or treat others should be the way Jesus would do it. What a challenge and delight to love out Christ's life.

17. How can your attitude toward the government and taxes improve? Pray for those in governing positions over you.

18. What does Paul teach us about our views of debt in verses 8-9? Make a few suggestions on how to apply that to your life.

19. Memorize verse 14. (Check here _____.) How would you answer someone who asks, "How do I put the Lord Jesus Christ on?"

20. List at least two changes you desire to take place in your life because of these verses.

    •

    •

Romans 13:1-14 Advanced Discussion Questions

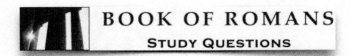

BOOK OF ROMANS
STUDY QUESTIONS

1. How are we to respond to those people who would encourage us to rebel against a wicked or corrupt government (13:1-7)? Might our response change if our own constitution mandates a rebellion against evil rulers?

2. Verse 8 says to owe nothing. What about loans and mortgages? What is this verse really trying to say?

3. How is debt related to coveting?

4. Explain how adultery, murder, stealing, and coveting each violate the principle of love.

5. What principles of spiritual warfare are stated or inferred from verse 12?

6. Are verses 12 and 14 related? Do you ever think of spiritual warfare in your daily life? Explain.

7. Explain the prohibition, "Make no provision for the flesh in regard to its lusts" (14). Think through your life and look for a hole or gap in your armor. How might this verse apply and how can you better protect yourself?

#28 Romans 14:1-12 Study Questions

BOOK OF ROMANS
STUDY QUESTIONS

RESPECTING OUR DIFFERENCES

Christians differ on many issues. Paul steps into this conversation in this chapter and paves the way to understand how we can live in peace with each other—even though we might differ from them.

- **Starter:** What are some issues that you differ with other believers? How do you presently deal with them?

A) The conflict (Rom 14:1-6)

14:1 Now accept the one who is weak in faith, but not for the purpose of passing judgment on his opinions. 2 One man has faith that he may eat all things, but he who is weak eats vegetables only. 3 Let not him who eats regard with contempt him who does not eat, and let not him who does not eat judge him who eats, for God has accepted him. 4 Who are you to judge the servant of another? To his own master he stands or falls; and stand he will, for the Lord is able to make him stand. 5 One man regards one day above another, another regards every day alike. Let each man be fully convinced in his own mind. 6 He who observes the day, observes it for the Lord, and he who eats, does so for the Lord, for he gives thanks to God; and he who eats not, for the Lord he does not eat, and gives thanks to God.

1. What is the first difference of opinion discussed in verses 14:1-4?

2. What kind of people are we told to accept (14:1)?

3. What condition is put upon the way we accept them (1b)?

4. Describe the two kinds of people and their faith mentioned in verse 2.

   •

   •

5. What does Paul ask both groups to do in verse 3? On what basis are they to do this?

6. What is the main point of his question in verse 4?

7. Paul goes from speaking about foods to what topic in verse 5?

8. Describe the two views Christians have toward treating certain days as holy days (5).

9. What is the most important principle both groups need to remember (5c)?

10. What makes a person's views "holy" and acceptable to the Lord (6)?

B) Personal accountability (Rom 14:7-12)

[7] For not one of us lives for himself, and not one dies for himself; [8] for if we live, we live for the Lord, or if we die, we die for the Lord; therefore whether we live or die, we are the Lord's. [9] For to this end Christ died and lived again, that He might be Lord both of the dead and of the living. [10] But you, why do you judge your brother? Or you again, why do you regard your brother with contempt? For we shall all stand before the judgment seat of God. [11] For it is written, "AS I LIVE, SAYS THE LORD, EVERY KNEE SHALL BOW TO ME, AND EVERY TONGUE SHALL GIVE PRAISE TO GOD." [12] So then each one of us shall give account of himself to God.

11. If we don't live or die for ourselves, for whom do we live (8)?

12. The Lordship of Christ is one of these debated issues today among believers. What was Paul's Lordship concept for believers (8)?

13. What was the overall purpose of Christ's death and resurrection (9)?

14. Paul asks two questions in verse 14:10. Write them in your own words.

    •

    •

15. Why are we not to judge our brothers and sisters (10c)?

16. Are Christians exempt from the need to give an account of themselves? Why (11-12)?

Summary

Evidently, Christians are expected to kindly treat and think of others, even with regard to issues on which they disagree. Isn't this a much easier approach to life than judging them?

17. What is the principle of keeping to one's conscience (5)? Give an example on where we can use this principle in the decisions a believer makes.

18. Do you live for the Lord in all your decisions? How does that supposed to work?

19. It seems like Paul is saying that though these issues should be taken seriously, it is more important to kindly treat and think of our brethren? Why is this so hard to do at times? Do you find it hard?

20. List at least two changes you desire to take place in your life because of these verses.

   •

   •

Romans 14:1-12 Advanced Discussion Questions

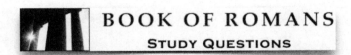

BOOK OF ROMANS
STUDY QUESTIONS

1. Why is the person who limits what he eats weak in faith rather than the other person who doesn't?

2. What differentiates moral issues from non-moral issues like the ones he has mentioned? Give three examples of moral and non-moral issues.

3. Is this teaching the same as what is being taught as 'tolerance'? Define today's notion of tolerance and explain.

4. A holy life is one which pleases God. How does this work out if there is no particular right or wrong way? Or is there?

5. Paul in verse 10 stresses that we are not to judge others because that is God's duty. How does that compare with Rom 12:19-21 where we are not to take vengeance?

6. Don't Christians escape the judgment? Look carefully at 14:10-12 before answering.

7. Have you ever seriously thought about giving a final account of
   your life? What do you think you will need to give an account
   for? How are you fairing? List one way to improve.

#29 Romans 14:13–23 Study Questions

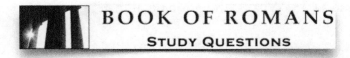

BOOK OF ROMANS
STUDY QUESTIONS

LOVING NOT JUDGING

Winning the person is more important than winning the argument! But it is more than this, we are to respect and love those around us–not act as their judge.

- **Starter:** Think of a time when someone was critical or judgmental toward you. How did you feel?

A) Refrain from judging (Rom 14:13-21)

13 Therefore let us not judge one another anymore, but rather determine this–not to put an obstacle or a stumbling block in a brother's way. 14 I know and am convinced in the Lord Jesus that nothing is unclean in itself; but to him who thinks anything to be unclean, to him it is unclean. 15 For if because of food your brother is hurt, you are no longer walking according to love. Do not destroy with your food him for whom Christ died. 16 Therefore do not let what is for you a good thing be spoken of as evil; 17 for the kingdom of God is not eating and drinking, but righteousness and peace and joy in the Holy Spirit. 18 For he who in this way serves Christ is acceptable to God and approved by men. 19 So then let us pursue the things which make for peace and the building up of one another. 20 Do not tear down the work of God for the sake of food. All things indeed are clean, but they are evil for the man who eats and gives offense. 21 It is good not to eat meat or to drink wine, or to do anything by which your brother stumbles.

1. What does it mean to judge another (14:13)? Provide an example.

2. Instead of judging one another, what are we asked to do in verse 14:13? What is the meaning of that?

3. Give an example of a stumbling block.

4. What is Paul so sure of in verse 14a? What does he mean by this?

5. What allowance does he build into his certainty of what is right (14b)?

6. What law am I breaking when I make an issue of food to the point I hurt my brother (15a)?

7. Write down a few synonyms for the word 'destroy'? Why might Paul use such a strong word in verse 15b to describe the situation?

8. Verse 16 is a powerful and practical principle for our lives. Write this verse down and give a practical example of this.

9. If eating and drinking are not the most important things about the kingdom of God, what is (17)?

10. What two things are we to pursue (19)?

11. Even if we think something is okay, such as eating foods, it can become evil. How so (20)?

12. Would you say "gives offense" (20) and to cause another to stumble (21) are the same things? Explain.

13. What does Paul ask us to refrain from doing if it causes our brother to stumble (21)?

B) Summary life principles (Rom 14:22-23)

22 The faith which you have, have as your own conviction before God. Happy is he who does not condemn himself in what he approves. 23 But he who doubts is condemned if he eats, because his eating is not from faith; and whatever is not from faith is sin.

14. What shapes a Christian's personal standard (22a)?

15. What makes a Christian happy (22b)? Explain what this means in your own words.

16. What brings condemnation upon a Christian's behavior (23)? What does he doubt?

17. The phrase, "Whatever is not from faith is sin" (23) summarizes well this chapter. Explain it in this context of eating foods.

Summary

Christians will at times run into people who differ in how they express their faith–what they watch, eat, drink, etc. Support them even when their standards differ from yours but keep faithful to the standard that God has put on your heart.

18. We can sin even if we do not do anything against our personal conviction. This is because what we do affects others. Are there areas of what you watch, how you say something, where you go, what you drink or eat, what you wear, etc., that could cause other believers to struggle with their faith? Share.

19. We might be on the other side of the fence where what people lead us to compromise our faith. How can the scripture, "everything not from faith sin" help us (14:23)? List the areas that you tend to compromise. How can you stand firm?

20. Can our standards change for the better as we grow as a believer? Can they change for the worse? If so, how?

21. List at least one change you desire to take place in your life because of these verses.

Romans 14:13-23 Advanced Discussion Questions

BOOK OF ROMANS
STUDY QUESTIONS

1. Do you have a problem with judging other Christians and making sure they meet up to your standards? List at least three principles from this section of scripture that would help you to have a proper attitude toward them.

2. Relate an incident where you saw a brother/sister stumble. What could have been done to prevent that?

3. We are an indulgent society where we tend to go beyond what we think is right or good. How can the phrase, "everything not from faith sin" help a person govern how much he eats, drinks, plays a computer game, etc.? Do you treat excessiveness as sin? Explain.

4. One of the biggest problems in the West is that we think we are free to do what we want. How does this passage challenge this?

#30 Romans 15:1–13 Study Questions

LOVE'S GREATER CALL

Christ has gone ahead and set a wonderful example to accept others as they are. The new life in Christ revolves in love—caring for those of weaker faith, different race or background, etc.

- **Starter:** Share an example of a person who went out of his or her way to help you with something. What did you feel as a result?

A) Pleasing one's neighbor (Rom 15:1-4)

^{15:1} Now we who are strong ought to bear the weaknesses of those without strength and not just please ourselves. ² Let each of us please his neighbor for his good, to his edification. ³ For even Christ did not please Himself; but as it is written, "THE REPROACHES OF THOSE WHO REPROACHED THEE FELL UPON ME." ⁴ For whatever was written in earlier times was written for our instruction, that through perseverance and the encouragement of the Scriptures we might have hope.

1. How would you define or describe the strong believer (1)?

2. What kind of weaknesses do we see in other believers that Paul might be referring to in verse 1?

3. "Just please ourselves" (1) is a apt description of our modern society. What is the problem with that mentality?

4. Finish this statement, "If we are strong believers, then we have a special call to _____" (1).

5. What is the difference between "good" and "edification" in verse 2?

6. Why should we go out of our way to help others (15:3)?

7. What can we look forward to in our reading of the Old Testament Scriptures (15:4)?

B) Being of one mind (Rom 15:5-13)

5 Now may the God who gives perseverance and encouragement grant you to be of the same mind with one another according to Christ Jesus; 6 that with one accord you may with one voice glorify the God and Father of our Lord Jesus Christ. 7 Wherefore, accept one another, just as Christ also accepted us to the glory of God. 8 For I say that Christ has become a servant to the circumcision on behalf of the truth of God to confirm the promises given to the fathers, 9 and for the Gentiles to glorify God for His mercy; as it is written, "THEREFORE I WILL GIVE PRAISE TO THEE AMONG THE GENTILES, AND I WILL SING TO THY NAME." 10 And again he says, "REJOICE, O GENTILES, WITH HIS PEOPLE." 11 And again, "PRAISE THE LORD ALL YOU GENTILES, AND LET ALL THE PEOPLES PRAISE HIM." 12 And again Isaiah says, "THERE SHALL COME THE ROOT OF JESSE, AND HE WHO ARISES TO RULE OVER THE GENTILES, IN HIM SHALL THE GENTILES

HOPE." 13 Now may the God of hope fill you with all joy and peace in believing, that you may abound in hope by the power of the Holy Spirit.

8. Perseverance and strength come through reading God's Word, but why is this emphasized here (5)?

9. Instead of looking down on different individuals, what should our attitude be (5)? Does that mean we are to think alike or what?

10. What is our purpose of being of the same mind (15:6)? How does being of "one mind" enable us to have "one voice"?

11. How does Paul summarize these teachings in verse 7?

12. The principle set out in verse 7 is elaborated in verses 8-13 for what two different groups (15:8 & 9-12)?

   • 15:8:

   • 15:9-12:

13. Verse 8 says, "Christ has become a servant" to both groups. How does He do this?

14. What stands out most to you from Paul's benediction in verse 13?

Summary

Paul not only tells us not to judge but how to get rid of a judgmental spirit. Don't act like judges because we are not. Instead, we can love and accept others just as Jesus did.

15. In verses 1-2, Paul records a new approach to life, "not just please ourselves... please his neighbor for his good." Think about your spouse, colleague, child, and others and see if you have consistently adopted this new mindset.

16. Through what power are we able to love those <u>who</u> have different views (15:13)?

17. Do you think this new attitude: love those that Jesus loved can replace your thinking? How will that work when you feel controlling, demanding, critical or angry?

18. List at least two changes you desire to take place in your life because of these verses.

    •

    •

Romans 15:1-15:13 Advanced Discussion Questions

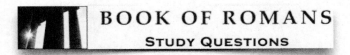

BOOK OF ROMANS
STUDY QUESTIONS

1. Define hedonism and observe it around you. How does its seeking self-pleasure mentality differ from those who seek the good of others (1-2)?

2. How did Paul summarize the main purpose of the Old Testament scriptures (4)? How would you have summarized it before this comment?

3. Read through the verses having to do with the Christ serving the Gentiles in 9-12. What do they have in common? How might these verses relate to what Paul has earlier shared his burden about wanting to save the non-Jew?

4. Unity was powerfully taught through two phrases, 'the same mind' and 'one voice.' (5-6). Reflect on the unity of the church you attend and the church in your city. What stops the unity from going to a deeper level? Pray for it, starting with a confession.

#31 Romans 15:14-33 Study Questions

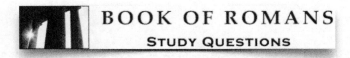

BOOK OF ROMANS
STUDY QUESTIONS

MISSION REMAINING

We often think of God's will as His specific plan for our lives, but we should first seek what He wants irrespective to our lives. Only then can we seek God's strength and wisdom to work with Him.

*   **Starter:** What is one question you have about God's will?

A. The basics of God's will (Rom 15:14-19)

15:14 And concerning you, my brethren, I myself also am convinced that you yourselves are full of goodness, filled with all knowledge, and able also to admonish one another. 15 But I have written very boldly to you on some points, so as to remind you again, because of the grace that was given me from God, 16 to be a minister of Christ Jesus to the Gentiles, ministering as a priest the gospel of God, that my offering of the Gentiles might become acceptable, sanctified by the Holy Spirit. 17 Therefore in Christ Jesus I have found reason for boasting in things pertaining to God. 18 For I will not presume to speak of anything except what Christ has accomplished through me, resulting in the obedience of the Gentiles by word and deed, 19 in the power of signs and wonders, in the power of the Spirit; so that from Jerusalem and round about as far as Illyricum I have fully preached the gospel of Christ.

1. Does Paul have a negative or positive attitude toward the brothers and sisters (14)?

2. List the three characteristics Paul sees in the believers (15:14).

   •

   •

   •

3. Why did Paul write so boldly in the book of Romans (15)?
   What does he mean by that?

4. As time allows, read about Paul's calling to be an apostle (Acts
   26:12-18) and explain how he is being faithful to the purpose
   God commissioned him (15:15-16).

5. Write in your own words the analogy Paul used to understand
   his ministry (see verse 16). What part of the analogy are the
   Gentiles?

6. Is it right to be boastful? Explain Paul's attitude toward this
   and his ministry (17-18).

7. How was Paul faithful to the test he mentioned in verse 18
   (see 19)? As time allows, check a map.

B. The specifics of God's will (Rom 15:20-33)

[20] And thus I aspired to preach the gospel, not where Christ was
already named, that I might not build upon another man's
foundation; [21] but as it is written, "THEY WHO HAD NO NEWS
OF HIM SHALL SEE, AND THEY WHO HAVE NOT HEARD

SHALL UNDERSTAND." [22] For this reason I have often been hindered from coming to you; [23] but now, with no further place for me in these regions, and since I have had for many years a longing to come to you [24] whenever I go to Spain--for I hope to see you in passing, and to be helped on my way there by you, when I have first enjoyed your company for a while-- [25] but now, I am going to Jerusalem serving the saints. [26] For Macedonia and Achaia have been pleased to make a contribution for the poor among the saints in Jerusalem. [27] Yes, they were pleased to do so, and they are indebted to them. For if the Gentiles have shared in their spiritual things, they are indebted to minister to them also in material things. [28] Therefore, when I have finished this, and have put my seal on this fruit of theirs, I will go on by way of you to Spain. [29] And I know that when I come to you, I will come in the fulness of the blessing of Christ.

[30] Now I urge you, brethren, by our Lord Jesus Christ and by the love of the Spirit, to strive together with me in your prayers to God for me, [31] that I may be delivered from those who are disobedient in Judea, and that my service for Jerusalem may prove acceptable to the saints; [32] so that I may come to you in joy by the will of God and find refreshing rest in your company. [33] Now the God of peace be with you all. Amen.

8. What was Paul's aspiration as a minister of the gospel (20)?
    Why? Where did he get his inspiration from (21)?

9. What reason did Paul give for not going earlier to Rome
    (20-22)?

10. Why does Paul want to visit Rome (23-24)? What other
    intention does he have?

11. What is Paul's explanation for delaying this trip to Rome (25-26)?

12. Why did Paul think it was appropriate for the Gentiles to make an offering to the Jews (26-27)?

13. Did Paul still expect to be able to visit them (28-29)? How did his aspiration (20) affect his plans?

14. Describe the manner Paul called them to pray for him (30). What does he mean by that?

15. What did Paul ask prayer for (31-32)?

Summary

Start by seeking what God wants. See what He is doing and join in. This mindset enabled Paul to powerfully serve God. Our desire to conform to God's will should greatly influence our decisions.

16. What is something that God has done in or through you (cf. 17-19)? Do you 'boast' about God's work in your life? What guards do you need to set up when you do this?

17. What is the most significant lesson from this lesson that you have learned about God's will?

18. Paul was working hard to fulfill God's ambition to reach the world with the gospel. Notice that others could join the apostle in his work—"to strive together with me" (30). In what ways have you joined God in this urgent mission to make disciples around the world? Do you think you need a specific calling to do this?

19. List at least two changes you desire to take place in your life because of these verses.

-
-

Romans 15:14-33 Advanced Discussion Questions

BOOK OF ROMANS
STUDY QUESTIONS

1. Out of the three characteristics listed in 15:14, which is most true of you? Which is most lacking? Praise God and seek Him for more grace.

2. Paul had a call to preach to the Gentiles but notice how he refined his goal or vision to focus on reaching those Gentiles who had not received the Gospel, "not where Christ was already named". Do you think it was right for Paul to redefine his life purpose? Explain.

3. Paul stated, "from Jerusalem and round about as far as Illyricum I have fully preached" (19). What do you think he meant by "fully"? Review the Book of Acts to examine his missionary journeys.

4. There is a great movement today to reach all the "unreached people" of the world with the gospel (see 21). Has this vision taken root in your heart? Why or why not?

5. Notice how Paul uses "will of God" in verse 32. Do you think
    it is something Paul knew would happen or was he sensitively
    trying to make it happen?

6. Paul explains his call to ministry (15:14-19) and shows why
    this call (15:20-25) has kept him from visiting them (15:26-33)
    and yet later enabled him to make plans to visit them. What
    are some principles about discerning God's will from this
    larger passage?

#32 Romans 16:1-27 Study Questions

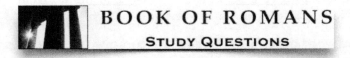

BOOK OF ROMANS
STUDY QUESTIONS

COMMUNITY SPIRIT

Much can be learned from the Christian community in Rome as well as Paul's heart of working together with them.

- **Starter:** Briefly share about one person in church that has positively impressed you and one that has disappointed you.

A) Working with God's people (Rom 16:1-16)

16:1 I commend to you our sister Phoebe, who is a servant of the church which is at Cenchrea; 2 that you receive her in the Lord in a manner worthy of the saints, and that you help her in whatever matter she may have need of you; for she herself has also been a helper of many, and of myself as well. 3 Greet Prisca and Aquila, my fellow workers in Christ Jesus, 4 who for my life risked their own necks, to whom not only do I give thanks, but also all the churches of the Gentiles; 5 also greet the church that is in their house. Greet Epaenetus, my beloved, who is the first convert to Christ from Asia. 6 Greet Mary, who has worked hard for you. 7 Greet Andronicus and Junias, my kinsmen, and my fellow prisoners, who are outstanding among the apostles, who also were in Christ before me. 8 Greet Ampliatus, my beloved in the Lord. 9 Greet Urbanus, our fellow worker in Christ, and Stachys my beloved. 10 Greet Apelles, the approved in Christ. Greet those who are of the household of Aristobulus. 11 Greet Herodion, my kinsman. Greet those of the household of Narcissus, who are in the Lord. 12 Greet

Tryphaena and Tryphosa, workers in the Lord. Greet Persis the beloved, who has worked hard in the Lord. [13] Greet Rufus, a choice man in the Lord, also his mother and mine. [14] Greet Asyncritus, Phlegon, Hermes, Patrobas, Hermas and the brethren with them. [15] Greet Philologus and Julia, Nereus and his sister, and Olympas, and all the saints who are with them. [16] Greet one another with a holy kiss. All the churches of Christ greet you.

1. The word describing Phoebe is accurately translated either as servant or deaconess. How were they to receive her? How were they supposed to help her (16:1-2)?

2. Why were they supposed to help Phoebe so much when she came to them (16:2d)?

3. What did Prisca and Aquila do for Paul the apostle (16:3-4)?

4. What was going on in the home of Prisca and Aquila (16:5)?

5. What word does each verse from verse 6-16 all start with? Next to the names below, write down what is associated with each of them.

   • Mary:

   • Andronicus and Junias:

   • Ampliatus:

   • Urbanus:

   • Stachys:

- Apelles:

- Herodion:

- Tryphaena and Tryphosa:

- Persis:

- Rufus:

6. How did Paul greet the church (16)? How might you translate that into your culture?

B) Sheltering God's people (Rom 16:17-20)

[17] Now I urge you, brethren, keep your eye on those who cause dissensions and hindrances contrary to the teaching which you learned, and turn away from them. [18] For such men are slaves, not of our Lord Christ but of their own appetites; and by their smooth and flattering speech they deceive the hearts of the unsuspecting. [19] For the report of your obedience has reached to all; therefore I am rejoicing over you, but I want you to be wise in what is good, and innocent in what is evil. [20] And the God of peace will soon crush Satan under your feet. The grace of our Lord Jesus be with you.

7. What warning did Paul give the church in verse 17?

8. What are these men like (18)?

9. What good thing did Paul hear about the church in Rome (19)?

10. What are two things he wants them to be characterized by
    (19)?

11. Write down the benediction in verse 20.

C) Establishing God's people (Rom 16:21-27)

21 Timothy my fellow worker greets you, and so do Lucius and
Jason and Sosipater, my kinsmen. 22 I, Tertius, who write this letter,
greet you in the Lord. 23 Gaius, host to me and to the whole
church, greets you. Erastus, the city treasurer greets you, and
Quartus, the brother. 24 [The grace of our Lord Jesus Christ be
with you all. Amen.] 25 Now to Him who is able to establish you
according to my gospel and the preaching of Jesus Christ, according
to the revelation of the mystery which has been kept secret for
long ages past, 26 but now is manifested, and by the Scriptures of
the prophets, according to the commandment of the eternal God,
has been made known to all the nations, leading to obedience of
faith; 27 to the only wise God, through Jesus Christ, be the glory
forever. Amen.

12. What are the names of Paul's possible relatives that know the
    Lord there (21)?

13. Who is mentioned in verse 22? What was he known for?

14. Verses 25-27 also serves as a benediction. (Some ancient
    manuscripts also include verse 24 part or the benediction).
    Who is it that establishes them (25-27)? What does this mean?

15. Is the mystery spoken of in verse 25 now known or still unknown (25-26)?

16. How are the scriptures being used (25-26)?

17. What does Paul wish God to gain (27)?

Summary

Paul's famous message to the Romans ends here. This clear defense of the faith in Christ has helped millions of believers over the years to grasp the glory of the Gospel of Christ and has provided them adequate knowledge for themselves to proclaim and defend the Words of life.

18. Which greeting is most significant to you (6-16)?

19. What would you want to be known for? What is one step you can take to get further there?

20. Which aspect of evil in the world troubles you most? Do you ever think of how Jesus' coming will thoroughly crush that evil? Explain.

21. List at least two changes you desire to take place in your life because of these verses.

Romans 16:1-27 Advanced Discussion Questions

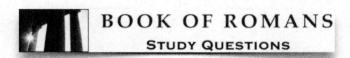

1. What is your philosophy of the church? Many believers only see themselves as spectators rather than coworkers. Are you a coworker? Check out Eph 4:11-13 and reflect on Paul's expectation of church members.

2. How does verse 20 allude to Genesis 3:15? Didn't Jesus already overcome the evil one? Explain.

3. Jesus is fully committed to His bride, the people of God. How does Paul reflect that commitment in his care for the people of God? How would you rate your own commitment to the local assembly? Are you devoted to her despite her many flaws?

4. Some suggest Paul looked down upon women. Observe Paul's comments he makes in chapter 16 about women. How can we use this to quiet such comments?

   • Phoebe Some(1)

   • Priscilla (3)

- Mary (6)

- Rufus' mother (13)

5. Where else in Romans is God's grand purpose discussed? How does 16:25 relate to salvation?

6. Why is there this emphasis on revelation and mystery (25-26)?

7. Why do you think Paul makes a stress on the 'nations' in verse 26?'

8. Think back over the teachings in this book. Share one way you have been significantly "established" (25)?

Appendix: About the Author

Paul has worked as an overseas church planter during the 1980s and pastored in America during the 1990s. God called him to establish Biblical Foundations for Freedom in 2000 and since then he has been actively writing, holding international Christian leadership training seminars and serving in the local church.

Paul's wide range of books on Christian life, discipleship, godly living, leadership training, marriage, parenting, anxiety, Old and New Testament and other spiritual life topics provide special insights that are blended into his many books and media-rich training resources.

Paul has been married for more than thirty-five wonderful years. With eight children and three grandchildren, Paul and his wife Linda continually see God's blessings unfold in their lives.

For more on Paul and Linda and the BFF ministry, check online at:
www.foundationsforfreedom.net

Printed in Great Britain
by Amazon